Gary Hill

Edited by Robert C. Morgan

A PAJ Book

The Johns Hopkins University Press   Baltimore + London

© 2000 The Johns Hopkins University Press
All rights reserved. Published 2000
Printed in the United States of America on acid-free paper

9 8 7 6 5 4 3 2 1

The Johns Hopkins University Press
2715 North Charles Street
Baltimore, Maryland 21218-4363
www.press.jhu.edu

Library of Congress Cataloging-in-Publication data will be found
at the end of this book.

A catalog record for this book is available from the British
Library.

ISBN 0-8018-6401-1
ISBN 0-8018-6402-x (pbk.)

Frontispiece: Still photograph from Gary Hill, *Incidence of
Catastrophe,* 1987–1988.

Permissions credits may be found on page 349.

Contents

II   Interviews

III   Gary Hill's Writings

Photograph gallery follows page 178.

Acknowledgments

I wish to thank the editors of *PAJ*, Bonnie Marranca and Gautam Dasgupta, for inviting me to prepare a book on the work of Gary Hill. I have long admired their critical and historical work in avant-garde theater and performance art and their persistent openness and careful discretion in coming to terms with new ideas and issues that expand the frame or the proscenium of what this art might be. Thanks to Linda Tripp, Maura Burnett, and Sam Schmidt at the Johns Hopkins University Press for their help as consultants and editorial assistants. I am indebted to Mr. Donald Young and his staff at the Donald Young Gallery in Chicago, especially Andrea Moody, for their help with photographic and textual material on the artist. George and Susan Quasha and Charles Stein showed me hospitality as we discussed, along with Gary Hill, many of the important issues related to both the earlier and the recent work. I wish to thank Rayne Roper Wilder for her courteous help and attention, and of course Gary Hill for his commitment and sustained interest in this book from the outset to its completion. His work has inspired the impetus to make it all happen. Most of all, I wish to acknowledge the dedication of my assistants, Cynthia Roberts, Leigh Winter, and Carla Gannis, and especially, Stefano Pasquini who has the supreme ability to make all the subtle details of such a project come together. Without his attention to such matters, the book would not have happened.

Gary Hill

Robert C. Morgan

Gary Hill: Beyond the Image

I must become a warrior of self-consciousness and move my body to move my mind to move my words to move my mouth to spin the spur of the moment.

—Gary Hill, *Site Recite (a prologue)*

Video art is a term that has been bandied about in the art world for nearly three decades. Much of the work that has come under this category has been intensely involved with issues in art, ranging from purely formal ones to more specific political concerns. Some of the work labeled "video art" is commercial in its intent, although video links have also focused on alternative means to disseminating ideas. In addition, video art offers a necessary response to the accelerating effects of television on our culture, indeed, a response to the imposition of the media on all walks of life.

There have been many approaches, many intentions, and many critiques given to video art—not only as a medium, but as a form. The controversies surrounding the electronic image in art have only been exacerbated with the development of digital and computer technology over the past two decades. There is clearly a performative component to much of the video art produced since the moment of its inception, as well as a strong conceptual aspect. It is within the context of these issues that I want to address the work of Gary Hill, the subject of this collection of texts and images, who has emerged in recent years as one of the leading practitioners and thinkers in video art today.

Gary Hill's introduction to video art came about in a rather oblique way. Like some video practitioners, he was initially attached to the plastic arts; but in other ways his discovery and development of the medium were somewhat atypical. Born in 1951, Hill grew up in Santa

1

Monica in southern California on the edge of the Pacific Ocean. Santa Monica is known as a beach town with an extensive beach culture. As an adolescent, the artist spent a good deal of his time surfing the waves—a highly athletic (and, to a certain extent, aesthetic) activity in which Hill developed a certain finesse and proficiency. The experience of surfing had a tremendous impact on Hill, one that would enter into his work as an artist, as he came to understand the properties of video time as somehow synchronous to the effect of being "inside" a wave or what surfers often call the "green room."

In an essay by Robert Mittenthal, included in this volume, there is a discussion directly related to Hill's application of surfing to the medium of video. Being inside the "green room" is when the surfer stands on the board inside the wave waiting to feel which direction the wave is going to roll. Hill describes this experience as waiting for the initial tug, the force of motion that will eventually pull the surfer through the wave. According to Hill, this is the moment of revelation—what he defines in an installation from 1993 called *Learning Curve (still point)*. Mittenthal goes on to suggest that "Hill's description of the green room is linked to Heidegger's notion of clearing, that moment when the 'obscuring curtain of things' is lifted."

In high school, Hill aspired to become a sculptor. He especially idolized the work of Picasso. His early work involved wire mesh and various other materials that emphasized the process of construction. This suggests a tendency that the artist would pursue later in his more mature career with video, namely, the self-referential aspect of the medium. It can be designated as one of Hill's first and most recurring themes. In 1969, he left California at age 18—never having pursued a college degree—and came to the Northeast, settling in upstate New York near the Woodstock area. By 1971 he had become involved with a local video organization (Woodstock Community Video) and was working specifically with the production of sound tapes. Within three years, he had become coordinator of the Artists TV Lab in Woodstock and concurrently realized his first video installation—in fact, an extension of his earlier sculptural concerns—a piece called *Hole in the Wall* (1974). The work involved cutting an actual hole in the wall of the building at Woodstock in which he fit a video monitor. The tape that played on the monitor was a literal documentation describing the process of the artist cutting through the wall to make the hole in which the monitor was placed. Again, the self-referential idea resurfaces as a hybrid between sculpture and video.

At the time Hill was not aware of conceptual art nor was he aware of the early work of Robert Morris, such as *Box with the Sound of its Own Making* (1962), a piece roughly comparable to Hill's, at least on a structural level, but from twelve years earlier. Yet, within a few years, Hill developed an extraordinary knowledge of the technical capabilities of the video medium, in addition to developing a clearer understanding of art in relation to the medium. The fact that his *Hole in the Wall* was not well received or understood by the Woodstock community of videomakers suggested something very important to the young artist: that making art and making video programs were not at all synonymous. Although his technical knowledge of video had progressed astronomically, Hill did not feel that this in itself was enough to make art. Although the technique came relatively easily to Hill, the real challenge lay ahead of him in terms of how to develop a statement, a point of view as an artist, without confusing the medium with the artist's idea.

In 1975, a year later, Hill conceived and directed a series of intermedia performances in Woodstock, called *Synergism,* which brought together dance and music with video. In doing so, he was able to realize a new direction in art. He also became an artist-in-residence at the Experimental Television Center in Binghamton, which continued through 1977. That year he established the Open Studio Video Project in Barrytown, New York, as a way of offering an alternative to the obsessive focus on technical matters being offered in Woodstock. This eventually led to a visiting associate professorship at the Media Center of the State University of New York in Buffalo (1979–80) and eventually a visiting professorship at Bard College in 1983. In the meantime, Hill was being invited to panels, appointed to boards, and given artist-in-residencies, both nationally and internationally. By the early 1980s, his work had entered into the lexicon of video art. He was showing both single-channel tapes and video installations in various prestigious art centers and museums. In 1980, he was selected for the "Video Viewpoints" series at the Museum of Modern Art, New York, and in 1983 he was given a retrospective of his videotapes at the American Center in Paris and an installation at the Whitney Museum of American Art. Since the mid-1980s, Hill has established himself as one of the major voices in the art of video. He has had major exhibitions and retrospectives of his work at important museums in Europe and in the United States, and has been the recipient of numerous awards, including the coveted MacArthur Award (1998).

One of the first noticeable themes in the work of Gary Hill is his concern for the self-referentiality of the medium, a notion that evolved from Hill's earlier concerns as a sculptor. There is also the obsession with time, the focus on specific intervals of time, as a means of raising consciousness about the reception of information being delivered in relation to the medium. Third, there is the theme of language. For Hill, as we will see, language is inextricably bound to time. Language occurs in time, and time is essential to our comprehension of language. Video is a medium that can make this clear and in the process of making it clear can elevate the consciousness of the receiver (the subject) to nearly inspired heights. Fourth, there is the "neo-metaphysical" aspect in Hill's work that is often denied by some theorists who are given to dismiss such notions as untenable in relation to the more rigorous semiotic constructs that are also available in Hill's tapes and installations.

This is to suggest a phenomenology of experience, in the sense that the philosopher Merleau-Ponty defines it, not only through the act of seeing but through the interception of language in relation to how to see. This aspect of Hill's oeuvre is not about separating the retinal, or purely visual aspect of art, from the nonretinal, or idea-based concerns of art, as defined by the artist Marcel Duchamp, as much as revealing the contiguity between the two. It is about restoring a sense of the tactile through the language of perception in an increasingly simulated, mediated, and dematerialized world; yet, at the same time, Hill is equally in favor of testing the limits of the tactile world. It would appear that he wants the truth from the manner in which we experience language and vision; and in wanting this truth, he desires the illusion of things to reveal themselves for what they are. In many instances, Hill will push language beyond the bounds of audibly or even cognitively defined receptivity in order to make this point.

Finally, there is the problem of the image—a theme of particular concern to Hill; that is, how to get around the seduction of the image? How to avoid the automatic presumption that the image or sequence of images can tell the whole story? This is where the conceptual roots of Gary Hill's art reside. His work is directed toward the structure of how we experience the image, not just toward an analysis of the image. The structure, of course, has everything to do with language, the way images speak, even in the silent intervals, the blank interstices between other images, what George Quasha and Charles Stein refer to as the "liminal," the in-between area or the threshold where language and image intersect.

Thus, there are five discernible themes in the work of Gary Hill:

one, the self-referentiality of the medium as understood through perceptual cognition; two, the viewer's phenomenological awareness of time-consciousness; three, the relationship to and interaction of language with the structure of experience; four, the neo-metaphysical issue of Being as affected by the mediation of technology and language; and five, the problem of the image in its parallel function to language.

What becomes apparent as these themes are revealed in Hill's video installations and single-channel works is how they are rarely isolated. The themes continually overlap and intervene. They repeat and reinforce themselves only to find a conduit or passage into another theme. It is the interplay of these thematic intersections that gives Hill's work a specific density of structure. In fact, it is never static and therefore less a structure than a system in which the parameters play themselves out.

For example, *Circular Breathing* (1974) is a large-scale black-and-white, five-channel projection/installation measuring 10 feet high by 35 feet in length, spanning across a darkened space from wall to wall. A laserdisc and synchronizer are programmed to place the images in their adjacent locations to one another. *Circular Breathing* is characterized by its calculation and stark simplicity, a kind of ultrarefinement of video installation in the context of narrative form. There is something about the imprint of these mundane images from everyday life, both indoors and outdoors. They are not alluring images, but compact ones, where there is both a compression of time and a refinement of intention. In fact, one might refer to Hill's images as ideograms in the sense of the language containing the image or, perhaps, it is the other way around. This kind of flow between images has an apparent irrationality, yet it is a flow that cements the piece into a total, wide-screen wholeness. There is a phenomenology here, a sense of the gestalt field, a sequential time/space field, digitally calculated, yet without a clearly defined formalist perimeter.

The structure of these sequences is reminiscent of some of Allan Kaprow's "activities" from the 1970s; they depict a structure through intimacy and repetition. One of the most striking sequences is of an older man in a boat sailing out into a bay or estuary of some type. The location of these scenes is never specific. Occasionally one of the five fragments will end, leaving a blank space on the wall between the others. Gradually, one realizes that the others are also "closing out" one at a time until they eventually start up again. What one is left with in *Circular Breathing* is the persistent phenomenon of seeing, the concept that Roget investigated in his experimentation with still images in motion in the 1820s. Hill's version is different, however, in that his persistence of seeing does not rely on still images but on digital images produced in time. In fact, it becomes a discourse of time itself, on acknowledging time as a relative state in relation to a presumed norm.

This further suggests that time is changing, and consequently our perceptions of time are changing as we acculturate to the media. The implication here is that the persistence of vision in the twenty-first century is more about adapting to a normative sense of biological time in relation to the circuitry that envelopes us; in other words, how do we find the stasis within kinesis, the language of the green room with the temporality of what we do and what we think we are doing? Mittenthal cites the famous passage by the media philosopher Marshall McLuhan: "Heidegger surfboards along on the electronic wave as triumphantly as Descartes rode the mechanical wave." The relationship between Heidegger and McLuhan is interesting and important for Gary Hill. It is the place where media reflects nature and where a new consciousness of language enters into the fold (of the wave?).

Circular Breathing gets at the "essence" of the phenomenological question as well. It is not only a question as to what the nature of Being within time is in the traditional Heideggerian sense, but a more dynamic construct related to how our awareness of time through media affects the way we understand and articulate our position in the world. In this sense, Hill seems inextricably bound to the secular notion of Being as discussed in Heidegger. Specifically, Hill is concerned with Being and time through the filter of the media. This is a central concern to Hill's video phenomenology and what differentiates him from other artists working in the media today. It is not just the "primacy of perception" (Merleau-Ponty) that concerns Hill, but how perception becomes mediated. This is more than just a technological issue; it is both linguistic and psychological or, perhaps, psycho-sociological. As Hill has made clear on numerous occasions, too much preference is given to the image, and not enough attention to the language that supports it.

Captions are not the issue here. Rather, it is an issue of how to give the text an equal status—a tension that consciously alters perception—that places the image in a perpetual state of crisis. Only when the image appears in crisis do we take the time to question it, to look at the image in a fresh way, to find its equivalence in language. How do we elevate the status of language in an age of image-bombardment where language is given a perfunctory status, one that is less than secondary? How do we give language a new kind of resonance, a reverberation between the passage of images, within time itself? It is within the context of language that images achieve a purpose, a sense of flow, a contiguity. It is the place where images pass by our receptivity, our conscious bearings. There is the assumption that they will appear and disappear in a virtual context. But what if images were so inscribed that they appeared to stand still, even for a fraction of a second, so as to question their veracity in relation to our act of perception? This is a method that Hill has employed consistently in his work since 1983, and it is the kind of directed self-examination within the context of language that gives his work the necessary tension that it has.

Hill's work is dependent on the context of seeing as an activity of time-consciousness. His installation *Tall Ships* (1992) at the 1993 Whitney Biennial was like an isolation chamber. Upon entering the darkened corridor, eyes had to adjust to the dim light of the video projections. Moving along the corridor, black-and-white images of people, spaced equidistantly on either side, advanced toward the viewer, then turned away. These ghostly images, like specters, were neither in color nor in sharp depiction. They seemed to float in the environment, yet always vertically poised. As viewers walked through the space, their movements triggered a mechanism that made the figures move.

In an interview included here, Hill explained the title to art critic Regina Cornwell. It related to a photograph he had seen of a tall ship taken in 1930 when these vessels were being removed from the Seattle harbor to order to construct a bridge. The appearance of these ships with their enormous vertical masts and full sails became an association, a metaphorical representation of the people he was videotaping for the installation. Again, Hill reveals his penchant for metaphor within the context of the medium itself. The metaphorical substance in *Tall Ships,* in addition to the impressive technical manipulation of the medium and the formal consideration given to the placement of the projected images within the elongated space, is what carries the piece beyond the ordinary. What may appear on one level as just another art world spectacle has a much deeper resonance, reaching through layers of careful decision making as to how the final effect might be incited within the phenomenology of viewing.

In *Viewer* (1996), another large-scale projection, the confrontational aspect of the work was difficult to avoid. A row of seventeen Hispanic men, all projected nearly life-size and in actual color, stand facing the viewer. This was accomplished by using five overhead projectors. By walking into the darkened space one catches the sense of waiting as these men are all looking for work, waiting for temporary employers to drive by and give them a day's assignment, that is, construction work, yard clean-up, moving, and so on. In *Viewer,* Hill replicated a situation that he had confronted himself on a diurnal basis in Seattle. He had seen a row of men gathered outside on the sidewalk near his studio and soon discovered their reason for being there. Drivers would literally pass by and illegally employ them, thus cutting costs in terms of the employer's business.

There is a sweeping theatrical quality in *Tall Ships* and *Viewer* while other works use a more intimate style of theatricality, one that is always conscious of the viewer. The engagement with time-consciousness is important in both types of work. The use of intimacy is evident in *Learning Curve* and *Learning Curve (still point),* both from 1993. *Learning Curve* uses a wide-angle, extreme horizontal projection of a breaking wave, videotaped in black and white. The projection screen is positioned at the end of an elongated school desk. The viewer sits in a grade school desk-chair with the desk portion fanning out to the kinetic depiction of the wave breaking on the screen in front. The image is taped with a loop, so that the same image repeats itself over and over, a technique Hill has used in other works as well. The second version, entitled *Learning Curve (still point),* is fundamentally the same idea in reverse; the desk-chair is the same except that the elongated portion of the desk fans inward to a small video monitor on which one sees the "still point" or the center of the wave before it breaks.

Another work on this scale is *I Believe It Is an Image in Light of the Other* (1991–92). Instead of sitting in one place, the viewer ambulates in relation to a scattered series of open books on the floor where over the texts are inscribed the nude images of bodies, thus showing the relationship between body and text, a theme that is involved with both language and metaphysics, yet also ineluctably held with a self-referential context. The open book becomes the screen for the body; the body, in turn, is the metaphor of the text. The narrative unfolds in relation to the two. Although one is "real" and the other virtual, the image and the text are inextricably bound to one another.

In this sense, Hill "performs" these installations from both a static and a kinetic point of view; but, in either case, there is the clear anticipation that the viewer will become transformed into a participant, not only on a physical or arbitrary level, but on the level of conceptual intrigue; that is, the viewer may feel the ideas on the level of a high sensory cognition which, of course, is different than merely "getting it."

Hill's works are not puzzles despite their labyrinthian solitude; they are works that require something from the viewer. In this way, Hill is indebted to Minimal Art and the kind of gestalt theories that this movement put forth; namely, by walking around the cubes or the tetrahedra you are in the space of an architectonic environment. These primary shapes offer a particular kind of gravitational pull. The space is intensified and pragmatically altered. The viewer's space or space/time changes from all angles as one ambulates around these fabricated structures. One's concept of the structure is only grasped on a conceptual level.

Clover (1994) is a work with roots in Minimal Art that is directly related to this phenomenology of seeing within a gestalt field. Mounted on a table so that the four uncased monitors are positioned between 5 and 6 feet, the average height of a person, each monitor reveals a man walking into the woods away from the viewer. The four monitors of a four-channel installation are placed in a quadrant, in fact, like a clover. Upon approaching the work, one hears the noise of leaves rustling underfoot. It is the combined noise of the four men walking at various times, presumably into the same forest. Each of the performers is wearing a shoulder harness with the video camera attached directly behind his head. The poet/critics George Quasha and Charles Stein explain: "We re-project the four path/leaves of clover pointing inward toward an unknown center, the life or course, which at the same time travel outward themselves projecting toward an open end." Quasha and Stein refer to *Clover* as a "mandala-like construction," meaning that the source of contemplation is somewhere in the center. The trick is to locate that center.

The mandala functions as a labyrinthian Buddhist icon where the subject enters from the periphery and gradually moves inward. There is a certain logic at the beginning, but as the "narrative" progresses the logic begins to form paradoxes so that the actual center is never apparent; that is, the center does not exist in literal terms. The subject is compelled to go beyond the logic in order to get to the center; but, in fact, the center is always intuited. What the subject is doing is moving into himself or herself. The mandala is essentially an outer guide to the inner self. Again, Quasha and Stein understand this open-endedness of *Clover* as linguistic to the following extent: "The syntax is axial: Antithetical (dialogical?) and (im)possible trajectories pursue their twin destinations: here at the crossroads, there in the missing middle."

The occasion of viewing these installations by Gary Hill—in Lyon (France), for example, where many of the foregoing works were exhibited—in a location outside the American context, and in relative isolation within the museum, may incite one to consider more actively the role of video in art. Video art is not merely the deployment of electronic and digital imagery in an institutional setting, founded on the basis of static aesthetic representations, but as an active force in the reinvention of how we understand the image/text as a paradigm within a globalized, mediated world ridden with deeply sublimated conflicts and denials. The unpretentious beauty and psycho-sociological impact of these installations of Gary Hill, in both form and concept, open the possibility for another level of intimacy in art—one that does not have to be about the spectacle as in the sensational effects of television advertising or the popular media. Rather, the impact of Gary Hill's work allows a slow passage of information to absorb its way into consciousness through a slow interaction between language and the virtual image within a physical space.

Gary Hill is interested in enunciating ideas that carry a subtle impact. In much of his work, one may easily experience the passage of time and in the passing one may feel the reverberation of language existing without having an obvious cause-and-effect relationship. It is the language of art expressed through the structure of a newly discovered intimacy, a structure of mind in relation to body, feeding through the channels of information dissemination, and finally becoming significant as art. This centering/decentering process, as seen in *Clover* and another related installation called *CRUX*, is symptomatic of Hill's method of thinking in relation to the video medium. It is particularly evident in how he deploys language as the medium (within the medium) to arbitrate the experience of what one is seeing. Language, for Hill, is representative of time, of the temporal process of seeing, or, from a Husserlian perspective, the fulcrum whereby one may discover a sense of "internal time-consciousness." But for this kind of ontology to occur, language may function as the conduit that takes the viewer to the threshold of this experience.

One of the best examples of this experiential phenomenon can be felt in *Primarily Speaking* (1981–83). Here the artist uses an eight-channel audio/video installation to set up a progression of equivalents between syllabic speech and imagery. As the viewer stands between the walls of the installation version of *Primarily Speaking* with its flashing video screens, using electronically generated color fields in relation to still video imagery, there is a sense that the screens are speaking. It is a kind of cacophony in that all the screens are speaking, although not necessarily to one another. Like an absurdist drama, the screens (characters) create their own monologues in relation to one another, playing off one another, but only in the most random sense. Most often, the medium of video represents a person speaking or a voice-over narrative as in the evening news; but in *Primarily Speaking,* it is the sensation of the monitors speaking without any secondary intervention in terms of pictorial representation or narrative captioning. Every syllable is measured according to each visible frame. The coherence of the image/text is direct, rather than indirect. We are being spoken to by the medium; this operation suggests the medium is a literal fact, a measurement of language itself. As the Dutch critic Willem van Weelden makes clear in his essay "Primarily Spoken," the experience of the viewer—or "spectator," as he prefers—is confronted with the ambiguity between the image and the text:

> The spectator no longer knows what came first: his text, the images on the tape, his own mental images, or the text read by Hill. This is important, because the creator is attempting to pursue the spectator as relentlessly as possible. In this tape, Hill has woven together absence and presence, essence and fact, time and space, meaning and sign, perception and imagination, speech and writing into a whole that is impossible to disentangle.

Primarily Speaking has an antecedent in another single-channel work called *Soundings* (1979). In the earlier piece, an image of a round uncased speaker is presented on the screen (a literal mandala). As the listener hears the voice of Hill reciting a text, related to the image and to the idea of sound, "a hand enters the picture" holding sand. It is apparent that the voice we have been hearing on the screen is coming through the speaker in that the center of the speaker is pulsating with the enunciation of each phoneme. The hand begins to drop grains of sand onto the speaker; the speaker, in turn, bounces the sand due to the vibration of the speaker's voice. More sand is deposited into the speaker until the weight of the sand covering the inside of the speaker makes it impossible for any further movement of the sand to occur. Sand fills the speaker as the voice is reduced to a muffled noise.

What *Soundings* has in common with *Primarily Speaking* (given, of course, the greater complexity of the latter) is the extreme literalness of the spoken text, as if to suggest that the image has a secondary role. What is interesting about this process is how Hill has deconstructed certain expectations about the function of video art as a generator of images or as a visual medium that extends the static frame of painting.

Video is quite clearly a visual medium; the point of Hill's discourse—his intention, in fact—is to play down the role of the image in relation to the text, a point he makes incisively in his interview with Lucinda Furlong:

> When you're trying to focus an idea, you're always in the context of everything else. All the external distractions are still going to exist, and they're going to affect that honed-in moment you're having. But the text is the heart of it. Language can be this incredibly forceful material—there's something about it where if you can strip away its history, get to the materiality of it, it can rip into you like claws, whereas images sometimes just slide off the edge of your mind, as if you were looking out a car window.

The vanishing of the video image is a fact. The image appears like vapor, then disappears; the signals are fleeting, not static. Hill has commented: "If I have a position, it's to question the privileged place that image, and for that matter sight, hold in our consciousness." What Hill is asserting here, as recently shown in *Midnight Crossing* (1997), is the need to establish a conceptual place for the image and thereby to understand that images cannot exist independently from language and still maintain the same significance. This may occur despite the random appearance of how images may occur in sequence.

The experience of watching video is not as neutral as it may seem. It is contingent on how the structure is conceptualized and how the images are manipulated within the structure: how the idea of an image informs our way of seeing. The critic Jacinto Lageira has made an insightful comment in this regard. In speaking of Gary Hill, Lageira asserts that "the term 'image' is not to be taken here as representation, depiction, reproduction, or imitation of what is perceived—a mental representation is clearly not an image, strictly speaking—but as a construction of our mind that we can formulate through language." This is precisely what *Primarily Speaking* is attempting to tell us. There can be no accurate understanding of one's experience of video in general terms any more than painting can be generalized. The experience is contingent on the formulation of images that operate on the basis of language. According to Lageira, to conceptualize video is to think of video imagery fundamentally as a language.

Today, the medium of video installation is a type of "sculpture in the expanded field"—a term employed by the critic Rosalind Krauss—in that real objects and performers may function in relation to the video monitor and in relation to the image(s) on the monitor(s). The use of video within the context of either a single-channel tape or an installation, as in the work of Gary Hill, relies on a specific structure and on a particular means of conceptualizing the language that will inform our experience. The installation, entitled *Inasmuch As It Is Always Already Taking Place* (1990), described by MoMA curator Barbara London, functions according to a specific structure that is contingent on the text of a specific idea. The piece is fundamentally a simulation of the human body. It carries a certain ironical essence not unrelated to Jasper Johns's *Target with Plaster Casts* (1955) or, for that matter, the object-shelves produced by Haim Steinbach some thirty years later.

In Hill's *Inasmuch,* we see a recessed compartment, built 5 feet into the wall, with an arrangement of "sixteen modified video monitors of various sizes, all removed from their casings." Each monitor, like the compartments at the top of Johns's target, reveals a different body part. In contrast to Johns's work, each part is visibly moving. There is an accompanying audio track mix of various sounds that suggest the experience of reading or of a mental reaction to something being read. This is most likely either extending the premise of or giving reference to an earlier tape, entitled *Incidence of Catastrophe* (1987–88). Whereas *Inasmuch* has a certain autonomy in that the signifiers give reference to one another, the earlier *Incidence* might be characterized as an imaginative acting-out of enduring sublimations, a represented state of mind, whereby Hill personally performs the suffering protagonist from the novel *Thomas the Obscure* (1941) by the French writer Maurice Blanchot.

What characterizes Blanchot's novel is a certain obsessive fascination with the abject. In this case, the character Thomas falls into a state of mental trauma where in the process of reading he becomes utterly and unequivocally absorbed in the text. As the critic/curator Lynn Cooke puts it: "Gradually Thomas's mind and body disintegrate as they are invaded and dominated by the voracious text: after robbing him of speech, it renders his mind incoherent and his body incontinent." The character literally becomes imprisoned by the text and he enters a fetal position on the floor, wallowing in his own excrement, and becomes victimized by a form of prelinguistic echolalia. Hill performs the role of Thomas in *Incidence* to the extent that he literalizes the actions of the protagonist. It is both deeply psychological and epistemological.

The intensity of Hill's videotape is a striking visual parallel to Blanchot, one that is heightened, in fact, by the performance of the artist as the solipsistic protagonist. In this way, *Incidence* becomes a powerful indictment of speech turned inward upon itself—indeed, upon the body—thus, an allegory of the solipsism of language; but it is also a discourse on consciousness, on the nature of mental retreat, the place where language disappears, the vortex where all sensory cognition is lost; and within this lost terrain, this primordial prelinguistic rattle, language still functions as the ultimate recourse to communication, the most primal, the most fundamental evidence of the body, lost and without deference to its own desensitized system of unconscious yearning, the yearning simply to be.

The writers of the works in this volume, including the artist himself, maintain a point of view that reflects this exchange between language and image. What comes to the foreground in Hill's aesthetic is a command of the medium as a means to sensitize—indeed, to sensualize—our perceptions, thus allowing language to feed into the sensorium of the mind, to the awareness of our innate sense of language as a fundamental premise. This is the crux of the matter: how to get to the point of that synaptic charge, that "still point" in the wave where we feel the tug that tells the mind and body which direction to go, to get into the flow, to discover the ride through the crest of Being. It is the synapse between the image and language, the open liminality where the threshold of language meets the genesis of the image evolving and dissolving through time. Neither is subservient or acquiescent toward the other. They stand or float on equal terms. So, we are back to surfing in the metaphysical sense, and to the metaphor of the green room—the perpetually moving state of consciousness that governs our knowing which direction to go. Being within the wave is an arbitration of consciousness where the work of Gary Hill takes us into a new time/space.

I Critical Essays

Barbara London

Video Spaces:

Gary Hill

The first time Gary Hill arrived to install *Inasmuch As It Is Always Already Taking Place* (1990) at a museum, he brought close-ups of a body recorded on forty different video loops. He selected sixteen to play on individual rasters—monitors stripped of their outer casings. The rasters, ranging in size from the eyepiece of a camera to the dimensions of an adult rib cage, were set on a shelf recessed 5 feet into the wall, slightly below eye level. Hill ran each loop on a screen that matched the size of the particular section of the body recorded on the tape. As he positioned the monitors, moving them around with the objectivity of a window dresser, it seemed he was actually handling parts of a living body: a soft belly that rose and fell with each breath, a quadrant of a face with a peering eye like that of a bird warily watching an interloper.

The components of the body displayed in *Inasmuch*—Hill's own—are without any apparent distinction. Neither Adonis nor troll, neither fresh nor lined with age, the body suits the endless loops, suggesting that it exists outside time, without past or future.

The arrangement of the rasters does not follow the organization of a human skeleton. Representations of Hill's ear and arched foot lie side by side; tucked modestly behind them is an image of his groin. Within this unassuming configuration, each raster invites meditation. For example, on one screen a rough thumb toys with the corner of a book page. In its repetition, the simple action of lifting and setting down the page functions like a close-up in a movie. Further, by concentrating the viewer's attention on such a rudimentary activity, the movement, as in a slow-motion replay, takes on the significance of an epic event.

Originally published in *Video Spaces* (New York: The Museum of Modern Art, 1995).

On a torso-size screen, smooth, taut skin stretches over the ridges of bones that shape the human back. The image fills the frame, and the monitor, given its equivalent size, is perceived as part of the body: an enclosure, a vessel, no longer something that simply displays a picture. Raster and image exist as a unified object, as representation, as a living thing.

Long, nervelike black wires attached to each raster are bundled together like spinal cords. Snaked along the shelf, the bundles disappear from view at the back of the recess. Although unifying the system of monitors, this electrical network emphasizes that the body parts are presented as extremities, without a unifying torso. The hidden core to which the components of the body are attached serves as a metaphor for a human being's invisible, existential center: the soul.

Although none of its segments are "still," the installation has the quality of a still life. Typically, the objects in still-life paintings are drawn from everyday life—food and drink, musical instruments, a pipe and tobacco. Their placement appears arbitrary, and they do not communicate with each other. Often set out on a platform or table, the elements are positioned within arm's reach and appeal to all the senses, especially to touch and taste. *Inasmuch* has most in common with a *vanitas,* a category of still life in which the depicted objects are meant to be reminders of the transience of life. In place of the usual skull and extinguished candle, *Inasmuch* depicts an animate being whose vulnerability underscores the mortality of flesh.

A textured composition of ambient sounds forms an integral part of the installation. For example, the sound of skin being scratched or a tongue clicking inside the mouth, although barely recognizable as such, is orchestrated with recordings of rippling water and softly spoken phrases. Within this uniform soundscape, the looping of the sound track combines distinctive notes in a pulse that reinforces the living quality of the installation.

In *Inasmuch* Hill has reduced the requisites for "living" to visceral sounds and, more important, physical movement that has no end. However, the ceaseless activity is an illusion, in that each component exists only as a seamless loop of 5 to 30 seconds in duration. Creating such a loop—one that seems to go on for eternity—involves a bit of a trick: the videotaped image has to match exactly, in position and in movement, at two places on the tape. The segment between these two shots is cut, and the tape spliced into a loop without a discernible beginning or end. Otherwise, for example, if the thumb were to lift the page and then "jump" back to repeat the action, or if the torso should rise slightly and then abruptly rise again, the piece would become a sort of Sisyphean depiction of endlessly repeated activities.

Inasmuch recalls an age when art was thought to be an illusion, a trick played on the senses. Here, the images are not illusory, but time itself is hidden from the viewer, in the way that segments of time are made to appear limitless. In folding time back on itself, a seemingly simple concept, Hill has fashioned a creature whose humanness poses an existential challenge.

Jacques Derrida

Videor

. . . So one would say. It seems to me, at least, that this is the case: quite singular operations, more and more numerous, put to "work" the new "video" power, the possibility which, in an apparently empirical fashion, is called "video." But I say "it seems to me that . . ." since I am not sure that I have at my disposal an adequate concept for what today goes by the name video and especially video art. It seems to me—that we will have to choose from among three rigorously incompatible "specificities." To go quickly by using common names, let us say that these are (1) the specificity of video *in general;* (2) that of video *art;* (3) that of such works, or the putting-to-work of a general technique that is called "video." Whether it is shared by these three possibilities, or whether it is proper to each of them, the aforesaid specificity would suppose the determination of an *internal and essential* trait. Now, despite the upheavals in progress, the use of a different technique or of new supports—

—But which ones exactly? What is a support for video?

—I am still wondering what these things have in common: for example, video grafted onto the ordinary use of television, surveillance video, and the most daring research, called "video art," which still remains confined in rather narrow circuits, either public or private, and whose "pragmatic" conditions have nothing in common with the other finalizations of video. The possibility of multiple monitors and of a freer play with this multiplicity, the restructuration of the space of production and performance, the new status of what is called an actor, a character, the displacement of the limit between the private and the

Originally published in *Passage de l'Images* (Paris: Musée National d'Art Moderne, Centre Georges Pompidou, 1990). Translated by Peggy Kamuf.

public, a growing independence with regard to public or political monopolies on the image, a new economy of relations between the direct and the nondirect, between what is carelessly said to be "real" time and "deferred" time, all this constitutes a bundle of considerable transformations and stakes. If, however, video can play such a visible role here, at a new rhythm, it is neither the sole nor the first technique to do so, which, at least for video art, is an external determination. Once again, it seems to me therefore (*mihi videor*) that there is no essential unity among these things that seem to resemble each other or that are assembled together under the name of video.

—But perhaps the video event, among others, reveals precisely the problematic fragility of this distinction between an internal determination and an external determination. That would already be rather disturbing . . .

—So why then do you say, quite rightly, "among others"? In any case, we would agree, I think, that giving up specific identity doesn't hurt anyone, and perhaps it's better that way.

—On the contrary, it always hurts a lot, that's the whole problem—

—Why should it still be necessary to try to identify? Especially in this case, why should one have to zero in on the irreducible property of an "art"? Why try to classify, hierarchize, even situate what one still likes to call the "arts"? Neither opposition (major/minor, for example) nor a genealogy ordered with reference to the history of supports or techniques seems pertinent any longer in this regard, supposing that they ever were. And if the very concept of the "beaux-arts" were thereby to find itself affected in the dark core of its long life or its nine lives, would that be such a serious loss?

—One could say that my uncertainty in this regard—it has a long history but it keeps growing, it is both uneasy and joyful—has been encouraged by the experience of the "video" simulacrum into which I have seen myself, modestly, swept along for a little while now, ever since I was given the chance to participate, or rather to figure in *DISTURBANCE* by Gary Hill. Better still, ever since I seemed to see (*videre videor,* as Descartes would say)[1] my simulacrum do no more than pass by there, risk a few passing steps that would be led elsewhere by someone else, I didn't know where. Narcissism set adrift. I owe this chance not only the way one owes a chance but the way one is obliged by another to be involved in an experience, without knowing it, without foreseeing it—an experience that combines in such an inventive fashion luck with calculation and *tuchè* with *anankè*. But, for that very reason, I was in no position to talk and, finally, I had no desire to do so. The blind passerby was hardly even an extra; as to what may be said about that, others have done so with better results than I might even attempt, in particular Jean-Paul Fargier in "Magie blanche."[2] On the other hand, concerning that which cannot be said about it and which remains encrypted in the bodily contact with another simulacrum, with a text that, as I was told and as I believed up until the last minute, was "apocryphal" (the more or less improvised choices that I dictated to myself, almost without seeing—only once—in truth, let be dictated to me like the truth of oracular symptoms in the space of my own familial, tattered gnostic, those raveled fragments of the Gospel according to Thomas that Gary Hill put into my hands, the interrupted premeditations and the sheer chance of improvisation, the hasty crossing of repetitions or rehearsals in the course of an irreversible scene, which is to say unrehearsed, live, direct but without direction, in a direct that was to get carried away with itself, from itself in the course of a simulacrum of performance or presentation that would reveal that there is not and never has been a direct, live presentation, not even, as Virilio ventures to put it in a very fine text, a "presentation . . . [of an] electro-optical milieu,"[3]) of that which, therefore, cannot be said about it and that regards only me and mine, I will say nothing. And for lack of time, I will also reduce to silence a whole possible rhetoric on the subject of, precisely, "video silence," of video "mystique," in the sense that Wittgenstein speaks of "mystique" when he says that concerning that about which one cannot speak, one must remain silent. Here, what one cannot "say" other than by showing it, or rather by putting on a quasi-presentation in video on the subject of video, must be silenced. One must put up or shut up, that is, do it or be quiet, take into account, as Gary Hill does, what happens to language through the "video" even (parti) . . .

—Ah well, but a moment ago you were saying that you did not see yourself as capable of speaking of an identity—already identifiable, already assured—of the "video" event . . .

—Not yet, one must take into account what happens to language (partitioned or distributed, cut, strung or tacked together, delinearized, palindromanagrammatized in more than one language and passing like a serpent across seven monitors at the same time) through the "video" event . . .

—But are you sure there is only one monitor, right here, and one line? What do you think you see?

—. . . anything but a mutism, a certain "being silent" of this writing—new but very impure and all the newer for that—which stages discourses or texts that are thought to be of the most "interior" sort. Is it just by chance that Gary Hill solicits, among others, gnostic texts or the writings of Blanchot? One never sees a new art, one thinks one sees it; but a "new art," as people say a little loosely, may be recognized by the fact that it is not recognized, one would say that it cannot be seen because one lacks not only a ready discourse with which to talk about it, but also that implicit discourse which organizes the experience of this art itself and is working even on our optical apparatus, our most elementary vision. And yet, if this "new art" arises, it is because within the vague terrain of the implicit, something is already enveloped—and developing.

—But someone who was neither an actor, nor an extra, just barely a passerby mobilized by a new interplay of the alea and the program, couldn't he say something about the way in which "video art" affects the essential status of its interpreters (I do not say its actors, even less its characters, one would say they are just barely its human subjects)? Whoever appears or sees himself appear in a video work of art is neither a "real person," nor a movie or stage actor, nor a character in a novel.

—Are you talking about video art or about the art of Gary Hill?

—As this was my first video passion (passion in the sense that, seeing myself passing by reading in front of a camera against an absolutely white studio background that made me think, I don't know why, of the cemetery in Jerusalem seen from the Mount of Olives, I was all the more gravely passive in that I did not know what Gary Hill would do with what I saw myself doing without seeing myself, with me and mine, with my words, the words that I borrowed, selected, recomposed, repeated, nor what he would do with my passing steps whose rhythm was all I could calculate, not the trajectory, and in fact this image was swept along by a well-understood path of necessity, from alea to alea, there where I could in no way have foretold or foreseen it would go, but passion also in the sense that right away I *loved* it, that is to say, as always when one loves, I right away wondered why I loved *that*, what or whom I loved exactly), I will say only a few words very quickly on the question that, like everyone, I have asked myself and am still asking: if it is an "art," that, and an absolutely new one, especially with regard to the analogues that are painting, photography, cinema, and television, and even the digital image, what would compose this irreducible difference, that very thing? What is going on there? What went on with me? What happened to the passerby that I was, using my body, my passing steps, my voice as no art, no other art, so one would say, would have done? It seems to me. Difficult. I tried out all the possible analyses—forgive me if I do not repeat them here—nothing worked; I could always reduce the set of components of this "art" to some combination of givens older than *that*, video "properly speaking" as art "properly speaking." So one could say that the question is badly put.

—Let us suppose Gary Hill to be exemplary here . . .

—No, not exemplary, otherwise you are going to end up back with the same classical problematic that you want to avoid; no, not exemplary, but singular, idiomatic, his work, each of his works is found to be singular and sweeps the general technique called video along in an adventure that renders it irreplaceable, but irreplaceable among other irreplaceables, other unique effects of signature, even if it puts to work many other things, many other "arts" that have nothing to do with video . . .

—All right, but you are still insisting on the "work," on the shape of its unity, on the idiomatic singularity of the signature, as if it were self-protecting and self-legitimating, in an internal fashion, whereas today events called "video" can lay bare symptoms that are far more disturbing and provocative; for example, those that lead us to think the singularity of "works" and "signatures" beginning with the very thing that institutes them and threatens them at the same time. Supposing that there is an effect, so it seems, as an effect and as the simulacrum on the basis of which we are speaking, some work and some signature, let us then start out from this reminder: Gary Hill was to begin with a sculptor, and a sculptor who was first of all tuned into sonority, indeed to the singing of his sculptures, in other words to that unheard-of technical prosthesis that, at the birth of an art, grafts an ear onto an eye or a hand, right away making us doubt the identity, the name, or the classification of the arts. But he is also one of the few, I do not say the only, "video artists" who is now working, even if he has not always done so, with discourses, many discourses (this is a "new" visual art that—and it is our first enigma—appears to be one of the most discursive), and not only with discourses but also with textual forms that are heterogeneous among themselves, whether literary or not (Blanchot, the Gospels, for example), that seem to be altogether at odds with such a working, with what one thought "video" art had to be, especially if, as seems to be the case, they are anything but the simple pretext assumed by the videogram.

—This obvious fact perhaps calls for the following hypothesis—I indeed say hypothesis, maybe even faction: the specificity of a "new art" —or, in general, of a new writing—is not in a relation of irreducible dependence (by that I mean without possible substitution or prosthesis) and especially of synchrony with the emergence of a technical generality of a new "support." One would say that the novelty remains to come, still to come with regard to a technical mutation that, by itself, could give rise to the most mechanical repetition of genres or stereotypes, for example, narrative, novelistic, theatrical, cinematographic, or televisual . . .

—So it would take time, a kind of latency period, to render the new support, the new technique indispensable, irreducible . . .

—No, not a homogeneous period of latency, but the history of an active, vigilant, unpredictable proliferation that will have displaced even the future perfect in its grammar and permitted in return a new experience of the already identifiable "arts," and not only the "arts," another mode of reading the writings one finds in books, for example, but of so many other things as well, and this without destroying the aura of new works whose contours are so difficult to delimit, that are delivered over to their social spaces, other modes of production, of "representation," archiving, reproducibility, while giving to a technique of writing in all its several states (shooting, editing, "incrustation," projection, storage, reproduction, archiving, and so on) the chance for a new aura . . .

—But there would have to be another name for that, other names for all these things, it seems to me . . .

—I wouldn't say that that is indispensable; one would have to see. It seems to me that . . . . see how Gary Hill makes secret names and dead tongues resonate on his seven monitors . . .

Notes

1. Second *Méditation,* quoted by Jean-Luc Nancy who writes in the course of his analysis: "The *videor* is the illusion which, through an extraordinary torsion or perversion, anchors certainty fully in the abyss of illusion. The place of the *videor* is indeed painting, the portrait, at once the most artificial and the most faithful of faces, the most unseeing and the most clairvoyant eye" (*Ego Sum* [Paris: Flammarion, 1979], pp. 71–72).

2. In *Gary Hill, DISTURBANCE (among the jars),* Musée d'art moderne, Villeneuve d'Ascq.

3. Cf. Paul Virilio, "La Limière indirecte," *Communications* 48, "Video" (1988), pp. 45ff. The point would be to engage a close discussion around the

very interesting but very problematic notions of "telepresence," of "present telereality in 'real time' that supplants the reality of the presence of real space." Already problematic with regard to video in general (the principal, even unique object of Virilio's analysis), these concepts would be even more so, it seems, with regard to the putting to work of "art" video, as well as the type of simulacrum that structures it.

Jacinto Lageira

The Image of the World in the Body of the Text

The history of thought has followed two main paths in its relationships with the world: one consisted in seeing in the human mind only a reflection or a relatively faithful copy of the realities which were external to it and to which it conformed; the other maintained that, on the contrary, our conception of the world depended on the intellectual construction created in order to understand it. In both cases, the tool which serves to support the ideas and images of the world is language.

From the start, the representations which we have of it are closely mixed up with the methods and processes which allow us to see, feel, and experience it, and language is at the heart of what makes sense in the world for us. We are as dependent on it as we are on the images of reality which it enables us to grasp through voice and writing, body and gesture, for what we perceive of ourselves and others, of things and actions, is modeled by a language whose mobility matches the shifting nature of the images. But these images, which seem to be organized by the things themselves, do not reach us as natural data, since they constitute themselves in accordance with the forms and frameworks which are applied to them. When voice and writing delimit subjects of thought or the displacements of our body in space, they immediately inscribe us in an image of the world which is incessantly renewable and perfectible.

To speak of "image" in connection with Gary Hill's work cannot, therefore, be a simple play on words, insofar as his work offers us a fundamental trait of human beings: their capacity to construct the world of objects through language. In this second path followed by the artist,

Originally published in a show catalogue of the Centre Georges Pompidou, Museum of Modern Art, 1992.

we must distinguish the video image from the symbolic, signifying image (picture) which we develop from reality and which we project mentally. The image is not only that of the film which develops its own language: it is also a vision of the world presenting itself in linguistic forms. It is not that the world is in a coded form that has to be deciphered, but there is a kind of fusion possible between world and language, which has to do with putting into words the actions and events that we perceive. It would be very hard for us to say what is totally outside language in the world, since while discoursing we also project a symbolically constituted world which allows us to conceive and understand the things that present themselves to us. But the interpenetration of signs and objects increases at the same time as it reveals the contingent nature of this relationship. The fact that the image of the world is an artificial construction of the mind reveals at the same time a certain stability in language in relation to the evolution of things and the finiteness of this same language as part of a vaster whole which it cannot entirely represent through symbols. Playing with these two poles through multiple texts and images, Gary Hill's work seeks to understand their mechanisms, but also to explain why no vision of the world can exist outside language, inasmuch as it is not a heterogeneous assembly of objects but can only be called world because language enables us to construct its image. We must discard the idea that the image of the world is to be reified by video technology, for this is only one tool among others, manufactured in order to understand our context and our environment. If *video* in Latin means "I see," seeing the world through television or film images no doubt influences our perception and our conception, but it does not fundamentally change our wish to construct intellectually a coherent image of the world outside all instrumentalization. It is precisely because we are creatures of words and writing that we have been able to make tools that are simply an extension of these first capabilities of language, and which in their turn serve to create other tools. If ideas do not relate directly to objects but to other ideas, the tools produced by language can, however, manipulate other objects by producing forms and images that are nevertheless linked to language. To be sure, the objects or tools constructed by G.H. have an aesthetic function and set out to integrate the world and the language of art, but *by referring* to the world outside and to natural language. Going beyond an individual quest, in his way G.H. explores a primary, universal condition: we cannot escape from language and the world, or exist without them.

To us, all this seems quite normal. As normal as the images of everyday life which G.H. shows us in his works. On the other hand, what seems less banal and obvious is the fact that this world, which is our environment and was already here before we arrived, is never perceived naturally but always through artificial frameworks. Our only point of reference and connection is thus never understood and felt in itself: we make images of it. And the work of G.H. does not naively use images of the world as an inexhaustible material to serve artistic ends, but rather makes this relationship its driving force. For whereas the work of art can develop its own *language,* quite different from the one we speak or write, the world, on the other hand, appears originally in its brutal materiality, its powerful and indifferent Nature.

What, then, are the reasons that prompt us to construct symbolic languages in order to understand the world in which we evolve? According to one of the hypotheses put forward by some philosophers, this is due precisely to the fact that no *intrinsic* relationship exists between the world and our language; if that were the case, we would certainly not resort to symbolic systems in order to explain it to ourselves, because we would *be* the world, as it were.

This problematic of the world understood as the only reality to which we are necessarily connected, while our language is independent of it, occupied Wittgenstein, for example, all his life; one can find this reflection, among others, in his *Philosophical Remarks:* "There is an incessant renewal of the attempt to define the limits of the world in language and thereby to make it evident—but it cannot be done. The world is self-evident, and this is expressed precisely in the fact that the world is all that language has—and can have—to refer to (*bedeuten*). In fact, given that it is only from its reference, the world, that language receives its way of referring, one cannot conceive of a language that does not present (*darstellen*) this world."[1] But since there is a partition line, a different essence belonging to language and world, how are the connections established between the *images* produced by language and the world itself?

The term *image* is not to be taken here as representation, depiction, reproduction, or imitation of what is perceived—a mental representation is clearly not an image, strictly speaking—but as a construction of our mind that we can formulate through language. If we find some of these questions in the work of G.H., we must nevertheless take care not to see it as an illustration of philosophical or literary theories; it is simply the convergence of ideas on the same problem, apparently so simple, that continues to provide food for contemporary thought: How is the image that we have of the world constructed?[2]

Although the images one sees in the work of G.H. are in the first place images of reality, they are also and especially *the image of the act which consists in constructing* the objects and frameworks in which they occur, the actual staging of this symbolizing activity. G.H. offers an oeuvre capable of referring to everyday, personal, philosophical, or literary language, while re-creating, over these preceding versions, a new unpublished version in which the images of the world contained in these discourses themselves become pieces of other images of the world. We often find ourselves in the presence of things and beings in their supposed natural state, only to perceive at once that everything that we see—and *a fortiori* everything that we understand through language—is only a symbolic reformulation which is different in all respects from what these things and beings are. The belief that we are simply receiving images of the real world is revealed to be an illusion, for we project worlds onto the one which is already given and which always appears through a preexisting grid. By weighing up what is given and what is constructed, G.H. relates the naturalness of the world and the artificiality of art and attaches language to the world in order to extract its meaning.

Voice

From his first attempts to his recent works, G.H. has worked on a register of human or natural sounds, stopping more particularly at the voice which, from simple phoneme to speech, is given with the image: "Sounding the image, imaging the sound" (*Soundings*). The voice is in the image, follows it or else gives rise to it, precedes it or completes it, but the image is also in the voice. Their simultaneity, achieved through the mingling of the texture of the image with the texture of the voice, throws into perfect relief the natural character of speech discoursing on things, as the conventional system of words which serves to describe them. The images of things that appear on the screen take their rhythm, form, and meaning in and through language, they seem to be inseparable from it, indissociable, and that without any mystical or ontological act of naming, for the words uttered are not the things and even try to set aside any coincidence between signification and object. The voice and the word are mediations which enable us to go beyond visual realities, while also being tools for exploring these realities to which the mind cannot be indifferent, inasmuch as they form part of its subjects of thought. A superimposition of image and voice considered as matter and material is needed in order to extract their differential processes more effectively, for some of these works consist in showing that the voice is not connected to reality but comes looking for it, the better to rid itself of forms already given.

G.H. pays close attention to volume, vibration, pronunciation, intensity, and inflection, in order to establish certain sound correspondences between the materiality of the world and the physicality of the voice. The forms he gives them are never fixed, and although one can find certain analogies between the timbre, pitch, and warmth of a voice and the images with which it is articulated, one can equally put forward contrasting examples with disturbing, haunting voices which produce a sensation of unease. Most of these voices (those of the artist or actors) are voices off and are naturally out of sight, but they are nevertheless present in the image phonically in order to accentuate its resonant handling, its expressiveness, the effect of dramatization, what we might call the "optophonetics" of the image. In the recent works, the images of reality—pond, bridge, house, path, forest, rain, car—are not accompanied by their natural noises, as if the human voice had to replace them. But it is not a question of making verbal what is mute in Nature through speaking instead of things and objects, since the appearance of the voice in their midst marks the insuperable distance between the naturalness of what is and its perpetual reformulation through our words. The very materiality of the world sets itself against them, because despite the fact that our voice is the fruit of education, work, and apprenticeship, and so of an artificial system, it is a part of *our materiality*, and our world is literally embodied in it.

The voice has to turn into sonorous matter in order to distinguish itself from or oppose itself to the world *almost* on the same level, for visible matter responds to phonic matter. The physicality of the voice is related to images and not to other noises or sounds, because their texture alienates the image through their rough nature. The noise of the waves or the wind makes no sense because it is not a sign, whereas images, on the contrary, even when they are of natural elements, nearly always make some reference to the passage of man and, like the voice, bear more or less visible traces of some work. The selection of words and ways of saying them thus correspond to the selection made from the stock of images of reality and their editing, showing the spectator the result of a series of constraints and determinations. The point of connection between sight and voice, between what is perceived and what is named, is their very functioning: seeing things is also speaking of them; speaking of them already involves arranging them in accordance with the images and archetypes that are peculiar to us. It would be tempting, therefore, to see in the linking of images a syntax similar to that of language, which would provide a partial explanation of the simultaneous appearance of words and images, one addressed to the ear, the other to the eye. However, voice and word do not make the world happen in images but actualize the sense we give them, and thus mark a difference not only in terms of the material form given but also in their nature. The elements of the world are subjected to a succession of sounds, words, and phrases, sometimes independent of their proper connections.

While our gaze is continually solicited by what is visible, a voice permeates our hearing as if it were trying to hypnotize us. More often than not, speech carries on an autonomous discourse on actions and states of the mind or body, as if it was acting on the brain of the listener, while leaving aside fragments of things that take place before his eyes, or sometimes only showing him a white line turning on a black background as in *Processual Video*. However, if the physicality of speech cannot be made concrete in visible images, it is capable of creating new mental images. The voice suggests, creates an imaginary space, projects a world in the listener's mind which, more often than not, has no direct or metaphorical correspondence to the images taken from reality. In these cases, the voice does not try to describe or transform it, but to make itself one with its materiality through rhythm, texture, and pitch, and seeks to insinuate itself into the listener's mind in order to take possession of him, like a puppet on whose behalf it speaks.

The viewer follows the voice as it is the only signal in a blinding confusion of images. In *Around & About,* the appearance of shots of an interior coincides with the syllables pronounced; table, chair, cupboard, or window are absent as referents, but present through their direct relationship with each word pronounced. Their visual existence is thus not really what is displayed on the screen but the mental correspondence established by a rhythmic sequence of sounds which makes sense only for us, that is to say, which makes sense only through language and not through a relationship with the world itself which, in fact, produces no sounds or noises. The rhythm of the voice compels the world, through the images which are connected to it, to follow its tempo. The struggle between the two material aspects of voice and image—taken only in their interplay of colors, masses, sonorities, conjunctions, and cross-references—is redoubled by the question of the actual meaning of what is proffered.

If the attempt to establish correspondences between the materiality of the world and that of language underlines the physicalist aspects of voice, phonemes, and various small units of sound, it is not only a matter of carrying out a plastic study of sounds and images—even if this is fundamental—but also of marking out the frontier between the artificiality of language and the naturalness of the world. Speaking of what we find around us does not consist only in establishing our position in our thoughts or in relationship to our body but also in taking hold of reality. On one level, by manipulating this reality through playing with confrontations of the rhythms of voice and images, G.H. would tend to make us believe that speech literally makes the world move, but on another level the content of the discourse that it may carry on shows that it makes the world explicit as image. Their development also seems to be connected, since clear images are consonant with a simple discourse—as in *Primarily Speaking,* where the words *red* or *blue* are contemporaneous with the colors named which appear on the screen—and a more elaborate sequence of shots interact with a more complex language (*Site Recite*). G.H. thus seems to rediscover in the development of his work the process of apprenticeship of any human being confronted by the world. The child's wish to know the names of things is not focused on knowledge of the names for their own sake, but on the objects they denote. The more numerous the words, the greater the world of possible, manipulable objects. The apprehension of things visually, corporeally, acoustically, through the filters of voice and word, thus coincides with the development of the materiality of the world and the materiality of our linguistic system. To speak is to project our phonic form and meaning in order to cover up the materiality of the world.

Writing

The immanence of the voice in what takes place visually puts us in a state of empathy with the works, so natural does it seem to us that *one speaks* and that one *speaks to us* about things of reality. We identify immediately with this voice which recites the states of the world to us, as if it was yet another of its states. But we are only in the field of the *phone,* an aspect of language which has absolutely no need of any kind of material image in order to circulate as sign. The manual or electronic writing which now appears on the screen in certain works brings us back to a spatialization of language, an inscription of the language we speak, but showing not only the various forms and typographies of writing, but equally the noncorrespondence between the visualization of the signs and the sight of the image. Initially, it seems to be the opposite: writing merges into a wave, a tree, a body, blends into the object perceived so as to constitute a part or an extension of it. Writing in its turn becomes an image. As with our voice, this takes place thanks to our body and is displayed in a space outside ourselves which appears as the place where our abstract ideas take concrete form, as if our brain, by displaying itself, was externalizing itself in greater topologies which it could only just contain in its infinite smallness. Such a fusion always remains material, and could not account for the fact that only writing can speak simultaneously of itself and of something else just by imaging itself before our eyes. Writing becomes an image which reflects itself. In the viewer who reads the words that pass before his eyes; in the voice which is their dependent aspect and which can repeat phonically what one reads on the screen; in the image of a page of text that one reads aloud or to oneself; between two screens that then act as potential mirrors. By exploring all the possibilities of reading and speaking in *DISTURBANCE (among the jars),* G.H. shows objects and actions that can refer directly or metaphorically to what one sees, while giving clear primacy to writing and its symbolization at the expense of reality. In this work, gnostic texts are used which were rediscovered in some jars in 1945 at Nag Hammadi in Egypt. The coexistence and simultaneity on the seven monitors of phrases which one hears and others which one reads, some that one interprets or that one translates into one's mother tongue as they scroll by, shows the interdependence between what is seen and what is said. Vision is understood only because it reads, and the words exist only insofar as they are perceived. The movement of the hand writing on the screen, the voice off declaiming the text, the words to be deciphered in real time, the preponderance of an image to be read are one and the same project which consists in affirming that seeing is firstly seeing a meaning. Through writing we see meaning take shape in characters, words, and sentences, while through the voice we *hear* it. Writing has the advantage that it can be a phonetic retranscription of the voice at the same time as it spatializes itself visually and no longer vocally. And also that in silent reading the writing keeps quiet. It transmits what it has to say only through the eyes.

Unlike the obsessive voice *imposed* on the spectator, with an intensity and a power that he cannot master but whose rhythm he can easily follow, the reading of the text—even if it is displayed at a normal speed—disturbs its understanding, hence its language, hence the perception of the whole. As soon as writing is added to the voice, the observer who, as well as viewer, is constantly called upon as reader, speaker, and listener, is outmatched. Because writing brings together all these forms, it overflows the cognitive capabilities of the viewer obliged to follow voice, writing, and image, their interpenetration and their self-interpretation. Linguistic interpretation of one system of signs in another, but also an interpretation in the musical sense of the term, since all these linguistic tools sometimes perform together; thus one discovers a correspondence between sound or voice as a material entity and its retranscription in visual notation.

At this stage, the image might approach a system of writing by recording the visible, setting down objects, things, or people, itemizing their words and actions; but this is an illusion. Although the set of images may form a *language,* the configuration is nevertheless not that of our mother tongue. The visualization of the signs of graphic or mechanical writing and the sight of the image do not address the same organs or the same cognitive structures, and they do not bring us within a unified temporality. Even if the magnificent "verbi-voco-visual" symphony of *DISTURBANCE* throbs with a homogeneous development, the writing does not act on us in the same way sensorially; it requires the hand, an activity of the body, and not the relative passivity of hearing. The gesture of writing mobilizes our limbs as if we were thinking directly with our hands, which trace the signs of what we think. The immediacy of this transmission is similar to speech, with the difference that writing requires a graphic system which comes and sets itself in the heart of objects and rivals them as object. The patterns of letters and words are objects created by man, artifacts, codes constructed with a view to substituting for things. The recourse in these works to visual palindromes, reversals of letters, words, or sentences, and their disappearance and materialization on the screen emphasizes their characteristic of manipulable object. Like the pieces on the chessboard of which Saussure speaks in connection with the elements of language, the set of signs and scripts can occupy one place, then another, and can be displaced within certain limits.

With alphabetical or ideographic systems, one can literally trace their graphic representation in space, as the representation of our ideas, since these "objects" have validity as something else. More than the voice, the written sign spatializes thought, printing it on a page or on the screen, and in the same movement, the thought thus retranscribed affixes its mark on things and beings like a seal on a block of wax. This is possible only because it too is located in space.

In certain respects, and this is verifiable in certain installations (*And Sat Down Beside Her, CORE SERIES*), the analogy with writing occurs precisely in a kind of *paging*—rather than staging—of screens and images in their own space. As if it was a question of fixing words and sentences on a page where it was necessary to determine the format, the size of the characters, the weight of the paper, the spacing between the letters and in the margins, by placing screens on which there is a flow of images of the world and texts that relate to it, G.H. places words and images of words in the world itself. The world is a place about which one writes and speaks, and in which one puts what has been said or written. Occupying a place by writing on it thus represents an advantage in comparison with the evanescent presence of the *phonē*. Whereas the voice is lost in a perpetually immediate story, writing accumulates and memorizes our representations and images in a space containing symbols. And yet they are indissociable, since the voice is articulated with objects in the world according to a temporal axis, and writing comes and takes its place among them following a spatial axis; time and space thus reunited in the tapes and installations form the true image of language.

But this image is shown only in fragments, pieces, parts, details, for all language cannot be contained in a single image. Systematically it exceeds our intellectual, corporeal, and verbal capacities, just as the richness of the world in return exceeds the possibilities of being symbolized by it. For all that writing is a convention, a human artifice capable of being called into question, a fallible instrument, nevertheless, confronted with the images of the world which exceed it in quantity and forms, it can write their story. By comparison with the ontogenetic side represented by the voice, which is immediately present with things and attends their birth, as it were, writing is the phylogenetic side which gathers them together after the event, after reflection. Not only is writing not present and not directly involved in actions and events but, what is more, it drops them into an abyss, historicizes them, transforms them into the image of itself: a mute language.

Text

Text is mute language par excellence. During solitary reading, the space occupied by the page illuminates our gaze, it passes immediately through our eyes and reaches to our brain.

"Imagining the brain closer than the eyes," this is the last line of *Site*

Recite. The text holds the attention through the meaning it contains, but also through the space that it occupies. And this on two accounts, since an image of what one perceives is formed in the brain and the ideas transmitted by the text are arranged within its folds. Skimming through the spaces occupied by the texts, transforming them, destroying and re-creating them, but also skimming through knowledge and ideas. That is why G.H. uses multiple texts—literary, theological, philosophical, and personal—recognizable by all, whatever their language and culture. The universal scope of the contents but also of the formal arrangements of the text shows through this very aspect the experience that each individual can have in terms of the two modes, voice and writing, individual and plural, for the reading of the text brings us into the presence of a Story, while at the same time isolating us from the rest of the world and drawing us into its own world. The text is thus the bearer of its story, its language, and its knowledge.

The gnostic texts in *DISTURBANCE* are evocative of such a challenge. Dating from the first century of the Christian era, they are considered heretical by nearly all religious movements, and one might maintain that the very essence of a general knowledge of the texts is the fact that their interpretation leads to controversies. The textual source selected by G.H. is thus already, in itself, subject to conflicting interpretations, which presupposes some knowledge. With this work we are inclined to believe that for G.H.—following the example of a certain Jewish line of thought for which obedience to the Torah is more important than God himself—the Text supplants the Being in accordance with which it is constituted. The fact that he had used gnostic texts which attack Christian dogmas on which Western religion has been based for two thousand years and which call into question the very writing of the events in the Bible or in the Evangelists shows the degree to which the *questioning* of the text is primordial for G.H. For the text, whatever it may be, only truly takes shape in the acts of reading and commenting, which add, subtract, and deform the content through the inevitable process of interpretation. The spectator who views the installation forms part, in turn, of the chain of possible interpretations, and in this particular case, as in certain others, this is a positive aspect transmitted by the text and taken up no less overtly by the reader; the understanding of the text may become more and more complex but gradually it sheds light on its content. But G.H. ponders over another more absurd aspect, linked with the possible disappearance of the text as such and going hand in hand with the blinding effect of the image.

To isolate these questions, he became interested in the writings of Maurice Blanchot and especially the work of fiction *Thomas l'Obscur*,[3] which he has used several times, as in *Incidence of Catastrophe*, which shows the intermingling of text and body, word and flesh, to the extent that the writing ends up by transmitting its dereliction to the body of the actor (G.H. himself), taking him back to an original state, and his language to sounds as yet without significance. While one sees Thomas naked, lying on the ground amidst his excrement, the text of *Thomas l'Obscur* passes over the walls of the room he is in, as if it had literally taken possession of the body and was dragging it down with it in its disaster. The texts and images drive Thomas toward nothingness.

By confronting a thought which exists only because it tends toward its disappearance, a text which exists only because it speaks of its own obliteration, G.H. questions the two sides of language, maintaining that the construction and interpretation of any production of meaning cannot be constructed without words, that even vision could not exist without them but that reading and knowing already imply driving the text toward its limit, driving the images toward nothingness. A true "imager of disaster," G.H. shows the possible obliteration of the real image and text, but especially the obsessive fear that they may disappear symbolically from the horizon of thought. This infinite anguish comes from the fact that we can speak of what is around us, give names to what we see, while also speaking of our own discourse. By doing so, we touch on an essential part of language, which is this capacity for reduplicating discourse within discourse. One of the themes in the work of G.H. consists in grasping the mechanisms of this phenomenon of splitting, duplication, self-reference in language according to various modalities by connecting them through vision, and in apprehending the meaning of language insofar as it questions itself.

By using, in the installation *Between Cinema and a Hard Place*, passages from a text by Martin Heidegger, "The deployment of language," taken from *On the Way to Language*,[4] whose starting point is a poem by Hölderlin, G.H. tries to approach this question of the text speaking of another text through thought expressed by poetic speech seeking precisely to escape from the categories of writing and text. This could be summed up in a formula by Heidegger: "Speech speaks." What is speech (*Sprache*) which knows it speaks? In this installation, it is not a matter of an adaptation or exegesis but rather of taking the very road, as it were, of the philosopher when he ends up in the region of being where thinking and poetry are close to one another. The text seeks to delimit the space occupied by this closeness, without thereby assigning it precise locations, without applying to it parameters and units of measure, for it is precisely this closeness in speech that is not understood and not expressed in space-time.

However, an interplay of nearnesses and closenesses is here put into images, simultaneously between the different spaces and temporalities of the videotape itself and especially between the space-time of the text and that of the installation, which sometimes coincides with what is said, sometimes moves away from it. The monitors are placed like stones marking out the perimeter of a property, but their technology utters speech that speaks of its being without physical limits. Reflecting ironically on the space occupied by speech, on its deployment in proximity, on references to pure nature or to nature worked by man by displaying a sequence of images of stones, twigs, clods of earth, indoor plants, fields, mountains, houses—as many spaces placed in the monitors with calculated, prepared times—*Between Cinema and a Hard Place* makes speech say that it can say itself through technique. The images which pass across the monitors, showing several fixed shots and approach shots of reality taken by the camera, enable us to appreciate physical distances and sizes, while the sentences proffered seek, on the other hand, to cancel out the supposed separations and topologies in this linguistic space where the closeness of thinking and poetry might occur. The heart of this proximity cannot be reduced to calculations, since in the final instance it is simply a matter of "setting out on the road," of an open questioning of language about its essence: speech which knows that it speaks.

The installation, which also suggests that language can be defined in a space, points to this fundamental idea that we cannot escape from language, nor exist outside it. Certainly, Heidegger's philosophy cannot accept that the language of thought should be subservient to technique, and still less that speech should be deployed within this technological space where images which belong to the "state of being" tend to come close to thought. However, in no way does G.H. wish to comment on the text he uses as material, by telling the truth about it or about language in general. Seeking to explore the processes of language production and reception through many languages, inscriptions, and literary genres, he wishes to throw into relief the facets of language when it speaks of speech or speaks of a text in which it is reflected. This work based on Heidegger's text is one of its facets, but it is not the ultimate reason for language.

Furthermore, this extract from the philosopher's commentary on Hölderlin's poem has been selected for its inner quality, the beauty of the text uttered. This text which speaks of another text sets thoughts in motion all the more because it is agreeable to the ear and charming to the eye as it spatializes itself in our thoughts and in the physical world. Caught between cinema and reality, between image and text, we are obliged to acknowledge that everything that is presented to our senses and which occurs in the space where our body is located can be put into language.

Body

At the turning point between language and feeling, gesture and writing, phonatory machine and living flesh, technological extension and solipsism, the body is the link which connects us to the world and its image. We are in the world through our body. If we were only brains plugged into machines, our vision would be quite different. Now, this image passes through our perishable body, which suffers and enjoys, expresses its enjoyment, as also its fear of becoming nothing but a heap of dead flesh.

In the work of G.H., despite his recourse to religious texts or to Blanchot's "disaster writing," it is not so much a question of guilt in relation to the body as of the simple realization that the body lives and dies. Like a text, it has a beginning and an end. But although texts can form part of an infinite production, our body is unique and will not be followed by another. Mirroring the language and texts which appear only in bits and pieces, the uniqueness of the body is here broken up, fragmentary, shattered, passing through various stages of composition and dismantling in which the *membra disjecta* are continually reassembled in order to serve for a new dispersion.

In *Inasmuch As It Is Always Already Taking Place* we find, in a few simple images, the unique and the organic, the body scattered and the body technicized, mixed up in such a way that one can no longer make out the smallest segment that contains the whole of the largest piece as an enlargement of the tiniest element. Since each screen contains the whole and its parts at the same time, the piece echoes to us the image of the living body which is ourselves and whose parts and whole we are able to touch and see at one and the same time. In these technologically recomposed images of the body, we now seem to return to the stage of the mirror in which we finally saw the image of ourselves as a whole which we believed was in pieces. In this image of an unknown body we also recognize the reflection of the "symbolic image" of our body, not the one which is real and living but the representation we have of it. The spectator's body is thus both in the image and in the physical world; the work, which is itself almost material like a body, produces a mental image of its flesh in the spectator.

The seventeenth-century theory of the "man-machine" thus unexpectedly reappears, but this time it is no longer the body itself which is compared to clockwork and a mechanism; the extensions which it has manufactured for itself *become* a technological projection of the body which continues outside itself by adding on pieces, installations, monitors, electrical circuits, computers, capable of reconstituting it. In the same way that voice and writing are the materialization of the language of thought, electronic circuits and connections are the fulfillment of certain potentialities of the body in an exterior which is, nevertheless, quite distinct from it, because it is redistributed insofar as it is imaginary and transmissible to an observer. When one speaks of a set of writings or work, one speaks of a "corpus"; one could thus take the work of G.H. literally as a "corpus," his own body represented, transformed, metamorphosed by machines. This similarity is reinforced by the fact that the artist lends his voice or his body to certain characters and he himself devises the technical system which makes it possible to produce the work. By disassembling and deactivating certain processes, remaking and reconnecting circuits, programming and schematizing functions, G.H. is simply recomposing his own body.

The installation *CRUX*, with its four monitors placed in the form of a cross—one for the head, two for the hands, the last one for the feet—presents this process of destructurization and reconstruction for, right in the center of the work, at the "crux," there is nothing else but the wall, the rest of the actor's body (G.H., once again) being absent; only the images of the extremities of the body appear. The piece shows a walk through some woods to reach the ocean, in which one can see the feet walking, the head moving, the hands pushing aside the branches.

In order to carry it out, G.H. had made up a kind of framework to support the cameras attached to the extremities of his body, which could thus film him during his progress. The image of the middle of the body is not absent because of the installation, but as a result of a choice in the process of filming, and it is up to the spectator to recompose the missing image, which is no longer just the image of a real body but is also the symbolic body which it projects on what it contemplates. The muscular effort to clear a path through Nature reveals that the missing image of the body is absent in the installation only because it has confronted the world and has been placed there knowingly. The body is therefore not an abstraction: the image of one of its parts truly forms a body with the world.

For it to be possible to take it to pieces and put it together again in images—following the example of voice, text, or writing which is dismantled and reconstructed—the body must be living, it must be able to disappear like the printed text on a page which one has just turned over. But the body, and the world, are not texts already constituted for reading; on the contrary, they are the source for images of writing and reading.

The work of G.H. speaks precisely of the interchange through images of the body and the world, and in this connection it is necessary to distinguish between certain *transmitting* parts of the body and certain *receiving* parts of the body. We have already seen that the voice transmits and the ear receives, and the hand writing a text transmits it, and the eye reading it receives it. The head is a part which naturally, biologically, possesses the two capabilities, which G.H. transposes into images, in an analogical or realistic way, by thus extending his body with this machine.

At the start of the 1960s, the very perceptive Marshall McLuhan was already speaking of the media as extensions of our senses and our nervous system, not only on a conceptual plane but also on a simply sensory plane, the two interpenetrating each other.[5] In certain works by G.H. one finds an approach similar to that described by McLuhan, now established as classic, which is simply the "objective" description of the functioning of man.

In the 1976 preface to *Understanding Media,* he explains how his intuitions were corroborated by neurosurgery: "The left hemisphere is quantitative and the right hemisphere has to do with visual space, while the global, simultaneous side of the right hemisphere is also that of acoustic space. Visual space is continuous, homogeneous, sequential and static, while acoustic space is discontinuous and dynamic. The right hemisphere is the domain of interaction between *content* and *form* (face and background, both medium and message), for it is the place of perception of the *Gestalt,* and that of analogical, discontinuous, symbolic structures." The visual and verbal functions, sound, voice, and writing, which we execute thanks to our body, are thus the externalization and application of the modes of functioning of our central nervous system. It is in the installation *Primarily Speaking* that we find most clearly these interactions and connections, which materialize on a larger or smaller scale the structures of the two hemispheres of the brain and their ways of functioning. The spectator being in the middle, a row of four television screens is set on his left, a row of four more on his right. When he hears a voice coming from the left, he sees images moving on his right, and vice versa; pieces of writing which pass from one monitor to another as a single unit of sentences are then mixed with voice and images which, however, are introduced on various levels.

The mouth is another part of the face which particularly interests G.H., since, more than any other part, it is the transmitter of the thoughts which *form* in the brain and which it externalizes from this event by meaningful articulations of sound. But this remains attached to physical phonation and vocalization, as witnessed by a certain technization of the fragmented body at the end of *Site Recite,* with its mouth in which we seem to find ourselves when it pronounces the final words, "Imagining the brain closer than the eyes," which is only a mechanical mouth imitating the working of a human mouth. This robotization of the buccal part of the body is an essential element which reminds us that language is also an artifice, yet produced by chemical matter. Situated inside the mechanical mouth, the spectator recognizes himself in its words, in its language, and we then pass into the symbolic body of the other, reach its brain and access its thoughts. For the other is also a body which I touch, a mouth which speaks to me, a brain which externalizes itself.

Dialogue

In order to place ourselves in between language and language, it is not necessary to breathe the air of the high peaks of philosophy. In acts of everyday language, this can take a more mundane form which is no less essential, when we are really caught between the two languages which are the other's and mine. This language of the other is first of all that of the text written by an author, in this case G.H., for the tapes and installations—sometimes comprising autobiographical passages, relating relational problems, or speaking of the images themselves— which address the spectator as interlocutor and not a mere receiver. The language of which they are composed, transmissible as medium and as message, is dialogue insofar as it requires at least two instances in order to exist as such. There is a *transmission* and a *reception* at the time of the verbalization of the image. As soon as the spectator looks, his vision immediately finds itself caught up in various levels of discourse, and as most of the texts bear on ordinary experiences, easily recognizable actions and feelings, through what is said we share the same world of reference.

The texts read or spoken exist in a procession through time which, to remain active and meaningful, has no other place than the spectator's power of abstraction and memory. It is not only his gaze that is sought, it is equally his ability to store information, data, without whose multiplicity he could not reconstitute what he sees. The continuous apprehension required by the tape is necessary for its complete understanding, but through this very fact, it overwhelms and absorbs the spectator on the conceptual level and makes him a participant or witness of his own development despite himself. The purely cognitive aspect of language, the simply verbal exchange, is thus put forward in relation to perception, and the immanent understanding of what is seen favors intellection at the expense of sensation.

G.H. gives an important place to the interchange with the other when the voices on the tapes address an imaginary person, someone who might also be the spectator, as for example in *Around & About:* "I would prefer to reach an understanding with you in a way on which there would be no going back, a way of being with you which would be the only one possible. When I came, I had no way of knowing it would be like this . . . I have tried to imagine you in various ways, to think of what your reaction would be, and that is also what has to be thought of now. I have never lost sight of this. Simply, I have nothing set aside for me or you. The sensation of time pressing, there is always time to see it coming. I would like to avoid that for the moment. But perhaps that is what you are waiting for; you wait and listen."[6]

The voice addresses the spectator who then becomes a "mediator" between various networks: image/voice, text/writing, reading/listening. The "mediator" in his turn becomes the second writer of a conversation between an "I" and a "you" which is transmitted not only through the voice but also through the materiality of the image and through written inscription. It must not be a sort of reflection of what he sees, reads, or hears; it must rather be highly aware of its own process of mediation.

These works place strong emphasis on the interchange with the spectator and thus touch on the nodal point of the nature of language, which is to be dialogistical. For the interlocutors, language is the distinctive feature of otherness: it is not an object but a mediation which enables them to understand each other. The three-dimensional experience of language that the spectator can have (image/reading/listening) sets him at the center of this conceptual space in the heart of which he manages and distributes the mental points of the different dimensions at the intersection of which he is. In order to confront the highly abstract nature of language, the "mediator" must make a permanent effort to reconstruct what he perceives, constantly updating images through language, following in real time the interplay between text and image which are projected at the same speed. He is no longer a spectator passively present while a tape is played, since his literal reading of the screen and his potential writing make him an active addressee who is obliged to have some backing if he wishes to carry on this strange dialogue. The reader/viewer thus fulfills one of the characteristics of language while discoursing in his turn on a text or a word which is addressed to him, and extends the dialogistical aspect. The Other does not reproduce but is a part of the exchange.

After the fashion of the language of which they are made, and for this very reason, the tapes created by G.H. can address a "you" while speaking of themselves. There is a coincidence between the event described on the tape and the instance of the discourse which describes it. It is one of the great achievements of G.H. that he has superimposed image and language on a single time, and has placed with complete appropriateness the technique of the medium and the significations which it transports, for it is also the nature of language to say something *about* something to someone, and the interchange in connection *with* something refers back to the materiality of the world, to language's hold on reality, and, in return, to the understanding of reality's hold on thought.

Metalogue

The notion and the term *metalogue* were created in the 1940s by the epistemologist Gregory Bateson. Numerous examples are given in *Steps to an Ecology of Mind*.[7] Metalogue is a conversation on problematical matters; it must be constituted in such a way that not only do the interlocutors discuss the problem in question, but also the structure of the dialogue within the whole is the exact illustration of the matter being discussed.

For example, in the metalogue *Pourquoi les choses se mettent-elles en désordre?*—which inspired the video with the same name *Why Do Things Get in a Muddle?*—a girl asks her father what muddle is, and as they talk, their discussion ends up by becoming muddled and incoherent: it images the content that was the point of departure. The dialogistical principle involved, which tends toward a clarification of the utterances, has its equivalent in the metalogue which is like its hidden side. The bad side of language, the area of misunderstanding, incomprehension, and destruction, are events taken into account by G.H. in the intersubjective relationship. These are language's faults, failures, and setbacks, which are hunted down in the discourses and texts. It is at the very moment when dialogue, reading, and writing tip over into entropy that G.H. intervenes in order to try to stick back together the scattered pieces, to explore what happens when violence is done to meaning. His videotapes are as if caught in a double bind, between dialogue and metalogue, the first trying to produce sense, the second moving toward the entropy described in *Why Do Things Get in a Muddle? (Come on Petunia)*. The metalogue, which by definition has a structure similar to its content, reappears in a number of his videos: the texts read or heard often correspond in their form to the remarks on the subject. Although originally metalogue only acquires its full dimension in a dialogue (but *written dialogues,* not spontaneous ones, as is the case with Bateson), G.H. seems to have enlarged this notion for his work on video. While preserving the dialogistical aspect with the spectator, the tape effectively develops as a metalogue, since the images literally do what the text says, and their formal framework is a perfect illustration of the content of what is written or read.

In *Happenstance (part one of many parts),* one can quote, among others, the moment when the words *vanishing points* appear, only to disappear again and thus fulfill the messages which the image gives us to read. The works are almost always conceived in a such a way that they seem to have been begotten by a generic metalogue, in which the coincidence between what is perceived and what is understood is such that these two instances function in themselves, and *at the same time* really yank the "mediator" into their world and make him a part of the metalogue. The "mediator" ends up by also *doing* and *writing* what the image that he views *does* and *writes.* The displacement performed will consist not only of the putting into discourse of the event but also of the putting into images of speech. The videos thus fulfill the definition of metalogue which is *to be in the image* of the problem being dealt with.

Another even more obvious example occurs in *Mediations,* where one sees a loudspeaker in a fixed shot and hears a voice coming from it. A hand regularly comes and puts sand on the loudspeaker, and the voice relates what happens in the picture: "a hand comes into the picture. I am a voice under the sand, a voice under the ground." At the end of the tape, the voice and the loudspeaker are completely covered by sand. While certain images and certain texts form a syntax in synchronization, others are diachronic, the images going in search of the texts or playing with their topological and semantic displacements. The metaphorical linking in *Primarily Speaking* plays with the syntactic metamorphoses of image and text, the words being related to the image, but through displacement: when the word *listen* is said, one sees a shell; the word *blood* goes with an upside-down bottle of wine; for the word *earth* there is a globe of the world, and so on. The paradoxes at the heart of the presentation of words and images—which seem to be sometimes in harmony, sometimes dysfunctional—are simply another aspect of metalogue, insofar as there is a perfect interweaving of the event and the discursive instant which says it, but always, and this is an important element, in relation to a specific event which involves people with the everyday aspect in real discussion, problems which refer to the most immediate reality.

One of the fundamental aspects of metalogue is that it involves the interlocutors in speech acts, but also in everyday actions, and it is precisely from these that their discussion is established. In other words, the interlocutors are physically involved, through their actions and gestures, their behavior, their attitudes, in the events of reality, and through a mirror effect the spectator is referred back to himself, to his presence before the screen, to his body, as if he was living immanently what he was witnessing.

Silence

One might believe that the silence in the last pieces was the logical outcome of metalogue, of the disaster of writing and vision, the dereliction of meaning, elements which served to constitute the image of the world but whose ultimate medium, the body, is inalienable. This latter becomes the place of silence. More often than not, moments of silence occur in conjunction with images of the body motionless or in action, for the latter is a living mass situated between language, constructed and artificial, and the fact of simply being there as a body, immersed in the natural world. Silence is the other side of the talking body, the condition which permits the appearance of the mute, purely visual image, the reduction of the image to its essence as image. Like these images taken back to their simplest expression as image, the body presented is reduced to its simplest expression: silence. But if one accepts voluntarily that objects or things in the natural world can be silent, it is more difficult for us to see simply a body sunk in silence. Just as language has no exterior, the body has no exterior. And in reality, if the combined images of the body and silence return recurrently, it is because we are dealing with the personal solitude of our body from which we cannot escape, we are dealing with the silence of our existence and of our unique, perishable body. This silence cannot be shared.

It can be seen. According to Michel de Certeau's elegant formula, a story consists of "a discourse articulated by bodies,"[8] and this applies even more to the film image, since in some pieces, such as *Suspension of Disbelief* or *Inasmuch As It Is Always Already Taking Place,* there is in fact a real mechanical articulation of meaningful images of the body. They seem to develop a language of gesture, behavior, and attitudes which is the silent opposite of articulated language or written language, and at the same time, they seem to become a surface for the text: the naked body as a metaphor for the blank page.

Certain projections of texts on images of body or face emphasize this possibility, all the more so since the text can be apprehended as a mute language, and in this sense it refers back to the body as the silent articulation of a story. For all that, it is not a question of narration—even if silence can be understood as a moment in speech, a pause which comes after or before language—but of a state. Rather than a blank in the voice or a space in writing, silence is a state of the body. When a person reads, sleeps, breathes, walks, all these physical states through which he may pass take place in silence; on the other hand, most of the time when one hears a voice one does not see the body of the person who is talking. While it remains in silence, what the body *tells* is directly integrated into the image and is no longer connected to an external text or speech.

This image stripped by states of the body which are articulated to other bodies but also to other images allows us to see even more clearly an essential characteristic of the work of G.H., rhythm. When the voice speaks, the hand writes, and the images are displayed, rhythm is so inherent in their ways of functioning that we immediately integrate it into our mental processes, so much do they coincide on this point. The rhythm of the images seems to be that of the thought which is enunciated. On the other hand, in certain works where silences play an important part, the rhythm is an *abnormal* succession of images changing from very slow to very fast, becoming inverted or affecting each other, without ever going beyond the optical capability of the human eye, and nearly always presenting the body as a kind of indicator of the state of things.

The spectator accustomed to works which marry image and voice or text will tend to see in the silent rhythm of the movements and gestures of the body an equivalent to the rhythm of the voice. But here, the rhythm is a purely visual transposition going beyond or falling short of the verbal or graphic rhythm, for if the natural flow of the voice is followed by a regular tempo of images, silence, in its turn, imposes quite a different tempo which strangely resembles, through its mere material transposition, the distortion of meaning which operates in the texts. The silence is not entropic or destructive, it is rather the placing between parentheses of speech and writing, a suspension and not a negation. If speech and writing are externalized outside the body and thanks to it, the silence of the body is not to be understood as the internalization of language. One cannot escape either from the body or from language, for what enables us to conceive and apprehend the states of our body is simply language; conversely, we cannot act and reflect outside the body.

The understanding, feeling, and experiencing of our body can only be effected through sensations, and the body is not merely an envelope of flesh surrounding our organs and our brain, our feelings and our consciousness, on the contrary, it is an incorporation of thought. This phenomenon takes place in silence. Here, the state of silence suspends the systems of language, the transmitting and receiving functions of the body, the gaze turned toward the word, in order to show them as pure images.

The pure image is an artifice which is revealed even better by silence and, once again, G.H. plays at the same time with silence as conventional sign and as natural state. For the silent image is in reality the only one which shows a unity which truly forms part of the world. Like the world, the body is presented in the raw state, with its sonorities and its silences, and although it is transformed by images into a cultural body, nevertheless it presents itself as attached to the natural materiality of the world from which it can never wholly be separated.

The World of Meaning

In the works quoted, G.H. constantly plays with their mimetic character—the irrefutable fact that we might recognize a partic-

ular object, that we might be able to identify ourselves with a particular experience—and their artificial character which challenges this first
approach. Through images of the world, where resemblances between
things and the way of seeing them and naming them seem to be self-
evident, there is a return to the distinctions one could see before between voice and writing, word and action, body and fragment. One
must distinguish between the simple technical recording of things,
their materiality, and the form which is placed upon them, in other
words, their signification. Although appearing just as it is, so to speak,
the evident materiality of things is not simply copied but transformed,
with precise aims which are far removed from the initial components.

The works thus swing between construction and destruction, between speech and silence, sense and nonsense, dialogue and misunderstanding, between absence and presence of the body—the organic and
mental data of the human being—the better to illuminate the functions
of language and of the work when the latter is presented as making reference to this very function. The voluntary mingling of organic parts
such as mouth, hands, brain, face, with the technological ones of networks and circuits creates several levels of interpretation insofar as the
term *function* is concerned. Transmitting or receiving organs, perceptions and receptions, encodings and decodings, body, image, and language possess functions which are different but not divergent. This is
doubtless one of the reasons which leads G.H. to establish separations
and dismemberments of the body and its organs, distinctions between
voice and writing, between the word and the action described, only to
stick them together again in order to construct an image (picture)
which is as complete as possible of what each part comprised in terms
of power. When these pieces of reality are reunited, they become something other than the sum of the parts: a symbolic image of themselves,
but also a new image which arises from the simple fact that they are
recomposed.

The act of reconstruction of plastic forms and contents thus constitutes the image of the generic world. There, too, G.H. plays both with
the conceptual frameworks in which the objects come to be situated,
the things and people of the world, and with the material frameworks
which he manufactures in the installations and tapes, without it being
a question of the metaphoric side of what the first ones would present
in their literal aspect. On the contrary, before an image is filmed and a
particular angle is decided on for a shot, predetermined physical and
intellectual frameworks are needed in order to apprehend this image as

symbolic image. Seeing and perceiving the world in images presupposes certain conditions so that it can appear in images (pictures), that is to say, so that it can be grasped as a sum of elements and actions which are comprehensible through the frameworks which we apply to it. The delimiting of facts and events operates first through the simple use of the camera, the televisual transmission of the images, of the spaces in the book as an object which also delimits texts in its pages, in the setting of the installations, in short, in the materiality of the physical frameworks in which the world finds itself enclosed, shaped, remodeled.

But we are not only dealing with filmed images of the real world, we are also confronted by a symbolized image (picture) of these images, and this is due to two ways of proceeding: one consists in going back to images of the real through direct reference—since what we see is obviously a chair, a face, a car, the ocean; the other makes the self-reference of language explicit when it refers to these images. On the one hand we have the irreducibly material and physical part, on the other hand the part of language which produces significations on these realities.

The fact that the world is independent, and totally indifferent to ourselves in the multiplicity of its forms, does not in any way prevent us from exploring it with the tools we have available. For G.H., it is clear that from the *material point of view* it appears only according to the way in which it is observed and manipulated: voice, writing, text, body, dialogue, metalogue, silence, for example, filter and produce different phenomena, since they are physically and functionally different. Depending on the works, one particular mode is called on more than another, a particular sensory organ is specifically made use of, certain textual structures and certain ways of pronouncing words are accentuated more.

This fairly recurrent distribution and classification of functions, cognitive and sensory capabilities, is not the result of an experimental work seeking new effects; this procedure sticks to the reality of the world and to our own reality. Just as we do not act or think by mobilizing all our senses, our body, and our ideas with equal intensity in all cases, the reality which we then construct thanks to them as we go along is made up of pieces which are more or less complex and more or less rich.

By favoring certain plastic processes in his works, G.H. emphasizes certain ways of constructing the image of the world which are specific to art, since it is also a question of an oeuvre which is deployed above all in accordance with aesthetic forms in which the rules and aims are not the same as in science and technology. The way of looking, for example. This seems evident, but on considering the cognitive and phenomenal interrelationships among eye, mouth, and ear—located on the head which coordinates perception, speech, and hearing—and the body which interacts physically with material objects and conceptual objects produced by thought during writing and ideating, G.H. seems to establish a sensible distinction between the upper and the lower parts of the body. The head is not the pilot of the body-machine which simply executes its orders, but the latter does not function in these works with cognitive aims—establishing meaningful connections among language, things, and beings—but with *referential* aims.

In these works, the body appears as the link which connects us to the world and thanks to which we can make reference to it, despite our language which is completely independent of it. The body is not itself the reference, and without it we could not ask ourselves the question about the reality of the external world in time and space. But it is in this paradoxical situation where it tends to melt into the nature of things—which explains the wish to set against them the destructurization and recomposition which are a product of a fictitious anti-natural order—and where it can be captured as an object in the world by other eyes or another body. The body well and truly establishes a *material connection* with the world, but its gestures and displacements are directed and thought beforehand in a meaningful way which by convention is alien to this materiality. And G.H. takes care not to leave it in a state of total nakedness; whether through the rhythm of the mere images when there is silence, or by direct contact with language by projecting phrases on faces or making a person struggle with a text, he brings it back to its role of mediator between materiality and meaningfulness. At one moment or another, the body always ends up stumbling on something written or spoken, for it is not an object taken from the world but an object of language. Hence, it becomes a subject of language. Following the logic of the works of G.H., we are not brains connected up to other brains living in a universe of abstractions, but people who address other people in connection with the common world in which their body is located. It is in this sense that the body is a passage for language. Moreover, the world described in the images of G.H. is not possible or parallel; it is always a question of the everyday world, the one which is at hand, which we regularly frequent and about which we talk to others.

There we come to another essential point: we do not construct the world through a solipsistic language, but thanks to the language of a community which comes to an agreement on defined principles and relationships. The image (picture) of the world is thus not constructed principally from the world itself, even if it may refer to it, but takes shape from other languages to which other constituted images are addressed.

At this stage, everything that we have been able to see of images of reality is now understood differently. For example, even if our body is in the world, interacts with it, and is a physical part of it, the thing which enables it to refer to the world is clearly language which, itself, is not found ready-made in the world. The latter has no need of the mirror of language which we may hold out to it, which only reflects the image manufactured by ourselves. Equally, the transformations which the texts already existing may undergo in these works, or those written especially for their creation, show that the world of first references is not that of reality but that of linguistic meanings which we establish by convention based on language itself. The pragmatic relationship with the world thus does not take place only during manipulations of images of reality, their transformations, the distortion of texts and words, interchanges having objects and actions as subjects, but above all when one language is in the process of taking shape in another language.

In the process, although the images appearing in the works are made from a reality connected with language, and which the latter manipulates, as it were, through images, the matters and events of the world remain materials which one can seize and whose significance one can transmit without thereby making language one of these manipulable objects. By contrast with the things or bodies to which the images in the videotapes and installations make reference, language is not a material like the others, since it is the only instance of being able to speak simultaneously of what is external and of itself. Whether this be in a metalogue or in a piece of writing which tends to do away with itself, language can always resort to self-reference, and it is in this form of self-comprehension that we find the clearest appearance of the idea that it is not only a symbolic construction but that the world itself enters within the frameworks of this construction.

The fact that while talking or writing one can refer to the world and at the same time be aware of this action is fundamental for the meaning that we integrate into our environment and our context. For we do indeed speak of something *between us* in connection with the world, but by exchanging our images of the world and not only the objects and things that it contains. The self-referencing nature of language now takes us further, since the ability of discourse to divide is reflected by a language which, although respecting the same principles and rules, is *another language* because it is the language of another. A person to whom a constituted image is addressed does not necessarily apprehend the world in the same manner; but if his language makes a different image of it, the image is nonetheless not divergent. By looking at images, works, we are led to compare them with the images which we too project of the world, and with the language which serves us as a framework for understanding and reference. So we establish connections between images, references, bodies, things, language acts, in order to address them to another language which knows how to analyze the connections thus established.

In this pragmatic exchange of languages and images between the work and the spectator, we rediscover the dialogistical dimension which we have been dealing with and whose main aim is to give meaning not to the world itself—even if it can organize itself according to our criteria—but to give meaning to my language/image when it goes looking for another vision of the world. The world can only create meaning because we give it meaning. And if it is not knowable in its ultimate reality, to which we constantly return and through which we live, we can at least say that "in itself" it does not possess any significance. The real, living world, physical and material, is non-sense. Thus, to project a world onto a world, an image onto images, is not a trivial reductive act, it is an act essential for our existence.

And all the work of G.H. is centered on the construction of the world of sense, the symbolic world which we create from start to finish and which enables us to perceive and conceive the real world. Without a predetermined world picture, it cannot be apprehended, and therefore even the images of reality which are given to us on the screens or in the installations are a consequence of it. Even if they may be its point of departure as a material reference, in the final instance the true reference is that of the multiple meanings which circulate in the heart of language. But we do not live in a system of symbols outside the world, where languages are only logical forms without content. Although they have a validity of their own, by projecting our mental world, our aim is to lay hold of reality and manipulate it, while making the reasons for this procedure explicit. In the works of G.H., this self-referencing aspect is always advanced, in order to show the extent to which the world at which our gaze is directed is perceived from the viewpoint of another world: the world of our meaning.

Notes

1. Ludwig Wittgenstein, *Philosophical Remarks.* Barnes & Noble, New York, 1975.

2. Following in the line of Wittgenstein's questionings one can find thinkers such as Cassirer, Heidegger, and, more recently, Goodman, Hintikka, and Putnam.

3. Maurice Blanchot, *Thomas l'Obscur.* Gallimard, Paris, 1950.

4. Martin Heidegger, *On the Way to Language.* Harper & Row, New York, 1971.

5. Marshall McLuhan, *Understanding Media: The Extensions of Man.* McGraw-Hill, New York, 1964.

6. *Around & About.* 15 min. 1983. extract from the text by Gary Hill.

7. Gregory Bateson, *Steps to an Ecology of Mind: Collected Essays in Anthropology, Psychiatry, Evolution and Epistemology.* Chandler Publishing Company, New York, 1972.

8. Michel de Certeau, "Des outils pour le corps," in "Panoplies du corps," *Traverses,* nos. 14–15, CCI. Centre Georges Pompidou, Paris. April 1979.

Corinne Diserens

Time in the Body

Naked to the sky
What you hide
What is veiled
All will be revealed
The first, Raphao, began by creating the head;
Abron created the crown, Maniggesstroeth created the brain
Asterekhme, the right eye, Thaspomakha, the left eye
Ieromunos, the right ear, Bissoum, the left ear, Akioreim, the nose,
Banenephroum, the lips
Amen, the teeth, Ibikan the molars, Basiliademe, the tonsils,
Akhkha, the uvula
Adabam, the neck, Kahaaman, the spine, Dearkho has the throat
Tebar, the right shoulder and the left shoulder, Mniarkhon, the
right elbow and the left elbow
Abitrion, the right forearm, Euanthen, the left forearm, Krus cre-
ated the right hand
Beluaé, the left hand, Treneu, the fingers of the right hand,
Balbel, the fingers of the left hand
Krima, the fingernails, Astrops, the right breast
Barroph, the left breast, Baoum, the right armpit, Ararim, the left
armpit . . .

DISTURBANCE (among the jars)

Originally published in *Gary Hill: In Light of the Other* (Oxford: The Museum of Modern Art; Liverpool: Tate Gallery, 1993). Translated from the
French by Charles Penwarden.

Gary Hill's video *Incidence of Catastrophe* (1987–88) ends with an image of the artist's naked body curled up like a fetus. He is drained, exhausted. Everything he has read in Blanchot's *Thomas L'Obscur* has become physical symptom. He is haunted, trapped by the text, suffocating. Stammering, convulsive, his body has broken down—in a state of collapse close to Bataille's, that of a man emptied and thrust before destiny by a story read in a trance. He has become so caught up in the reverie that is the book that he can no longer stop reading. Drunk, he is adrift on the waters of the ocean that Thomas, where he sat, was already contemplating, and that recur at several points in *Incidence of Catastrophe,* the ocean from the beginning of *Processual Video* (1980): "he knew the ocean well." Hill renews the theme of the voyage of initiation, and every journey in this world is an exploration of the mind. The body, which has become a wreck doomed to solitude, does not reside in the movements of waves but in uncertain, stagnant waters. The sea withdraws, life ebbs from him.

As sometimes with Eva Hesse,[1] the body is seen as a system that procures various evacuations, secretions, and disjecta. Hesse noted in her journal: "Revealing the past—and thus overcoming this shit—purging it by this entrance into the future—wholly and forever!!!" These final images of *Incidence of Catastrophe* bring to mind Marcel Griaule's analysis of the ambivalent cultural status of spit, as both stain and purification:

> Spit goes with breathing, which cannot leave the mouth without becoming imbibed with it. Now breath is the soul, so much so that some peoples talk of "the soul at the front of the face" which ceases to be when breath can no longer be felt. We say "to breathe his last," and "pneumatic" ultimately means "full of soul."[2]

> *Incidence of Catastrophe* came about from having a unique and powerful experience while reading that particular book. As you read this book, it reads you. It personifies that kind of enfolding of physicality back onto consciousness that is so indigenous to video—there would have been no way not to have done something with it. Being the protagonist was not a choice. I wasn't about to verbalize my experience of this book to a third person; I wanted to confront this text and its body (the book) as another real body (myself). (Gary Hill)

As Bachelard suggests in *La Poétique de la reverie* (On Poetic Imagination and Reverie), if we accept the hypnotic effect of the page of poetry, our remote dreaming self is restored to us. A kind of psychological memory, which brings back to life the Psyche of old and recalls the being of the dreamer we once were, sustains our reading dream. The book has spoken to us of ourselves.

> But what are we seeking in artificial paradises, we who are mere armchair psychologists? Dreams or daydreams? Which documents are the most vital to us? Books, always books. Would these artificial paradises still be paradises if they were not written? For us readers, they are paradises of reading.
>
> . . . Yes, before the advent of culture, the world dreamed abundantly. The earth gave birth to myths and myths opened the earth so that its lakes could gaze like eyes at the sky. A high destiny rose from the abyss. At once, myths found human voices, the voice of man dreaming the world of his dreams. Man expressed the earth, the sky, the water. Man was speech and spoke for the macro-anthropos that is the monstrous body of the earth. In primitive cosmic reveries, the world is a human body, human eyes, human breath, human voice.

Again, washed ashore by the waves, it is the body that reads, but this time it is fragmented, decentered in a "reflexive space of difference through the simultaneous production of presence and distance" (Hill) which we also come upon in *Inasmuch As It Is Always Already Taking Place,* which comprises sixteen cathode ray tubes—light-emitting elements of television monitors, of various sizes between ½" and 23", niched in a wall, their frames filled with life-size images of parts of a naked body. Only one, very small monitor shows the image of a text with a finger following the movement of reading. The gaps between these "naked monitors, their glass organs exposed,"[3] vary, and yet they appear to form a single whole, one that radiates a cold light, that murmurs and breathes in the depths of the wall. The light shines out of the abyss, all that shines sees.

In her remarkable essay, "Gary Hill: Beyond Babel,"[4] Lynne Cooke notes that:

> *Inasmuch* . . . posits a very different form of absence, one that reconfigures this notion of loss of centre into an impregnable solitude. . . . This tableau is accompanied by a barely audible soundtrack on which a murmuring voice pulverised into what Hill calls "the debris of utterance" is almost obliterated by the rustle of turning pages and other ambient sounds. This ceaseless yet indecipherable monotone in which phrases seem simply to spill out of the

mouth by rote serves to draw the spectator close to the chamber in which the monitors have been arrayed like still life elements.

This is not the body of *Incidence of Catastrophe*—"like a drowning man who goes down with his hands clenched, as one drowns because unable to lay one's body down as peacefully as in bed . . ."[5] In *Inasmuch* life does stretch out within him; it is a more contemplative, hypnotic work, one that emerged after the Hill/Thomas experiment, and in which the body compels thought.

Writing about Michelangelo Antonioni, Gilles Deleuze echoes Blanchot's words on fatigue and waiting:

The body is no longer the obstacle separating thought from itself—that which it must overcome in order to be able to think. On the contrary, it is that within which thought must plunge if it is to attain the unthought, which is to say, life itself. It is not that the body thinks, but that, in its stubborn obstinacy, it compels thought, forces one to think of that which eludes thought; life. Rather than life being summoned before the categories of thought, thought will be thrown into the categories of life. The categories of life are precisely the attitudes of the body, its postures. "We do not even know what the body is capable of"—be it in sleep, when drunk, in the midst of effort or when resisting. To think is to learn the potential of a non-thinking body, its capacities, its attitudes or postures. It is through the body (as opposed to through the intermediary of the body) that cinema celebrates its nuptials with mind, with thought. "Give us a body, then": is first to set a camera on an everyday body. The body is never in the present, it contains the before and after, the fatigue and the wait.[6]

To set a camera on a body: that is exactly what Hill did in *CRUX* (1983–87), when he fixed five cameras to himself. *CRUX* marks a significant return to the human body, which had disappeared from Hill's work after his early experiments with his own body and a video camera in the 1970s. It marks the return of the artist as performer with the alternating roles of actor and medium, capable of both seeing and showing, and of being seen.

I must become a warrior of self-consciousness and move my body to move my mind to move the words to move my mouth to spin the spur of the moment. (*Site Recite [a prologue]*)

The idea is not to follow and track down the mundane body, but to have it undergo a ceremony which affects both sounds and gestures, making the body a grotesque from which there then emerges a gracious body. It is the transition from *CRUX* to *Incidence* to *Inasmuch,* in which the body finally floats, gently palpitates, murmurs, breathes—slowly, patiently, draining meaning to the end or the origin of language and being.

> The direct time-image always takes us into that Proustian dimension of time in which people and objects assume an importance quite out of proportion to their spatial one. Proust talks in cinematic terms of Time setting its magic lantern on bodies and making different shots coexist within depth.[7]

Hill retains only that aspect of space which adheres to bodies. He composes his space from disconnected bits linked only by a single gesture. Here is his description of *Inasmuch:*

> Their arrangement as such is one of accumulation—a pile up. They appear as a kind of debris—bulbs that have washed up from the sea. Each one is a witness to a fragment of a body—perhaps a reclining figure, a man reading, a corpse, etc.—forever rendering actual size ad infinitum (ie a 1-inch tube displays a portion of a palm of a hand, or perhaps an unrecognizable terrain of skin; a 4-inch tube displays part of a shoulder or an ear; a 10-inch tube emits the stomach and so on). Each emission bares little movement (whether it be a wavering gaze or the murmur of the body remains unknown). The movement objectifies itself within a closed loop with no beginning and no end. The anatomical site is incessant, however fragmentary.[8]

The expression *pile-up* recalls W.S. Wilson's analysis of the work of Eva Hesse:

> She conceives of art (and life) as an investigation, construction—in the etymological sense of the word (from *struere*, to pile up, and *con*—which implies with or together) and as knowledge*: the subject constitutes itself in experience, it comes into being in the event of the work; the event as the emergence of a form/movement, of a form in movement, in-finite and derisory as well as necessary.[9]

In Hill's work, attitudes and postures turn toward that slow theatricalization of the body Deleuze spoke of in relation to Morrissey and

---

* *Translator's note:* The original French word for knowledge, *connaissance* (which is close to co-naissance, or co-birth) brings out a further connection which the English word does not allow: between knowledge and construction, and knowledge and birth—the constitution of self.

Warhol and Cassavetes, with his fatigue and waiting but also the moment of relaxation and the play of the basic, fundamental body.

Here the work has undone history and action, and even space, to penetrate to the attitudes and categories that put time in the body, and thought in life. There is a process whereby bodies are constituted from the neutral image, the black or white screen. The problem is not the presence of bodies, but of a belief which could restore to us the world and the body from what signifies their absence.

Notes

1. "Marcher sun un fil," Catherine David and Corinne Diserens, in *Eva Hesse*, IVAM, Valencia/Galerie nationale du Jeu de Paume, Paris, 1993.

2. Ibid.

3. "Disturbing unnarrative of the perplexed parapraxis (A Twin Text for DISTURBANCE)," George Quasha, *Gary Hill, DISTURBANCE (among the jars)*, Musée d'art moderne de Villeneuve d'Ascq, 1989.

4. "Gary Hill: Beyond Babel," Lynne Cooke, *Gary Hill*, IVAM, 1993.

5. *L'impossible*, George Bataille.

6. *L'image-temps*, Gilles Deleuze.

7. Ibid.

8. *Otherwordsandimages*, Video Galleriet/New York; Carlsberg Glyptotek, Copenhagen, 1990.

9. *Eva Hesse*, op. cit.

Stephen Sarrazin

Surfing the Medium

Toward Language: The Invisible Performance

Like most artists of his generation working in video, Gary Hill was involved with another medium before discovering electronics. He was a sculptor, using at first copper-coated steel rods and later on wire mesh.

The sculptures made with wire mesh are those which have been reproduced occasionally in articles and interviews; they reveal Hill's fascination with the work of artist Frank Stella, and his idea of bringing painting out in the physical space, distancing it from its surface. His access to video came with the decision to move from the West Coast, from the sea, to the East Coast, to the forest, in the early 1970s.

It was by attending the Arts Students League, in Woodstock, New York, that he encountered the Woodstock Community Video, formerly New York's People Video Theater. This proved to be the first of Gary Hill's chance encounters with art, culture, language, and video, which would reoccur continually during the next decade. Unlike many artists of his generation, Gary Hill was not consciously aware of the evolutions in contemporary art; he had been sculpting for years before discovering Minimalists such as Robert Morris, Donald Judd, and Carl André. One significant reason for this, outside the relative isolation of Woodstock, which was as much of a retreat as a center for experimental culture, is that he quickly abandoned the idea of a formal university education (let us remember that artists of the previous generation held such training in high esteem. Bruce Nauman got his master's degree, Frank Stella and Carl André were Yale graduates, etc.). Thus Gary Hill

Originally published in *Gary Hill, Chimera* monograph, 1992.

went through the hazardous process of creating, at first, by intuition. There was much "rediscovery" involved in his output, finding out that someone else had the idea first. For instance, when Gary Hill came to ask the Woodstock Community Video if he could borrow equipment, one of the first things he did, without anyone telling him to experiment with this concept, was to tape himself in front of a monitor which was showing a previously taped image of himself. Of course, Vito Acconci had been working within such a situation for about three years before Gary Hill decided to do it. But Hill would not engage in a dialogue with his own image, he would not be heading toward a concept of the body owing to theories of reflections, of how video as a medium was able to expand what performance artists had been doing previously on the stages of public spaces. On the contrary, he was to remove himself from the space of the monitor, although he was to leave something behind.

It is worth examining for a moment how much video has changed in the past fifteen years. Consider for instance that Rosalind Krauss, in her seminal essay "Video: The Aesthetics of Narcissism," wrote that "most of the work produced over the very short span of video art's existence has used the human body as its central instrument . . . in the case of work on tape this has most often been the body of the artist-practitioner. In the case of video installations it has usually been the body of the responding viewer" (pp. 180–81).

Since then we have witnessed, in a very short period of time, bold new directions as artists were no longer confronting their image to the one appearing on a monitor, but to various histories of moving images (as in the works of German artists Klaus vom Bruch and Marcel Odenbach, where archive footage, excerpts from classical cinema, etc. constituted a body against which the artist was to locate himself); this represents a second-generation legacy of performance art on video. We have also seen how the medias have taken back the medium and its technological potential and could not care less about issues of aesthetics; the concerns have to do with entertainment, polishing and upgrading the digital capacities of definition, editing, and so on. As for the installations, the past decade has seen the progressive disappearance of closed circuit installations, as these early forays into interactive works have given way to more sophisticated systems, while the aesthetic of video installations as an art object grew in complexity and diversity. Obviously, we may not include Hill's tapes in any of these categories. But there is one direction that video took, which is not considered, and perhaps excluded, from Rosalind Krauss's considerations: image processing, and underestimating Woody Vasulka's contribution to an epistemology of electronics. In retrospect, however, Krauss may be noted for not having spent the time to address what was being done in that area of video, as very little of it is now worth discussing, except within the context of video's history. But Vasulka's experiments did contribute largely in showing Gary Hill the way toward his subject.

The first intuitions of what that subject would be had to do with the relationships between sound and image; Woody and Steina Vasulka naturally function as models of such investigations, as their work was founded on the principle that in electronics, the signal was able to produce both sound and image. The major step lay in making images with sound. Or at least determining the existence of an image through the objective length of time of a sound: another sound, another image, or the transformation of the image with a new sound; discovering that the Vasulkas were working in such a way was a coincidence. Each became aware of the other, but examined sound differently: for the Vasulkas, sound was to become the invisible architecture of the image, while for Hill it came to function as movement. Again in retrospect, we may see how Gary Hill's tapes, which were created by himself, like much of what was being done by artists who were combining performance and video, began to reflect on the concept of presence. Thierry De Duve, in his *Essais Datés* (éd. de la Différence, 1987), spoke of performance as the art of the "here and now" and of the pertinence of presence in any discussion of performance art. But he did add that contemporary philosophy regarded presence as a suspicious concept; philosophers such as Derrida and Heidegger (who will play a crucial role in Hill's intellectual evolution) doubted and challenged presence, eventually deconstructing it to the point where presence became the site of its opposition: void, absence, and so on (De Duve's *Présence Impossible,* pp. 160–63, in *Essais Datés*). From 1974 to 1978, Gary Hill removed himself, as an identifiable subject, from his tapes, concentrating in such pieces as *Air Raid* (1974), *Mirror Road* (1976), *Bathing* (1977), and *Windows* (1978) on organizations of images in sounds.

He was undertaking the task of deconstructing the image/sound structure which has dominated most of what has been done with moving images. The image itself was a sign of presence and these early works display as much weariness toward any image, as artists like Acconci, Jonas, Campus, and the like showed toward their own video reflections.

The sounds used by Gary Hill were those of his immediate surroundings, as well as electronically generated music, and silence, up until 1978. His explorations in image processing led at first to the texture
of the electronic image: vertical scanning of the lines, experimenting
with negative images of the black-and-white ones video could only produce when independents were first able to have access to equipment, as
well as testing feedback, solarizing, and so on. *Air Raid* and *Mirror
Road* are representative of this, yet one must pay attention to the fact
that even here these tapes are not primarily preoccupied with image
effects: each shot and effect are barely on the screen for a few seconds,
this aesthetic is at once removed from the "long take" strategy inherent
to performance videos, from Acconci to Nauman (Bruce Nauman, in
an interview given in the Spanish series *El Arte del Video* explained that
he had been influenced by Andy Warhol's films, in which actors and
performers did things until the film ran out. The length of Nauman's
early tapes was thus determined by the time the tape lasted, which was
generally 60 minutes), as well as from what was at the time one of the
major video aesthetics, Paik's "effects assaults" and the cult of post-production. In those two tapes by Gary Hill, the image revolves around
one sound which is central to the tape; in *Air Raid* one sees interiors
and exteriors, and what people are doing within those spaces during the
time a siren goes off, while *Mirror Road* splits the screen in two, examining the simultaneity of movements going forward and backward
(along a road), which is at the core of major works like *Why Do Things
Get in a Muddle? (Come on Petunia)* and *URA-ARU*. In *Bathing* and
Windows the image processing goes a step further as Hill begins working with the first color video cameras which were available; Hill has
said about *Bathing* that it played with conventions of painting and
video's capacity to reproduce "tableaux." The tape consists of a shot of
a woman taking a bath; the sound track is simply that of the water running. By varying the size of the shot throughout the tape, Hill is obviously playing with the first convention of painting, which is delimita-
tion of surface; the second concerns the representation of a nude figure
(this is in fact one of the very few cases of a nude female body throughout all of Hill's productions); the third deals with more contemporary
preoccupations as they concern flatness of surface on one hand, and the
"industrial" idea of massive repetition of works with slight modi-
fications from "tableau to tableau" (the Warhol paintings). Video is at
first a flat medium, and Gary Hill demonstrates this each time he
freezes the bather into different color patterns, but more important,

with each interruption of the act of bathing comes a further "disinte-gration" of the figure until it is reduced to pixels. And organizing pix-els, as well as the medium's horizontals and verticals in space, will be-come the next step in the quest for a subject.

We should note here that several of the artists working in video ex-perienced an explicit fascination for the technology, and were at first involved in an essentially modernist activity as they sought an "elec-tronic" specificity within the medium. This would go on until the artist had found his own project/agenda. Bill Viola's break with technology was brutal, and aside from slow-motion control and working on the materiality of the image, its texture, he was never to use explicit post-production effects again. With Gary Hill, the break will not constitute the same type of event, as the technology keeps on leading him toward language. With the tapes that follow *Bathing,* he begins to meld pixels and lines with sounds; *Electronic Linguistics* and *Sums & Differences* sig-nal the identity of the work to come, and with which he is generally as-sociated. These two tapes introduce us to Hill's logic of sound: the im-age either changes completely or is transformed as it exists with each new sound. With the "linguistics" tape, it moves essentially from one image to another: black-and-white electronic effects.

Hill's linguistics at this point have nothing to do whatsoever with theories and philosophies of language as we have come to understand them through the texts of Jakobson or Austin, but with a language of the medium, another vocabulary for art. In *Sums & Differences,* which is his most ambitious tape until then, we have shots of musical instru-ments which follow each other: percussion, wind instrument, key-board. One begins little by little to "listen" to these images, as their editing attempts to compose a work of music (Hill by that time was taken by the music of composers like LaMonte Young, Terry Riley, etc.; as were artists like Bruce Nauman and Vito Acconic). The pace of the editing accelerates, creating more complex rhythm structures, the sounds merge into an ensemble. The "differences" in this tape have to do with the number of frames Hill is removing from each shot as the sounds pick up speed; the sums are represented by the presence of all instruments in a single-screen image; the shots of the instruments are divided into vertical or horizontal fragments which try to keep up with the speed of sounds. As we may now see, time had various methods of infiltrating video productions as well as discourses on the medium: from the real-time experiences of Nauman and Acconci to Hill's edit-ing ideas, one could either develop an analysis which was determined by the uncut representation of real time, or another which concentrated on the existence of an object (sound or image) in time.

Nauman's case is extreme in that his performances lasted as long as the recording medium did, but to this dependence on the apparatus Nauman added the use of a paradoxical space inside the image, locating the camera at unfamiliar angles so that the representation of the event on a monitor would not correspond to the "shape" of the event: for example, in his *Bouncing in a corner*, the camera's axis shows him bouncing off a corner wall, a vertical action, on a horizontal plane; the artist's body is dividing the screen in two. But like most artists Nauman was associated with, his works, whether sculptures or tapes, were part of a larger scheme, a list of possibilities; Nauman's tapes were either about standing, sitting, lying, and so on. Gary Hill eventually used this "listing" technique in the tape *Primarily Speaking,* as a blueprint of what was possible. However, most of the performance videos had another approach to time; generally the length of the tape was determined by the event. The tape would last as long as it took for the event to accomplish itself. Whether it was Acconci or William Wegman, the event was singular and could last several minutes if not hours (Acconci), or just a few seconds or minutes in the case of Wegman's conceptually comic skits, which were certainly distancing the artist from the tapes of people like Richard Serra, Peter Campus, Nancy Holt, and the like. Although it's fair to say that John Baldessari also investigated the possibilities for humor within conceptual art, as the tape *I am Making Art* demonstrated.

Gary Hill brought another distinct identity to these events which were no longer based on the figure of the actor-artist. He introduced the voice and its movements in time. We did not see Gary Hill in the tapes, but we heard his voice, and his voice was performing. Having gone through the experience of sound, the image was now about to refine its availability through abstract narratives Hill would soon be creating. The tape which initiates this project is a piece called *Full Circle* (1978). In it we see the image divided into an upper and a lower half; the upper half is again divided in two: in the right corner we find a processed black-and-white image of the artist, kneeling; in the left corner we see a line produced by a modulator. In the lower half of the image we see both hands of the artist picking up one of those copper rods, it's a close-up color shot of what is taking place in the right-hand corner. As the hands are attempting to make a circle with the rod, we hear Hill's voice making sounds, trying to find the one sound which will produce the most accurate circle on the modulator, in the left-hand corner. By the end of the tape, image and sound have barely coincided. The physical gestures remained the same—making the circle—but the image of "sounding" the circle was in constant transformation. Gary Hill had found something. Two more tapes will follow, which in effect will be teaching the image how to speak. With *Primary* and *Elements,* both from 1978, Gary Hill uses the pronunciation of words which we could possibly locate within the prehistory of language: in *Primary,* which lasts 1:40, we have a close-up of the artist's mouth reciting colors: red green blue. The editing structure is similar to the one in *Sums* in that the sound represents an image (when the mouth says red the image turns red, when it says blue it becomes blue . . .) and the editing is accelerated until we are no longer able to distinguish the image from the sound. The mouth serves to give an image of the words, it acts as the other side of the sound. Gary Hill will keep on developing the use of speed edits; one example of how much his approach has evolved may be found in the 1989 tape *Site Recite,* which will be discussed in the third part of this essay. In *Elements,* he recites "air, fire, water, earth" over processed images which approximate the texture of each element; in any case, the transitional movement from each element is a flowing one, even though the voice-over is interrupted, repeated, manipulated.

Equal Time (1979) signals the task of writing. Gary Hill begins to conceive short narratives, acutely describing the acts of seeing and listening. These narratives may be about social gatherings, about objects such as tools or household appliances; some of them were also autobiographical. It would seem easy in retrospect to say that these texts anticipate Hill's encounter with Maurice Blanchot; nevertheless, when examining the stylistic concerns apparent in the brief tales recited in *Equal Time, Processual Video* (1980), *Videograms* (1980–81), one cannot help but remark on the intensely objective descriptions of what is taking place, which in turn give way to a "swelling" of meaning, a "flooding" of the senses which will later express themselves, in the tapes and installations after 1984, as figures of intoxication, disaster, and chaos. But in 1979, Gary Hill relies on the Rutt/Utra processor in order to produce the images which would try to follow and at times represent the flow and content of the narrative. The text always came first, laboriously, as Hill eliminated all unnecessary words, spaces . . . The intangible and ephemeral images which followed either transformed themselves so as to "represent" the pace of the narration, or changed into connotations of what was being described. Of course, the images are modified by the vocal performance; while the artist is not visible, the results of the act of speaking may be witnessed on the screen, and Hill explores a number of "talking" sounds, from the murmur to the flat-voiced monologue, singing, tongue in cheek, clinical delivery, and so on. But there is never any screaming. However, this strategy does reveal a willingness to privilege the mouth, "the dirtiest place of the body" (as Gary Hill says in the *El Arte del Video* series). In fact, once he will return to figurative work, the mouth will often appear shot in close-up, in *Mouth Piece, Commentary* and *Around & About, Primarily Speaking, Tale Enclosure, URA ARU, Incidence of Catastrophe,* and *Site Recite.* In *Videograms,* he describes kissing as the act of two amphibians destined to live on the face, which are gutting and devouring each other. Diane Ackerman, in her *Natural History of the Senses* (Vintage, 1991, pp. 108–10), insists on this idea of sensual appetite in the act of kissing, but when Gary Hill describes it it sounds much closer to the opening shots of *URA ARU,* when the knife is slicing open the belly of a fish.

What is interesting about those particular tapes (we could add *Black/White/Text* and *Happenstance* [1980 and 1982–83] to the list) lies in the idea that they are traces of performances, documents, very much in a Derridean fashion, that allow for a resistance to a complete erasure of memory. It was impossible to transfer directly onto tape the images produced by the Rutt/Utra processor, and Gary Hill had to place a camera in front of the machine's screen in order to record them (the Rutt/Utra scan processor functions through raster manipulation, changing the parameters of the display of the video signal; as Christine Tamblyn explains, "the images can be stretched, compressed, twisted, rotated, etc.," in "Video, An Historical Sketch," in *High Performance,* issue 37, 1987). Thus not only is the nature of these images quite fragile, but their paths toward meaning involved assistance, a supplement. There is already here the theme of the struggle "to get the words out." But the struggle of language is not the only act of representation involved in these tapes; we may also argue that the language produces "landscapes," "interiors," that it is attempting to exist within a space, which would be, for the time being, that of the monitor. In this respect, I would suggest that Gary Hill's work explores this "physicality" of language, as do the extraordinary paintings of Ed Ruscha, and the sculptures, neons, drawings, installations, and so on, of Bruce Nauman. While there is an undeniable preoccupation with the dematerialization of the art object so that the idea becomes the privileged proposition, such artists challenged both the notion that language was an immaterial form and that the loss of the visual linked to conceptual art was compensated by the idea of "art as idea." As Thierry De Duve mentions in *Au Nom de l'Art* (ibid., p. 125), artists like Ad Reinhardt or Joseph Kosuth were "repeating" Duchamp's gesture of removal and re-assignment, relying on Duchamp's legacy of "anything is art."

But Ed Ruscha brought language into the visual, not only creating horizontal landscapes for words which become objects, but postulating the idea that words have their own "colors," their arrangements in terms of spatial tensions as well as in terms of structures of meaning. Furthermore, the size of Ruscha's paintings is often determined by the manner in which language is organized on the canvas. Although Gary Hill was not representing words in those processed tapes, the language was responsible for the spatial organization of the image, and Hill plays with words, or connects words which may not produce "sense" but create other experiences of reading; like Ruscha's *High Speed Gardening* or Hill's *A Voice in the Sand,* from *Mediations* (1979–86). Afterward, when he did begin to show words in his work, he often relied on puns, idioms, and so on. However, Hill's production does not have the same "joyous" quality that Ruscha's has, nor is it explicitly and publicly violent as Bruce Nauman's videos and installations. It is a significantly more interiorized relationship to meaning, possibly closer to the sensibility of conceptual artist Robert Barry (one may think of his 1971–72 piece, *It Can Be,* which consists of eighty slides of text, which begin with "it can be started," move through "attacked, ignored, alone, denied, affirmed, accepted . . . and stopped"), whose art eventually retreated in an almost completely uncommunicable interiority. But then again Hill's work constantly tries to carry out into a physical space that lack of communication, the struggle to say and mean something. In recent tapes and installations, such spaces have a tangible geography, unlike the Rutt/Utra pieces; they move from the sea to the forest, to interiors, and out again, underlining in the process Hill's own physical displacements, from the West Coast to the East Coast, and back again to the Pacific shoreline. Curiously, the sea and the forest are also crucial metaphors for two thinkers whose reflections and writings he has translated into images; the sea for Maurice Blanchot, and the forest for Martin Heidegger. Somewhere in between these two figures we find that of Jacques Derrida, in whose theories of deconstruction Gary Hill found a system which formulated the objectives of another direction his tapes were taking.

I've tried to show how Gary Hill, through the act of exploring how to work with language and the image, came to be involved in aesthetic concerns shared by many artists of the late 1960s and 1970s. But I would suggest that the first of his significant contributions to a reflection on the image took place with the tape *Soundings* (1979) which showed, one shot at the time, what happened to the image when something was happening to the sound. The tape consists of physical acts on a number of speakers: flooding them, driving nails through them, setting them on fire. By virtue of how the sound source was being aggressed, the image/representation of that sound was obviously modified in the process. This is shown in a manner reminiscent of *Full Circle,* in that we only see the hands of the artist entering the frame, as each act is performed on the speaker. The artist's voice accompanies these gestures, telling how they are "sounding the image, imaging the sound, locating the sound with my voice, imaging my voice . . . "; ultimately that voice has a skin, the inner carton of the speaker which Hill is touching, piercing, covering, and so on. This tape may act as the first step into what will become an explicit signature strategy, syntaxic editing: the image changes literally when the sound tells it to do so. In 1986, Gary Hill isolated one figure of disaster for the voice, in his reconception of *Soundings* which is called *Mediations:* in this 4:45 tape, we see a close-up shot of the speaker, and a hand keeps entering the frame, carrying sand which it pours over the speaker, eventually covering the speaker completely. This is a one-shot tape, and the text which is heard tells of the voice being buried; at first we hear the voice bouncing the grains of sand in the speaker, then the voice struggling to be heard as it is half covered, until finally, when all one sees is a flat and full image of sand, the voice emerges, with difficulty, through the sand. Curiously though, when the burial is completed and the volume is lowered, the sound becomes clear again and allows Gary Hill to perform this difficulty to get through the image.

What he has done here consists in deconstructing the relationship between sound and image. Derrida's method finds its origins in the domination of speech over writing, how to present as primary something which metaphysics holds to be in second place. For instance, writing as the bastard son of the logos (see Geoffrey Bennington and Jacques Derrida's collaboration, as they go over Derrida's theories in "Jacques Derrida," éd. du Seuil, in the collection *Les Contemporains,* 1991; for a discussion of deconstruction, see pp. 43–64). For Derrida, writing will eventually refer to the manner in which speech has come to function. The 1980s were to see a number of artists engaged in the pursuit of deconstructive practices within the contexts of specific mediums, or of the art system and its structures of economy, gender, power, and the like.

In the case of film, television, and video, the image has generally dominated the sound; sound was there in most instances as a "coating" for the image (even though there were such notable exceptions as Tati, Tarkovski, Lynch . . .), while in video the image is the site of post-production and picturality, incrustation, and layering. Gary Hill's tapes turned this structure around, and in a number of instances his voice does function as writing, as when Derrida speaks of writing when one cannot talk, when obstacles, as in forms of distance, prevent the voice from being heard. Hill will be sensitive to this idea of obstacles, beginning with the use of figures of isolation, then on to signifiers of chaos and disaster at play in the image itself or in the recording process of the image.

Isolation, first, in the sense that the early experiments with sound and language rely largely on the development of the deconstruction mentioned above, and on the singular performances of Gary Hill's voice. But *Soundings* introduced suggestions of a more affirmative intimacy, it established materializations of meanings, and the sound + the image + the concept contribute to their constructions. In 1980, Hill produces *Processual Video, Commentary,* and *Around & About* in which the isolation begins to change into solitude, and will eventually lead toward themes of incapabilities of communication. *Processual Video* is a processed image piece, in which the visual changes are following the speech patterns more closely. This time, Gary Hill's text introduces the element of autobiography within the larger context of a precise phenomenon; just as the voice was the subject of *Soundings,* so is the vision, and how it is experienced, the focus of *Processual Video.* We listen to those accurate descriptions of nonevents quoted earlier, such as "the outline separating the pristine blue sky and distant peaks never seemed to stabilize"; or "the maintenance crew was still covering the run with snow" and see white lines against a black backdrop move in rhythm to the narration. But this time, Hill is adding lines like "he knew the ocean well, he grew up there and observed the waves daily, the water always returning, informing the shoreline, feeding the waves back into themselves." Raymond Bellour has already mentioned that the "He knew the ocean well" line anticipates Hill's *Incidence of Catastrophe* (see R. Bellour, *Video Writing,* pp. 421–44, in *Illuminating Video*) but before the encounter with Blanchot, and how it will lead the artist to a production of silence, we must first encounter works like *Around & About* and *Primarily Speaking*.

In a much quoted interview with Lucinda Furlong (in *Afterimage*, vol. 10, no. 8, March 1983), Gary Hill explained that *Around & About* was addressed to a particular person, at a time when a relationship was breaking down. He had been making tapes for about eight years, and the audience was about to encounter in *Commentary* (made a week after *Around & About*) the one who had been speaking while only showing his hands or his mouth. The tape was shot in his office when he was teaching in Buffalo, where the Vasulkas were also located. The text one hears starts off with: "I'm sure it could have gone on another way, a completely different way, a way that hasn't come to mind but that's a given. One can never observe all the possibilities and go onto the next." At first glance, that way would appear to be the direction the images are taking: they change with every syllable or one-syllable word, and throughout the tape they find new ways of existing within the frame, from left to right, right to left, reconstructing the shot of a wall, as if each word were a brick, starting from the center of the frame and "spiraling" out into a full image. Now the syntaxic editing strategy is expressed in its purest form, as the vocal performance carries a certain speed which the montage reproduces from movement to figure (from lateral displacements to stacking constructions). The montage is further enhanced by the randomness of the image content: Hill is recording, one shot at a time, everything in his office—chairs, lamps, the walls, clothing, and so on. In the accompanying piece, *Commentary*, which relies on the same strategy, Hill includes himself, close-ups of parts of his face in the 0:40 tape, and there are brief instances when the voice and the image of the one who is speaking connect and this is a first, even though Hill says in the tape: "No one is connecting, no one is feeling the attempt of connection." But this has more to do with the nature of the relationship which is alluded to; in *Around & About*, Hill says: "I mean if you want to leave you can do that or you can just turn off. I'm not trying to say that I'm indifferent. I just think there's a way here . . . I've never lost sight of that. I don't think there's been a loss of anything." This piece also included a technique which was developed in *Primarily Speaking*, as well as in *Site Recite*, which is rapid focusing on an object. This technique serves a punctuation function, it "underlines" dramatically what is being said at the time.

Primarily Speaking represents another major step in the progression of Hill's concerns. It is at once a more sophisticated piece of syntaxic editing, and a blueprint for much of what will follow later, notably installations. It also reveals the artist's increasing willingness to move from the clinical to the intimate. Using two image sources located next to each other at the center of the frame against a television test card backdrop, which has come to symbolize the void on television (this color grid appears on the screen when programs go off the air; the image stays that way until they come back on). There's obviously the idea here that television can really begin to "show and tell" once it leaves a time and space (within its scheduling grid) to do so. It's Hill's most explicit "media" tape. It lasts 18:40, during which time the two image sources are having a dialogue; Hill takes the syntaxic editing one step beyond, from the monologue situation of the previous tape to a more intricate interaction between two frames. The dialogue is composed of idioms responding to each other, which functions on the idea of "words not saying what they mean," of how easily a situation in which there is confusion over the simplest statements may arise, how there may be a hidden meaning behind a word which had not been taken into consideration previously. . . . Gary Hill made up a list of idioms, just as he tried to come up with enough images to keep up with the exchange. Some of these follow a deliberately random pattern, while others become parodies of their original meanings by virtue of the idiom which coincides with them. In some instances, they are as insidious as many current language productions, which emerged while painting was enjoying its comeback on the art market in the late 1970s–early 1980s. One practice of language and art is now linked with awareness, denunciation, and protest, as we've witnessed in such diverse works as those of Muntadas, Tim Rollins and K.O.S., Larry Johnson, Jenny Holzer, Mitchell Syrop, Louise Lawler, and Barbara Kruger of course. Just as I suggested that the art of Ed Ruscha and Bruce Nauman was bringing substance and matter back into the object of language (taking some distance from Kosuth, Barry, Weiner), so do these artists, who were recognized in the 1980s, take language in another visceral direction. Gary Hill didn't go in that direction, although this tape was the first sign of his visual acknowledgment of the outside world, without effects, that is. This is achieved by moving from one space to another, from the water to the countryside, from a drive along a road to interior scenes of eating, sitting, lying down, and so on. However, we must insist here on the idea that in spite of all these movements (lateral pans and moving camera shots, moving from the foreground to the background of the image/no dolly being used here . . .) the spectator, like the image, isn't getting anywhere. And the accumulation of idioms, which serves at first to establish an impression of familiarity, soon contributes to this lack of progression. It anticipates the disembodied walk in the forest, in Hill's 1987 installation *CRUX*, in which the logic of a point-of-view shot is completely shattered. In fact, one finds in *Primarily Speaking* a few shots of the feet walking through water, much like the ones always present in the installation (which will be discussed in the third part of this essay). Movement in space is thus clearly determined by whether or not communication has been achieved. If confusion is to result from an encounter, between two persons, between two sounds or images, between a sound and an image, then movement will cease to be linear. This concept will invest practically all of Gary Hill's pieces from 1984 to 1990. How does the body move about when it is such a potential site of chaos?

Collisions of Meanings

I mentioned earlier how Gary Hill repeatedly encountered artists, writers, and thinkers who became fundamental to his development: these meetings were often the result of coincidences. There was always someone to tell him about Derrida, Blanchot, or Gregory Bateson. But his own work was naturally articulating concerns similar to those at play in the texts of those thinkers. What had become quite apparent in this articulation was the expression of what is termed the postmodern, and which after more than a decade of discussion has come to signify a crisis in Western representation, its authority and universal claims. Stemming from the deconstruction of the modern order of the arts based on the Enlightenment order of distinct and autonomous disciplines, this postmodern expression sought to address issues of crisis and catastrophes brought about by the incapability of modernism's cultural agenda to confront a changing social context (ten years later, Hal Foster's compilation, *The Anti-Aesthetic,* published by Bay Press, remains one of the most useful references in any discussion of the postmodern). While not being explicitly political in nature, tapes such as *Why Do Things Get in a Muddle? (Come on Petunia), URA ARU,* and *Incidence of Catastrophe* are clearly involved in a breakdown of representation, and what Hill had been expressing in his work was the capacity to speak. But they seem lucid enough to suggest that the postmodern project has had a tougher go of it with the reconstruction aspect of this aesthetic contract; postmodernism was not positioning itself simply as an avant-garde, it came into the art world with a purpose.

With those three tapes, Gary Hill found a vocabulary of chaos figures which was going to transcend the single-channel pieces and find another space within the context of new installations. I should add here that while he made seven tapes between 1984 and 1990, twelve installations were created during the same period. Returning to this trilogy of the struggle for meaning, the first thing we may notice is that Gary Hill is no longer working alone, and the second lies in his resistance to mise-en-scène. Made with no funding, *Why Do Things Get in a Muddle? (Come on Petunia)* is a 32:00 "adaptation" of a Gregory Bateson metalogue, taken from his book *Steps to an Ecology of the Mind;* Bateson was one of the founders of the communication theory termed "cybernetics." What Hill is attempting to do here is reproduce the structure of the metalogue, its identity, through image and sound; in some ways he begins to remove himself from the characteristic properties of video as a medium, and even further from any notion of film language as it is understood in the organization of shots (size, camera movement), scenes, direction of actors, and so on. A metalogue is an exchange between at least two persons, and the form this discussion takes on mirrors what is being discussed. For Bateson metalogues were representations of entropy, and artist Robert Smithson, whose art and writings had an influence on Gary Hill, wrote that entropy was the cause of time for man. In *Why Do Things Get in a Muddle? (Come on Petunia)* a daughter asks her father this very question, and as the dialogue progresses we are made to see and hear what each character has in mind when speaking of what is a muddle and what is tidy. The daughter, who takes on the additional task of becoming "Alice," from Lewis Carroll's *Through the Looking Glass,* was played by Kathy Anastasia, who was the artist's wife, and the father was played by sound poet and performer Charles Stein, whom Gary Hill had met through George Quasha. Neither of them tries to act; the conceptual intention present in Bateson's proposition of logic as a frail state, informs their performances. Throughout the first 10 minutes of the tape, Charles Stein is reading his lines directly from the book.

In Gregory Bateson's text, the discussion is initiated by the daughter asking the father about something she saw at the beginning of an animated film: the letters which constitute the title of the film are all mixed up but end up moving correctly next to each other so that the spelling of the title is accurate. The father explains what probably happened: the filmmakers first shot the title written correctly on a flat surface, then moved that surface around, still shooting, so that the letters would get mixed up. Afterward they ran the film backward, so that each letter gave the impression that it was looking for its right place to be, so that the title could be tidy. It is this dimension of meaning which Hill explores in this piece: Is there a more appropriate direction for language if it seeks to achieve meaning? He goes on to reproduce the technique discussed in the metalogue, but whereas the text describes a process of writing as the signifier of language, Hill's tape applies it to the voices of the performers. Questions and answers move in two directions, forward and reverse, and end up colliding within the piece. In order to do this, Gary Hill had the father and daughter recite the lines normally, while in several other key moments during the tape, events were moving backward. He had written part of the text phonetically in reverse, and recorded the voices in the standard way, then played the tape backward so that one would hear the text moving forward once again; more than 20 minutes of this 32-minute piece are in reverse. There is a third element in the constitution of this chaotic development: to the ambiguities present in the attempt to define "muddle," as a noun and as a verb, and to the recording techniques, Hill adds excerpts from Lewis Carroll's *Through the Looking Glass,* notably the passage in which Alice loses the ability to name things. Kathy Anastasia is also dressed as the Alice character, and is surrounded by card games, a chessboard, wooden figures representing the mad twins, and so on. While this tape does ask the question "Does language reveal more if it moves in another direction?" it offers neither affirmation nor negation. But it did reveal, for the artist, that words took on other identities when seen, written, and spoken backward. It's interesting to note that a few years later, David Lynch used a similar recording technique in several episodes of his series *Twin Peaks* (which was shot at Snoqualmie Falls, near Seattle), which also produced a challenging network of correspondences among sound, image, and performance. So *Why Do Things Get in a Muddle?* is a first attempt at mise-en-scène, and therefore it's a tape about a learning process, but the lessons in language and image are taught backward. If we were to examine Gary Hill's tapes from that perspective, specifically those that were shot with a camera, rather than those made with the Rutt/Utra processor, which are clearly about electronically generated forms transforming themselves within a context of simultaneity, we would rapidly get caught up in the aesthetics of experimental cinema (and Hill has expressed appreciation for such filmmakers as Michael Snow and Stan Brakhage), especially that of structural film, as it's been discussed by P. Adams Sitney, a form of filmmaking essentially concerned with the exploration of a formal aspect (as with the "camera movement" films of Michael Snow).

Yet, the *Come on Petunia* tape triggers a will to sophistication, and Hill's next piece, *URA ARU (the backside exists),* displays a new preoccupation with composition, effects, the "beauty" of a shot, and so on. In 1984–85, Gary Hill lived in Japan, under a Japan/U.S. Exchange Fellowship. The *URA ARU* piece primarily came out of the *Muddles* experience, and Hill set out to find words in Japanese which had a correct sound and meaning when pronounced backward; this is what he called the acoustic palindrome. Thus the project was a further investigation into the idea that a word holds more than meets the eye, and the ear. A Japanese poet, Shuntaro Tanikawa, helped him sound out the words in Japanese, pointing him to those capable of producing images and folding into each other's meanings, for example EMA/offering-AME/rain, or ASU/tomorrow-USA/melancholy. These are precise palindromes, in that once the first and last letters of a word trade places, they still produce a word. In the case of an acoustic palindrome, a word which is pronounced normally becomes another word when pronounced backward. However, Gary Hill represents each word graphically, and the letters of those whose spellings differ in reverse become visual elements which contribute to the composition of the image. For instance, we find a shot of a Noh actor moving laterally, from left to right, and as he walks he leaves a trail of letters. They spell "that woman." The tape is reversed and this time the letters spell "ano(that) onna(woman)." Obviously, the manner in which the letters move around, throughout the tape, is reminiscent of the Bateson metalogue, but they introduce figures which Gary Hill will use in future projects, namely, all of those around Maurice Blanchot's *Thomas l'Obscur.* The most striking one is possibly the shot of a spider's web with words sliding from it, which looks ahead to the 1990 installation *And Sat Down Beside Her.* As the tape progresses, we become increasingly aware of such finds; they appear in image layerings and superimpositions, in square insets, incrustated at the center of the image, representing another space in which the Noh actors may perform. They are also present in the use of a meticulous control of slow motion, of forward and reverse movement: from the sharp quality of his previous syntaxic editing, Gary Hill moves on to a much more fluid aesthetic, which doesn't mean that it's more serene. The speed and urgency which characterized the previous tapes has not left these pieces, but perception has changed, as for the first time in a tape, Hill shows physical contact between two persons

(the "sweet mountain/floor passion" passage). It is also the first tape in
which there are more than two performers (besides the Noh actors, we
find once more Kathy Anastasia, and Don Kenny, who had been living
in Japan for over twenty-five years, and who was instrumental in introducing Gary Hill to the Japanese actors). Nevertheless, he has not
abandoned the idea of language as struggle, as the opening shots of
URA ARU demonstrate: the first shot is a close-up of a hand slicing
open the belly of a fish, the shot is reversed, sealing it, then opens it
again, while the second shot is a close-up of a mouth. It's the knife cutting the fish which signals the tape to "talk." Hill was able to do post-
production for this tape at the Atsugi Sony Plant, thanks to a Sony
grant; for a month he was to work every day with three 1-inch machines and an editor which had built-in dissolves and wipes. What
Gary Hill learned from this technology and its possibilities took full expression in his following tape, which may be one of the few truly great
works produced in video.

In the mid-1980s, a colleague of George Quasha from Station Hill
Press gave Gary Hill a copy of Maurice Blanchot's *Thomas l'Obscur*
(other titles by Blanchot, who writes fiction as well as essays, include *La
Part du Feu, L'Ecriture de D'ésastre*). The Thomas character and the experience brought on by the reading had a determining influence on
Gary Hill. From the 1986 installation, *In Situ,* to the 1990 piece *Inasmuch As It Is Always Already Taking Place,* a number of works refer to
that book. Hill gave his reading of the text in a 43-minute tape called
Incidence of Catastrophe, in which he plays the part of Thomas. The
chosen pages describe Thomas's experience of the sea and swimming in
it, the restless and uneasy nights which follow, a dinner with other
guests in a hotel where he is staying, and the "illness" brought on by
reading a book, alone at night in his room. The illness is one of the
senses: Thomas suffers from a flood of meaning, he is inundated by experiences. Each physical and sensory event, from the sensation of being
in water, to the language he hears at the dinner table on to the act of
reading, overwhelms him. Meaning is disintegrated as it's being constructed; the mind, like the body, is apt to drown, sink in the initial
pages, until it breaks down completely by the end of the tape. While
there are no explicit references to the book Thomas is reading in Blanchot's text (although one perceives that what Blanchot is doing consists
in portraying the character as an incarnation of reading and writing
within one body), in Hill's tape, the artist as Thomas is reading Blanchot's book, and uses the language in it as "triggers" for representation,

and for the progressive loss of control of body functions. The body becomes the site of catastrophe and disaster, no longer able to articulate. The tape is in essence inspired by Blanchot's book, but Hill adds some of his specific concerns to it; each part of the book becomes a space in which to perform and to develop his vocabulary of chaos. A list of signs is inscribed within the tape, establishing a series of parallels between the book as a physical object, its content, the print and the pages, and physical events, environments, such as a forest of shrubs, beaches, the sea, and so on. Gary Hill called upon a director of photography for this tape; it was the first time he did this. Rex Barker did the lighting and a number of hand-held and dolly shots. But Hill did the editing, using fades to black, dissolves, frame edits, but one operation stands out from the process, the soft-edged wipes. These are being used to bring images of waves rolling over certain portions of a page which is being read. This figure is used continually throughout the tape. *Incidence of Catastrophe* opens with a shot of the water going back to the sea, and in its flowing movement it breaks up the sand banks; if one looks carefully, we see, mixed in those grains of sands (the grains of voice from *Mediations*) letters and fragments of words. As we encounter the text, through macro shots of the pages, we see how a word calls forth its analogy, either through one of those wipes, or through a physical movement, as when the camera pans over a passage in which we may read "eyes fixed": although this is meant to represent Thomas's intense point of view, and his increasing incapability to focus on anything, we hear the hands setting the book down, again and again, but it refuses to stand still and results in a sensation of vertigo which will overtake him as it turns into a disease. At other times, the camera stops on the word *flood* and the waves roll over the pages. This water imagery will gradually invade the scope of Thomas's experiences, as in the scene in which he is unable to sleep, turning violently in his sheets, and which Gary Hill edits back and forth with shots of himself drowning. Another example worth mentioning may be taken from the dinner scene: Thomas is at the table picking his teeth as he's reading his book; Hill superimposes a shot of typewriter keys, which moves on a tighter close-up of the open mouth in which we see the waves rushing by, carrying the sand with them.

This is another representation of the inability to master the text; from the one finger inside the mouth, linked to the typing key, we move to the uncontrolled current making language impossible. There is one remarkable scene which is signed by Gary Hill: it begins when Thomas has difficulty in simply turning the pages, he can't go forward.

This cuts to Thomas running through a forest of shrubs, and in the course of trying to extract himself from this site, his body is marked by the sharp branches cutting into his skin. Later on when we return to the book, we see a finger cutting itself on a page, and this incites another desire to flee, but this time the flight is represented as movement which does not lead anywhere. The shot consists of Gary Hill running, and a light is shone occasionally on him to show that he is moving. Little by little, he comes closer to the camera, until we see his face flash up in pain. What is particularly impressive is the use of sound; we hear a sequence of steps in the act of running, creating a rhythm, which is in turn repeated throughout this passage, changing slightly as Gary Hill is nearing the camera. And the shot which follows immediately is that of a needle skipping at the end of a record, and on the rotating record we're able to discern a reflection of the space in which the next scene is about to take place. It is the dinner scene, the only one in which we actually hear people talking, since up until that point Hill uses the sound of the water, his breathing, the pages turning. This scene proves to be the breakdown of Thomas. Assaulted by all the sounds produced by the acts of eating and speaking, Thomas drops to the floor and begins to hallucinate (another hallucination of this character will be at the core of the installation *And Sat Down Beside Her*). The tape ends with Thomas in bed, trying to read once more, but this time the excesses of meaning literally make him sick. *Incidence of Catastrophe* closes with the celebrated scene in which Thomas becomes the senseless text himself, which is poked, like the book was, by a stick attached to the camera; Thomas has lost control of his body functions. Just as the text was constantly represented as rushing water, the complete loss of language takes on the form of the body discharging its fluids; these are the last residues, the last traces. The only time we get to hear Thomas takes place in the final moments, as he makes a series of undecipherable sounds until the pages of the book are superimposed as the walls of the room in which he has collapsed. This textual architecture will offer the artist radical new directions for setting the image within a space as the text becomes materialized into an installation.

Tapes Keeping Quiet, Objects Learning to Speak

If we look carefully at the opening shots of *Incidence of Catastrophe,* those of the water rushing back to the sea, while breaking apart the sand banks, we notice that Blanchot's text is softly superimposed, but there is one word which we can make out: *silence.* As I mentioned earlier, from the *Muddles* tape on, we no longer hear Gary Hill's voice. Between 1974 and 1986, Gary Hill made seven installations, three of which are related to single-channel pieces (*Around & About, Equal Time,* and *Primarily Speaking*). Three other works were done with live cameras (*Mesh, War Zone,* and *Glass Onion*), while his very first installation, *Hole in the Wall,* was a site-specific single-channel work. However, I will concentrate here on a discussion of the post-1986 installations, and from these I will make a selection in order to insist on the recent changes in the artist's relationship to language (notably in its path toward silence), as well as to underline his contribution to the evolution of the video installation as an art object.

These recent works express a coherence which allows for important connections within the construction of what now appears to be a fully mastered and mature aesthetic, as one piece develops one specific concept while announcing another which is eventually addressed in a following work. A quick example of this may be found in the formal concerns shared by the 1983–87 installation *CRUX, Incidence of Catastrophe,* the 1989 tape *Site Recite,* and the 1990 installation *Inasmuch As It Is Always Already Taking Place. CRUX* is a five-channel installation, in which the five monitors are arranged in the shape of a monumental cross. The upper monitor showed Hill's head, while the other four showed hands and feet; all of these images were recorded simultaneously as the video cameras were attached to his body. What is disturbing, however, in this piece is the absence of the body. During 26 minutes, we see him walking through a dense forest on a small island, from the ruins of a castle to a shoreline. While the perspective of the movement is reminiscent of some images from *Primarily Speaking,* the struggle represented in this piece (the difficulty of making his way to the shoreline) anticipates the scene in *Catastrophe* in which Thomas runs through the shrubs. This disincarnated body is also the Blanchot body, from *Thomas the Obscure* to *The Last Man.* For just as the absent body in *CRUX* leads to the collapsed body of *Catastrophe,* so does the latter point to *Inasmuch As It Is Always Already Taking Place,* which consists of sixteen television tubes positioned in a horizontal inset in a wall; each monitor shows a part of the body according to scale. Finally, this last piece shares formal concerns with one of the two tapes made by Hill since 1989, *Site Recite* (the other is *Solstice d'Hiver,* commissioned by the French cultural channel, La Sept, for a series called *Live,* in which artists working with film, photography, and video were invited to do a 60-minute take. La Sept has never showed the tape). *Site Recite,* which is a 4-minute tape commissioned by TVE (in Spain) for its *El Arte Del Video* series, shows us another horizontal surface, a table, on which are set various objects: stones, pieces of wood, bones, skeletal heads of birds, and so on. The table functions as a repository and as a cemetery, as another site of chaos. These objects are spread out on the table in a composition akin to that of the installation, and while both pieces refer to a specific formal preoccupation found in cinema, they are in essence representations of a novel reflection on the nature of perspective in video. The installation with its rectangular inset recalls the cinemascope format, yet the sixteen television tubes are arranged in a three-dimensional composition "inside" the wall; the spectator's gaze moves from left to right, but it also moves forward and backward. In the tape, which is accompanied by an introspective text, written by Gary Hill and recited by actor Lou Helter (who was in *Incidence of Catastrophe*), we see the camera moving in a circular dolly, stopping at several key points around the table and focusing back and forth on the objects set on the table: the focal length goes inside the image, then back again to its periphery. The impression produced by this process is that of a long take, but by looking closely at the focusing operations, we realize that a meticulous editing is taking place; Gary Hill does speed edits from one focal length to the other, accelerating in the process the circular dolly movements. These works, and those which follow, constitute a network of meanings within an image, but Hill, who previously investigated the idea that meaning within the image could be determined by the direction that image took in the monitor, is now exploring directions outside the monitor. *Site Recite* was originally conceived as an interactive disk piece, and this movement of meaning was eventually to be taken over by the spectator, as he saw fit to go from one point to another.

Recent developments in video art have seriously threatened the existence of single-channel tapes. These past few years have signaled a change in the reception of this art form. Gary Hill (as well as other artists including Bill Viola, Klaus vom Bruch, Marcel Odenbach, Dan Graham, Matt Mullican, Gretchen Bender) has achieved notoriety within the structures of contemporary art (galleries, museums, magazines) due to the interest generated by installations. Naturally, the art world's increasing tolerance toward pluridisciplinary productions has contributed to this little space allotted to video (within this logic, the work of Bruce Nauman plays a greater role than that of Nam June Paik). Thus a wider audience, and not solely that of festivals, may have an opportunity to discover this artist's tape production. It is necessary to understand the reasons behind this rekindled enthusiasm for larger-scale video pieces in order to fully measure what Gary Hill has accomplished. Until recently, few institutions were able to define a clear policy toward media and television on one hand, and experimentation and creation on the other, often letting artists indicate directions (the ones that did have a position, like the Whitney, the MoMA, the Stedelijk were "influencing" several other museums). One could posit that two distinct groups have emerged, one which did not wish to have its output assimilated by traditional art mechanisms such as exhibits and acquisitions, opting rather for a proximity with television, whether this took on the form of a radical critique or of an explicit complicity. The second group located itself closer to the context of contemporary art and aesthetics. Still, in spite of the will expressed by artists to participate actively in such debates and projects, many institutions chose to develop video departments and show tapes and installations under a designated term and banner, and in an isolated context. Showing video next to other types of practices (painting, sculpture, photography, non-video installations) is a relatively recent phenomenon. In the past, most video creations were often placed in exhibits for their novelty value; this raises once more De Duve's imperatives: Is "novelty" video's function in the "whatever . . . as long as it's art" proposition? Has this changed? How has video as an art form succeeded in gaining credibility beyond its link to conceptual art? Most likely through artists who appeared with precise aesthetic agendas and strategies and who were successful in making the transition from single-channel tapes to installations. The perception of Gary Hill's work has been increasingly displaced from that of video art to art made with video. Many characteristics have been assigned to video in an attempt to locate its specificity: from real time and simultaneity to apparent signifiers of technology, contemporary art sought to locate the practice of video within a number of discourses, including that of the icon (the immediacy of the reproduced image) and that of power (the economy of high technology). Although Gary Hill's output has not been immune to this type of classification, it has challenged efforts to make it "say" something definite. In other words, there is a difference between hearing "he said this" and "it sounded like he said this." Hill's body of work was never about "to keep its word." As we've seen, his strategy is not based on the construction of meaning but on its insidious unraveling. It has continually provided an experience of chaos, notably through the fractal quality of his editing techniques, and in this sense it does matter that the artist has established a sophisticated relationship with the tools of video. Such control of the medium has made it possible to have something chaotic happen to meaning, as in the mise-en-scène of the speech act and its direction, which came to function as a strange attractor, as the hidden pattern of order within disorder.

The presence of Maurice Blanchot, with his discourse of catastrophe, disaster, and fire, and the manner in which it has been linked to postmodern thinkers such as Jean-François Lyotard, Jean Baudrillard, and Paul Virilio, could have initiated a closer scrutiny by critics and curators, who began examining his work in the context of a more aesthetically elaborate context. This triggered an immediately positive effect in that the artist would be able to move on to more ambitious and more technologically intricate pieces; to work with video is to work with tools, forms, and images, and not exclusively with concept. The timing was auspicious since artists working close to the technology were well aware that the tape as a creative medium would probably disappear by the end of the century. Unlike cinema, video (electronically generated images) has unceasingly challenged the medium through which it presented itself. Gary Hill, who worked with tape for more than fifteen years, is now using laserdiscs which are controlled by a computer matrix. Reduction and miniaturization are dimensions which are now explored by installation artists, especially Gary Hill. For instance, *And Sat Down Beside Her,* and *Inasmuch As It Is Always Already Taking Place,* both done in 1990, reveal a radically new idea of scale. *And Sat Down Beside Her* refers to the Little Miss Muffet nursery rhyme ("along came a spider . . .") and to a passage in Blanchot's *Thomas the Obscure* which describes an hallucination Thomas has about a spider. The installation is divided into three parts: at the center we find a long and delicate glass tube hanging from the ceiling (the spider's thread); at its extremity hangs a 1-inch television tube revealing a close-up of a typeset ball. This image is shown on the floor through a projection lens; it continually turns on itself, "weaving" the text which has been applied on the floor in a circular pattern. To the left, we find a four-inch television tube, suspended from the ceiling over a table. A projection lens is located through the corner of the table and we discover the projection of a close-up of a woman's face on an open copy of Blanchot's book. The book itself is set on a small chair; the legs of both the chair and the table are shaped in order to convey the physical presence of the spider. Finally, to the right of the central web, we find on the floor two 1-inch television tubes, and four projecting lenses showing two different image sources: shots of Blanchot's texts are projected on the corner of the wall (see the closing shots of *Incidence of Catastrophe*), creating another web of sense made out of eight different images, suggesting the four pairs of eyes one finds on a spider. By using this figure, Gary Hill succeeds in merging a number of crucial references in his work and introduces us to the next direction he is about to take. The spider passage allows Hill to represent one of Derrida's other major contributions to the quest for meaning: etymology (as demonstrated in a number of texts in which the philosopher explores what lies behind the chosen title for an essay; this also informs the tape *URA ARU*), which is linked to the act of weaving. The spider is also present in Nietzsche's *Zarathustra,* in which it represents a figure of poison, a whirling of the senses, of revenge. Both Blanchot and Derrida are certainly Nietzscheans, and it is Thomas's heightened sensibility that Gary Hill represents as a disease. This idea of language as a "poison" was already present in the 1988 installation *DISTURBANCE (among the jars),* commissioned by the Centre Georges Pompidou. The texts used in this piece are part of the fifty-two texts (gospels) found at Nag Hammadi, in Egypt, in 1945; they are the foundations of the gnostic perspective on Christianity. Jacques Derrida appears in this installation as one of the performers. The scriptures are about destruction as they weaken established meanings and references which circulated largely through language (the Mass, the preaching, etc.); they are also traces of another history and memory. Jean-Paul Fargier has written a religious analysis of this work (see Magie Blanche, in the catalogue of the Musée d'art moderne, Villeneuve d'Ascq, 1989, and not his text on Nam Jun Paik, in *Chimera* 3 bearing the same title), but I perceive this collaboration between Hill and Derrida to be about "belief" rather than "faith." What should things mean if they were kept hidden for centuries, and how are we to say them? There is an archeology of sense operating within the seven monitors of the installation, and when Derrida encounters other performers, as his image moves from one monitor to another as it asks "how to pray," he could as well be asking "what is believing," not in a religious manner, but as a cognitive process. Some time before participating in the *DISTURBANCE* project, Derrida had published a volume of poetic writings called *Feu la Cendre,* in which is articulated the notion of "ash" as a representation of disintegration. In the installation, Gary Hill selected passages from the Gospel according to Thomas, in which Jesus speaks to Thomas, and when the disciples ask him what Jesus said, Derrida answers: "If I were to tell you one sentence, you would take stones and throw them at me, and fire would come out of these stones and consume you."

These installations implode within the category of video art and are now participating completely in what is at stake within contemporary art. They may also be divided in two specific areas of investigation: one which continues to explore the frontal dimensions of the moving image and another which fragments in a three-dimensional space the continuity among images. Works such as *BEACON, Split Time Mystery* (shown in Vienna in 1991), *Suspension of Disbelief* (Hayward Gallery, London, 1992), *Between Cinema and a Hard Place, Tall Ships* (for the 1992 Documenta), and *Inasmuch* each dissect aspects of this frontal formalism. Pieces like *CRUX, I Believe It Is an Image in Light of the Other* (Donald Young Gallery, Seattle, 1992), *And Sat Down Beside Her,* and the *CORE SERIES* touch on the physical interruption of the image. Naturally both areas communicate with each other, as well as with the earlier works, as I've explained. Furthermore, such objects distance themselves from the use of massive equipment and the necessity to fill up a space completely. They are fragile and refined gallery objects on one hand (and this is an important step taken, which makes it possible to reach another kind of audience for this medium: Gary Hill's idea of a fragile architecture for his works of frailty are as significant as Dan Graham's elaborate passages within a gallery space, although Hill does not consider in the conception of his art the economy of aesthetic receptions), and on the other hand they are charged with a menace and affection. What is most striking, however, in all of these pieces is the sound; it no longer serves its initial purpose. In fact, Gary Hill's art seems to move toward silence. This may be explained in part by a transfer of the way sound was being used onto the image containers themselves, as in the case of *And Sat Down,* or *I Believe It Is an Image.* In the case of the *CORE SERIES* and *Inasmuch* and *Suspension of Disbelief,* the technology increases the editing possibilities suggested earlier on by language. From 1986 to 1991, Maurice Blanchot was a crucial reference, and the piece *And Sat Down Beside Her* seemed to conclude a series which began with the installation *In Situ* (1986, the first work which refers to Blanchot).

Beyond the isolated passage from *Thomas the Obscure* at the center of the work lies a question which infiltrates the next installations: From which direction does meaning come? Does meaning exist simultaneously on horizontal and vertical planes? The representation of the spider's web hanging from the ceiling signals the idea of the hanging image, used once again in *I Believe It Is an Image in Light of the Other*, which projects images of bodies (from an object which recalls an aqualung), of a chair, on open books (the book is Blanchot's *The Last Man*). The reference to the monitor as a container for the images is annihilated, just as it is no longer the site of elaborate editing. I believe this is a truly revolutionary act, the implications of which have totally escaped the field of virtual realities. *CORE SERIES, Between Cinema and a Hard Place, Suspension of Disbelief,* and *Split Time Mystery* have done away with this equation: multiple monitors = multiple channels.

Reflection on the capacity of motion within the frame continues to be severely hindered by the single screen; even those simulations made for scientific purposes, which allow for a mesmerizing number of perspectives inside and outside a subject, remain confined to a traditional idea of continuity, fluidity. These new works by Gary Hill allow new technology to do something different with an image, positing in the process another discourse for the analysis of digital technology, one which would not focus exclusively on the relationship between high-tech and its idea of image as artifice. The new premise in this exploration into the language of images is the need for "multiple" screens. The *CORE SERIES* consists of a pair of small monitors placed next to each other at an angle suggesting an open book. The seed for such an object was already present in *DISTURBANCE (among the jars)*.

Images are now contained on one tape; in this sense, video returns to its origins, which consisted of "recording" the image. However, the editing now exists as a computer matrix which controls the switching from monitor to monitor. The more elaborate piece, *Between Cinema and a Hard Place,* obviously holds more than one image source, but the basic concept is the same. On one object from the *CORE SERIES,* we see a board attached to the camera as it pans back and forth in an empty room. There is a glass of water on the board. The switcher appears to be removing some images out of the thirty images per second, so that a constant flickering appears on the monitors. The experience is phenomenologically unsettling; upon seeing the piece for the first time, it takes a moment to rationalize whether it is the eye or the mind which understands the concept of simultaneous interruption and continuity. Somewhere in the time of this tape, some images have been spilled.

More recently, Gary Hill has become interested in the philosophy of Martin Heidegger, notably his texts on art and technology (at a time when most media artworks being financed and produced cannot be separated from the "politically correct" agendas, Hill's preoccupation with Heidegger appears to have caused controversy). This is a logical step in moving away from Maurice Blanchot and Jacques Derrida; the ideas which have made their way into his art are those that concern Heidegger's discussion of the proximity between poetry and thought. His critique of technique may also be located in the act of replacing multiple channels by a matrix. In spite of the threat of viral assaults, pirating, and the like, the matrix holds an aura: videotapes which may be reproduced over and over are not concerned with this will to uniqueness. However, it becomes clear that without this matrix, *CORE SERIES* and *Cinema* cease to exist. Conceptually, it contributes to further discussions on the nature of the work of art as private property. Furthermore, with an installation such as *Cinema,* Gary Hill points to the weight of established forms, such as film and television editing. The next logic of the image could be about displacement rather than artifice.

Presently, much of the art world's interest in electronics is focusing on the "nature" of the image, elaborating yet another theory of the artifice, the simulacra (interactive works, simulation, virtual realities . . .) and it may take more time before this community acknowledges the implications of Gary Hill's breakthrough, recognizing such works as significant steps in the investigation of the language of images (the text used by Gary Hill in the *Cinema* installation is taken from Heidegger's *On the Way to Language;* it is a discussion of Hölderlin, taken from the *Bread and Wine* elegy, the verse in which Hölderlin speaks of "words which must like flowers grow" is examined. Heidegger discusses how poetry and thought are seemingly located in the same surroundings; "each step taken forward in that direction is a step back to where we already are." This allows Gary Hill to work at once on representation and illustration: the gardening shots are the grooming of words, while several moving camera shots suggest the similarity of surroundings, from mountains to fields, and so on. There are constant reminders, however, that proximity does not signify "merging": shots of fences, hedges, all of these are signs of separation, of distinctness. As for the illustration of the step forward/step back, each category of moving camera shots is ultimately sent back to the series of monitors on the right side—there are twenty-three monitors in all, placed in three separate rows on a floor—making its way back to the left side where no further movement is possible). His images are fragile, removed from the burden and number of equations necessary to the post-production of digitally created images. However, an object from the *CORE SERIES* indicates that this proximity between poetry and thought, between a shot of a glass of water, or of a leaf, and the software moving these images from monitor to monitor, can remain a source of revelation.

The silence which has progressed throughout these recent works has placed Gary Hill in the company of artists quoted earlier, like Bruce Nauman, Ed Ruscha, Robert Barry, and the like. This may have been the result of the "dispositifis" having "words" with the issue of language. Sound may eventually reappear in upcoming projects, but presently these new concepts are soaring and one may wonder if they'll ever hear sound the same way again.

> *"quick, a glass of water, I can't say, at the level of my mouth"*
>
> —*Inasmuch As It Is Always Already Taking Place*

Raymond Bellour

The Matrix

Why *Picture Story*? Because these words, in the opening title, delineate a text and a program which the work itself is charged with recognizing and executing.

Picture: image, painting, film: everything that is framed and displayed. *Story:* everything that is told, true or false.

A small lemon-yellow cursor glides toward us and then retreats, transforming and becoming larger as it travels through the empty space of the bluish screen. A word ("horizontal") is inscribed inside this square micro screen, which grows larger and turns into a rectangle that becomes more and more elongated, squeezing the word inside it until the word coincides with its meaning. This form, or screen, withdraws into the distance, becoming tiny, and the word disappears; what is left is a simple mark against the blue background (losing its yellow color, the mark turns a neutral white). At this point a brick-red hand, doubled by a fantastic shadow, seems to pass underneath the mark left by the cursor; presumably holding a pencil that the spectator doesn't see, the hand doubles the cursor's mark with another one that wobbles a little but is still clearly inspired by its model. As soon as the hand-drawn mark has been made, the machine-mark is retracted, withdraws, returns to its original form and surrenders to the power of the new word inscribed inside it. Subsequently, until almost the end of the tape, each new word will originate directly from the cursor as it disengages from the line that temporarily holds it.

When the hand first appears, a voice pronounces several words which will be joined by others each time a line is drawn. Three dis-

Originally published in a catalogue from The Long Beach Museum of Art, 1994. Translated by Janet Bergstrom.

jointed sentences are formed this way, and at the end of the third, the tape is over (7 minutes). Here, the text can be cited in continuous sentences, but one needs to remember that during the tape, the words are produced one by one (with the exception of a large part of the last sentence, which is read very quickly), and the sequence doesn't really make sense until the end. This also holds true for the entire operation of the "program." ("Four letters in the alphabet possess a quality significantly different than the others. When upside down or backward their character remains the same. The letters are H, I, O, X, or HI OX . . . furthermore O and X may be turned 90 degrees in any direction and still contain their original meaning.")

Two things are immediately apparent. The hand-drawn mark, which is the same color as the hand that traces it, seems to emanate from the hand. Along with the hand and the voice, it comprises a kind of virtual body (those who know Gary Hill's voice will recognize the way its presence gives his tapes a unique tempo, directly engaged in the process in which it is one of the elements). On the other hand, as soon as the second mark is made, a little above the first but longer, one is struck by the contrast between the form (horizontal) and the meaning ("vertical") of the word which is created this time. This excess creates a situation of semantic inversion with respect to the first mark. Thus, from the beginning, the body or the (virtual) subject of the experience is brought back to a succession of logics that are stacked up without excluding one another. An open logic.

Twenty-one words are written in this way inside the screen of the cursor, thereby allowing the drawing to be made as well as the project to be carried to its conclusion. Here are the words: beneath the simplicity of their appearance everything contributes to a program: (horizontal/vertical/height/width/scan/slew/triangle/envelope/summing/ bias/cycle/hold/sequence/event/character/plot/development/form/content/concept/vision).

With the exception of the first two, which are adjectives, all these words are nouns. But none is the name of an object—those objects that Swift had imagined being carried by the inhabitants of Lagado in order to avoid deceptive games between meaning and sound. These words designate abstract givens, concepts, if you like (and the word *concept* is operative since everything here designates). They define reality in general. But in the aleatory opening, one can distinguish three levels that relate directly to the process taking place. The first refers to operations that are effected before our eyes. For example, "summing" refers to stacking the logics at work in this program. "Slew" (pivot, turn) refers to the movement the cursor makes on the screen. But the term also refers to the fact that the words can appear reversed (like a mirror image) inside the cursor as well as upside down. (This can be seen in the way the opposition *horizontal/vertical* is represented.) The second aspect of this list is the recording of numerous characteristics attached to machines of vision. So, "picture" (painting, photo, cinema, video, etc. . . .), everything that makes one think about vision—the word *vision* itself ends the list—for instance, the image of this elliptical body that draws and speaks. The words chosen often encompass simple forms (the first four thus qualify as elementary coordinates of perception); they can designate a more specific mark ("scan": the process that constitutes the video image itself). Finally, many of the words in the final third of the list refer to the idea of story, event, character, in short, of fiction (that's the "story" side), sometimes suggesting more precisely a story in images ("sequence"). Let's move to the end of the tape, where all the elements in play are brought together in an unusual kind of suspense. What does one see, what does one hear at the end of a journey that, for a long time, seems to hold no surprises, that allows the spectator/reader to reflect gradually on what he discovers as well as what he forgets (the words, the sentences, and the abstraction of a process that is physically imposed—but because video is a conceptual art, and not a very public one, concrete traces can be found, if only modest documents accompanying the projection where one can read, as here, the text that was spoken and the list of words.

At the moment the voice pronounces the two syllables that bring together the four exceptional letters ("HI OX"), a yellow ox appears in the middle of all the red lines that have accumulated. This apparition changes everything, the way a joke can be suddenly illuminating. Two meanings are immediately suggested: first, the meaning of the two words made by these four letters which have the singular quality of remaining identical whether they are reversed or upside down. This is important: these letters are therefore less purely symbolic than the other letters of the alphabet: they are more plastic, more mobile, and can therefore take part in the figuration that is interrogated here. The appearance of the ox underscores this very well. While it is a drawing, an image, it does exactly what the two letters (OX) that compose it can do, namely, turn in every direction—and in doing so, acquire a quality that is as much virtual as it is a mediation between a visual representation and an abstract meaning (the question of the sonorous dimension of the word and its effects as such on the image with respect to the materials that compose it, the question that has preoccupied Hill in other works, remains in suspension here).

The second meaning has to do with recognition. Up to this point, the pattern of intersecting lines has remained rather enigmatic, but one suddenly recognizes, because of the placement of the ox, an enclosure within which the ox is located. Thus, one touches on the question of schematization, which is of such importance (as Christian Metz saw clearly) in linking "the perceived and the named": the schema passes as if without transition (in particular because it transcends the analogical opacity of images linked to photographic reproduction) from the order of pure abstraction to that of intelligibility as soon as the eye and the mind recognize a "real" image in it—that is to say, a nameable object, the arbitrariness of the word coming with all the weight of its meaning (concept) to inhabit an image which didn't preexist it in that form. The schematization here, banal, belongs to the drawing, even if it seems to originate from the cursor and the machine that animates it: remember the hand making the marks. That's where the finesse in having opted for two colors, red and yellow, becomes operative. The ox playing in its pen, this crude image, originates from the hand that draws (itself preprogrammed by the trace of the cursor attached to the words that are lodged inside it, but distinguished from them by its red color); but it also originates from the cursor that produces the words in that the yellow background seems to be distinguished from the words themselves in order to inspire the color of this ox.

We should remember the source of the lines of the enclosure and the ox that revolves inside it. They come from the words, the concepts inside the cursor, from which they are detached and transformed into micro elements of a virtual image which is suddenly actualized. They come from other words too, from the brief commentary stating the properties specific to the four letters that bring them into the story which is suddenly able to be represented by this image. The image comes to us therefore from the words and even from the logic that relates the letters to each other. But it is also created by the voice that enunciates the proposition, from the hand that takes over the marks from the machine and affects them with its own color (red). And the concepts themselves are created from a color, the yellow of the cursor, and are similar to the blue background of the screen that sets off this yellow.

Several things should be noticed, signs of a work dedicated to the relationships among the body, the voice, sound, and meaning (perhaps this follows directly from the conceptualization of this "program"). First, the idea that there are, most important, face to face, the body, a body, and machines (video, computer, etc.). Between the body and the machine (as between the machine and the body) exists a relationship of transformation (collusion, seduction), to the extent that this relationship allows only the mimicking and the conceptualization of the transformation that takes place within the body itself, the sentient and thinking body, between the assertion of the word and the assertion of the image. For the machine (the new machine) has the singularity of rendering sensible, perceptible, and perhaps intelligible, these transformations which, in various ways, collide and accumulate. From the virtualities manifested in this tape, one has the impression that what is being evaluated here, finally, is the very process of being or of existing in this historical age in which, increasingly, the machine is becoming the interactive double of every body.

The impact of *Picture Story* comes from beginning with the most remote elements possible and linking them in a way that creates a mystery, constructs an event, and begins a story that becomes a pure network of relationships: a program. A word is created inside a cursor that is displaced and its residue left as a mark, a process that is profoundly alien to the recovery of this mark by the hand that forms an image and a "story" bit by bit to illustrate the figural properties of four letters of our alphabet. Yet . . . filling in the distance between these heterogeneous dimensions by playing them off against each other is the act through which the thought makes visible the nearest as well as the most distant of the elements that give it physical form. In that, *Picture Story* is the matrix for every work to come by Gary Hill. A little toss of the dice.

Willem van Weelden

Primarily Spoken

Call/Resonance

Primarily Speaking (1981–83) is the resonance of a desire to speak. The tape begins with the words:

Well . . .
you know what they say . . .
we've all heard it before . . .

One sees a drop falling into a pool of water. In the pause that follows the word *well,* concentric circles ebb from the spot where the drop landed. If the spectator interprets the word *well* as a noun rather than an adverb, it acquires the meaning of "spring." This opening image could then be understood as a metaphor for the spring of speech and the dying fall of its echo. In an interview with Lucinda Furlong, Hill says: "*Primarily Speaking* is probably the most complex work I've done. It still isn't finished. Its complexity gets subverted by the use of idiomatic expressions. I still haven't unwound it because it exists on so many different levels."[1] As long as the echo of the work resounds, its original pronouncement is forever merged with and inseparable from the labyrinthine murmur of its interpretations. An ideal spectator, like the creator of the work, has freed himself from a uniform reference to reality with the intention of unraveling whatever meaning can be discovered in the work. The spectator no longer knows what came first: his text, the images on the tape, his own mental images, or the text read by Hill. This is important, because the creator is attempting to pursue the spectator as relentlessly as possible. In this tape, Hill has woven together absence and presence, essence and fact, time and space, meaning

Originally published in an exhibition catalogue from the Stedelijk Museum, Amsterdam, Kunsthalle, Wien, 1993–94.

and sign, perception and imagination, speech and writing into a whole that is impossible to disentangle. This indecisiveness in establishing a uniform interpretation causes one to concentrate more and more closely on the sound of Hill's voice. As if his voice could do one justice in the new dimensions that have come into being in the relationship of words and images. But what does one hear?

> there are no tell-tale signs
> to speak of . . .
> I wonder if a better thing
> to do is refrain
> from speculation . . .
> hang in there
> but hold back
> not get caught up
> in the missing link syndrome

Nietzsche proposes a remedy for the apathy that can result from indecisiveness and static:

> Erst *Bilder* zu erklären, wie Bilder im Geiste enstehen. Dann *Worte,* angewendet auf Bilder. Endlich *Begriffe,* erst möglich, wenn es Worte gibt ein Zusammenfassen vieler Bilder unter etwas Nicht-Anschauliches, sondern Hörbares (Wort). Das kleine bißchen Emotion, welches beim 'Wort' entsteht, also beim Anschauen ähnlicher Bilder, für die *ein* Wort da ist— diese schwache Emotion ist das Gemeinsame, die Grundlage des Begriffes. Daß schwache Empfindungen als gleich angesetzt werden, als *dieselben* empfunden werden, ist die Grundtatsache. Also die Verwechslung zweier ganz benachbarter Empfindungen in der *Konstatierung* dieser Empfingdungen; *wer* aber konstatiert? Das *Glauben* ist das Uranfängliche schon in jedes Sinnes-Eindruck: eine Art Ja-sagen erste intellektuelle Tätigkeit! Ein 'Für-Wahr-halten' im Anfange! Also zu erklären: wie ein 'Für-wahr-halten' entstanden ist! Was liegt für eine Sensation hinter '*wahr*'?[2]

Thus, the primary sound of speech is connected with the sensitivity of primary listening. Hill spoke more than ten years ago, and we, the listeners, begin by finishing what he started.

Frame Provocation

Everything speaks and everything has ears. Those whose lips are dumb, talk through their hats with their fingers. *Primarily Speaking* was created in the period in Hill's work in which he used the video image as a syllable. Sequences of image-samples accompany the text spoken by Hill like a perfectly synchronized simultaneous translation. The sequences of images that "look like what is being said" are divided up between two rectangular frames in the middle of the monitor. These sequences run along like lapdogs, absorbed completely into their owner's movements, aping them and yelping along with them as they walk. But, like dogs, the images don't succeed in being a perfect reflection. The images remain images and tell a story of their own. The suggestion is more of "doubling" than genuine fusion. The background is a test card (vertical, colored bars like the test card used by the BBC), that changes into abstract animations during the video. Like the images, the sound is distributed through two separate channels. Each (left and right) alternately steers the images in the frames. Thus, a suggestion is created that the two frames[3] and their corresponding sounds are complementary and engaged in a dialogue, and produce a commentary just as the text does: an interior dia-/trialogue. The text increases the oscillatory effect by continually changing back and forth between an I, a YOU, and a WE form. At times it seems as if the spectator is being directly addressed, provoked; at times, the YOU seems to refer to the other frame. This causes the spectator to continually check the images for divergence and commentary as she or he stumbles after the text. The spectator seems to compare the modulations of Hill's voice with the "modulations" and rhetorical repetition effects of the images. The spectator seems to be searching for an answer to the question: Which voice inhabits which media space? And the question of how close to allow the voices to get to the setting. The search for purity, for primary, essential speech is impossible in the multiplicity of interwoven voices and influences.

Even if only for fractions of a second, the images antecede, move in a different time frame, another universe of meaning, because we listen first and then retrieve the images from oblivion to use as "afterimages" in interpreting the combinations. The same thing happens in a disco when dance partners react to each other's movements only in the second place. Their primary reaction is to the music. Research of the relationship between text and image thus becomes a function of the analysis of sensory perceptions. In this regard, McLuhan speaks of *sense ratios*.[4] As information is offered visually or auditorily, a shift can occur within the "sense ratio" in a visual or auditory direction, creating a different kind of "rationality." This is a point of departure for reflection on media-circuits and an impulse for a theory of translation.

Since Duchamp, art is concerned with the metabolism of one medium within the other. For Duchamp, this consisted mainly of metaphors borrowed from physics: gases could become fluid or solid. The question here is how a spoken text becomes a video image, computer animation, written text, or montage. One's focus of attention shifts continually between media levels. So much is happening at once that the choice of what one pays attention to determines the meaning one perceives (McLuhan's *subjective completion*). This means that as a spectator, you quickly become aware of how you watch, which translations and interventions you register and endow with meaning. The greater the complexity, the more structure and mise-en-scène is needed in the medium in order to make those interventions accessible and the more the accent comes to lie on following the structure of one's perception. In this sense, *Primarily Speaking* is a mirror that renders visible the perception of the spectator. This provokes the desire to intervene. To replace obedience with deeds, to participate: interactivity. But the linearity of the video sermon prohibits this. The tape adheres too much to a pre-text, a script, to allow this.

In an interview, Hill confides in Lucinda Furlong:

> I really constructed the text. It wasn't like writing. (laughs) When I was doing the text, I thought of Matisse's cut-outs, these re-energized primal shapes. Idioms seem like language cut-outs. Once you get inside of idioms, they're incredibly rich. Television is the most advanced communication system and yet it's one big idiom. Everything that's spewed out is one big idiom—the corporate world takes on how life should be.[5]

But the text (the recorded sound track of the spoken text, including voice modulations and intonation) used by Hill can be seen as a script. Yet a script is the result of the script writer's mediation between the two worlds of text and image. Like a genuine tightrope-walker, he attempts to preserve the balance between text and image with writing acrobatics. But the gravity of the images pulls him down.

His circus number precedes the video performance. It takes place within the framework of the medium itself. In spite of intentions of breaking out of the borders of the medium and moving toward an approach to the spectator, the narrating script writer remains confined within the closed system that this medium is. The script is part of the INPUT needed to become OUTPUT and program. A script is half text for a yet-to-be-performed play and half apparatus programming. The *script writer* is thus a mixture of a dramatist and a not-completely-automatic *word processor*. His text cannot stand on its own. Even in a radio script, a script without images, the text only exists within the context of a broadcast. If the text were to stand on its own, it would be a *bad* script, one that fulfills its program-determined function inadequately. The comparison of a script with a drama text indicates a radical change in our mood. We no longer live dramatically, but programmatically—in the text of *Primarily Speaking,* this is stated:

> We have our choice
> living in suspended animation or under
> the auspices of supply and demand

Dramas are behavior, while programs are guidelines for behavior. A dramatic attitude to life is based on the belief in the uniqueness, the irrevocability of every act. It is the attitude of historical awareness. The programmatic attitude to life is based on belief in "die ewigen Wiederkehr des Gleichen," the arbitrariness of every act. It is the attitude of posthistorical awareness. A script is a pre-text. In both senses: an excuse/deception and a preliminary text/script. It is lines of letters being transformed into images, being recoded, quite literally in the case of *Primarily Speaking.*

At one point in the video, Hill says:

> point blank
> who are you
> I mean it just this one time . . .
> we don't have to split hairs
> or anything within reason
> who
> are
> you

As television spectators, we are used to this admixture of provocation and seduction, of which we cannot tell if we or the medium itself is the object. In the latter sense, *Primarily Speaking* is a rendering of a rhetorical interrogation by the medium of itself, an analysis in progress: a medium provoking itself into giving feedback. Because Hill's own voice is not emphasized; the voice in the tape is virtually synthetic, as anonymous as possible. A disembodied voice, as it were, a voice as a phenomenon that interrogates the series of technical images.

The spectator is provoked and seduced into determining the intimacy of this voice in action: determining the degree to which he or she is prepared, capable, of being absorbed, becoming part of the composition that is the medium.

Interface—Recall

There is singularly nothing that makes a difference a difference in beginning and in middle and in ending except that each generation has something different at which they are all looking.[6]

Primarily Speaking is a half product in the sense that it is both a work of video art and displays similarities to a television program. Yet a spectator will quickly recognize it as "art" and as such, will probably interpret it as a criticism or at least a commentary on commercial television.

From the beginnings of video art, there have been artists who imported television into art culture. Some fifteen years later, we've become used to the presence of televisions as alternative bearers of information in the museum. The museum became a living room where not only paintings were hung on the walls, but where one could also find a television set offering an alternative program one could not get at home. The television as tool thus also became an art icon. This gradual acceptance made it increasingly difficult for artists to make strategic use (tactical television) of the medium within the museum. The television, once the mascot of information liberation of the "global village," changed from a social-critical instrument into a remembrance that seemed to take its place alongside other monuments of preliterary culture, once it had been placed in the museum. Among other things, this has caused an increase in installations in museums by video artists. Installations can only exist in museums or spaces or institutions that resemble them. But in the specialization of the art field, these alternative sculptures are forced to obey production values using high-tech standards. The enormous costs incurred by such high-grade equipment can only be met when institutions like museums or industry vouch for them.

Hill has also shifted to these kinds of presentations (somewhat more of a natural step in his case, considering his background as a sculptor). He has chosen the installation version of *Primarily Speaking* above the linear videotape version. Hill himself compares the spectator's fixation on the two frames in the monitor in the videotape version to putting on blinders. Moreover, the effect of distraction from the text is amplified by the images in the installation version, because one's attention as a spectator is even more divided. There is a speaking and a listening wall. The spectator is literally caught between them. This creates a greater physical involvement in the work, creating a completely different kind of perception and aesthetics. The multiple monitors have provided the multivocality of the work with a place of its own. An element of spatial direction has also been added to meaning in the work.

The multivocality of the tape version is more reminiscent of contemporary computer interfaces for multimedia. The installation version might be interpreted as an alternative interface. The important difference between such computer-supported universes of information and Hill's work is that in the latter, one remains a spectator who cannot intervene in Hill's mise-en-scène. The process of endowment with meaning occurs without the possibility of action with direct visible results in the work. In other words: the interactivity of the work is of an extremely discrete, voyeuristic nature. Hill's work seems to be undergoing a gradual change in relation to the spectator, considering that past installations like *Tall Ships* did contain an element of interactivity. Moreover, the roles have been switched: in installations like *Primarily Speaking,* the spectator is the silent partner, whereas in *Tall Ships* it is Hill who does not use spoken language. It is probably this silence that allows the spectator to talk back with movement.

But just as with broadcast television (in Europe, in any case) Hill's work seems to be in a germinal phase in this respect. But his works are important for the development of alternative interfaces—interfaces that allow not only more specific forms of information transmission, but also research into the increasingly complex language of images.

In *Mythologies* (1957), Roland Barthes claims that the myth is depoliticized speech.[7] He does not mean that the myth denies facts; on the contrary, he envisages purification and establishment in nature and eternity. By opposing an activity to it that is focused on simplicity and essence, myth puts an end to the complexity of human behavior. The world is then bathed in naturalness. Things then seem to be imbued with self-evident meaning. Meta language is the reserve of myth. People's relationship with myth is not one of reality; it is one of use. Myths can go underground for a time and then return to reassert their power. Gertrude Stein writes about works that were first refused, then accepted and declared "classics." The quality of the classic is beauty, but she says:

> If everyone were not so indolent, they would realize that beauty is beauty
> even when it is irritating and stimulating and not only when it is accepted

and classic. Of course it is extremely difficult nothing more so than to remember back to its not being beautiful once it has become beautiful.[8]

These words certainly apply to *Primarily Speaking*. The influence it has,
or can have, is dependent on the extent to which Stein's insight holds
its ground. When one interprets the ideal spectator as an ideal interface, then one can expect a new translation when he or she once again
engages in explication with this work. An interface is an accomplice-
mediator who stands guard over a permanent transformation of
thought in action. An interface causes the memory of its own creation
to dissolve. Maybe Hill has provided such an ideal interface. Otherwise, we must make space in our nervous auditory ducts for the drone
of Pan, the Greek god of the ear: *"Ajoutez la résonance!"*

Notes

1. Lucinda Furlong, "A Manner of Speaking: An Interview with Gary Hill,"
Afterimage 10 (March 1983), pp. 9–16.

2. Friedrich Nietzsche, *Werke IV, Aus dem Nachlaß der Achtziger Jahre Briefe
(1861–1899)*, Karl Schlechta, Frankfurt/M, 1969, pp. (III) 431–32 (23–24).

3. Derrick de Kerckhove, *Brainframes, Technology, Mind and Business*,
Utrecht, 1991, p. 31. This could be a reference to the two sides of the brain. In
Joseph Bogen's theory, the right side of the brain processes time-independent
configurations, while the left is occupied with processing of series of stimuli in
a definite chronological sequence. The problem with these theories is that they
are mainly based on the Western approach to language. Cultures with languages that are written and read in other directions will be harder to include in
such hypotheses.

4. Marshall McLuhan, *Understanding Media*, New York, 1964.

5. Lucinda Furlong, "A Manner of Speaking: An Interview with Gary Hill,"
Afterimage 10 (March 1983), pp. 9–16.

6. Gertrude Stein, "Composition as Explanation," in *Selected Writings*, New
York, 1972, p. 516.

7. Roland Barthes, *Mythologies*, Paris, 1957, p. 294.

8. Gertrude Stein, op. cit., p. 515.

Robert Mittenthal

Standing Still on the Lip of Being:

Gary Hill's *Learning Curve*

In his preface to the monograph titled *Surfing the Medium,* Gary Hill reveals his surfing roots and acknowledges the presence of "the surfing mind" in many of his works. A *surfing mind* may sound a bit "kooky" to the uninitiated, but it does make sense in relation to the way Hill describes surfing's "green room": it is the moment of ecstasy—being inside the question that asks of itself while revealing itself. This process of immanent revealing is what drives Hill. From the chaos of ocean, waves are revealed. This is as religious as Hill gets. He has educated himself in the reading of these revelations.

> When the surfer stands and looks down the face of the wave he knows he is on the way to being there. He is lifted in the process of entering the extant question of Being. It is not about whether he makes it to the green room or not, for it is all grounded in the process of becoming with the wave. Is not the television display with its spray of information another green room of sorts that we've lost control of, that has "closed out"? (The surfing term for waves that are too big for a particular location and collapse without any form.)[1]

Hill's description of the green room is linked to Heidegger's notion of clearing, that moment when the "obscuring curtain of things" is lifted. Indeed, Hill opens the preface with a quote that foregrounds his involvement with Heidegger. These first few words from Marshall McLuhan would make a fitting tabloid headline: "Heidegger surfboards along on the electronic wave as triumphantly as Descartes rode

Originally published in a catalogue from the Henry Art Gallery, University of Washington, Seattle, 1994.

the mechanical wave." In "becoming with the wave," Hill tucks Heidegger under arm and heads out into the electronic surf.

With *Learning Curve*, Hill is trying virtually to enact that perfect wave that "appears to stand frozen in its own becoming as if it were requesting existence from the world." Hill has designed an industrial-strength school-chair to support a huge desktop that resembles a desert or beach, rising up and out until it reaches a curved wall that forms the horizon-line for a looped projection of a seemingly endless breaking wave. The expanse of whitish stained wood emphasizes the separation between viewer and image, between the material (chair) and the immaterial (wave image).

Besides the obvious reference to surfing, *Learning Curve* puns on the slide-in functionality of the school-chair, which wraps around the student in a suggestive curve and, if viewed from above, resembles a cross-section of a wave. While a *learning curve* is a projection or quantification of how quickly someone will be able to acquire a particular skill or ability, video feedback resembles a kind of *learning* in that it involves a dialogue between being and becoming. Hill describes this nearly instantaneous feedback loop as a "near future" that simultaneously absents and makes present the camera's subject.

Learning Curve has an imposing presence which calls up particular narrative associations. To students forced to sit through hour after hour in room after room, the school classroom can become a kind of dystopia, whose artificial, imposed structure can only be overcome by the mind. Faced with *Learning Curve*, one might think of an interactive video game, but here, instead of losing oneself in the thrill of trying to survive in a rigidly rule-governed visual space, we are faced with an image of relentless steadiness. There is no game and no diversion, only a kind of confrontation between chair and wave. One may well wonder: something is there, but is anything happening?

To sit in *Learning Curve* is to become part of the piece; one is physically supported by the same object that focuses one's attention on the pure visual space of the projected wave. The chair forces the viewer into a single-point perspective, where time seems slowed down. Conversely, speed is exactly what television relies upon to eliminate the time to think. In *Learning Curve*, sensory diversions are minimized, so that one's perception of the wave easily becomes abstracted or estranged. Heidegger suggests that in order to see the truth in mere things, just such an abstraction is necessary.

Much closer to us than all sensations are the things themselves. We hear the door shut in the house and never hear acoustical sensations or even mere sounds. In order to hear a bare sound we have to listen away from things, divert our ear from them, i.e., listen abstractly.[2]

This renewal of perception is at the heart of Heidegger's claims about art. However, Hill is not interested in renewing the viewer's perception of a wave, or in helping us see what makes the wave *wavy*. Rather, Hill wants the viewer to see something else, to find a mental path, any mental path, but not one that he would want to predict or dictate.

If we are able to see the wave abstractly, we may be, after Heidegger, *on the way to thinking.* The desktop physically connects the viewer to the projection of the wave at the same time as it separates him or her from it. Sitting in the frame of this chair, another perceptual frame opens; one enters the ground of the piece, where seeing can become "a sort of touch . . . a *contact* at a distance."[3] If *Learning Curve* is about anything, perhaps it is about one's ability to read and write one's self. Those who insist only on *looking* will likely be baffled and disappointed.

The second piece of the series, *Learning Curve (still point),* uses the same school-chair design, this time with an extended desktop that narrows to a point, resembling an old-fashioned surfing long-board. In what from some perspectives seems an optical illusion, a disproportionately small monitor sits precariously out on the toe of the board, spitting light out at us from an image of the green room. One imagines a California schoolboy daydreaming of surfing, suddenly called upon to answer one of his teacher's queries. *Still Point* suggests the physical motion of standing to answer. If the secret of poetry is, to paraphrase poet Charles Olson, learning to dance sitting down, one can say that *Still Point* invites us to leap upon the desktop and ride our minds wherever they might take us.

The third piece in this series, *Learning Curves,* is a proposed installation at the École Nationale Supérieur de Mécanique et Aérotechnique in Poitiers, France. Hill has designed an extended desktop that will connect four or five chairs similar to those used in the first two pieces. However, unlike the flat surfaces of these desktops, here the desktop will be shaped by the interactions of the various chair-sites. Hill proposes to make an analogue for the complexity of wave currents. There will be one monitor for each chair to serve as a mirror for the viewer to contemplate. According to Hill, the perspective each chair provides is to be isolated from the other chairs' perspectives. This echoes Maurice Blanchot's fascination with the solitary gaze. Hill wants to elicit an interminable gaze, "when what is seen imposes itself on your gaze, as though the gaze has been seized, touched, put in contact with appearance."[4]

This is not the first time Hill has used a single-point perspective in an installation. In *In Situ* (1986), he positioned a monitor, speakers, four fans, and a spotlight so that they focused on a single armchair. The chair invites the viewer with a curious "too-small" seat cushion, as if this cushion were a frame within the larger frame of another armchair. Photocopies of images from the video float down to an area rug, which is cut to match the dimensions of a television monitor. The videotape begins with images of Hill's eye blinking, as if something horrible had entered it. Images of Hill reading, trying to eat, are interrupted by a loss of equilibrium. As if tumbling off a wave, Hill falls, pulling a table-cloth with everything on it down with him. Voices from the then-current Iran-Contra hearings are slowed down so that they seem disembodied. When the monitor switches off unexpectedly, we are left in silence, looking at ourselves in the reflection of the empty tube, the remnants of the "news" on the floor around us. When the video suddenly returns, it is each time in a smaller frame.

In Situ goes to great lengths to physically confront the viewer with various events, from the shrinking start/stop news images on the monitor, to the paper erratically jettisoned and blown around the room by the fans, to a sound source hidden beneath the seat cushion. Forcing the viewer to see where she sits, *In Situ* literally jars her out of the seat. In contrast to this framing frenzy, *Learning Curve* employs far less aggressive means to alienate the viewer. Creating an immobility that he hopes will fascinate and/or disturb us, Hill pursues what Blanchot calls the "ultimate form of communitarian experience, after which there will be nothing left to say, because it has to know itself by ignoring itself."[5] Mirroring the viewer's position, *Learning Curve* and *Still Point* provide sites for thinking, inviting us to lose ourselves in our own gaze.

In Michael Snow's film *Wavelength*, the camera takes a real-time plunge into a photograph of waves. This sudden climax occurs when, after more than one-half hour, the picture frame finally reaches the water, leaving the viewer gasping for air. Conversely, *Learning Curve* resists any sudden climax, presenting a wave ceaselessly curling toward us. Hill's *Learning Curve* series invokes a steady state, all middle ground, where there is no beginning or end, where there is no climax (or all climax).

Hill's suspicion of visuality is an undercurrent in many of his works: "If I have a position, it's to question the privileged place that image, and for that matter sight, hold in our consciousness."[6] Like the Greeks, we tend to think of understanding as a kind of seeing. While most video disembodies sight, relying on the image to titillate the viewer, Hill foregrounds the physical *seeing* of the image. He would remind us that the eye is flesh and that the body is both perceiver and perceived, both subject and object. This separates him from those who, after Blake, enamored of the image, pursue a kind of *received* or visionary experience. Against Blake's infinite Vision, Hill proposes that we imagine "the brain closer than the eyes."[7]

Notes

1. Gary Hill, preface to Stephen Sarrazin's *Surfing the Medium* (Montbéliard: Chimera monograph no. 10, Edition du Centre International de Création Vidéo Montbéliard, Belfort, 1992), p. 9. All unfootnoted citations are from pages 8 and 9.

2. Martin Heidegger, "The Origin of the Work of Art," in *Basic Writings* (New York: Harper & Row, 1977), p. 156.

3. Maurice Blanchot, *The Gaze of Orpheus* (Barrytown, N.Y.: Station Hill Press, 1981), p. 75.

4. Ibid.

5. Maurice Blanchot, *The Unavowable Community* (Barrytown, N.Y.: Station Hill Press, 1988), p. 25.

6. Interview with Stephen Sarrazin, in *Surfing the Medium,* p. 84.

7. Gary Hill, *Site Recite* script, quoted in *Gary Hill* (Paris: Editions du Centre Pompidou, 1992), p. 32. Hill's reference to "dormitories of perception" in this text plays off Blake's "doors of perception."

George Quasha

Notes on the Feedback Horizon

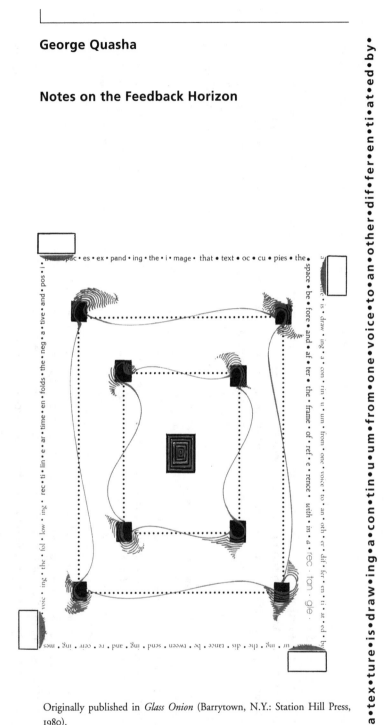

Originally published in *Glass Onion* (Barrytown, N.Y.: Station Hill Press, 1980).

While reading this talking about Gary Hill's GLASS ONION please notice that you are inside the rectangle of the printed text. ☐ You can only *imagine* the sound of my voice, implied by the title *Talking* whether, for instance. Its dominant timbre resembles the sound of a garbage truck, an alarm clock, a dog barking, a child crying, a lover complaining, or the artist himself in a late night conversation about the intentions of his work (recorded now on tape and playing back in the living room)—or all of these sounds at once (as sometimes happens in life). ☐ What can be said about a topologically self-interfering media installation; or the perception of a field of nonrepeating relationships among sounds, images, words, and anyone(s) present; or the "reflexive apperception" of *retangularity* that seems likely to occur in the mind of any alert participant . . . ☐ In what sense can language embody the rectangular? ☐ This question comes up in thinking about the verbal text ("representing" video feedback), printed at our left as the outer boundary of the diagram, which, in the installation, crawls horizontally across the bottom of each of the 4 monitors (defining the corners of the largest rectangle)—*the periphery.* ☐ In what sense is language the *periphery* of the event it describes? ☐ You have to be there. ☐ Imagine that you are standing outside the space of the work, faced with the choice of whether to enter (we can take nothing for granted). ☐ Does it matter how you think of the outer skin of the Onion (*it is golden and not edible*)? ☐ If it is a *threshold,* perhaps the "inside" is tabernacle, shrine, ark, bridal chamber . . . ☐ If it is a *horizon,* perhaps a sky into which the sun will soon rise, or else a black hole . . . ☐ If a *fence,* perhaps another person's backyard, pasture, prison, or stockpile of stolen goods . . . ☐ If a *limit,* perhaps the work of art is the space in which we cannot be more wrong (or lose more) than we already have . . . safe at last. ☐ Suppose you were discouraged by this speech from attending the installation, would this be an instance of language as barrier, veil, box? ☐ Would it be more encouraging to have a clear description so that you knew what to think before going in (in which case would language be less of a wall?)? ☐ Let's try. ▦ *(To protect*

•meas•ur•ing•the•dis•tance•be•tween•send•ing•and•re•ceiv•ing•mes•sag•es•voic•ing•the•fol•low•ing•

the unwilling reader we are screening the following technical description: in order to hide behind this screen, avoid the video gray and return to the photo black.) ▬ Physically the installation consists of 4 rectangles on the "outside," the 4 monitors: next, 4 speakers; next, in the center, a single monitor. ☐ The central monitor and 8 speakers are on the floor, facing up. ☐ Facing down from the ceiling, a camera with automated zoom ranges from all the way "in" (filling any screen with the image of the central monitor-screen) and all the way "out" (filling any screen with the image of the whole installation from the "outer" rectangle to the "center"). ☐ The central monitor (upon whose rectangular face you gaze by facing down and whose perfect image you interrupt in the eye of the overhead camera as it communicates with the peripheral monitors) shows successive embeddings and transformations of electronically generated rectangles (a 3-minute loop). ☐ These expanding and shrinking recorded rectangles (like the real-time image from the overhead camera, on any one of the 4 monitors) expand and shrink in general sync with the sound tracks. ☐ These tracks are measured according to the slow and deliberate "vocoded" enunciation of the 3 syllables of *rec•tan•gle.* ☐ Is it helpful to know these things in advance and in this way (and, if so, helpful for what)?

☐ The electronically modified voice (via the Vocoder) of the artist (it's not quite human) sets the measure for pulsating changes with the rhythmic pacing of *rec•tan•gle,* and, in each of 5 other tracks, embeds progressively larger phrase units from the verbal text, proceeding backward from the end-word "rectangle" (in multiples of 3 syllables). ☐ The 6 tracks sound through 2 channels, one on each of the 2 "rectangles" of upward facing speakers, and move, like the monitor images, in a circle around the center, according to the rhythm of the 3 syllables ☐ thus Track 1 (on Channel 1) says *rec•tan•gle;* next, Track 2 (on Channel 2) says the next 6 syllables (double of Track 1) from the end *with•in•a•rec•tan•gle* (now Track 1 repeats the 3 syllables of "rectangle" twice to fill the larger measure but at the same rate of enunciation, so that the last word, *rectangle,* becomes synchronous on 2 tracks) next Track 3 (back to

i•mage

rec•ti•lin•e•ar•time•en•folds•the•neg•a•tive•and•pos•i•tive•spac•es•ex•pand•ing•the•i•mage•that•text

Channel 1) says the next phrase (doubling the 6 of Track 2) *the•frame•of•ref•e•rence• with•in•a•rec•tan•gle* (now Track 1 repeats the 3 syllables 4 times and Track 2 repeats its phrase twice); and so on until the whole text is distributed into 6 tracks each one of which both doubles the number of syllables of the previous phrase and repeats itself as the next phrase comes up, filling out the measure. ◻ The "exact rhyme" of multiple repetitions of the end phrase increases in length and number of voices. ■ Is this clear? ◻ The more I tell you the more confusing it may get. ◻ The more I try to say the longer my sentences become, as language tries as usual to blurt out the whole truth, only to discover that it has obscured what really matters. ◻ What really matters? ◻ You have to be there. ◻ If you have been reading the text on the diagram and glancing at the graphic relationships you have been breaking the rectangle of this text in something like the way that any perception inside the installation is immediately broken by shift in location of the "*text*." ◻ What is a text? ◻ Latin *textus,* meaning Scritural text, says "woven thing." ◻ Perhaps the whole installation is a single weave, constantly changing (Penelope making and unmaking her design, awaiting her beloved who never arrives). Not a "single" but a "poly" sentence: in electronic time-space the syntactic is replaced by the synaptic—leaps, disappearances, and then residua in the mind. ◻ Not one text, one God, but many texts, many Gods, half-seen, half-felt, impossible to grasp except as the apperception of articulated time-space. ◻ Rectangles, and there are no rectangles. ◻ You have to be there. ◻ You stay inside as long as you do (this is personal), and you are part of the design (you see yourself disrupting the rectangle in which you see yourself seeing yourself). ◻ Perhaps you are aware that the verbal text (a texture is drawing a continuum from one voice to another differentiated by . . .) is a fairly "literal" description of video feedback. ◻ But all concepts fade in electronic time-space. ◻ Rectangles disintegrate as consciousness shifts. ◻ Minute time-delays of the video camera looking at itself on the monitor create feedback. ◻ As the overhead camera zooms in to the point where its frame approaches frame

oc•cu•pies•the•space•be•fore•and•af•ter•the•frame•of•ref•e•rence•with•in•a•rec•tan•gle synchrony with the frame of the monitor, it arrives at the Feedback Horizon. ☐ The rectangle is blown away, the image breaks up, is no longer rectangular, the middle comes out (*we have been waiting all our lives for this*), flipflop pulsations, the periphery caves in, englobes, enfolds on itself, gets globular, goes blank . . . residual texture. ☐ It's as though, staring itself in the eye until all surfaces catastrophize, the image can no longer hold the information of its pure reflection. ☐ In what sense can the mind monitor its own activity? ☐ Does it know itself only in bouncing back from an other? ☐ Can it think itself directly, and what happens when it tries? ▤ *reflection upon reflection* ▤ At the Feedback Horizon it gives in, it gives it up, the mind! ☐ The camera is like any person who stands long enough before the mirror, eye to eye. ☐ This electronic phenomenon is not new but is of the nature of video itself. ☐ Does it mind? ☐ Reflect upon it. ☐ I myself am talking to myself but what is that person in the mirror trying to get across? ▮ John Lennon died while this piece was in the final stages of realization. ☐☐ Everything interferes with everything. ▮ Each layer of the onion is reflexively new. ☐ The phrase "Glass Onion" occurs in one of his songs. ☐ Now even my own television set is sometimes a Glass Onion. ☐ I am writing this speech previous to the installation which you may or may not attend: who am I to talk? ☐ All the available information cannot be perceived at any one moment, all the thoughts cannot be thought at once, nor all the feelings felt. ☐ Our representations are generative and incomplete. ☐ Certain words jog up across the screen, leaving vestiges. ☐ Brackets and vice versa. ☐ "It's a mazeless maze." [Patricia Nedds] ☐ "Amazing maze" without walls. [Susan Quasha] ☐ A "Klein maze," all enclosing paths continuous with all others, impossible to visualize (the diagram is only a prejudice, mind imprisoned in concept and soon set free). ☐ If the total configuration of all relationships of sounds, images, and perspectives suddenly repeated, you would never know it. ☐ If you are inside the piece, wherever you are standing and "apperceiving" is now the outside the Onion, now a fold within it, now the center, alternately and at once. ☐ If you are reading this piece you are not there. ☐ You are here. ☐ Or there may not be any *where* to be. ☐ "Language cannot *be* that rectangle." [Gary] ☐ "There is no rectangle." [George] ☐ "Right." [Gary] ☐ Maybe. ▮

John C. Hanhardt

Between Language and the Moving Image:

The Art of Gary Hill

Am I ready to answer the essential question: What is writing? But it presupposes the power to reply and who could possess it?

—Edmond Jabes, *The Book of Margins*

Central to Gary Hill's project as an artist is the negotiation of the processes that link language to the moving image. His works reveal a fascination with the exposure of the essential relationship between language and our cognitive formation of images, with the exploration of the materialism of writing articulated through video and multimedia installation. This primary concern with the vital power of the word is located in a poetics of language that finds its fundamental expression in the incorporation of the body as an idea and ideal into the aesthetics of the text. Extending this aesthetics, Hill carries the self into the larger context of the public sphere and the history of the word as logos. The irony in his work is derived from the potential threat of the erasure of language within the very technologies he employs in his art making; his aesthetic investigations are based on a philosophy of language and expression that seeks to recode technology through a logos of a poetic language of imagery. This tension between modern technology and the primary philosophical roots of *techne* as a poetic of language and meaning is the space negotiated by Hill in his art. In this space, by turning the camera upon and into the self and the other, Hill eradicates the traditional boundary between subject and object, body and technology, word and image. With the aim of providing a context for Hill's work, I want to comment on these merging themes by exploring the relation-

Originally published in a catalogue from the Henry Art Gallery, University of Washington, Seattle, 1994.

ships between a selection of Hill's projects and various other artworks and objects.

The first illustration in this investigation of works connected to Hill's art is a phantasmagoria from the eighteenth-century Belgian creator, Etienne Gaspard Robert (Robertson). In his precinematic magic lantern demonstrations, Robertson created spectacular installations in which images of skeletons and the dead, projected into the smoke-filled space, floated ghostlike above the spectators. In American artist Raphaelle Peale's *Venus Rising from the Sea—A Deception (After the Bath)* (1823), a similar play with the themes of illusion and reality, desire and spectatorship, is achieved through the trope l'oeil canvas which masks its presumed subject (the body behind the sheet); Peale uses his uncanny artistic skills to simultaneously hide and reveal the object of our gaze.

In juxtaposing these two works from the late eighteenth and early nineteenth centuries, we are faced with the everyday realist style of Peale's canvas and the spectacular illusionism of new technology in Robertson's theater. These works foretell the crisis in representation created by the photograph and motion picture, a crisis being played out today as electronic-image technology assumes new dimensions of power in our culture, further diminishing the boundary between the "real" and "unreal." Peale's play with the image that records at the same time it conceals its subject explores the epistemological limits of realism; this type of image has been at the center of the debate surrounding the photographically/cinematographically recorded image and its relationship to the "objective" representation of the world around us. Robertson's theater of illusionism playfully articulates and anticipates the spectacle contained within the projected film image and the later proliferation of television screens and the power they have for creating apparent truth. Both Peale and Robertson are offered here as emblematic texts of the diminishing boundary between real and unreal explored in Hill's videotapes and installations. Hill's vision becomes fittingly relevant at this critical time in the history of art and technology as his aesthetic draws on a variety of metaphorical strategies to revise the relationship between the image and the means of its creation.

In Hill's exploration of these creative and destructive forces of technology, the body becomes a metaphor for language and a means for exploring the spectator's reception of the aesthetic text. His installation *Tall Ships* (1992) and his single-channel videotape *Site Recite (a prologue)* (1989) are particularly interesting in their placement of the body at the center of perception and representation of the spectator's point of view. In *Tall Ships,* images of bodies, hovering in near three-dimensionality on the walls of the dark corridor, approach and pull the viewer into a shared space; there the viewer is engaged in an intimate dialogue of gestures and facial expressions. The silence of the images reinforces their presence while their gestures convey deep longing and an isolation relieved only momentarily as the viewer shares the space with them. Like Robertson's phantasms, Hill's apparitions elicit a strong response from the viewer, who is launched into a sort of primal discovery of the images and recognizes in them the same desire for an intimacy with the moment and with the other.

Site Recite (a prologue) articulates a representation of the Renaissance "wonder cabinet" filled with lost and remembered objects. Upon the screen, images shift in and out of focus as the camera lens becomes an eye recording objects; the sound track, through its unique use of language, layers the experience of perception and reception of the image as a complex text of meanings. Placed on a rotating disc, the skeletons—the shifting signifiers—circle in and out of the camera's eye, which eventually shifts to the dark interior of a mouth, looking from the inside through a web of tongue and teeth, out. The camera develops into a simulacrum of the body as its lens becomes the mouth and the eye, both the articulator and observer of the world, and it approaches a phonetic vision in which image and word are fused. A metaphor for this fusion is the body as both image and articulator of speech, a speech consisting of a language which circles back to represent and ultimately embody the image; here, the language of words and images circulates through the videotape, representing and ultimately embodying the phenomenology of observation. Hill's postmodern spirits, like Robertson's precinematic ghosts, are fused to their technological counterparts, and receive their living breath from the medium even while overcoming that medium in terms of its traditional usage.

The first philosopher to use a typewriter was Friedrich Nietzsche, who in 1879 experimented with the rounded keyboard. Nietzsche's decision was motivated by his increasing blindness, as the organization of the keys permitted a tactile means for an organization of his writing. I use this typewriter, its instrumental embodiment of language, as an instance of technology at once being shaped by and shaping language. In its spatial organization and displacement of language from the mind to the page, it reflects Hill's exploration in his videotapes and installations of how to make concrete the processes of cognition. Nietzsche, the great postmodern philosopher and assailant of the sacred traditions of academic philosophy, began to reshape his discourse through the instrumentality of this first technology for writing: the typewriter, the immediate precursor of the word processor. The word processor further transformed written language, from the typewriter's static sheet of paper to the word processor screen, which allows the easy shifting and reorganization of language. Hill's art, too, reshapes the discourse of the traditional cinematic order of frame sequences into that of the fluid time and space of the video universe; his cognizance of philosophy and the tradition of the word places his writing and image making in the precarious realm between tradition and revolution, written language and moving image.

Primarily Speaking (1981–83), one of Gary Hill's early video installations, plays with the movement of words and images. The installation consists of two long wall units positioned face to face, each equipped with four built-in monitors masked to be flush with the surface. Words and phrases are aurally presented and integrated with solid fields of color and images of objects and scenes on videotape. The articulation of images and sounds is formed by the changes in sequences of the videotapes and sound tracks between the two wall-like structures. This rapid and precise movement between color fields, images, and words, combined with the shifting position of the listener/viewer, results in a proliferation of contexts—and thus the contents—of the various elements.

The physical depiction of semantics in *Primarily Speaking* moved to another more literary level in Hill's *URA ARU (the backside exists)* (1985–86). This spectacular videotape employs formal and rhetorical strategies to explore word meaning in its treatment of a selection of Japanese words as palindromes (words that read the same way both backward and forward and that Hill further breaks apart and re-forms). In the tape, which consists of a series of visual-verbal haiku, Hill employs great economy of action and technique; the printed word moves through each scene, echoing the spoken word. The result is the inscription of language into the visualization of its own meaning.

In *Primarily Speaking* and *URA ARU (the backside exists),* language is rendered *material* as images representative of it extend from the optical enclosure of the monitor and into the installation space, which is the spectator's space as well. Hill's transposition of language into a visual medium reconstructs the language of video art itself. Like Nietzsche's typewriter which made visible the thoughts of the near blind philosopher, Hill's video works make manifest his uniquely expressed view of the relationship of word to image. His understanding of video technology is expressed in his ability to remake these instruments into a supportive complex of poetic interrelationships.

The artist's place within the context of the artwork is a complex cognitive issue. The physical stance—of the painter before the canvas, the writer bent over her paper, the sculptor contemplating his materials—reflects physically the question of where the artist stands in terms of the work, but there are also the spatiotemporal and ideological positions when the work of art is viewed in this social context. Hill's art constructs a variety of metaphorical strategies with which to represent the body's position within society; he achieves this via his rendering of video into a technology usable as a means of individual creative expression.

At the written heart of American democracy is the Declaration of Independence, written primarily by Thomas Jefferson. Jefferson embodied an eighteenth-century ideal which replaced a narrow view of the self in favor of one of the self as part of something greater, exchanging tunnel vision for a broad multiperspective stance toward the surrounding world. Jefferson's Monticello, built on a hill from which a physically broader view was possible, was an architectural expression of that desire, as was his invention of the swivel chair. The swivel chair's arc of movement permitted Jefferson to physically shift his writing body and point of view from the locked position of a single aspect to numerous other ones; this is symbolically fitting as this was probably the chair in which he drafted the Declaration, the written testimony to his engagement with the democratic ideals of the new Republic, and with an all-encompassing and less self-interested perspective (a distinctively greater perspective than, for instance, that of Bentham's architectural panopticon, which afforded society a limited yet controlling view of prison life).

Art—also as architecture and design—embodies ideals and ideology. Hill's videotapes and installations bear a relationship to this distinctively American poetics of expanding the view of the self through an open exploration of language and image making. In *CRUX* (1983–87), this idea of image making is taken one step further with the image's making of itself, a complex negotiation of the traditional concepts of subject and object as discrete entities. Here, Hill himself controls—via his positioning of them—the five cameras: two focused on his arms, two on his legs, and one pointed up to his face. The cameras accompany the artist as he crosses a ruined building in a rural setting, turning him into the ironic subject. The five video channels thus recorded are played on five monitors suspended against a wall and synchronized to represent the movement of the body over the torn landscape. The constant replay of the installation conveys the sense of a technology open to all, a generous means for the construction of a vision. Hill's remaking of the technology into an instrument of poetic inquiry with the potential to express the quest for an ideal, and not simply mercantile, vision of television and society is parallel to Jefferson's creation of the Declaration, which also was, in a sense, an instrument of poetic inquiry for a nation then just beginning to identify itself. Jefferson's chair, whose mobility allowed for a generous view of the world around him, becomes a physical embodiment of the Constitution's own inclusiveness and support of a democratically viewed public sphere. This is echoed in Hill's installation *Learning Curve* (1993), in which the old-fashioned school desk and chair embody, in their view of an ocean wave's endless movement, the expanded vision of personal experience and public history that is the necessary foundation of our perception and understanding of the present.

In the 1980s, video installations moved to the forefront of new expression in contemporary art. Nam June Paik, Bill Viola, Dara Birnbaum, and Gary Hill created large and compelling bodies of work. At the same time the art market and artists' careers were expanding, expressing a new surge of interest in artistic culture, best manifested in the rapid construction of museums during the decade.

Today, the art world is once again in flux; art continues to flourish in terms of abundance but the markets are changing. Anselm Kiefer's extraordinary installation *20 Jahre Einsamkeit* (Twenty Years of Loneliness) *1971–1991* is composed of the refuse of the artist's studio, objects related to his artistic past ranging from actual works of art to raw materials and balls of dirt and sunflowers from the place where he lived in Germany. In the installation, the canvases and other materials that distinguished Kiefer's art are piled to the ceiling in a mute and moving testimony to the creative ideals of the previous decade. Kiefer's reflection on the painter's canvas and materials as a kind of detritus of the imagination is an ironic and poignant meditation on the creative process and the materials an artist chooses to work with. His installation lays bare the contents of his studio and is, in a sense, a laying bare as well of a life, of the realization of the self he is today and of the precarious flux of the artistic venture. A space that could have been cold and impersonal is hauntingly personalized.

I am suggesting that Hill's art is itself a mediation on being an artist and the struggle to remake technology into a poetic instrument. Like

Kiefer, Hill confronts himself in his art as a thinking being seeking to strip it of the decorative and ephemeral so as to retrieve a sense of self and memory. For Kiefer it is the poetics of a personal history and painting; for Hill, the poetics of language and media.

Hill's art does not face the crisis of a questioned and eroding art form and tradition, but the challenge of renewing tradition and charting a new horizon of possibility. Indeed, he transforms the technology of video, carrying it away from the conventional categorization and usage of art and television and into the intimacy of the artist's studio and imagination. By stripping the monitor and camera of their conventional applications, he re-creates cathode ray tubes so they become a contemporary language which allows the moving image to enter into the discourse of sculpture and installation, and of self-inquiry. In this regeneration of the medium through a philosophic strategy of image making, Hill has recovered the place of language and origins of technology in a metaphysics of *techne*. His installation *Between Cinema and a Hard Place* (1991) consists of twenty-three monitors positioned to create a demarcated space with rows like that of a field. The work adapts Heidegger's *The Nature of Language* into its self-questioning meditation on the marking of space and time, language's earthly roots, and disrupts the mechanics of the cinematic sequence of moving images and spoken text, and thus its own flow, to bare the nature of a technology at odds with itself.

"As soon as we try to reflect on the matter we have already committed ourselves to a long path of thought," Heidegger wrote. Thought is commitment, language, a precious vessel for thinking, images need words in order to be understood. This sequence of demands, commitments of both time and energy, has led to Hill's artistic release of a body of work fragile in construction but strong in its resolve to resist the easy consumption of ideas. This is perhaps most eloquently articulated in his videotape *Incidence of Catastrophe,* one of the handful of major works created within the discourse of single-channel videotape. This work uses as its inspiration the writer/philosopher Maurice Blanchot and his text *Thomas the Obscure.* In this epic work the artist himself is enfolded within the phenomenology of the written/printed text; as his body and eye merge to become one, the screen struggles with the folio sheet, the press-type on the page—with the impression of language on our consciousness.

In his exploration of the age-old debate between word and image, Hill's aesthetic language has retrieved a hope for art. As Kiefer symbolically rebuilds the aesthetic discourse of painting in a Homeric pyre of fragile canvas, Hill, our most visual of new image philosopher/artists, also reconstructs the aesthetics of the video medium with his brilliant solution to the dilemma of being an artist in the fin de siècle: the placement of the body at the center of the process that links language to image, poetics to poetry, and the words we speak to the tongues we embody.

George Quasha and Charles Stein

HanD HearD / *liminal objects*

Mesologue

Imagine yourself walking into this gallery, and through the door you catch a glimpse of a large head focusing on an open hand. The sheer mass of the image, the scale, the presence is *impressive*—all the more so because onlookers standing nearby are "hand-sized" by comparison. As you gaze into this projection, it takes on an enigmatic life of its own. Now you get farther inside the room, and moving through the middle of this medium you find more large and living human heads, half-turned away from you, "middling" in a similar inquiring posture before raised hands. There's a pointed stillness, yet the room seems *ready for action,* poised for the big event. But what is it? Where could it be, especially in light of the fact that nothing *more* seems to happen. . . . Could it be that we—the possibly perplexed negotiators in *media space*—carry the key to a *missing event?* . . . as if we ourselves are guardians of a Mysterious Object whose very existence is suspect? . . . as if, accordingly, we comprise a community of silent witnesses, members of a linking space, which offers nothing to our identity except a sense of open-eyed resonance—a strange and radical affinity, like that between tall ships in the moonlight, or people simultaneously reading the same words in the same book at different places on the planet. . . .

Reading Matter/Readable Space

Those familiar with Gary Hill's work may wonder why HanD HearD/*liminal objects* does not offer a text as the linguistic

Originally published in *HanD HearD/liminal objects* (Paris: Galerie des Archives; Barryton, N.Y.: Station Hill Arts of Barrytown, Ltd., 1996).

point of orientation, since texts used in this way have seemed essential to what he does. We have grown used to thinking of his work as, in part, an extended meditation on texts and textuality in interaction with other communicative and representational contexts. For instance, there are texts—reading matter—accompanying video images, physical books on which video images are projected, oral readings as auditory components of video installations, works that are themselves "readings" of texts, and so forth. In HanD HearD— as in *Tall Ships* (1992)—the only textual element is the title. (Similarly, there is no sound track, yet the title refers to auditory experience, and indeed listening, like reading, is a vitally important, albeit subliminal, dimension of the work.) While there is no explicit reference to a text or textuality, this work—which is only minimally (yet critically) an *installation* as opposed to an *exhibition*—is somehow *textual*. And in fact this somewhat mysterious truth—what can only be called the textuality of the space—makes it meaningful to discuss this work in the context of spatially disposed art —art that we commonly know by the unfortunately limiting name *installation*.

If HanD HearD/*liminal objects* is a text, then each room is a readable unit or assemblage of units. We may view the two rooms in this gallery as part of the same installation or, to break that conceptual mold, *work-event*. And, although they are entirely separate works, we might read them as, say, chapters or poems in the same book. The "filmic" projections and computer-generated images relate to each other as elements in a text, albeit a curious and arguably *sui generis* text. Most important, the *space* of the installation is itself an extrapolation, even a *projection,* of a certain experience of the "space" of a text. So that, although we seem to be looking at *image projections,* it may be truer to our experience to say that we are looking at *text-space projections.* Or, more radically: we are *inside the projected space,* itself a *virtual text.* The "images" we see are *syntactic nodes and points of orientation.* Although they depict familiar things—hands, a wheel, a bed, a house—they are not "ordinary objects" separate from ourselves as "viewing subjects," so much as image-complexes, almost verbal terms in a process of reflection.

If HanD HearD/*liminal objects* is a text, then we are readers rather than viewers. But not ordinary readers. Rather, we are *virtual readers,* meaning that by the very act of being there we engage a *possible text,* and this text is the space itself in which we discover ourselves and others in a particular way. This discovery is the natural result of a mode of

HanD HearD
liminal objects

presence experienced uniquely in the very moment of "reading" the text-space. And unlike most reading experiences the only thing repeatable about such a text is this fact: *the radical uniqueness of a moment of engagement in and of which we are, at the very least, co-creators.* We are the *possible artists* of our own presence in the space.

Considering more particularly the piece HanD HearD, we discover that its way of being a text imposes nothing on the mind, yet it offers an *image* (a hand in front of a person's face) as a possible *posture* of awareness. And because the "text" has no "content" other than this posture, it grants the participant *direct access* from the beginning. But access to what? to *interactive space*—interactive, however, not in the fashionable sense of menus of options that trigger, say, hypertextual paths, but in a radical sense of *nonseparable agency*. With the latter, artistic content is not ultimately distinct from the registration of experience. And in such space "artistic vision" is not mediated by the sheer objectivity, the "opacity," of a work, but by the quality of presence of the participant: the work is "transparent" and we are the mediators. Moreover, the work "happens" by virtue of our intervention, and in a way not quite true of most art "it" is not really there without us.

HanD HearD's particular status as text derives from the way in which it disposes "the image." Consider the scene. Larger-than-life projections of five individuals gazing at their hands, oriented in and around the corners of an irregularly polygonal room, seem *almost* photographic, *almost* stills. But they are breathing. And they are still as only living beings can choose to be still. They are *not* moving in "real time," so that deeply they seem somehow not to be in time at all. They are almost *not happening,* because this is recognizably *not* how things take place in "real life." A person gazes at a hand that must be his or her own, but the angles and proportions are such that the hand almost seems to belong to an other. Or is this the case because this kind of gazing is *almost* something people do not do? It could be anyone's hand. No one's hand. A Surreal hand. An alien hand. The image of the sound of one hand not clapping, or the converse. A severed hand or a hand severed from its status as image. Cut off from use. A-technologically focused manual dexterity. Utterly flesh, even fleshy. Senseless, sensuous, sensual. Or:

A hand whose resonance is a state of listening,
a listening hand in a silent state.

To listen to this hand being looked at is to be inside the hand itself. In short measure, is this not as much my hand as the other person's? I watch it from within my own hand, just as the hand seems to be watching (or listening to) the watcher. This all has to do with the way we "take in" what happens around us—whether by habit or by special orientation. Much as the poet John Keats's "Ode on a Grecian Urn" instructs the reader in how to read the poem by directly reading the urn itself, in HanD HearD, "the scene" prevails upon the viewer, induces the precise mode of attention true to its nature. It virtually instructs (you) the viewer in how to hear it / (you) the listener in how to see it. It initiates you into its modality of showing being, shows you how to reflect what it shows, inspires reflection, reflects inspiration. It holds itself in view, and it is the view it holds.

I am holding up my hand (without moving my body) as I attend this work; that is, to grasp the work I imitate it bodily in the mind. This sympathetic embodiment is a "practice" implicit in the image, an entrainment. To practice in this way I go "inside"—but inside what? I'm confused, subject and object fuse. What constitutes appropriate understanding before an ambiguous projection? In time I discover a necessary ambi-valence in my own disposition: It wants to call what I am experiencing

projective amphibole,
a great ontological net cast in a textual open space.

In a single "throw" I trap:

State of body, state of mind, posture of soul, spiritual angle of incidence:
a hand facing a head with an open ear,
caught in the unmoving turn.
[hand heard]

In what Frame of Mind, what portraiture of incarnate intelligence, is this hand held?

The artist pictured
with a hand-held image, even.

Is this a state of hypnotic trance? Philosophical inquiry? Physical examination? Simple observation? Active imagination? Contemplation (*samadhi*)? The unnamable—or all the names of history? All of these, none of these: absolutely any. This is the open object, interactive with the open subject:

The liminal state.

Liminality

A *limen* in Latin is a threshold. While its current usage is principally behavioral with respect to the threshold of a physiological or psychological response, in fact, liminal or borderline states are anywhere that something is about to undergo a phase transition or turn into something else. They range from the ordinary to the extraordinary—from, say, the everyday hypnogogic state between sleeping and waking to the "final" margin between life and death. We tend to set these all-important states in opposition to each other as though their borders were clear and absolute, but when we study liminal states we may discriminate virtually limitless nuances, even to the point of challenging the major distinctions themselves. With respect to the distinction "life and death," for instance, Tibetan Buddhist philosophy discusses highly nuanced in-between states called *bardos,* the knowledge of which theoretically equips one to exercise profound and consequential choice in phasic transitions that the ordinary opposition does not recognize at all. Comparable distinctions are now made, for instance, in Western therapeutic bodywork such that intervention in borderline "body-mind" states allows far-reaching pattern-transformation. These liminal interventions challenge the normative "scientific" distinction between body and mind. What is conceptually difficult in observing liminal states is that even fundamental distinctions like *space* and *time* come into question. Where are we and when are we in the in-between? In what sense is what we observe "really there"? Or is it only *liminally there?*

"At the still point, there the dance is,/But neither arrest nor movement," writes the poet T. S. Eliot in *The Four Quartets,* a powerful evocation of transtemporal awareness: "To be conscious is not to be in time." This vision of suddenly realized timelessness raises the issue of the liminality of time. While deriving from Dante's vision of eternal stillness in the last canto of the *Paradiso,* it interestingly resonates with "still point" in other, apparently unrelated contexts far from the rarefied world of sacred poetry. Perhaps least expected is its use as a technical term in therapeutic bodywork (e.g., in craniosacral therapy, an offshoot of osteopathy). Here "still point" refers to a momentary suspension in the body's "fundamental pulsation" (the "craniosacral rhythmical impulse"), mobilizing the system's inherent ability to correct its own imbalances. Paradoxically, the still point's *liminal* awareness is connected to a sense of *whole*ness—that is, *in the margin we find the threshold of an experience of totality.* So to be *at the limen* does not mean to be off-center or moving away from centrality. For the still point is anywhere that the discovery of the threshold takes place: center and periphery are one *in the present moment.*

Gary Hill's interest in this species of *integrative liminality* shows up, for instance, in his 1993 piece with the related title *Learning Curve (still point),* particularly its image of an endlessly breaking wave, an interest derived from years of Pacific Ocean surfing. For the surfer, balanced "stillness" is the key to entering the "green room," the interior of a cresting wave, and remaining there as it rolls toward shore. This ecstatically sustained moment of being inside the state of "continuous wave" now contextualizes the whole of the activity of surfing. The experiential knowledge of riding the green room—its secret *juissance*—is what lies behind a sort of "surfer's obsession." And this is one model of what it is to *declare liminality as a possibility of Being:* special knowledge of a nonordinary state attracts one back—you might say it calls one home—to an apparently marginal zone. We speak of the one who intentionally returns as an *initiate,* one who hears and responds: the *beginner* of the work.

There are works of art that require initiation. This does not mean that they require explanation, special consensus, or any other prescriptive bearing. It does mean that one must discover an *appropriate mode of entry* which is more than informational. This can involve radical reorientation, as in the case of HanD HearD, which directly (but noncoercively) introduces us to the posture of awareness appropriate to our participation in the piece. In a certain sense the piece is this process of orientation, rather than "visual objects" calling for observation. The objects are, in this sense, orientational nodes—points that conduct the participant to a noetic state. They are signposts of liminality. Since they do not absorb and contain your gaze, but instead reflect it back, the gaze is *retained* within the state of alert presence. Objects that are only liminally what they seem to be may lead to some measure of open reflection. And in this reflective retention of "looking energy," the objects invite inquiry into their very nature—a process of inquiry that, the truer it is, the more nearly "endless" is its state. Liminality could be described as the state in which reality questions itself, inquires into what it is to itself.

Consider again the scene. You enter the room and find five larger-than-life wall projections of hands held up to "face" the half-turned faces (seeming to turn *away* from us). In a manner of speaking, the *hands face.* Alternatively we could call this piece:

Facing Hands

At any given moment we are looking into the face of a hand. In so doing we take on the posture of the head, whose face we do not quite see or only liminally experience, a head facing a hand. *Facing Hands* implies a pure dialogue between hand and face, linked by the ambiguity of *facing.* In a true dialogue the sides do not fully exist separate from their interaction. They enjoy *double unity,* bi-unity, fundamental ambivalence. And they share with us this state, giving us a virtual model of our reciprocal connection with them: we are to them as they are to each other. I face the hand on the wall; the hand faces me; I am faced; and so on. *The grammar of the space is wide open.* The room is a poem-in-process, the key to which is *reciprocity.* And we are reciprocating here—carrying on the work, giving it its *further life*—by "reading the room" in some of the ways possible. Of course we may or may not end up "believing in" these hermeneutic options. What then is the value of such textual multiplicity? Perhaps our view resembles that of the poet William Blake: "All things possible to be believed are images of the truth."

Hall of the Gods

You enter the hall: figures lining the walls are huge enough that you could virtually be held in hand. Multiple beings. Are these gods? We remember the long halls (memories of being a child in some of the world's greatest museums) filled with massive Egyptian statues, where scale is a key to divinity. We feel *in their hands*. To some this is powerlessness itself; to others, an opportunity to get a sense of other-dimensional space, a *linking space* in which one understands connection with *possible beings*. Scale—how it seems to be in relation to how *we* seem to be—is not entirely physical, and transformation of the relationships can be a function of intangible factors—energetic, psychological, textual, postural. . . . In the *transvironmental* halls of Egyptian gods and HAND HEARD alike, alteration of scale happens in such a way that our whole inner orientation shifts with respect to the "world" around, challenging the relative ontological status of the viewer and the viewed. The shift, the reorientation, the transvironmental moment, the linking —still point.

Liminal Objects

A large wheel rolls through a bed without severing it. Two hands coming together go right through each other. A rotating house reveals and conceals a brain its own size, which passes through its walls. A rotating column crosses directly through a chair. What are we looking at?

This is a question that never quite leaves our minds as we look at the four animated video images displayed on monitors and designated as *liminal objects.* This is a potentially open series (arbitrarily limited here to four) of what might be called *object-events*—miniature looped narratives of short duration. They involve two items each (house and brain, wheel and bed, column and chair, hand and hand) whose repetitive interaction and circular logic constitute a thing-like whole. Their identity as recognizable objects oddly combined is never separable from their origin as computer-generated animations.

Unlike the extravagances of the ubiquitous presence of computer images, Gary Hill's four enigmas are oddly understated. They are only liminally fantastic. They hover at the margin of impossibility. They offer a disciplined perplexity grounded in the ordinary. Their violations of the canons of reality might under certain perceptual circumstances almost risk being overlooked. These are scarcely jailable offenses. Indeed we could almost grow used to them. One could even grant them a certain status: simulations of possibilities inherent in the real. Such is their strangeness that the more "normal" it looks—falling well below the standard of weirdness common to the root technology—the more disturbing these images become.

At the same time, these images of the liminally real call out to be *read.* Although the bent of the technology is toward representation, the images hardly represent objects as such. We are not drawn to think of specific real houses, brains, beds, and so on, but something perhaps symbolic. Yet neither the context nor the character of the images supports referentiality. If they momentarily act as familiar signs, they quickly bounce back to themselves, seemingly pointing to their own riddle of existence. If we are in the presence of symbols, then this is an open *symbolism.* Yet this species of openness differs from that associated with certain Symbolist creations, what has been called the "symbol of indeterminate reference," wherein, for instance, a poem might stand for an almost identifiable condition, psychological or social. Similarly, it differs from the post-Symbolist developments, like Imagism, the "intellectual/emotional complex" with its own kind of specificity of open reference. The other obviously related genre of images, the Surrealist, which on the face of it perhaps most resembles these object-events, is far more "committed" to some reality presumed to be more intensely real than the ordinary; indeed, it functions psychotropically as intensifier, whether oneiric, transpersonal, political, or whatever.

By contrast to the other image genres, these *liminal* objects stand as *virtual symbols,* indicators of possible objects, yet knowable only in the interactive condition of image-eye-mind. If they call out to us to *read* them, they do not let us rest in our reading, but demand of us that we *read on,* eventually to *read our own reading.* They put us in dialogue with our own interpretative process, as though in some sense we are implicated in the objects. If *they* are strange, we must be analogously strange. They mirror our liminality. To parallel William Blake, all things possible to be invented are images of ourselves—our "technological" selves, creators of the world.

So whatever we say about these objects is implicitly followed by the qualification, "but only liminally so." To perform this act of intellectual honesty is a step toward transforming our temptation to determinacy, closure, and positive assertion, in favor of open inquiry. These *liminal objects* inspire us to guard against the definite interpretation that suppresses an open field of possibilities. More important, they bespeak a domain of their kind, the liminal state itself, a balancing act along the junctures of unknown versions of the real, "presence of mind in a tough situation"—the open condition itself.

So we could say that the liminal state produces *liminal feedback.* That is, the images *read back into us,* operating on a level that is both more arcane and yet *intuitively more direct* than that of ordinary, interpretative thinking. In certain ways these images are distant cousins of the emblems associated with Renaissance alchemical writings. There is the suggestion of mysteries, subtle enigmas, and hidden ontological possibilities. And, although these undisclosed matters seem open only to the "initiated," the images carry within their own graphic qualities and sequential structures everything necessary to bring the viewer to "initiation." Only here in Gary Hill's work the event is a *virtual initiation*—direct introduction to the open field that lies below or beyond any specifiable induction.

Thus, where the images (whether alchemical emblems or liminal objects) hint of secrets, in their very act and mode of suggestion they supply the means of revealing the secrets they embody. They do not lead to something outside themselves, but to that of which they consist. It is debatable whether any text can disclose the cryptic references or parse the subtle doctrines to which such images might allude. Rather, the images speak directly. They call for participation more than understanding. While dislocated and lacking context, they are resonant and invite a kind of listening. To what end? Goethe spoke of an "exact percipient fancy" with which he reckoned we could glimpse unknown realities. We would add: realities of which we are liminally co-creative.

Said *liminal objects* Appearing on the Screens:

Wheel, bed, house, brain, column, chair, hands—all doing utterly unpredictable things, now rendered oddly inevitable. . . . In the present limitations of time and space we will only address the latter object-event:

Hands

Two hands, clearly of a single person, performing the "impossible" movement of passing their fingers through each other. Something that we know cannot be seen is precisely what we are seeing. Instead of supplying the object that in our minds we know "must be there" amid the largely unfamiliar image data, we must subtract from the all-too-specific image what we know in our minds "can't be there." Yet more than seeing we are sensing, unaccountably getting the feeling of what it would be to actually *do* such a thing. This eerie identification stems from the phenomenology of perceiving another person's body: the very fact that I have hands means that, if only subliminally, I know through *my* hands what is happening to *other* hands. Perhaps this is an instance of *morphic resonance* (to borrow a concept from biologist Rupert Sheldrake)—a term for the "field effect" in how things indirectly influence each other. It addresses the impressive phenomenon of shared sensitivity among members of a *kind,* the way *like affects like* even when seemingly at variance with causality, circumstantial evidence, and linear logic. Certainly it has to do with *entrainment*—the natural tendency toward getting into step with others. Is our easy induction into the nearby activity of sympathetic beings evidence that we unconsciously seek out essential sameness?

What, if anything, about these perplexing hands *is* "the same"? their rather mechanistic animation hardly advertises *anima* or spiritual kinship. These are not the hands of some possible "soul mate" or ours (as could be the case in HAND HEARD). The very idea of feeling connected here borders on the bizarre. And that's just it: the degree of disturbance aroused by such an *unlike* object is itself somehow alluring here. It calls out for an unfamiliar identification, a sort of *projective sentience.* You watch those quiet, deliberate, *simulated fingers,* those delicate digital manipulations, painstakingly pass right through each other. And while it's hardly a miracle for an animation (a mere *'toon,* as it were), it nevertheless calls up the imagination of a possibility—a phantom capacity, summoned into the nearness of our awareness. It is as if we were being submitted to the rigors of a proprioceptive logic, a logic of identification, in which our fingers think inside their emerging rhythmic entracement, "If *they* can do that, so can *we!*" And why not effortlessly penetrate the flesh? Why not manifest this interior spaciousness? Once this line of inquiry picks up steam it gets to be rather *natural.* . . .

And maybe this is what seems to be "the same": a natural capacity for unlimited intimacy. Some truth that only hands know. . . . Is it that certain communicative movements between them summon their internal life outward toward the objects they handle? Is the ability of hands to interpenetrate a reminder of abilities we have lost—to pass into the interiority of each other through a level of mutual contact that dissolves boundaries? Contemplating these "strange hands" I flash on a "primordial" capacity that—I come to realize—is a common currency of dreams—penetration of walls, the power to soar above trees, intimate projection into the body of another. . . . Can mere physicality suspend so splendid a claim? Is not the self-declaration, as I startle awake inside my dream—*Of course I can do this!*—at least as natural as finding oneself awake outside the dream?

liminal objects make us wonder what, if anything, is not liminal.

The Question Concerning Technology

Martin Heidegger's *The Question Concerning Technology*, along with other texts reflecting on the ontological significance of the technological as such, has served as a focal point for Gary Hill's recent work on this complex issue. For Heidegger, the essence of technology is a movement in history that progressively takes possession of Being itself, an appropriation performed by increasingly subjecting Being to calculation and control. Within the "Frame" (*Gestell*) of the technological, according to Heidegger, only what can be calculated—represented by mathematical coordinates—counts as real. Technology in this essential sense is not what it appears to be—the hardware, the software, and the general collection of procedures and apparatuses designed to produce objects on demand. It is rather the underlying ontological assumption that only the calculable is real.

For Heidegger, Being is not encompassed by the technological, although our awareness of this truth is seriously at risk. There is a way beyond the truly monstrous consequences of a world fully appropriated by the technological, but it is hardly simple. It consists in a realization within thinking itself—a poetic, mediative thinking that inquires more profoundly into Being's essence, displacing the technological Frame. Gary Hill's direct invocation of this aspect of Heidegger's work signals his own interest in a transformative relationship with the technological—to preempt, so to speak, what would preempt us, by turning technical means toward open ontological inquiry.

The stand against submission to the technological "Frame" is no simplistic or Luddite opposition to technology. Heidegger, in fact, warns against direct opposition that would inevitably enclose itself within the frame it defies. The point is akin to Blake's insistence that when we use our enemy's means we become the enemy. If we fight technological manipulation and control merely by trying to control it, we unwittingly further the technological. There's another possibility, however, which has to do with the nature of Being itself—to participate by serving what the technological does not know how to encompass: *the art of the open.* This is an art of the threshold, the liminal possibility, an art of beginnings. It declares a context of radical inquiry and a space of continuous presencing before the unknown. It does not represent "reality," it presents possibility; not a claim of assessment, but a declaration of radical affinities.

Liminal Seer

Who sees? What sees? Who sees what sees? Etc.

The eye altering alters all. —William Blake

Accordingly: *who* does the seeing depends on the *state* of seeing.

So in my contemplation in the liminal state I am as much the seen as the seer. Who indeed sees? I see me. I see me seeing. I see me being seen. I am seen. I am seen through. I am the medium of seeing: the space of seeing, of the *work* in which seeing *is*—

Being seen

Lynne Cooke

Postscript: Re-embodiments in Alter-Space

"Anthropologists of possible selves, we are technicians of realizable futures."

—Donna Haraway

"Images are the dominant currency of communication," Margot Lovejoy argues in her book on electronic media and postmodern culture. This has resulted, she contends, in a crisis of knowledge that is in fact a crisis of vision: "We can only see the world by forming a picture through various specialized mediations."[1] Lack of a vision adequate to the electronic datasphere has led, in turn, Scott Bukatman concludes, "to a set of allusive attempts to reconstitute the space of the computer in human—biological or physical—terms; in other words, *to permit terminal space to become phenomenal.*"[2] Among those contributing to these attempts the work of artists is seminal, he believes, quoting in support J.G. Ballard's belief that the (science fiction) writer's role is to parallel the ontological redefinitions of the electronic era: "I feel that the balance between fiction and reality has changed significantly in the past decade. Increasingly their roles are reversed. We live in a world ruled by fictions of every kind. . . . For the writer in particular it is less and less necessary for him to invent the fictional content of his novel. The fiction is already there. The writer's task is to invent the reality."[3]

While granting the reality of the objective world, Maurice Merleau-Ponty nonetheless stressed that it is in the interactivity that occurs between the perceptible physical object and the perceiving motile subject

Originally published as "Who am I but a figure of speech?" in *Parkett,* no. 34 (1992), pp. 16–27. This version was published in the catalogue *Gary Hill,* Henry Art Gallery, University of Washington, Seattle, 1994.

that consciousness is instantiated. Phenomenology thus proposes that the status of being is not an absolute condition but one that changes relative to changes in the experience of the real. Irrespective of whether electronic "presences" can be said to exist in real spaces, experience of those spaces remains a "real" experience. Thus an examination of the cognitive processes of consciousness may be accorded priority over consideration of the veracity of any given external conditions. By focusing on the activity of a guided consciousness rather than on the absolute reality of the world "in itself," it may become possible to construct a phenomenology of those abstract and nonphysical spaces peculiar to electronic technologies. From this, definitions of both the modes of communication and the forms of social interaction they make possible may be constructed.

In *Suspension of Disbelief (for Marine)*, by suppressing the "willing" normally integral to this familiar phrase when titling a recent installation, Gary Hill suggests that conscious acquiescence will not be necessary: whether it is fictive or not, what is presented as real will be automatically, inevitably, even unavoidably, embraced as such. What was a goal for Ballard is for Hill, given his medium, virtually preordained. For, unlike current literature, reproductive technologies are among the principal conditioners of contemporary values and beliefs: their representations not only record objective reality but shape it to the point where they are frequently experienced as more potent than those provided by the everyday phenomenal world. As Vilèm Flusser argues, "The imagination functioning in technical images is so powerful that we not only regard these images as reality, but also live within their functions."[4]

Images of two bodies, the dominant one female, the other male, move across the screens of some thirty monitors which, stripped of their casings and attached edge to edge along a steel beam, create a potential linear continuum of electron space. The camera has lingered lovingly on these nudes: it almost nuzzles the skin in probing their surfaces, delivering the body to the gaze with a heightened immediacy. Seldom, however, do the forms glide along the chain of monitors in a smooth, continuous flow: their passage is constantly interrupted, spliced, cut, relayed, and replayed by means of a switching mechanism. Further complicating the spectator's perception of the "lovers" is the speed at which the images travel. So rapid is their passage that it becomes impossible to focus clearly on even a single frame, to fix it and hence appropriate it. Attempts to fuse the pair as a couple are equally problematic, for the overlapping, splicing, and intercutting of their individual anatomies postulates a connection very different from the conventional one melding discrete entities into a singular whole.

The bodies never blend, join, or fuse. The skin remains an impermeable boundary even when the body is fractured, its parts overlaid and intersecting. What seems to galvanize these rapidly sequencing images is, nonetheless, a desire for proximity, a wish to suppress separation. Vividly present yet frustratingly elusive, this seductive montage of swiftly shifting shapes at once conjures notions of togetherness and simultaneously redefines them. The accelerations, reversals, slowdowns, ellipses, and fragmentary arrests within the incessant flow conjure a stream of desire—the quintessence of eroticism. While seduction plays only on the surface, and coupling remains only tenuously proximate, this nevertheless does not signify the endlessly deferred merger that characterizes frustration. A dizzying, capricious, voluptuous, and ultimately delirious swirl, *Suspension* offers a sensuous paradigm for an ecstatic transcendence of the physicality of direct sexuality.

The intimacy which results from the camera's proximity to the bodies would seem to promise an eroticism of the kind conventionally linked to notions of voyeurism. What could have been private disclosures in the form of transgressive glimpses are, however, rendered spectacular by the overtly exhibitionistic presentation of the work. Far from surreptitiously revealing the clandestine, this installation has the grandeur and sweep of something deliberately devised to be seen. It offers a spectacle, in the sense that Guy Debord and others defined it: a surrogate self-contained form of reality.

The elevation of the monitors to overhead height, together with the vast length of the beam, keeps the viewer back in the cavernous space of the otherwise empty room, prohibiting any physical proximity to that which is viewed. The images hover luminously in the half-light, the darkened context further enhancing their intangibility and ephemerality. Unlike previous iconic depictions of lovers suspended in a timeless optical etheria, seen, say, in paintings of Paolo and Francesca by G. F. Watts, among others, this electronically manifest duo inhabits no coherent temporal entity. Their time and space (the space of kinesis) pertain to a nonphysical realm, that of electronic technology; these are the phantasmic spaces enabled by, and constituted through, communicative technologies. "[T]ime and metaphorical spaces for texts [and subjects] to unfold are the parameters I begin with," Gary Hill wrote recently. "It's a kind of telescopic time that makes the viewer aware of the process of seeing—of beholding the world through sight that exists in the folds of time."[5] Perception, and hence apprehension, remains rooted in bodily being, as Merleau-Ponty argued, yet that which is perceived belongs now to another reality. Vision is at once imbricated in the world and disembodied, embedded yet suspended, precluded from grasping what it surveys.

In its exclusive focus on the naked body viewed in close proximity *Suspension of Disbelief (for Marine)* (1991–92) bears comparison with *Inasmuch As It Is Always Already Taking Place,* which Hill made some two years earlier. Comprised of sixteen monitors varying in size from 0.5 inch to 21 inches, installed like a reliquary in a niche in the wall, this work transmits images of different parts of the human body life-size on each of its screens. By stretching the skin across the screens like a taut membrane, and by ensuring that the limbs disclose only abstract dark spaces in their interstices, Hill makes the forms vividly present to the viewer. Juxtaposed with these details of torso, organs, and limbs is an image of a finger laid on a page of text. A barely audible sound track draws the spectator forward in order to hear better the murmur of a voice almost obliterated by the rustle of turning pages and other ambient sounds.[6] This incessant but nearly inaudible speech finds its visual counterpart in the almost imperceptible motion of the anatomy. Such slight movement can be read as evidence simultaneously that the body is alive and that it is being observed. The act of visual interpretation can be understood as isomorphic to the reading of a text: just as reading creates the text, so seeing conjures meaning. In one of his most prophetic early works, Hill had asked "who am I but a figure of speech?"[7] This was in fact a rhetorical question, for much of the artist's work at that time was expressly focused on the generation of reality by language.[8] Subsequently, however, Hill affirmed on a number of occasions that the products of this verbal encoding may not be revelation, enlightenment, or clarification, but their very obverse. As seen in *Why Do Things Get in a Muddle? (Come on Petunia), URA ARU (the backside exists), Incidence of Catastrophe,* and above all *DISTURBANCE (among the jars),* language only too easily unravels, dissolves, implodes, or shatters into multiple contrary pronouncements. As speech disintegrates, infantile babbling, nonsense, and glossolalia ensue, freeing the body from the restrictions of the conceptual into the sensual embrace of anatomically generated sound. Given that speech has been pulverized in *Inasmuch* to what Hill calls "the debris of utterance," rather than incorporating the listener/viewer as it normally does, it serves now to emphasize a cleavage in communication: the body wrapped in its own "hum."[9]

Video has often been described as a medium of surface effects. The delimited scale of the monitor, together with the relatively poor resolution of the image and the constant motion of light particles all, as Jean Fisher argues, mitigate against viewers "entering" the image in ways akin to those by which they imaginatively inscribe themselves into filmic space.[10] Moreover, since deep focus translates poorly onto the screen, video operates optimally with a quite shallow depth of field. Thus instead of the viewer entering the illusory space of the recorded world, the motion and fluorescence of the photons propel the image forward so that it "invades" the observer's ambience. For most of its early avatars, Hill included, video was a medium that privileged time-based experience, with real time normally replacing the reality of actual space. Yet in his recent work Hill has steadily relinquished conventional usages and forms of time in order to explore more complex spatio-temporalities. In *Inasmuch* he capitalizes on these potentialities to great effect. Because the hand-held camera does not alter either its focus or its position, and because the recordings are continuously replayed, the flux of real time seems disconnected from the norms of daily temporality, collapsed into an eternal present. Each monitor is thus the site of the body which appears on the screens as immutably present and yet outside actual time. Its impregnable solitude reduces the viewer's role to that of mute witness at what Hill describes, disquietingly, as "the incessant, however fragmentary, anatomical site."[11] Presence is brought to betray a haunting absence.

Hill's most recent works reveal a growing preoccupation with place, space, and time, and in particular with the kinds of spaces inhabited by or made available through the new electronic technologies. *Inasmuch* has the proximity of a still life, but the site is not available to the body as a fully embodied agent. In *Between Cinema and a Hard Place* (1991) and, subsequently, *Suspension* and *Tall Ships* (1992), a more fully developed interplay linking actual and visualized spaces occurs as Hill capitalizes on the spatio-temporal malleability of the electronic signal. Like *Suspension*, *Tall Ships* has no verbal component, and so provides no possibility of overcoming estrangement via language. Projected directly onto the walls of the installation, the images have been freed into the materiality of real time and space. Walking the 90-foot-long corridor-like space of *Tall Ships,* the spectator is confronted with life-size figures who approach (and recede) apparently to intercept the viewer's passage.

But proximity fails to ensure connectedness. These sixteen figures of varying ages and sexes are first viewed from a multiplicity of vanishing points. Initially glimpsed small, as if seen at a distance, they rapidly draw near as if to effect what is the simplest of encounters, a one-to-one confrontation. As in many of Hill's previous works, relationships with the other are found necessarily to involve, if indeed they are not strictly confined to, forms of representation. On one level, such relationships might be described as projections. Here, exceptionally to date in Hill's oeuvre, the interface between the image and the actual becomes the site of potential interaction.[12]

In *Inasmuch* the relation between self and other is defined by the impregnable frontiers of the physical and illusory, which in this work lie at the interface between body and screen, skin and electronic surface. *Tall Ships* posits other relations by divesting the frameless continuum that is the hallmark of the video signal of its conventional physical constraint, the monitor. Whereas this might normally imperil the proximity of the image as it became absorbed into a continuous linear matrix, the fact that in this installation the projections are the sole source of light imbues them with an unexpected effect of embodiment in real space. Nonetheless, interaction cannot transgress the essential separateness of each protagonist: proximity does not vouchsafe connectedness. By contrast, *Between Cinema and a Hard Place* focuses directly on themes of division—more specifically, on frontiers in space—by setting up rapid and unpredictable movements from one kind of space to another at the same time as moving images from monitor to monitor. "Heidegger's use of nature as a metaphorical place of thought is intervened upon, with images of landscapes and pastoral scenes being interrupted by variable fencing, posted signs and other interventions of spatial temporal limits," Hill recently wrote of this work.[13] In this way various—and sometimes contradictory—levels of time are conjured.

The text and pre-text for this critique of "neighboring nearness" is a passage from Heidegger's "The Nature of Language," which Hill adapted for his sound track. The installation comprises twenty-three monitors of varying sizes laid out irregularly on the ground. In physically occupying an indeterminate space, the piece provides an apt metaphor for an extract which the artists describes as "question[ing] a strictly parametrical view of space and time, posing the possibility of a 'neighboring nearness' that does not depend on a spatial-temporal relationship."[14]

Tall Ships operates in real time and space, but with the aid of a complex technology manifests the other as an ineluctably but teasingly un-reachable image in projected spaces which are nonetheless extensions of the viewer's own world. *Suspension* and *Between 1 & 0*, by contrast, pos-tulate very different versions of subjects imbricated in electronic tech-nologies, and hence of the relationships—the "proximity"—they per-mit. For common to both *Suspension* and *Between 1 & 0* is a form of computer switching which renders their bodily subjects(s) radically un-like anything Hill had devised before. Eschewing identifications based in bodily-kinetic knowledge, Hill presents a relationship between the self and the other that is irremediably based in exteriority. In his early works this self is rendered locked in an essential solitude, to borrow a phrase from Maurice Blanchot who has been an important influence. Recently the impenetrable solitude which, for him as for Blanchot, lies at the heart of consciousness has begun to be reexamined as the body is inserted into the different kinds of non-Cartesian space facilitated by electronic technology. Precluded from inscribing him or her self into the novel spatio-temporal geographies which Hill devises (unlike many others working with virtual space who simulate actual space), the spec-tator is brought into an unfamiliar and uncertain proximity with the subject. Relaying images across banks of monitors in rapid but not nec-essarily linear succession, the switching mechanism creates a mode of temporality that has little to do with actual time, that is, with time lived (or recorded as in live relay). Likewise, the spaces opened in these works, if and when continuous, do not have the coordinates of Carte-sian space. In this way Hill's fragmentation and multiplication of bod-ily imagery in phantasmic spaces may be read as conforming to current notions of social identity in the technological era. In adopting such strategies of visualization, these works open to scrutiny the "spatio-temporal" zones of electronic sociality.

Vivian Sobchack's perceptive article, "The Scene of the Screen: To-wards a Phenomenology of Cinematic and Electronic Presence," pro-vides an invaluable discussion of the ontology of this kind of visual space.[15] In exploring the phenomenological distinctions that separate photographic, cinematic, and electronic "presences," she argues that only the space of the last is discrete, ahistoric, and disembodied. A record of human vision and presence, the photograph depicts a frozen moment from the past. In its immutability it, as Merleau-Ponty notes, "keeps open the instants which the onrush of time closes up forthwith; it destroys the overtaking, the overlapping, the 'metamorphosis' . . . of time."[16] Cinema enacts a present-time experience of physical, bodily spatial reality. Very different again is digital electronic technology which "atomizes and *abstractly schematizes* the analogic quality of the photographic and cinematic into discrete *pixels* and *bits* of information that are transmitted *serially,* each bit discontinuous, discontiguous, and absolute—each bit 'being-in-itself' even as it is part of a system."[17] In *Suspension* the scale of the electronic band is that of a cinema screen. Through the close alignment of the frames an almost filmic sense of connectedness in space/time is hypothetically established. Moreover, on at least one occasion in the cycle, a single shot moves continuously from monitor to monitor, creating a spatial analogue for the cinematic flow of frame after frame. Yet, ultimately, these allusions serve only to make more apparent the distinctiveness of the spatio-temporal matrices of electronic technology.

In *Between 1 & 0,* thirteen monitors are grouped on a wall in a configuration that resembles a plus sign. The viewer is confronted with a subject which is locked in what seems to be an unfinishable process of writing itself—literally *and* figuratively writing itself. Literally in the sense of employing codes integral to that system, and metaphorically in several ways. Although not easily identified precisely, the sound track (made by graphite scratching a sheet of paper) is obviously of something scraping itself along a surface, etching itself into existence. And the backward and forward movement of the frames on the sign may be likened to the process of beginning a sketch: the pen hovers, wavering, over the ground, searching for the proper point at which to begin the process of definition.

"[E]lectronic space," Sobchack writes, "constructs objective and superficial equivalents to depth, texture and invested bodily movement. . . . [C]onstant action and 'busyness' replace the gravity which grounds and orients the movement of the lived-body with a purely spectacular, kinetically exciting, and often dizzying, sense of bodily freedom (and freedom from the body)."[18] Devoid of center and ground, these phantasmic spaces have at best only a vector graphic simulation of perspective to guide a human eye that has become distinct from its corporeality, its spatiality, its temporality, and its subjectivity. In *Between 1 & 0,* as in *Suspension,* Hill constructs a disembodied space in place of a Cartesian one: "machinic" images spin across a field voided of spatio-temporal metrics in a vertiginous display of their very depthlessness.

No rapport connecting viewer and projection of the kind initially proposed in *Tall Ships* is possible in *Between 1 & 0.* But neither is there that divorce of the spectator inherent in the spectacle found in *Suspen-*

sion. In fact, this is not an installation, properly speaking: the work is best seen as a transmission *tout court.* Phenomenologically, the electronic is experienced as a discrete and simultaneous transmission, Sobchack argues, for "the materiality of the electronic digitalizes *durée* and situation so that narrative, history, and a centered (and central) investment in the lived body become atomized and dispersed across a system that constitutes temporality not as a *flow of conscious experience,* but as the *transmission of random information.*" The primary value of electronic temporality is thus the instant, she concludes: "Temporality becomes paradoxically constituted as a *homogeneous* experience of *discontinuity* in which the temporal distinctions between objective and subjective experience . . . disappear, and time seems to turn back on itself in a structure of equivalence and reversibility." Similarly, the nature of the space experienced is redefined, disembodied: "Without the temporal emphases of historical consciousness and personal history, space also becomes abstract, ungrounded and flat—a site for *play* and *display* rather than an invested situation in which action 'counts.'"[19] In *Between 1 & 0,* as befits a relationship with a sign, or matrix, the physical relation inherent in the phenomenology of perception has been abstracted, and temporality destabilized. Yet as in *Suspension,* seeing remains a highly participatory activity as the spectator relentlessly scans this configuration trying vainly to compress the whirling shards of information into a whole.

If in *Inasmuch* Hill disembodied the self, and in *CRUX* (1983–87) decentered it, in *Between 1 & 0* he might be said to have dismantled it. So rapidly do the microcosmic fragments of the body seen in close-up course across, and up and down, the surfaces of the monitors that it is difficult to identify them—with the notable exception of the teeth, whose intermittent yet recurrent presence reveals the program to be a circular one, one seemingly without beginning or end, origin or conclusion. Given the title as well as the interplay between absence and presence on the screens, several of which receive only a single frame lasting one-thirtieth of a second, this subject might be said to have been written literally in the coding of electronic technologies. Yet in being resolutely "between," the fragments could be said to refuse a unitary identity. "*Between* things does not designate a localizable relation going from one thing to another and back again, but a perpendicular direction, a transversal movement that sweeps one *and* the other away, a stream without beginning or end that undermines its banks and picks up speed in the middle," write Gilles Deleuze and Félix Guattari in their chapter in *A Thousand Plateaus: Capitalism and Schizophrenia* devoted to the "Body without Organs" (BwO).[20] Their discussion has great pertinence for Hill's piece, whose subject too is always in the process of becoming, and so precludes any straightforward way of conceptualizing it. For them the BwO is unattainable: it is a limit that is never reached, with no point of origin and no fundaments. Instead, "it proceeds from the middle, through the middle, coming and going rather than starting and finishing."[21] To establish a "logic of the AND" it overthrows ontology, and so it "is not at all a notion or a concept but a practice, [a] set of practices." They contend: "The modes are everything that comes to pass: waves and vibrations, migrations, thresholds and gradients, intensities produced in a given type of substance starting from a given matrix."[22] The better to illustrate this, they cite a passage from William Burroughs's *Naked Lunch* which (coincidentally) parallels the imagery seen on Hill's screen in striking fashion: "No organ is constant as regards either function or position, . . . sex organs sprout anywhere, . . . the entire organism changes color and consistency in split-second adjustments."[23] But equally apposite is their contention that "there are not organs in the sense of fragments in relation to a lost unity, nor is there a return to the undifferentiated in relation to a differentiated totality. There is a distribution of intensive principles of organs, with their positive indefinite articles, within a collectivity or multiplicity, inside an assemblage, and according to machinic connections operating on a BwO."[24] Thus, in the BwO "flows of intensity, their fluids, their fibers, their continuums and conjunctions of affects" replace the world of the unitary, centered subject.[25]

The body has traditionally been construed in manifold ways: as self, as historical object, as organic substrate. It is in terms of the third of these constructs that it has been most extensively examined in recent theory—tellingly, theory which situates it in relation to technology. Yet assessments of the value, implications, and consequences of the new electronic technologies remain in contention. For all their great differences, two of the most influential theorists of this discourse, Jean Baudrillard and Donna Haraway, are united in their recognition of the enveloping and determining parameters of a fully technologized existence that has forced a crisis around untenable definitions of the human, rendering technology and the human no longer dichotomized. Through the interface between technology and the human subject, new technological modes of being in the world are emerging, along with reconceptions of the subject as one in whom human and technology are coextensive, codependent, and mutually defining. In *Between 1 & 0,* Hill's body/subject/self may be said to have become a cyborg.[26]

In her suggestive article, titled "Virtual Systems," Allucquère Roseanne Stone charts the transforming effects of the new technologies on the character and locus of the social arenas of Western industrialized societies. In character, this has meant, she argues, "a change from individual or group interaction, which implied physical presence, to decentered and fragmented communication whose nature and quality took on rapidly shifting and fundamentally novel forms. In locus, it meant a shift from a physical space [to one] whose geographical coordinates resist traditional modes of representation."[27] "The kind and quality of human interactions created by these shifts—interactions of a character quite unrecognizable from the standpoint of geographically located agoras—have been described [and explored] in many different ways," she contends.[28] When manifest as interactive computer systems, they offer possibilities for a novel sociality that has been eagerly appropriated by a broad spectrum of interests ranging from the military, to institutions of psychology and education, and business. Among notable explorations in the fictive realm are those by the inventors of computer games, writers of science fiction film and literature, and visual artists working with multimedia.

Whether or not they dwell in "real" or "fictional" systems, the inhabitants of these technosocial spaces are new kinds of beings with whom interaction may be not only novel but, perhaps, transformative. For, as Stone argues, such exchange contains "the potential for emergent behavior, for new social forms that arise in a circumstance in which 'body,' 'meeting,' 'place,' and even 'space' mean things quite different from our accustomed understanding."[29] The binaries—1/0, plus/minus, etc.—which rewrite the body in computer code simultaneously redefine it, offering potent alternatives to the bounded individual as the standard social unit and validated social actant. For the subject in virtual systems may become uncoupled (from the living body), ungrounded, constituted solely through communication technologies. The history of such technologies is therefore one of tensions between selves and bodies, as the play of their interactions, separations, and fusions constantly broadens. Once the authorizing body can be manifested through technological prosthetics, agency in these spaces becomes proximate. This, in turn, entails, Stone contends, "that as these prosthetics become more complex, the relationship between agency and authorizing body becomes more discursive."[30]

For optimistic theorists like Haraway and Stone, "virtual systems and the social worlds they imply are examples of the flexible and lively adaptations that persons seeking community are beginning to explore."[31] They discern a potential range of innovative solutions to prevailing constraints in social interaction, whereas Hill's vision of these communicative capacities seems at present more ambivalent. His version of their erotic capability, adumbrated in *Suspension,* may be lyrical, just as his refiguring of the subject in *Between 1 & 0* apparently offers the cyborg a liberating "schizo" mode (in the sense outlined by Deleuze and Guattari), yet his embrace of the simulated remains qualified. At the heart of his doubt lies an ongoing struggle with the question of what the differences in our relationships with the simulated and the actual amount to. His refusal of any prescriptive answer suggests that these recent works are likely to prove but prologues to further reworkings of the structure of sociality and more detailed mappings of the geography of elsewheres.

Notes

1. Margot Lovejoy, *Postmodern Currents: Art and Artists in the Age of Electronic Media* (Ann Arbor: UMI Research Press, 1989); quoted in Scott Bukatman, *Terminal Identity: The Virtual Subject in Postmodern Science Fiction* (Durham: Duke University Press, 1993), p. 109. I am indebted to Bukatman's theses in more ways than this and the following citations indicate.

2. Ibid.

3. This statement, made in 1974 in a new preface to Ballard's 1973 novel, *Crash,* is quoted in Bukatman, op. cit., pp. 116–17.

4. Vilém Flusser, "The Status of Images," in *Metropolis* (Berlin: Martin Gropius Bau/New York: Rizzoli, 1991), p. 53.

5. Gary Hill, "Interviewed Interview," *Gary Hill* (Valencia: IVAM Centre del Carme, 1993), p. 152.

6. The impression it gives of hovering on the borders of intelligibility recalls Maurice Blanchot's evocative characterization: "Not speech, barely a murmur, barely a tremor, less than silence, less than the abyss of the void; the fullness of the void, something one cannot silence, occupying all of space, the uninterrupted, the incessant, a tremor and already a murmur, not a murmur but speech, and not just any speech, distinct speech, precise speech, within my reach." *Celui qui ne m'accompagnait pas* (Paris: Gallimard, 1953), quoted in *Foucault–Blanchot,* Michel Foucault, "Maurice Blanchot. The Thought from Outside" (New York: Zone, 1990), pp. 22–23.

7. *Primarily Speaking* (1981–83). In this tape, images were linked to speech in such a way that as each syllable was enunciated the picture changed. Impetus

to explore this and related aspects of the technology grew out of a concern, emerging in the 1970s, with investigating the specifics of the medium, a concern shared at that time by many pioneers working in this rapidly changing field of electronics. In Hill's video work from the late 1970s, sound was a key element; in the early 1980s it took on the guise of language and text, as well as speech.

8. Heidegger's notion, "Language is the house of being in which man dwells," has been central to much of Hill's thought, although he arrived at it via Blanchot, Ludwig Wittgenstein, and other writers rather than directly through the texts of the German philosopher. For a fuller discussion see Lynne Cooke, "Gary Hill: Beyond Babel," *Gary Hill* (Valencia: IVAM Centre del Carme, 1993), pp. 163–71. That this notion has continued to be important to Hill's thinking is evident from two pieces he has made recently: the four-minute tape *Site Recite (a prologue)* (1989) and *I Believe It Is an Image in Light of the Other* (1991–92). In *Site Recite*, language not only generates and shapes all, it threatens to consume all. For most of this tape the camera moves in a circular tracking shot that evokes an omniscient vision, or a model of a mind generating a world. During its final few seconds, however, an image of a mouth speaking, recorded from a point near the back of the tongue, is suddenly substituted for the displaced, and hence placeless, still life which had up to the moment been the sole subject under review. Its highly charged concluding statement—"imagining the brain closer than the eyes"—gives weight to Raymond Bellour's claim that "there is no visual image that is not more and more tightly gripped, even in its essential, radical withdrawal, inside an audiovisual or scriptovisual . . . image that envelops it." (Raymond Bellour, "The Double Helix," *Passages de l'Image* [Barcelona: Centre Cultural de la Fundacio Caixa de Pensions, 1991], p. 72). In *I Believe* seven canisters containing monitors and lenses are suspended over open books strewn on the floor in a darkened space. Images of the body and of writing are literally overlaid so that text becomes embodied and anatomy encoded in the printed script.

9. Gary Hill, "Inasmuch As It Is Always Already Taking Place," in *OTHER-WORDSANDIMAGES* (Copenhagen: Video Gallerie/Ny Carlberg Glyptotek, 1990), p. 27.

10. Jean Fisher, "V-I-D-E-O-Z-O-N-E," in *Topographie II: Untergrund* (Vienna, 1991), pp. 26–50.

11. Gary Hill, *OTHERWORDSANDIMAGES*, p. 27.

12. By contrast, *Site Recite*, subtitled *(a prologue)*, was originally meant to be an interactive video, that is, to provide a context in which viewers could enter and move around according to their own impulses. Through a kind of phenomenological insistence, it would have been able, Hill hoped, to "make participants aware of their own mediation process." Quoted in Christine van Assche, "Interview with Gary Hill," *Galeries Magazine*, December 1990/ January 1991, p. 141.

13. Gary Hill, "Between Cinema and a Hard Place," unpublished text, 1991, unpaginated.

14. Ibid.

15. Vivian Sobchack, "The Scene of the Screen: Towards a Phenomenology of Cinematic and Electronic Presence," *Post -Script,* 10, 1990, pp. 50–59.

16. Maurice Merleau-Ponty, "Eye and Mind," in *The Primacy of Perception,* ed. James M. Edie (Evanston: Northwestern University Press, 1964), p. 186.

17. Sobchack, op. cit., p. 56.

18. Ibid., pp. 57–58.

19. Ibid., p. 57.

20. Gilles Deleuze and Félix Guattari, *A Thousand Plateaus: Capitalism and Schizophrenia* (Minneapolis: University of Minneapolis Press, 1987), p. 25.

21. Ibid.

22. Ibid., p. 153.

23. Ibid.

24. Ibid., pp. 164–65.

25. Ibid., p. 162.

26. In her now celebrated text, "A Cyborg Manifesto: Science, Technology, and Socialist-Feminism in the Late Twentieth Century," Haraway starts from the premise that the cyborg (a term she analyzes at length) literalizes the inseparability of the human and machine in a symbiosis of body and technology from which she formulates a potential utopian future for this mythic state of being, one which will elude those racial, gendered, and class-based dichotomies that have lain at the very heart of western culture. Donna J. Haraway, "A Cyborg Manifesto: Science, Technology, and Socialist-Feminism in the Late Twentieth Century," reprinted in *Simians, Cyborgs, and Women: The Reinvention of Nature* (New York: Routledge, Chapman and Hall, 1991), pp. 149–82.

27. Allucquère Roseanne Stone, "Virtual Systems," in *Incorporations,* eds. Jonathan Crary and Sanford Kwinter (New York: Zone, 1992), p. 609.

28. Ibid.

29. Ibid., p. 610.

30. Ibid., p. 616.

31. Ibid., p. 620.

George Quasha and Charles Stein

projection:

the space of great happening

If someone asked me, "Where do you take place?" I might answer, "Here, where do you think?" This is not a question that automatically makes sense. I don't necessarily think of myself as an *event*—a "taking place" within an environment. In addition, the question is different in every context. If I'm an actor on a stage, my "eventuality"—my event-reality—is self-evident because it is spatially and temporally framed. I may witness myself, for a change, somewhat as others do, especially if I'm used to hearing or seeing taped versions of my performance. Likewise if I'm playing tennis, even though I'm hardly watching myself, I am performing within a context that sees me as an event and that promises reflection—I will be *replayed* in mind, in recording, in report, in assessment, and so on. I am aware of my eventuality by virtue of replayability and reflection. My fear or hope of assessment—I want to win, communicate, look good, and so on—fuels my connection with the frame of the event. I stand within a projection, and take place accordingly.

This account, simple and abstract as it is, suggests that we are art-beings who exist in relation to more or less continuous projection of our own event. What we actually do in that projection is open to interpretation from many points of view—psychological, geometrical, aesthetic, ontological—depending in part upon the declared frame. Sometimes the frame itself is ambiguous or otherwise *open,* in which case the meaning of our happening is also "open"—which can mean anything

Originally published in English and Portuguese in the catalogue *Gary Hill: O Lugar do Outro [Where the Other Takes Place]* (Centro Cultural Banco do Brasil and Museu de Arte Moderna de São Paulo, Rio de Janeiro, 1997), pp. 35–57.

149

from *free* and *possible* to *catastrophic* and *mad.* If in such a situation someone asks me "where" I take place, I may no longer say "here" as though it meant something clear.

Imagine that you are entering a long dark hall in which the only light is the measured occurrence of small luminous spots along either side, at about eye-level, on the walls. As you approach you see that each "spot" is a person in the distance (seated, standing, or reclining), who, in response to your presence, "gets motivated" and walks toward you, then stands in front of you, eye to eye. Here you remain, faced with this other person—"no one special," just himself or herself, like the guy or girl next door finally coming to meet you face to face. Strangely familiar. Yet completely other. It has its own light, this *other,* the only light there, which plays on your surface and the faces of the visitors in the room, like moonlight—a cool and thinly resonant light, a space consisting of residual light that seems to call up one's emotions for no reason but that the space is empty (emotion is one way nature has of abhorring a vacuum!). And here we are, viewers (*voyeurs/voyageurs*) in this darkly illuminating space with the consistency of water and the tendency to drift and a slow welling up of feeling in waves moving *between us* and *the projected* other, like ships signaling half-seen, half-known ships. Tall ships.

Tall Ships (1992). We have been imagining—you might say, projecting—a visit to Gary Hill's installation piece bearing a Turneresque name that might make us expect an archaic landscape. What we get is something closer to an archetypal mindscape—like entering a birth canal in reverse, or descending into the Underworld with Ulysses, or dreaming an encounter with ghostly yet vividly *personal faces.* Moving thus in the silent territory of mind, we easily find ourselves replaying the encounters, "re-projecting" them as mental events—as though, once having viewed the Mysteries, we are now initiates and retain the human flavor of these unidentified but unmistakable entities. Dreamy, yes, but once you have met these beings in the intimate dark, you're not likely to forget them. (How many human circumstances can that be said about?) If this is projection, then how does it differ from life itself?

Ambiguously, or, we might say, only liminally. Once we have crossed the threshold of *Tall Ships* we are qualified to observe: projection goes on all around us and all the time, but most poignantly it leads the way, *it goes before us.* (We are, after all, a race of moviegoers, and we expect nothing less than life writ large on the great luminous space *out there*—sky, screen, (sur)face of the other. And as art-beings, we may even have a certain right to the expectation.) So, obviously we put off as long as possible asking the impossible question, *What is projection?*

Quick impossible answer: *projection is what makes reality surface.* (A dolphin breaching the water.) *It does so by surfacing reality.* (Asphalt or gold leaf, same difference.)[1]

Or, stating it graphically to retain the torque of ambiguity in the problem:

$$\frac{\text{projection is what makes reality}}{\text{surface}}$$

Is reality what is cast upon a surface, as the word "*project*" (to "throw forth") might suggest? In this case, reality is in the projector (the artist, the film or recording medium, the machine) and the surface is a neutral receiver—the "silver screen." Or is reality what is brought up—made to disclose itself—from *beneath,* from the unrevealed or unconscious or otherwise unknown? In this case the projector is the *spur,* the instrument of cutting through the surface or boundary that holds back the real, and the artist is the liberator or agent of release.[2] Or is the art-act *liminal to both* of these, the cultivation of the ambi-valent *between,* the medium as middle and the edge of (inter)activity?[3] If this third possibility is so, then in the graphic formulation above, the horizontal line stands for *one's presence*—the view of the viewer viewing, the (inter)space of the great happening that is the release of what is "normally" held from us. This is the space—the event horizon—where it is possible to know, more simply, and liminally.

$$\frac{\text{reality}}{\text{surfaces}}$$

As you voyage down that long hall, yourself a tall ship catching the light of the other by which you orient *yourself* in the confusing dark, you take place as the twin of a possible person—the projection that comes toward you, a sort of angelic messenger bringing you news of what you have unconsciously cast before you.

Je est un autre.

—Arthur Rimbaud

It seems to me I take place out there.

—Robert Duncan[4]

Projection—to think or say this word is to participate in a confusion, at least potentially. It stands for something the mind does—*we ourselves do*—pretty much all the time. It also stands for the mechanism and medium, psychological or physical, that implements it. Perhaps such a crossing of domains accounts in part for the immense power that artistic projection has for us. Projection as metaphor and means has had a unique appeal from Plato's cave to camera oscura, Proust's Magic Lantern, the silver screen, holograms, and video installation. Its attraction as a possible domain seems to combine what somehow belongs to us with what is utterly other and out there.

When a video projector casts the image of a person on a wall, we are never unaware that we are viewing a projection. Yet in works like *Tall Ships, Viewer,* and *Standing Apart* the person is also experienced as real, even somehow as more real than a person standing nearby. For a moment the projection co-opts the space of the real. Undeniably there is a special intensity that intentional projection invites, obviously lacking in our casual interaction with people. *Tall Ships* extends this truth by provoking an encounter so curiously real (although the figures appear in black and white and not very finely focused) that some viewers find themselves involuntarily responding as though a stranger had walked right up to them. The projection is charged by its *resemblance* to the real, its momentary confusion with the real, especially when the real does something we try to keep it from doing—confronting us face to face. In *Viewer* too there is an uncomfortable intensity, of something a bit too real, as seventeen (all male) waiting day-workers stare at us as we pass, their eyes following us everywhere and their lives, their *wanting,* pressing against us. It's as though they were projecting back at us.

Perhaps all of these projection-works by Gary Hill—especially *Tall Ships* due to its effective "interactive" mechanism—demonstrate the instant "feedback" quality of intensive projectivity. It's as though the projection draws you out into a kind of identification with the other, only to come back at you with its difference—or rather *your* difference. But difference from what? Not, surely, just one's difference from the other, which, on the face of it, is hardly news. No, what the feedback brings us is, as it were, *our difference from ourselves.* And that's *poetic news* (to paraphrase Ezra Pound)—"news that stays news."

To be learning of one's difference from the "oneself" that one thinks one knows, is new every second of the way. So it is that the feedback is a mirroring, but a mirror that reflects truth which, without reflection, is hard to see. *Poetic?* Yes, but only in the root (the true) sense of something *made*, a created truth. This is the work *on* oneself that is also work out of oneself as the art-being responsible for the projection. I may be a mere viewer gazing upon the *artist's* projection, but if it *gets* me, bounces me back to the *instantly present reality of myself,* then I begin to wake up to my role as projector of the projection of the other. I'm a shared reality, co-holder of a space of great happening that is shared otherness and participated difference.

Of course this sounds like double-talk, and for good reason—it is. To speak accurately about *projection* in the fullness of its interactivity between viewer and viewed is to harness the *twinning* force of language. This is the energy of doubling—of which a palpable embodiment is *Standing Apart,* wherein the "same" person witnesses himself (and we witness him witnessing himself witnessing us, etc.). To be sure, there's something eerie about such "twinning," but what is it, after all, that's uncanny about twins? "Identical" twins are distinct human beings who seem to do an impossible thing—share an identity. Here the very difference between "the different" and "the same" becomes confounded. The *"confusion"* is literally the case: each takes his identity from the other. Twins often experience heightened intersubjectivity under quite ordinary circumstances—a projection/counter-projection—and this may explain why the metaphor of "twin" and "twinning" is so enormously attractive in certain kinds of art. There's more than etymology at stake in the connection between *twin* and *twine* (intertwine) and the vine-like torsional force behind the double-talk inspired by projection.

We are noticing that the phenomenology of projection has a parallel dimension in ambivalent (torsional) language—words and syntax with an apparent double meaning, as though a verbal event turns on its axis and shifts its semantic force. Gary Hill's language—in his own prose statements, his use of verbal and textual material in his work, and in his titles—belongs to the world of poetry. Likewise the images and narrative structures throughout his work (beginning in his single-channel videos) belong to the poetic domain. Poetry we define as "conscious speaking with listening," in the way it seems to turn around inside the speaker/listener's ear.[5] His title for the collected single-channel work, *Spinning the Spur of the Moment,* combines the notion of torsional force with that of penetrating and awakening intervention concentrated in an instant of time. The implication is that a *projective act*—whether verbal, imagistic, or narrative—disrupts the plane of perceived reality by introducing a "fold" in the place of the normal distinction "subject" and "object."

Consider in this regard both the title and the tortuous narrative of the single-channel video *Incidence of Catastrophe* (1987–88; 43:51), which, in the way it uses material from Maurice Blanchot's fiction *Thomas the Obscure,* creates a sort of "double" of the mysterious French text—a topologically catastrophic rendering of a text as the site of creative/decreative self-interference.[6] This work, in which the camera veritably ravishes the printed page with acts of reading and brilliantly lit page-handling, prefigures the later installation work involving projection of, and onto, text: *And Sat Down Beside Her* (1990)[7] and *I Believe It Is an Image in Light of the Other* (1991–92).[8] In these installations (in which one walks around illuminated objects, sensualized surfaces, readable things, imagized texts) it's as though the viewer entered directly into the world of *Incidence*[9]—oneself as the angle (view) of incidence or projective force—whose incursion into the still (and moving) life of the *gathering of things* creates . . . *Catastrophe,* that is, utterly particular meaning folded into the surface of the world. A reprojection of the world as *lived space,* sat down beside.

Parataxis—the juxtaposition of phrases without the use of logical connectives (site-specific language)—is especially common in the oral storytelling mode of laying out incidents with no logic but that they're there, and it expresses the arrangement of *events* as though they were *things.* In these projective installations involving a display of (illuminated) objects, things seem to talk back, as though they were events, at least potentially. The site recites, to borrow the title of Gary Hill's single-channel videotape—*Site Recite (a prologue)*(1989; 4:05). The space speaks, like a voice from beyond the grave (voice-over), through things and the "little deaths that pile up": bones, butterfly wings, egg shells, seed pods, crumpled notes, skulls—things acting like words uttered in quick views. Likewise in *Inasmuch As It Is Always Already Taking Place* (1990) the parts speak—body parts, one body with many voices, the multiple personality that any*body* inevitably *is* through the multiplicity of one's self-projections. (Isn't personal self-projection really site-specific?)

Here in *Inasmuch* the "projection" implicates a deeper fact about surface-viewing than the literal one that video or film projects onto a surface. The piece consists of a sixteen-channel video/sound installation comprising 0.5-inch to 23-inch black-and-white television tubes. These are positioned in a horizontal wall inset, somewhat below eye level—an *inj*ection, an in*spur*ation, a concave "project." The body, dismembered like Osiris,[10] livingly and breathingly displays itself, a *nature vivante* of actually life-sized parts. (Is the eternally absent procreative member inversely present here as video lens?) The fragmented body projects a *possible* body, body as field, as murmuring self-textualizing space, a body knowable as the mind knows itself. *Body as projection of mind,* thanks to "art-being's" long lineage from Osirean myth to Cubist painting, is not limited to any specific logic but can imagine possible wholenesses, and so enjoys the permission to lie about as it likes. And say what it wants (lacks).

> What kind of syntax/synapse serves
> an open field in-
> vaginating toward a
> possible center?

> —Ontonymous the Particular

From single channel (one birth canal) to multiple channels (confluence of twinning possibilities), Gary Hill's work evolves structurally and technically toward open projectivity and awareness by field. In the four-channel installation *Clover* (1994), the voyager, a "viewer" in the woods, is seen from behind. The camera is attached to his back and shows head and shoulders against the "background" of "oncoming trees." He walks away from "us," the "viewers," toward an unknown point *out there.* The background is the *in*ground into which *viewing* makes its incursion, a continuous conscious projection *through* the video tube *into* a world that (like the actual meeting point in *Tall Ships*) never arrives.[11] Or four worlds, as we see in our circumambulation of the four 20-inch monitors, each displaying a different man walking out into the approaching woods . . . Journeying around the mandala-like construction, as though performing our own slow round-dance, we re-project the four paths/leaves of clover pointing inward toward an unknown center, the life or source, which at the same time travel outward, themselves projecting toward an open end. The syntax is axial: antithetical (dialogical?) and (im)possible trajectories pursue their twin destinations:

> here
> at the crossroads,
> there
> in the missing middle . . .

Notes

1. The English verb *surface* is multivalent: "to surface" means (1) [intransitive] To rise to the surface; to emerge after concealment: *the diver surfaces;* (2) [transitive] To apply a surface to: *surface a road (with asphalt).* In the two graphic formulations that follow, the word "*surface*[s]" below the horizontal line can also be read as a noun.

2. Gary Hill named his three-volume laserdisc of collected single-channel video works, *Spinning the Spur of the Moment* (Voyager, 1994). Interestingly he had considered giving the installation *Viewer* the name *Cast,* which would have the double meaning of "project (= throw forth)" and "a surface impression formed in a mold."

3. A limen in Latin is a *threshold.* The notion of liminality has played a key role in our discussions of Gary Hill's work; see especially our *Gary Hill: HAND HEARD/liminal objects* (Station Hill Arts of Barrytown, Ltd. & the Galerie des Archives, 1996).

While the current usage of the term *liminal* is principally behavioral with respect to the threshold of a physiological or psychological response, in fact, liminal or borderline states exist anywhere that something is about to undergo a phase transition or turn into something *other.* What is conceptually difficult in observing liminal states is that even fundamental distinctions like space and time come into question. *Where are we and when are we in the in-between?* In what sense is what we observe "really there"? Or is it only *liminally* there?

4. Rimbaud (1854–91) in his famous visionary letter to his teacher says, "I is an other." The American poet Robert Duncan (1919–87) made the quoted remark in a lecture, probably in the 1960s.

5. The link between Gary Hill's work and the world of innovative poetry is a matter of historical fact which the artist has discussed many times and which we, in our nearly two decades of collaborating with him, have experienced firsthand. While he has not been particularly influenced by the poet Charles Olson (1910–70), the latter's work and ideas have reached him indirectly. We intend at a later time to explore the connection between video projection and Olson's influential notion of "Projective Verse" (1950) (most available in *The Selected Writings of Charles Olson,* ed. Robert Creeley [New Directions: New York, 1966]).

6. Gary Hill used the Robert Lamberton translation of Blanchot's *Thomas l'Obscur* originally published by David Lewis, Inc. (New York, 1973) and subsequently by Station Hill Press: Barrytown, N.Y., 1988 (original French edition, Gallimard: Paris, France, 1941). *Thomas the Obscure* has a "twin" text in the *Gnostic Gospel of Thomas;* Gary Hill used material from the latter, itself rich in "twin" symbolism, in the seven-channel installation, *DISTURBANCE (among the jars)* (Paris, 1988, in collaboration with George Quasha).

7. Three-part mixed media installation with content derived in part from *Thomas the Obscure* by Maurice Blanchot in which the narrator imagines he

sees a woman in the form of a spider. Gary Hill creates sculptural analogies to the form of arachnids, and in one part, a video image of his own face is projected onto an open book set upon a chair.

8. Seven-channel video/sound installation, with seven hanging 4-inch black-and-white video displays and a projection element consisting of seven modified video monitors and projection lenses placed inside seven black metal cylinders which hang from the ceiling. The only source of light in the darkened room is from the images of different parts of a male body, and a chair, projected onto open books lying on the floor. The texts illuminated by the images are excerpts from a Blanchot fiction, *The Last Man,* in the Lydia Davis English translation (Columbia University Press, New York).

9. "Incidence" in English is multivalent: (1) happening; (2) frequency of occurrence; (3) the incursion of a projectile (spur) or radiation on a surface; (4) angle of incidence. (In the projective installation *Remarks on Colors* [1994; 45 min.] the young girl, reading in real-time Wittgenstein's text of that name, pronounces "angles," "angels"—angel of incidence or incidence of angels? To paraphrase Rilke, any angel *is catastrophic.*) "Catastrophe" is used most importantly in its topological sense of a discontinuity in a process that gives rise to an unanticipated circumstance or form.

10. The ancient Egyptian god whose annual death and resurrection personified the self-renewing vitality and fertility of nature: murdered by his brother, Set, and dismembered into fourteen parts, his body was spread across Egypt, eventually to be regathered by Isis.

11. The sense of suspension—compare the four-channel installation with thirty monitors, *Suspension of Disbelief (for Marine)* (1991–92)—is never far from the center of the process in Gary Hill's work: the labyrinthine journey (*Withershins,* 1996); the state of "still point" in riding the perpetual wave (*Learning Curve [still point]*, 1993); the endless cycling of self-dividing/self-reversing and indeterminate image accumulation (*Circular Breathing,* 1994), etc. At issue here: the *retention of energy,* memory, and awareness, a holding in the middle of the process, and the discovery of alternative modes of focus. Such is "the space of great happening" in the oscillation of projection/counter-projection.

Arlindo Machado

Why Do Language and Meaning Get in a Muddle?

There is one perhaps not very orthodox but strategically efficient way of introducing Gary Hill to the Brazilian public. Due to the circumstances of our cultural history, Brazil has been a particularly fertile ground for experimental poetry, that poetry which does away with the resources of sound, images, kinetics, and audiovisual synchronism, in order to produce a concentrated expression of the feeling/thought/imagination complex in a creative approach. The polemic and fertile tradition of concrete poetry, with its unceasing multiplying of followers and detractors, has accumulated a long discussion about what the most contemporary poetic form might be, and about the arsenal of significant resources which the poet can nowadays adopt thanks to the expansion around us of electronic/digital means.

Well, in order to place Gary Hill within an already familiar discussion, we can begin by imagining him a poet of the media age; *poet* because, like all poets, he concentrates his inquiries on the role and meaning of *language* within our culture and other human contexts; *media age* because, although books and the written word continue to represent strong references, his working materials are video pictures and sounds, electronically generated characters and forms modeled by computers, with all their respective rhetorical editing and metamorphic resources. In fact, Hill's work is based on investigation into the specular and labyrinthine aspects of language, in an audiovisual and media "translation" of certain traditional poetic components such as palin-

Originally published in English and Portuguese in the catalogue *Gary Hill: O Lugar do Outro [Where the Other Takes Place]* (Centro Cultural Banco do Brasil and Museu de Arte Moderna de São Paulo, Rio de Janeiro, 1997), pp. 11–35. Translated from Portuguese by Lucy Needham.

dromes (words or verses which can be read both from left to right and vice versa, such as *live/evil*), anagrams (the transposition or shuffling of letters in a word or verse, such as sword/words), and plays on words in general, with a view to exploring the ambiguities and paradoxes of language, as well as undermining the institution of meaning. In an interview given to Christine van Assche,[1] Hill confesses that his main interests lie "in the moment approaching meaning and the moment when meaning begins to fade." He goes on: "I want to suppress the dualism of sense and nonsense, and see what happens inside the experience of language as meaning is taking root or being uprooted."

We are, therefore, dealing with all the more recent poetic experiments into overtaking the pragmatic and communicative limits of language, in order to see it as a fundamentally turbulent phenomenon, the main cause of human disorder, instability, and disclosure crises.

Naturally, the placing of Hill's work within the bounds of experimental poetry can present problems in certain situations or in some aspects. First of all, it is certainly paradoxical that Gary Hill's name is rarely (if ever) cited in discussion about the most decisive experiments into defining the direction of current poetry, even taking into consideration the fact that he has worked closely—in *Tale Enclosure* (1985), for instance—with well-known representatives of visual or sound poetry, such as George Quasha or Charles Stein. This fact is still more surprising when we consider that some of Hill's work, such as *Happenstance* (1982–83) and *URA ARU (the backside exists)* (1985–86), extracts all the possible consequences from the idea of integral media poetry, in which its linguistic and semiotic instances (oral, written, musical, moving pictural) reach an almost undecomposable synthesis and their highest degree of condensation and force of meaning.

In fact, I am unaware of any other work, within the unstable boundaries of experimental poetry, that has achieved the same degree of radicalism. On the other hand, simply the fact that Hill moves around in such a wide terrain, a spectrum ranging from video art to technological poetry and multimedia installations, and also because his art lies on the very edges of labels and specialities, so is not easily characterized, all this may explain the fullness and perfect roundness of his work. In best haiku tradition, each of Hill's works is an amalgam of such accurately combined sensations and ideas that the music is not relegated to mere background accompaniment, nor are the images just illustration of the text, the text an explanation of the image, nor the voice the verbalization of the written word. It would be difficult for this holistic quality to become evident in such a systematic way in the work of a creator who only defined himself as a poet, musician, or artist.

So we can view Hill's work as a systematic effort to create *video poetry*, which we can understand as a complex and meaningful system in which the written word, the spoken voice, and the image (figurative or abstract) maintain a tense dialogism with each other: sometimes complementing or contradicting each other, at other times oscillating in a nonsynchronized (but harmonic) fashion between pure visual or auricular sensation (the inarticulate and meaningless primal cry, the consonance of shapes and abstract colors) and philosophical discourse as understood in its conceptual dimension.

Happenstance is exemplary in this sense. Both its images and the text which interacts with them are electronically generated (by a Rutt/Etra synthesizer) and can therefore be converted into each other. The text explodes, melts, catches fire, and, when one supposes that it has now turned into pure images, its particles fly over the space appearing first as birds, then as ideograms of some unknown language, and, finally, as Western characters which spread out, are superimposed, inverted, and join up to form new words. The written and spoken sentences do not coincide, but combine in a certain counterpoint. Sometimes, the pronunciation of a word or syllable coincides with its visual appearance on the screen. At others, the pronounced word contradicts, mirrors, or inverts that which is being said in writing. During its rigorously condensed 6.5 minutes, *Happenstance* flows with a musical rhythm and structure, continuously alternating or transforming the visible and the legible. Like a black hole which sucks in all sense, the video evolves toward absolute opaqueness. "The words are coming/ Listen to them/ Nothing surrounds them/ They are open/ They speak of nothing but themselves/ With perfect reason," says Hill's voice on the sound track. If the signs murmur and ruminate their material features, it is not because they wish to say anything ("The silence is always there"), but because they endeavor to disentangle themselves from all their semantic burdens in order to at last convert themselves into that language being of which Valéry spoke.[2] "They (the words)," continues Hill in *Happenstance*, "sit like deer in a field/ If I approach them too quickly/ They fade into the quick of things."

URA ARU (the backside exists), in turn, is a radical reinvention of the palindrome as a resource for investigating the erratic adventure of meanings. During a trip to Japan, Hill was surprised by the enormous quantity of specular words in the Japanese language, in other words,

words which can be read backward, as in "ano onna" ("that woman"). With the help of experts in that language, Hill conceived a video in which the inversion of the tape movement allowed the reverse playback of both the words (written and spoken) and the dynamics of the images, but in which the inversion always resulted in a new sense. Sometimes the palindrome effect also contaminates the English, the language used initially just for subtitling and translating the Japanese mirror games, but soon drawn upon in order to construct inverted word pairs such as *live/evil,* or in order to interfere with the Japanese constructions through cuts and reediting. In general it is almost impossible to know, in each shot of *URA ARU,* whether the pictures and the words were registered in the order which we see them on the screen, or in the contrary direction, only to be inverted at the moment of being shown to the viewer. At any rate, the inverted world—the reversion of everything to the contrary—brings to the surface another dimension of reality, which we could never imagine living alongside our familiar world, a dimension which is the other of the same. By making words and things show their opposite two sides simultaneously, *URA ARU* forces us to see ambiguity in the very state of meaning. We recall that, according to Mikhail Bakhtin,[3] inversion has heuristic value in all culture: it allows us to take a divergent look at the world, a look not yet framed by civilization's halter, so as to make perceptible the relativity of values and the circumstantiality of power and knowledge. But all this is articulated in *URA ARU* with a precision and economy the like of which can only be found in the Japanese art of haiku.

Before being able to make this dense and sophisticated work, *URA ARU,* materialize, Hill rehearsed with a previous experiment with inverted images and sounds, an equally important work known as *Why Do Things Get in a Muddle?* (1984), sometimes referred to by its subtitle *Come on Petunia* (which, with the shuffling of the letters at the end of the work, is transformed into the anagram "Once Upon a Time"). Fundamentally, the video is based on the first meta dialogue by Gregory Bateson,[4] with a little seasoning from Lewis Carroll's *Through the Looking Glass.* Bateson defines meta dialogue as a conversation whose presentation structure is capable of reflecting the problem under discussion. The conversation revolves around the problem of entropy: in the universe, there is a greater tendency for things to become disorganized and to lean toward chaos than the contrary. Sometimes, says Bateson, during movie credits before a film we see a bunch of shuffled letters, which then start moving around the screen changing position, until they form the name of the film. This could give us the impression that order is born of chaos. But this situation is only possible, he maintains, because movies invert the real process: in fact, the camera films the process of disorganization and shuffling of the letters backward, starting with the correctly written title.

Now, what Gary Hill does, remaining faithful to Bateson, is to reenact this dialogue between the philosopher and his daughter (the latter substituted in the video by Carroll's Alice) with a meta dialogue structure, in other words, "in a manner of presentation capable of reflecting the problem under discussion."[5] Thus, for the greater part of the video's duration, the images and sounds are inverted, in other words, we see and hear backward, with the tape running backward. But—and this is the video's most paradoxical aspect—at the time of recording, the actors (the poet Charles Stein and performer Katherine Anastasia) speak their texts backward, and also make their gestures and movement backward as well. Thus, by inverting images and dialogue which has already been inverted by the actors themselves, the camera ends up producing the contrary effect, in other words, it reconstitutes them in the original and "correct" order. But the reconstitution is an artifice which it is impossible to disguise: even if the movements are correct and the dialogues coherent and intelligible, it is clear to the viewer that everything is backward. It is as if an internal corrosion process contaminated all the dialogue and continually threatened them with dissolution. One never knows exactly which way the tape is running: sometimes, it wavers simultaneously between the two directions. When Alice says: "Here on the end of this shelf," the tape reverts to its initial direction, transforming *shelf* into *flesh,* and then *flesh* into *shelf* again and then again and again successively in endless motion, like an acoustic palindrome.[6] And so, the dialogues about entropy themselves end up suffering the effects of entropy and disarrange themselves, continually leaning toward incoherence and chaos.

The greatest dream of all artists since time immemorial has been to conceive an entire spectacle capable of synthesizing all the arts. This dream, which lies at the heart of Japanese theater, Chinese opera, Wagnerian opera, classical and modern dance, and talking motion pictures, is revived with full force in Hill's work, in a contemporary and electrified version. Eisenstein[7] called this systematic striving toward synaesthesic art "synchronization of the senses," art capable of invoking all the senses at the same time and synchronously. Many artists (including Eisenstein) made valuable contributions to this objective, but Hill has discovered singular and wholly elegant alternatives for making the voice, text, and image combine in a unique tessitura. The first of them simply consists of making some physical action (the pressure of hands or the cumulative weight of sand) interfere with the reproduction of sound from a loudspeaker. The idea is amazingly simple, but the result is explosive. In work such as *Soundings* (1979) or *Mediations* (1986), the timbre, pitch, volume, and intelligibility of the voice reproduced by a loudspeaker are modified as the apparatus suffers varied interferences operated in sight of the viewer. It is as if the image were capable of modifying sound. Another great contribution by Hill in this area (which was to become his registered trademark) was the discovery of an editing method which causes the duration of pictorial shots to coincide with the duration of syllables pronounced on the sound track. Thus, the flux of images is "punctuated," or marked rhythmically by syllabic time. One must consider, however, that there is already a change of focus in the acoustic level conception and this is exactly what aids the image synchronization: the syllables are pronounced in strongly marked rhythms, reminding one of the staccato technique in musical discourse. It is as if the voice were in fact more a percussion instrument than a mechanism for communication. Meanwhile, the images evolve in a much faster rhythm than in any conventional video, since the cuts occur at the speed of the syllables. In some cases, the time each shot remains on screen is beyond the limits of visualization, and it is just this effect of effacing the images which Hill wishes to explore. The images are forever placed on this misty frontier between the figurative reference and that opaqueness, which reduces them to pure textures or abstract stains. The results obtained through this method of synchronization are surprising, and can be seen in the various videos which adopt it: *Around & About* (1980), *Primarily Speaking* (1981–83), or *Site Recite (a prologue)* (1989).

In the first, we have an obsessively self-centered treatise, as if the video were reflecting on its own state of existence, permanence, and relationship with the viewer. "I mean if you want to leave," says Hill on the sound track, "you can do that or you can just turn off. I'm not trying to say that I'm indifferent. I just think there's a way here." Accompanying the rhythm of these words, the screen displays minimum fragments of almost unrecognizable objects which apparently have nothing to do with each other. Hill thus proposes a game with the viewer: that he or she tries to relate these fragments as far as possible and let the senses form and undo themselves in his or her mind, but without worrying about coping with it all. Something will certainly remain at the end of the experience. "I've never lost sight of that. I don't think there's been a loss of anything."

Primarily Speaking is a little more complex. Here, that which is synchronized with the voice is not merely the cut from one shot to another, but also movements (drops of water, for example) which occur within each shot. Here, instead of a plain image like in *Around,* we have a complex composition, obtained through the juxtaposition of two different images (separately edited "windows") and a background which ironically combines different details of the television color bars. On the sound track we also have two distinct voices which talk to each other (and to the images), confronting and transforming idioms, clichés, and current English phrases. The two voices are recorded in stereo in such a way as to allow the voice on the left to be synchronized with the right-hand image, and vice versa. There is an intricate process of interaction between the two images and the two voices: at times they complement each other, at others they deny themselves, invert their respective senses like a mirror game, or reveal that which the others tried to hide or disguise, and so on. Sometimes, the two voices enter a metalinguistic process and start discussing the almost chaotic situation which they are creating, not rarely interrogating each other, about the possibility of anything coherent emerging from it ("Double talking will get us nowhere," says one of the voices). But as in all of Hill's work, what matters is not actually getting anywhere, but experimenting with the paradoxical process of contradiction and dispersion of the meanings, and all its consequences.

In *Site Recite (a prologue),* the syllabic synchronization is no longer constructed through the editing or the internal movement of the images, but through focusing and blurring, which allow for the appearance and disappearance of pictures along the depth of field. The camera travels around a large round table on which scores of objects are placed, mostly the remains or pieces of organic forms (bones, empty eggshells, butterfly wings, creased paper, human and animal skulls), the majority of which are out of focus and impossible to identify. From time to time, the incessant variation in focus and the camera's movement make a few details of the object visible for a fraction of a second, and this movement of disclosure and defacing follows the paused rhythm of the oral speech. Here, Hill's text (recited by actor Lou Helter) is already far denser, much more polysemic and impenetrable than in any of his previous work. Just as the sophistication of his work with video has grown, Hill has also become an increasingly mature writer, whose discourse has lost its most immediate frames of reference in order to deal with and carve out complex linguistic forms. "I must become," says the voice on the sound track, "a warrior of self-consciousness and move my body to move my mind to move the words to move my mouth to spin the spur of the moment." At the disconcerting end of *Site Recite,* the camera places itself at the least possible and most unthinkable position in order to produce an image: in the interior of the mouth which speaks, making the point of view of the person seeing coincide with the point of origin of his or her voice, the place of the phonetic apparatus, as if it were possible to listen to what the eye sees, or see what the ear hears. Just then, the mouth opens, letting light into the speaking device, the tongue moves, and the teeth masticate the video's last words: "Imagining the brain closer than the eyes."

We come, finally, to Gary Hill's definitive tour de force in the field of video: *Incidence of Catastrophe* (1987-88). The work is based—sometimes strictly and at others loosely—on the novel by Maurice Blanchot, *Thomas l'Obscur,* as well as on the experience of watching his own son learn to speak. In fact, it isn't a translation or audiovisual version of Blanchot's work, but that which Haroldo de Campos[8] much more appropriately calls *transcreation.* Blanchot is anyway untranslatable into any form other than the verbal, since the world which he presents is a specifically *written* one, a world in which the words registered on the page are true characters, a *typographic* world, so to speak. Hence the double transgressive character of Hill's undertaking. In the novel, Thomas is to begin with concentrating on reading a book when, suddenly, he feels he is being watched by the words, as if they were eyes spying on him from the jungle of the text. Alone in his room at night, the character is attacked by a strange illness, a sort of logorrhea or verbiage, which causes him to hallucinate progressively as he gets deeper into the book.

The Thomas of the video also finds himself engrossed in reading a book, which is none other than *Thomas l'Obscur.* During the video's 43 minutes, Thomas becomes more and more tormented by the text, not by what it says, but by what it represents *physically* and by its *material* threat: the text (that is, the words, the phrases, the paper, and the pages) drive him into a world of nightmares, it becomes a forest of verbal signs where the character gets lost or drowns, a forest that cuts him, penetrates his body so violently that he becomes incapable of controlling himself. Thomas tries to vomit the text which has taken hold of him, but the verbal virus has dominated him and completely transformed him. The words start corroding. The metaphor of land sliding every time someone pronounces a word is called for to designate the demise of language as a bridge of contact between us, others, and the world. Left naked in front of the astonished guests at a banquet, Thomas is attacked by glossolalia and begins writhing on the floor, mumbling incoherent phrases as if he were returning to the origins of language. In the end, he curls up into the fetal position amid his own feces, at the same time wildly stammering meaningless words, and the pages of the book grow immeasurably around him, surrounding him, becoming, as Lynne Cooke[9] observed, a monumental structure of imprisonment.

Rarely has a text been shown on the screen with such corrosive force and rarely have the iconic, acoustic, and even kinetic aspects of words been shown in such structural evidence, placing their nerves on display. In each new work, Hill reinvents the course of poetry and gives his creative paths new direction, incorporating (but also subverting) the new technical possibilities of editing, synchronization, interference, and metamorphosis made available by new electronic and digital methods. During a discussion about Heidegger's ideas about art and technology, Hill[10] points out that the things he has been exploring in recent years are an attempt to demonstrate that, in a sense, video technology prompts a new poetic form which he defines as a sort of electronic linguistics. Just like our greatest writers and poets, Hill has gone to the extreme limits of the problems of language and meaning, above all, in its crises and problematic aspects. But, unlike philosophers and other poets, he has also taken the discussions about technological systems seriously and to their final consequences, above all into those nooks and crannies which affect sensibility and conscience. As Bruce Ferguson has said,[11] Hill is one of those rare poets who has succeeded in producing an authentic intertextual experience in the field of crossing representation with technology, and not merely the metaphor of one with the means of another. "For it is only by creating an actual situation of indeterminacy in which the audience can truly experience the effects of language and technology simultaneously that the possibilities of either can be assessed. And that their poetics may be felt."[12]

Notes

1. Christine van Assche. "Interview with Gary Hill." *Galleries Magazine*, December/January 1991, p. 77.

2. Paul Valéry. *Oeuvres.* Paris, Gallimard, 1960, p. 1324.

3. Mikhail Bakhtin. *A Cultura Popular na Idade Média e no Renascimento.* São Paulo, Hucitec, 1987.

4. Gregory Bateson. *Metadiálogos.* Lisboa, Gradiva, 1972, pp. 9–17.

5. Ibid., p. 7.

6. Steven Kolpan. "Bateson Through the Looking Glass." In *Gary Hill: Sites Recited.* Long Beach, Long Beach Museum of Art, 1994, p. 10.

7. Sergei Eisenstein. *The Film Sense.* London, Faber & Faber, 1968, pp. 60–91.

8. Haroldo de Campos. *Deus e o Diabo no Fausto de Goethe.* São Paulo, Perspectiva, 1981.

9. Lynne Cooke. "Ruminations on a Rapacious Loquacity." In *Gary Hill: Spinning the Spur of the Moment,* Holly Willis, ed. Irvington, Voyager, 1994, p. 9.

10. Stephen Sarrazin. "A Discussion with Gary Hill." *Chimaera Monographie,* no. 10, 1992, p. 83.

11. Bruce Ferguson. "Deja Vu and Deja Lu." In *Gary Hill,* Chris Bruce, org. Seattle, Henry Art Gallery, 1994, p. 21.

12. Ibid.

Heinz Liesbrock

Loss Illuminates

Midnight Crossing as an Approach to a Language of the Living and
The Dead

Gary Hill has inscribed his own dimension of depth into the
medium of video. Again and again, his work analyzes the customary
ways of using the medium, breaks through its endless, seemingly un-
problematic stream of images, and emphasizes the fact that the mere reproduction of what is visible, and the machine's alleged capacity for
simulation, are not sufficient to create an adequate horizon of meaning.
In his eyes, more is required if this machine is to be made into a driving
force for artistic cognition. Hill, as his works demonstrate, still regards
the camera and the screen as alien instruments. Although he is a master of the technical skills involved and of all the ways in which images
can be manipulated using the computer, in his hands these are nevertheless only tools, the real potential of which is still quite unclear and
needs to be freshly discovered in each work.

Through the way in which he shatters their image sequences until
they are seemingly unrecognizable, and significantly alienates the accompanying verbal text, his works refuse the quick comprehensibility,
the absorption into a one-dimensional narrative context, that the medium otherwise offers. And it is precisely the search for a dimension of
meaning in the images that is utterly their own, bringing out their
strangeness in contrast to words, that is a central concern in Hill's
work. In view of the flood of undifferentiated images, devoid of meaning, that accompany us in today's world, particularly through the in-

Originally published in *Gary Hill: Midnight Crossing* (Münster: Westfälischer
Kunstverein, 1997).

creasing omnipresence of television, tremendous emphasis is given here to the question of the remaining potential of the image, its special form of cognition and communication. "I think the most difficult aspect of using video in an installation is decentralizing the focus on the television object itself and its never-ending image. How does one get away from that everyday seduction of the continuous flow of images couched as information?"[1] To undermine the viewer's accustomed perceptual routine, to set in motion a new capacity for discernment, Hill has developed an aesthetic strategy involving multiple blurring of the image, distributing the image sequence over several monitors, and switching the set on and off. This rhythm is accompanied—also as a way of contradicting the logic of the images—by ambiguous verbal phrases, which often concentrate more on the material quality of the sound of language than on its semantic dimension. This systematic destruction of a false appearance of intactness in images at the same time describes the core of a coherent artistic language in the medium of video. This language appears to be a difficult one, precisely because it does not simply record a reality already known to us. Each formulation is at the same time a search, which is why it gives an appearance of stammering, progressing only hesitantly, pausing again and again to examine itself before preparing to speak once again. Analysis and poiesis, the construction and disintegration of meaning, form the interrelated facets of this conception of the work.

Midnight Crossing, like Hill's earlier works, expresses such a process of reflection and contradiction of the customary use of the medium. At the same time, the work has a special unity and even a monumentality of its own. The earlier dismantling of images and abandonment of the semantic primacy of language are replaced here by a concentration on more extended film sequences which, projected onto a single screen, are presented in an alternating rhythm with clearly articulated words and sentences. This structural change appears to be determined by a need to convey the question of the adequacy of images beyond the sphere of the aesthetic and of formal investigation, into a fundamental dimension in which reflection, emotion, and deep-reaching memory are inseparably bound together. In this way, an existentially attuned epic arises that tells of humanity's attempt to place itself in relation to external reality through the image, to clarify this essential point of contact between the inward and outward worlds. The examination of the image is therefore not primarily related here to any retinal activity in the eye—although this too, as we will later recognize, is subjected to an

acute test. Instead, the experience of seeing acquires a world-encom-
passing dimension. *Midnight Crossing* expresses a gaze that is explicitly
making an effort to depict—in the sense of forming an idea—and to
define what all the diversity of reality essentially means to it, and which
through this process is attempting to position itself adequately in relation to that diversity. A dialogue with the visible world is here simultaneously and explicitly a means of creating meaning. It is this element of
comprehensive orientation that determines every level of the work.

And this is why in *Midnight Crossing* the specific site of presentation
of the image acquires a significance, which is greater perhaps than in
any of Hill's other projects, for what we experience as the "work." In a
completely blacked-out room—in which usually we literally can't see
our hands in front of our faces—images are projected onto a screen set
up on an aluminum frame. This stream of images is interrupted at ir-
regular intervals by dazzling flashes of light, which are accompanied by
a voice speaking individual words, or a coherent sentence. When the
projection has been interrupted by the light, a new image is only established slowly, and it remains weak even though its sharpness of contrast
and brightness increase. This may provide an initial characterization of
the work.

For the visitor entering, the initially exclusive impression is one of a
massive, monumentally unstructured darkness. No opportunity for visual perception emerges beyond oneself, and only gradually does one
begin to perceive in the distance a diffuse image in the otherwise
blurred darkness. As its dimensions are impossible to guess at, the room
gives the impression of being darkness itself, a nonplace that provides
none of the distinctions familiar to us on which we base our sensory
orientation. The web of distance and closeness, brightness and darkness, the color shading that normally constitute objects with their own
characteristics, all have no place here. We have been robbed of a central
aspect of what constitutes reality for us. Without the capacity to see, we
feel helpless and in danger. "If I have a position," Hill once remarked,
"it's to question the privileged place that image, and for that matter
sight, hold in our consciousness."[2] This determined transformation of
a space in an art gallery, in which one is usually concerned precisely
with experiencing sensory differentiations, undoubtedly implies another
of those impediments to perception strategically deployed by Hill in
order to restore to sight a productive dimension that is otherwise sub-
merged. The whole point lies in the extremeness of the blackout. The
room is converted into a laboratory in which even the slightest percep-

tion of sensory differentiation requires an explicit effort—and in which, at the same time, our self-perception is enhanced, because the core of the dialogue with the external world that otherwise supports us has been disturbed. The same search for orientation that we suggested above as the theme of the image sequences has to be carried out by viewers entering the room, before they have found their bearings. On the way in, one is confronted in an utterly fundamental, genuinely rudimentary way with oneself—as a body, as an organism listening and feeling for its way and desperately looking for support in order to establish itself in a sphere that is alien to it. But this loss of the multiplicity of stimuli from the visual world causes an intense concentration in our entire perceptual apparatus, not merely the sense of sight, so that one's perception becomes receptive to the most delicate nuances. *Midnight Crossing* thus describes a zone of transition: beyond the structures that usually guide us, deprivation transforms itself into a wealth of perception and meaning. In this way, we are prepared for the special meaning that we are about to meet in the images.

Like the dark space surrounding us, the video sequences are also characterized by a special quality of compactness, a lack of sensory differentiation, which leads us beyond the horizon of everyday experience. It is only very slowly that they condense at all into a perceptible form. Hesitantly, a diffusely colored field forms out of the deep darkness—the first, weak source of light, which expands to the size of an oblong projection screen. What we recognize first is movement, and gradually this condenses into a contoured image, although we are still far from being able to say what it shows. More basic than this what, to begin with, however, seems to be the process of differentiation that is taking place along with each sequence. Out of the undifferentiated totality there arise movement, space, color, and shadowy shapes that then condense into landscape, animals, objects, human beings. We are witnessing a process of creation, and we are also explicitly contributing to it ourselves, since the ability of our eyes to adapt is challenged in an extraordinary way as they try to grasp the formation of phenomena out of darkness.

This strain on our visual ability to take things in continues when, at the end of each image sequence, the room is blazingly illuminated by a series of sudden flashes of stroboscopic light. For the first time, we can now more or less recognize the size and shape of the room and see the portable frame of the projection screen, like one from an open-air movie theater, and we realize there are other visitors to this strange and minimally equipped movie house. Hill has remarked that the movie theater is a place in which images and sight meet in an extraordinary fashion.[3] In the allusion to movies, what he is concerned with is surely the restoration of images in a quasi-mythical dimension that is defined in a purely sensory fashion, and which cannot be captured in conceptual and discursive terms. However, his target is also always the tense relationship between image and language. He brings out the different premises that underlie the two, placing them in a relationship in which they are incapable of simply dissolving into one another. His cinema is a reflexively oriented form that is not a blind victim to the sensory power of images.[4] Another central work of Hill's dating from 1991 is entitled *Between Cinema and a Hard Place,* and characteristically, in the case of this work as well, an artistic and a discursive form of cognition are placed in relation to one another. In this work, images from a natural, landscape-like sphere are "accompanied" by a passage from Martin Heidegger's essay "The Essence of Language," which conceives of poetry and thinking as two "ways of saying," as equally valid paths of assimilating reality in which "the letting-appear of the world occurs."[5] Poetry and thinking, a poetic point of view that is creative in the original sense of the word, and a reflective point of view, also define the structure of *Midnight Crossing.* The two points of view, as we shall see, share an equal interest in the process of cognition.

Of course, the sequences of images initially dominate our attention more strongly; their presence appears to be more immediately captivating than the few words, spoken together with the light, that interrupt their flow. But the images remain peculiarly silent about the basis for this impression. It is a silence that is not based on their acoustic muteness, but on the unapproachability with which they initially reject our attempts to categorize them and integrate them into our horizon of meaning. When the images, emerging out of utter diffuseness, begin to differentiate themselves from one another materially, we can certainly link what we see with words that seem to be familiar to us. We can recognize roaming dogs, a bird ascending in flight, a richly formed flower, a distant view over an asphalt road that reaches to the horizon; or we see a pair of clasped hands, a woman's face, a market square and a group of musicians playing. But at the same time, we are still aware that it is not really a question of this type of identification. The verbal approximation does not break through the strangeness of the images. More important than the names of the objects is the suggestive force with which these phenomena reveal themselves to us. The special intensity of a gaze is expressed through them, the unreserved attention of a perceiving subject to visible reality. To this perceiving subject, it seems to us, the world appears with the magical quality of a first moment, without a firmly defined horizon, not hemmed in by the pattern of categories in which the things we encounter usually already have a set place. Here, however, we seem to be witnessing a primordial orientation within an immense openness. We are observing the unfolding of a genuinely self-oblivious gaze that has brought no preconceived meaning along with it, except for an urgent interest in what it encounters. The first fenceposts are being hammered in that will define what "world" might mean. Accordingly, the camera often looks for things in close-up. The careful way in which it touches them recalls the groping of a hand that is not guided by a conscious eye. The camera moves with no regard for the physical unity of the phenomena, and the hierarchical concepts that usually help us to structure reality are still unfamiliar to it. As if in a dream, everything here seems equally significant. We see variety, but—whether living or not—it always reports one and the same.[6] What is visible and its meaning collapse into a unity. What it is cannot be separated from its appearance. The gaze lies in the midst of phenomena.

Evidence of one of the few genuinely successful encounters between poetry and the fine arts is found in Rainer Maria Rilke's letters, in which he describes the art of Paul Cézanne. This encounter provides a parallel that may help to explain the special quality of this type of "unconditional" experience of the external world. Rilke's reflections followed an encounter with Cézanne's painting during the first comprehensive exhibition of the artist's work at the Salon d'Automne of 1907 in Paris. A series of letters which he wrote almost daily to his wife, the sculptress Clara Westhoff, during a two-week period that October contain insights that open up new perspectives in the understanding of Cézanne's art, which was then not yet widely known—insights that have by no means been superseded in the art-historical study of Cézanne's work since that time. The intensity with which Rilke analyzed Cézanne's work was due to a related artistic problem that he was trying to work out at the time in his own writing. Cézanne's art seemed to him to provide a model solution to this problem, since he saw his own questions as already having been answered in it.

As the poet sees it, his own and that of Cézanne converge in a fundamental attitude that is defined both aesthetically, on the one hand, and morally and existentially on the other. This attitude can be described as an objective form of speaking that turns to outward phenomena with an unreserved openness that has left any personally influenced meaning behind it. In one central passage in Rilke's letters, animals, with their special relation to the world, serve as a metaphor for this objectivity. In a passage that recalls the roaming dogs in the first sequence of images in *Midnight Crossing,* Rilke quotes the painter Mathilde Vollmoeller on October 12 about Cézanne's way of looking at his motifs: "Like a dog, he sat in front of it and simply looked, without any nervousness or secondary intentions."[7] In Hill, too, as this passage once again makes clear to us, the boundaries between the world of human beings and the animal and vegetable kingdoms become permeable. Since these areas are categorically linked, a potential nearness to all phenomena opens up, and humanity with its meanings does not enter into this special sphere. This restraint is a precondition not only for the cognition of phenomena in their own right, but also the basis for the creation of an aesthetic form that is actually adequate to this insight, which Cézanne termed "réalisation." A few days later, Rilke speaks of Cézanne's art as a "work that had no preferences any more, no inclinations, no spoiled choosiness." He goes on, "It is this limitless objectivity, resisting any interference in a alien unity, that makes Cézanne's portraits seem so offensive and comical to people."[8] The personal element dissolves in an act of looking that is direct and discreet in equal measures.

The point of view that is formulated in *Midnight Crossing* is based on an escape from the conditions of personal identity—which is probably only possible momentarily. To shed that scaffolding of meaning and of conceptions of the world that primarily constitutes our self-image, and which we therefore like to see reflected in our discourse with external reality, also opens up the possibility of a seemingly intentionless form of looking, to which what is visible reveals itself in the special richness of its phenomenality. As Robert Mittenthal observes, the center of the work is in a state of presubjectivity.[9] The title of the work, which is borrowed from video technology, also suggests the degree to which a point of view of this type fundamentally deviates from the conditions of the experiential pattern that normally defines us. *Midnight Crossing* refers to a kind of time shift, the paradoxical moment at which an apparently perfect electronic time measurement drops into a "hole" when it is unable to capture a specific time point, and therefore has to leap over it.[10]

The semantic horizon of the term, however, can also include the metaphorical crossing of a boundary in a moment of intense dark-ness—not only implying an absence of light, but equally a gloominess of mood.[11] In this sense, the images guide our minds momentarily, again and again, to levels beyond daylight consciousness. We are then led into a zone between waking and dreaming—a zone that we also un-derstand, however, to be an oscillation between life and death. We see that in the urgency of their appearance, these silent images, with their latently blurred outlines,[12] are not only reporting a reality that has arisen *before* the formation of subjective categories. Instead, they must also be seen as an approach to the point of view that we might have *af-ter* the dissolution of our identities as persons.[13] From a sphere between life and death, our gaze turns back once again to phenomena that have now become physically inaccessible, and sees that they have been im-bued with a richness of phenomenality that we were not able to grant them in life because our gaze usually only brushed their surfaces. Every single dot in the images appearing before us is now equally endowed with life. In this retrospective gaze that is nevertheless wholly shaped by the present, what is visible finally becomes permeable to what had al-ways remained hidden from us, and phenomena become interwoven in their innermost natures. Suddenly, we find ourselves in an unreserved vicinity to all phenomena. In the face of death, we cease to feel as indi-viduals and perceive ourselves as part of life itself.

"Have you ever noticed the relationship between possession and see-ing—you see it and you gotta have it?"[14] Again and again, Hill uses the blazing stroboscopic light and the voice that speaks alongside it to pre-vent the viewer from dissolving completely into the images that float as if disembodied in the dark space. The image disappears, and for a mo-ment we only see the blacked-out room and the scaffolding of the pro-jection screen, before the light goes out again and a further sequence of images begins to shape itself in the darkness. But before the first out-lines of a new image become visible, we go on seeing the afterimage of the projection screen and the shadowy figures of the other viewers, which the intense light has impressed on our retinas, as if reminding us of the material and species-specific preconditions for sight. For a mo-ment, the afterimage mingles with the resuming projection. The text, written and spoken by Hill himself, sections of which accompany each flash of light, serves here not so much to create images by making them seem to emerge from the sound of the voice.[15] Instead, its role is more that of a resonance chamber, reflecting on the meaning of the se-quences of images as it accompanies them, explaining them or contradicting them as required. And the text has a markedly poetic quality. It cannot be tied down to a single semantic line, and remains constantly ambiguous, building its effect on the material quality of the sound of words as well.

Nevertheless, a few central lines of meaning can be clearly recognized without any need for speculation. One of these is certainly described by the initial orientation within a reality whose meaning has not yet been firmly established: a point of view that also influences the sequences of images. "something /. . . / perhaps / one is / . . . / him / . . . / he she" are some of the words spoken at the beginning, describing a questing and hesitant recognition of another being.

A phrase that can be read as a coherent sentence, although it is scattered over several passages, later describes the inner connection between darkness and light and the fascination of observing the constant construction and decay of meaning: "even darkness / imparted a kind of brightness hidden within itself / it said, 'all is possible' with cruel circularity." The painful realization that there has been a total dissolution of any viewpoint capable of providing meaning—a dissolution that suddenly begins to spread unexpectedly, and against which nothing can be done—then becomes clear in the following central sequence of words: "outside / the belief / everything is burning / being extinguished by the many different hearths / separate fires engulfing one another with cold passion / each one working wherever it likes as it likes." This passage could be read as saying that the images, too, fail to provide an adequate path, in the face of a reality that is no longer defined transcendentally. The images reject our desire to make them a kind of home. Any attempt to converse with them always ends in aporia. When we try to address them, our words always go into the void. As in all of nature, these too contain a core of decay: "abruptly I look up counting / a moth flies into my mouth / mistaking the numbed words for light."

Notes

1. "Gary Hill, Inter-view," in *Gary Hill,* exhibition catalogue, Stedelijk Museum, Amsterdam/Kunsthalle, Vienna 1993/94, p. 16.

2. "A Discussion with Gary Hill," in Stephen Sarrazin, *Gary Hill: Surfing the Medium* (Belfort, 1992), p. 84.

3. In an unpublished description of *Midnight Crossing,* Hill describes the movie theater as being "the site of pictures."

4. "And yet, although my art is based on images, I am very much involved

in the undermining of those images through language" ("Gary Hill, Inter-view," p. 14).

5. The essay "The Essence of Language" is included in Martin Heidegger, *On the Way to Language,* tr. Peter D. Hertz (New York: Harper & Row, 1971), pp. 101–4.

6. Cf. Hill's statement about the structural openness of *Midnight Crossing* (*Gary Hill: Midnight Crossing* [Münster: Westfälischer Kunstverein, 1997], p. 24). According to Hill, the image sequences and the verbal phrases are not con-ceived of as being exclusive. This does not make them accidental, but it does make them fundamentally interchangeable.

7. Rainer Maria Rilke, letter to Clara Rilke of October 12, 1907. Cf. R. M. Rilke, *Letters on Cézanne,* ed. Clara Rilke, tr. Joel Agee (New York: Fromm In-ternational, 1985).

8. Letter to Clara Rilke of October 18, 1907.

9. Robert Mittenthal, "Presubjective Agency: Outside Identity" (*Gary Hill: Midnight Crossing* [Münster: Westfälischer Kunstverein, 1997]).

10. Cf. *Gary Hill: Midnight Crossing* (Münster: Westfälischer Kunstverein, 1997).

11. "Midnight" is defined as follows in the *American Heritage Dictionary*: "1. The middle of the night, specifically 12 o'clock at night. 2a. Intense darkness or gloom. 2b. A period of darkness and gloom." *The American Heritage Dictionary of the English Language,* ed. William Morris (Boston: Houghton Mifflin, 1980), p. 830.

12. According to Hill, the brightness and contrast in the image sequences in *Midnight Crossing* reach a maximum value of 40 percent of the normal settings.

13. A statement by Hill also underlines his interest in these themes: "Rather than characters and locations, whether or not they exist literally, my subjects are more akin to entropy, memory, consciousness and death" ("Gary Hill, In-ter-view," pp. 14–15).

14. Ibid., p. 13.

15. Hill has said regarding this procedure in relation to other works, "Vocal-ization was a way to physically mark the time with the body through utter-ance—the speaking voice acting as a kind of motor generating images" (Ibid., p. 13).

Air Raid, 1974. Black and white; 6:00. Photo: Courtesy Donald Young Gallery, Chicago, Ill.

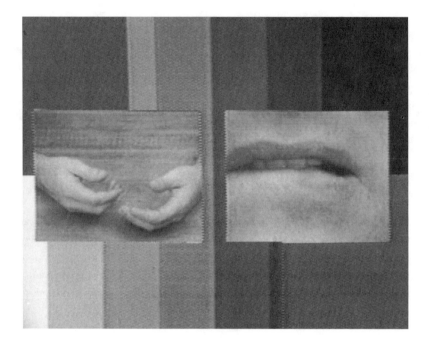

Primarily Speaking, 1981–83 (video still). Two-channel video/sound installation, two versions: 1. Eight monitors, four speakers, and controlling electronics; 2. Two monitors, chairs, and mirrors. Photo: Courtesy Donald Young Gallery, Chicago, Ill.

In Situ, 1986. Mixed-media installation: modified easy chair, modified monitor, six electric fans, sculptural elements, motorized paper feeder, controlling electronics, and speakers. Photo: Courtesy Donald Young Gallery, Chicago, Ill.

Incidence of Catastrophe, 1987–88 (details). Color; stereo sound; 43:51. Photos: Mark B. McLoughlin. Courtesy Donald Young Gallery, Chicago, Ill.

BEACON (Two Versions of the Imaginary), 1990 (detail). Two-channel video/sound installation: two television tubes mounted in an aluminum cylinder, projection lenses, motor, and controlling electronics. Installation: Stedelijk Museum, Amsterdam, 1993. Photo: Carl de Keyzer. Courtesy Donald Young Gallery, Chicago, Ill.

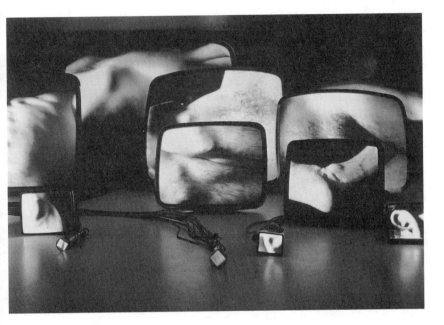

Inasmuch As It Is Always Already Taking Place, 1990 (details).
Sixteen-channel video/sound installation: Sixteen 0.5-inch to
21-inch black-and-white television tubes positioned in horizontal
inset in wall. Photos: Mark B. McLoughlin. Courtesy Donald
Young Gallery, Chicago, Ill.

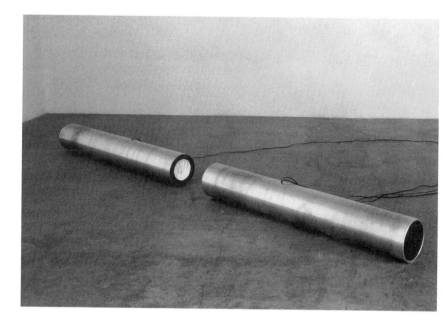

Cut Pipe, 1992 (details). Single-channel video/sound installation: black-and-white video monitor, projection lens, two aluminum cylinders, and three loudspeakers. Photos: Courtesy Donald Young Gallery, Chicago, Ill.

Tall Ships, 1992. Sixteen-channel video installation: sixteen
black-and-white monitors, sixteen projection units, sixteen laserdisc
players, and computer-controlled interactive system. Photos: Mark
B. McLoughlin. Courtesy Donald Young Gallery, Chicago, Ill.

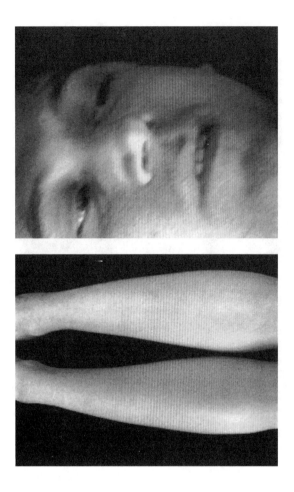

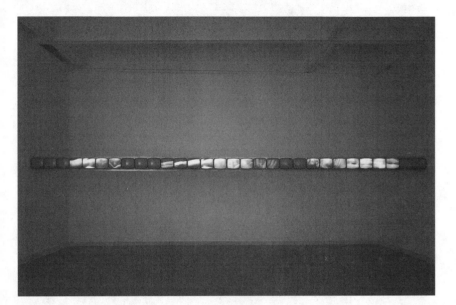

Suspension of Disbelief (for Marine), 1992 (details).Four-channel video installation: thirty 12-inch television tubes mounted on aluminum beam, four channels of video, four laserdisc players, and computer-controlled switching matrix. Photos: Courtesy Donald Young Gallery, Chicago, Ill.

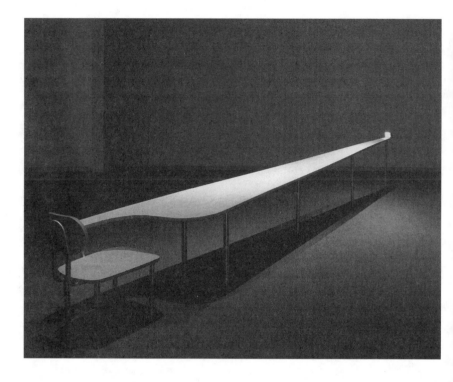

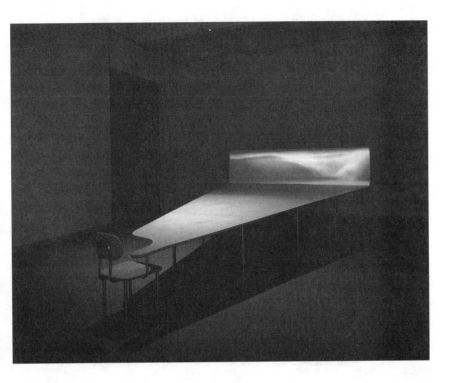

Learning Curve (still point), 1993. Single-channel video installation:
one 5-inch monitor, plywood chair/table construction.
Photos: Mark B. McLoughlin. Courtesy Donald Young Gallery,
Chicago, Ill.

Circular Breathing, 1994 (details). Single-channel video/sound installation: five color video projectors, laserdisc player, computer-controlled video switcher, amplifier, and two loudspeakers. Installation: Museum für Gegenwartskunst, Basel, Switzerland, 1994. Photos: Mark B. McLoughlin. Courtesy Donald Young Gallery, Chicago, Ill.

Withershins, 1995. Interactive sound installation with video projections: aluminum maze, electronic switch mats, two projectors, two disc players, computer-controlled location of sound on four speakers, two computers with sound cards, lights, synchronizer. Installation: Venice Biennale, Italy, 1995. Photos: Courtesy Donald Young Gallery, Chicago, Ill.

HAND HEARD, 1995–96. Five-channel video installation with
five color projections: five projectors, five laserdisc players, and
synchronizer. Installation: Museu d'art Contemporani, Barcelona,
Spain, 1998. Photo: Courtesy Donald Young Gallery, Chicago, Ill.

25:59:59:29 The Storyteller's Room, 1998. Twelve-channel
video/sound installation: twelve laserdisc players, twelve-channel
synchronizer, twelve 4-inch black-and-white monitors with
projection lenses and mounts, audio amplifier with multiple
loudspeakers, ten strobe lights, strobe controller, computer, foam,
rope, and miscellaneous cabling. Dimensions variable. Installation:
Capp Street Project, San Francisco, Calif., 1998. Photo: Ben
Blackwell. Courtesy Donald Young Gallery, Chicago, Ill.

Crossbow, 1999. Three-channel video/sound installation:
three 13-inch color LCD displays with built-in speakers, three
DVD players, synchronizer, and three DVD discs. Photo: Lynn
Thompson. Courtesy Donald Young Gallery, Chicago, Ill.

II Interviews

Lucinda Furlong

A Manner of Speaking

Although he is better known for his videotapes and installations, Gary Hill has also been prolific as a sculptor. Born in Santa Monica, California, in 1951, Hill moved east in 1969, and in the early 1970s began making videotapes at Woodstock (N.Y.) Community Video. Like those of many artists in the late 1960s and early 1970s, Hill's earliest tapes reflected a highly experimental approach in which the capabilities of various electronic imaging tools were explored. For the most part, this kind of video was visual in orientation, and Hill's work was no exception, drawing as it did on conventions of abstract expressionist painting. Eventually dissatisfied with the limitations of such an approach, Hill began to make tapes that integrated the audio and video components so tightly that sound became almost visually apprehensible. This concern—in which the immaterial is somehow made physical—is central to all of Hill's video installations and tapes, and to some extent, is derived from his background as a sculptor.

In his most recent work, however, language and thought—rather than electronics—are the immaterial entities that are given form. Hill's tapes since 1980 are of two types: short, descriptive, often convoluted passages which are sparely "illustrated" by abstract black-and-white imagery; and extended monologues that directly address the viewer, to which video is rapidly edited to the beat of Hill's voice. Although they differ greatly in tone, these tapes reveal Hill's exacting—almost obsessive —weighing of image and language as carriers of meaning. At the same time, they are richly evocative pieces that variously resemble poems, stories, and soliloquies. Hill's installations, too, bespeak his interest in setting up dichotomies between sight and sound, language and image.

Originally published in *Afterimage* (March 1993).

Hill has received production grants from the National Endowment for the Arts, the New York State Council on the Arts, and PBS-station WNET in New York. In 1981, he was awarded a video artists' fellowship from the Rockefeller Foundation. A 1982 recipient of the United States/Japan Exchange fellowship, Hill traveled to Japan in the fall of 1983. That summer he taught video at Bard College's M.F.A. program in video.

The following interview was edited from transcripts of two meetings in Barrytown, New York, on October 28, 1982, and January 5, 1983. The interview incorporates Hill's additions and revisions.

Lucinda Furlong: You worked in sculpture for a long time before you became interested in video.

Gary Hill: I got into sculpture in 1969, when I was 15, while I was still in high school in Redondo Beach. I had always been interested in art, and the brother of a friend of mine—Tony Parks—was a sculptor. He welded. I saw him working and was immediately drawn to the process. I had a summer job at a hamburger stand on the beach—a surfer's dream—so I saved money to buy welding tanks and started welding. Soon after that I was set up making sculpture in all my spare time, except for a little surfing. It's not that easy to give up.

Even though I had vague notions about the avant-garde, I really wasn't aware of American art. I was looking at Giacometti and Picasso. Picasso was a god to me.

I had lots of support from my friends and parents, in particular my high school teacher, Mr. Pelster, who just let me do my thing. He was a big reason why I even finished high school. I didn't see much point in it, and almost quit. When I got out, I saw a pamphlet for the Art Students' League in Woodstock, New York, which described it as an idyllic artists' colony. I came out for a month on a scholarship, but I didn't do sculpture. I just drew and painted, made thousands of drawings. Then I went back to California to go to a community college—partially for a draft deferment—but decided I would get out *another* way, and college definitely was not for me. I quit in about two weeks.

My teacher at the League—Bruce Dorfman—had invited me to work independently with him. So I packed my belongings and hopped in a driveaway car. I experienced my first fall, first snow, first being cold-as-shit, first super struggle. I didn't stay in that situation very long, though. I got jobs. Actually, I've been pretty lucky in terms of being able to do my work with very little struggle.

About that time, I began to see art in New York, and the thing that really overwhelmed me was a show at the Met called "1940–1970." It was the New York School. I was knocked out, and went through a lot of different attitudes in my own work. I still used the same materials, but I went from making cage-like structures with human forms—almost Bosch-like—to abstract biomorphic shapes mixed with geometric shapes. Pretty soon it was all geometric. I started using wire mesh, spray paint, welding armatures for shaped canvases which were incorporated into the work. I would make shapes, pile them into a corner, and then work with them later. It was like being my own factory. I went through a complete cycle of color. I slowly started to add color to the metal. I got very extreme using fluorescents, and later I toned down to metallics, essentially monochromatic, and finally back to the natural color of the material—copper-coated steel welding rods. I started improvising large constructions in the exhibition space, usually working off a wall and down to the floor into a kind of sprawl. I was working a lot with moiré patterns, and the sheer density of layers and shapes. Experimenting, burying myself in the process, working *all* the time. It wasn't intellectual. It was more like—how far can I take this material as a worker?

LF: How did you get involved with video?

GH: I got into sound first. I discovered the sculptures generated interesting sounds, lots of different timbres. The overall texture seemed to mirror what I was seeing. I worked a lot with loops and multitrack audiotapes, which later became an integral part of the sculpture.

Getting into video isn't so smooth in retrospect. I think at the time I was getting frustrated with sculpture. I needed a change. I was drawn more and more into working with sound. Around that time, Woodstock Community Video had been established. I walked up the stairs, knocked on the door, and said, "Gee, I'd like to try that. Can I take out a portapak?" So I did a performance/environment piece with a friend, Jim Collins. For four or five nights in a row, we painted colored rectangles in the town of Woodstock—all over everything, stores, private property, public property. They slowly appeared, 'til we got caught. I did a little—not really a documentary. . . . I just went out and talked about it with people, about what they thought. Should there be more colored rectangles? Should they go away? I really enjoyed the whole process, the experiential aspect of that little thing up there next to my eye. It seemed like there was a high energy connection to whatever I was looking at. I guess I became obsessed with that electronic buzz (*laughs*). It was like a synapse with the rest of the world in a removed way, yet attached at the same time.

So I exchanged work at Woodstock Community Video—recording town board meetings, or whatever Ken Marsh [the former director] wanted—in exchange for using the equipment. Sooner or later I got a job there, because NYSCA [the New York State Council on the Arts], which had been heavily oriented toward community video, switched to the art route—in video at least.

LF: When was that?

GH: Around 1973–74. I was given a salaried position as the TV lab co-ordinator, helping people to use the equipment. They had a few devices—a broken genlock unit and a keyer—put away because they didn't really work. So I asked Ken Marsh if I could come in late at night and see what I could make them do.

I totally got into that. Everything half worked. The keyers would put out really harsh, broken edges. I don't know *what* the genlock put out, but there was always something. I had monitors all over this little studio—rescanning everything, starting and stopping the tape, manipulating it with my hands. Everything was open. It was a very free feeling. Discovering how to manipulate this material was amazing.

I can remember being totally naked, lying on the floor with a tripod over my head pointing a camera down on my mouth and another camera lying on my stomach. I would make kind of a primal sound with my breathing, raising the camera on my stomach so that it would reveal my head from the bottom view, making this sound. This was all somehow mixed through a special effects generator. In a manner of speaking, I was practically fucking the equipment. Some time around then I made *Rock City Road* [1974–75].

LF: Were you colorizing the tapes?

GH: There was no colorizer there at first, but Ken was friends with Eric Siegel, and he got a Siegel colorizer fairly soon. About the same time, I found out about the Experimental Television Center [now in Owego,

N.Y.]. I didn't know about the equipment there; I just had heard that they had all these possibilities. With the tools I was using in Woodstock I saw an infinity of image-making possibilities, and they had a whole set that was much more sophisticated. . . . So I went up there and met Walter Wright [artist-in-residence at the Experimental Television Center from 1973 to 1975], and became very good friends with him. We did some multimedia performances together called *Synergism* [1975–76], with Sara Cook, a dancer in Woodstock. Then we started fantasizing about having our own machines, but it didn't really happen until 1976. Ken thought that Woodstock Community Video was going to be a media-organization-in-residence at Bard College. Everyone involved moved over to Rhinebeck, but it fell through at the last minute. So for a short time Barbara Buckner, Steven Colpan, and me all lived together as artists-in-residence. There we were in this big house and we weren't using all the rooms. I made Ken a deal—I asked if I could have David Jones come down to build some equipment, and I would pay extra rent [Jones, a video tool designer and builder, is now affiliated with the Experimental Television Center].

LF: What did he build?

GH: First we put together four input amps and an output amplifier. The main thing Walter and I wanted was a multichannel colorizer. Ironically enough, we never got to that. David had designed an analog-to-digital converter, which led to other things, culminating in a small frame buffer with a resolution of 64 by 64. One day I came home and David was gone. He had left the equipment on, and there was this digitally stored image on the screen of him smiling and waving. Suddenly colorizing seemed superficial, next to having access and control over the architecture of the frame in real time.

LF: Is that around the time you made *Windows?*

GH: No, the first tape I made using any digital processing was *Bathing* [1977], which was all done through the analog-to-digital converter. [In *Bathing,* a color tape shot in real time is intercut with stills rescanned with a color camera and digitized. Different placements of color and gray level are derived from rearranging the digital-to-analog output.] I'd record something, take the circuit board out, resolder the wires, and try it again until I got the images I wanted. It's just another way of working. It's like when I started at Woodstock Community Video: you mess around with the innards, where all this stuff really happens. It was a process of trial and error. Since I wasn't working so much with preconceived images, "control" wasn't a problem. There were always surprises—images that happened outside of control, things you wouldn't dream or think of.

LF: How did the converter change the image visually?

GH: Radically. It remaps the gray levels of an image and it also remaps the color you're mixing with it.

If it had any imposed framework, *Bathing* was centered around vague ideas of painting, taking traditional subject matter—a bather—and exploring it with the notion that any one frame could be a painting. *Windows* [1978] was the first tape in which I explored the idea of mixing analog and digital images together. I did it as a study for an installation that would have been similar in nature—dense, layered images, structured compositionally, but on several monitors. The images would pass between monitors, all under automated control. No tapes. I was still working intuitively, feeding off the images, seeing an image, liking it, working with it.

In those early tapes, though, I was distracted by the phenomena of electronics—several tapes were really part of that learning process. I'm glad I went through it—to have the knowledge and to feel free to do what I want within the medium. But if I never do something strictly imagistic again, it wouldn't matter. The knowledge of how things work is embedded now; it applies itself to whatever I'm doing.

LF: Those early tapes seem to fit what has become a genre of video art—image processing.

GH: I think there's a big problem even with the term. What does "image processing" refer to? Any tape that has processed an image electronically?

LF: It is too broad. It can mean video put through a time-base corrector or something that's been colorized.

GH: Yeah, but when someone says "image processing," what automatically comes to mind is a heavily mixed collage, like *Windows* (*laughs*), that I can't possibly decode—in fact I can't even see the point of using color. When you look at a painting, you can't always verbalize why the artist used a color or shape, but you feel some kind of visual tension, something getting at you. So much that I see that falls under "image processing" I can't even fathom.

When I first started working with machines, and exploring images— around the time I was working with Walter Wright—I remember him calling tapes *Processed Video I, Processed Video II,* etc. But process had no reference to machines. It had to do with the process of working, an improvisational situation in which devices could be patched in a number of different ways. Image processing suggests taking known or fixed images and processing them, sort of like food processing. I think for *some* people who are put in this category, it was an open method of working—dialoguing with the tools in search of images.

LF: Did others think of it this way, too?

GH: I don't know. The Vasulkas had to be among the first to experiment with the properties inherent to video. They were certainly more methodical than anyone else. Whatever machine they had, they explored it to the *n*th degree. When I think of their work chronologically, the development is razor-sharp, didactic, yet mysteriously powerful, especially Woody's. Steina, I think, became more idiosyncratic, and that's probably why they present themselves as two separate artists now. Between the two of them they've covered a lot of ground.

This experimental notion of dialoguing with tools has its tradition, though. It's like what filmmakers did. That's why—in the end—it was no longer interesting for me. Okay, it's video, it's electronic, it functions differently, it has different properties—but it's the same approach that photographers and filmmakers already applied. I started to see it as a dead end. I wanted to dialogue with my mental processes, consciously, self-consciously.

LF: How important do you think it is for viewers to know the technical circumstances under which a tape was produced?

GH: It's an element, part of the information that's valuable. But I think that for anything to work, it has somehow to translate that. Some works do and some don't; all the explaining in the world and all the complex electronics and knowing the insides of the machine won't do anything. It's a difficult question. You can't sidestep the mechanics of the medium, but it's not what makes something. A whole different shift occurs in putting a work together—materializing it—and perceiving it. If a piece really works for you, your response goes beyond a question about how it was made, although it might come up later as extra information.

LF: I agree, but it's something I think a lot about when I look at tapes that are exhausting or investigating the properties of video. They stop at a certain point. I "get it"—I understand what that tape is "about," and it ends there. It seems that *Primary, Elements, Mouth Piece, Sums & Differences* [all 1978], and *Objects with Destinations* [1979] not only investigate the properties of video, but how video and audio function both separately and as an integrated unit. They illustrate well how the two can operate on one another.

GH: But how video and audio function separately and together *are* the properties of video. What I was getting at is something else, granted a little more difficult to talk about. I think *Sums & Differences* really works in terms of sound and image actually becoming one another. [In this tape, four separate video images of four musical instruments and their corresponding sounds are sequenced together at a continuously increasing rate. Normally, a video image is scanned on the video raster at 60 cycles per second. As the rates of change increase, starting at about one cycle per second, switching becomes faster than the time it takes to scan the complete image. This produces an effect whereby all four images appear simultaneously on the screen in four, eight, twelve, etc. horizontal bars. When the switching rate is at higher frequencies, the different sounds, including the switching frequencies, become blurred into one, just as the different images become one image.] In that tape, audio and video can't be separated. There's a simultaneity of seeing and hearing.

If I were only investigating the "properties," I wouldn't have digitized the images, electronically generated the instrumental sounds, or used additional frequencies slightly out of phase with sync that slowly roll through the picture. These were also digitized, which created thin horizontal lines on the edges, that at certain times I associate with "strings." There's an overall energy constructed from a lot of subtle modulation. The question here becomes—Did I *add* things that weren't there, circumvent my own concept, seduce you, the viewer, into believing something that wasn't there? I think from this tape on a basic theme in my work became physicality. I no longer wanted to be behind the glass, playing jazz with my friends. I wanted to, you know, communicate—reach out and touch someone.

LF: *Picture Story* [1979] seems to represent a shift to how language is used to construct meaning. [In this tape, Hill's didactic voice-over describes a quality shared by four letters of the alphabet—H, I, O, and X. Whether they are written upside down or backward, their readability, and meaning, is essentially unchanged. As we hear this description, rectangles containing words referring not only to video, but to narrative and pictorial representation, randomly collapse into horizontal and vertical lines and points, whereupon a hand traces them. At the end of the tape, the four letters are used to draw an image of an ox. The letters thus form not only the basis of a story, but a picture as well.]

GH: It really wasn't a shift. Language simply became fair game, too. What I discovered in doing that piece was that there are these invisible properties—properties of language—that I could work with, rather than essentially mechanical or electronic properties. Structurally, perhaps even organically, in some way linguistics seemed related to electronic phenomena. I remember calling it "electronic linguistics." I really began to think of the mind as a kind of muscle, and wanted to physicalize its workings in some way. But I don't feel there was a jump from working with the elements of video to a plateau where I said, "Gee, I'm working with ideas now." I don't have any hard-and-fast rules about how I work.

LF: I'm not trying to impose any final categories on the development of your work, but as an observer of your tapes, I think that while your working process may have been the same, the end result isn't.

GH: In terms of development, *Ring Modulation* [1978] was just as pivotal as *Picture Story.* [In *Ring Modulation,* the video screen is divided into three sections. In the bottom portion, there's a close-up of hands holding a welding rod, attempting to bend it into a circle. As this happens, Hill's mouth vocalizes an "Ah" sound, which becomes distorted by the effort of bending the rod. In the upper portion of the screen, one box contains a full image of Hill bending the rod. The other contains a wavering circular image from an oscilloscope, generated by mixing Hill's unsteady voice with a steady electronic signal. If, instead of the voice, the second sound was a cosine of the first electronic signal, a circle would be produced.]

In *Ring Modulation,* there's a paradoxical struggle: trying to sculpt physical material into a circle and simultaneously trying to form a circle electronically with nonphysical material—waveforms. It's impossible to do. I did it as a kind of alchemical ritual, trying to change this "material." In this light, the copper coating of the welding rod took on other meanings in relation to the phosphorus green of the oscilloscope. When copper rusts, it turns green. *Ring Modulation* was, again, returning to working more physically, using sculptural concerns, getting back to things I had left hanging.

The installation *Mesh,* which I worked on during the same period, had similar concerns—trying to merge physical material and concepts into some sort of unifying tactile resonance. It was a fairly complex installation, in some ways a culmination of burying myself in circuit building. [In the installation, layers of wire mesh were mounted on walls; each layer contained one oscillator which generated a certain pitch depending on the size of the mesh. The pitch generated would pan between four speakers mounted on each layer of mesh. Hill used small (3-inch) speakers to give a metallic quality to the sound and to give the effect of the sound being "woven" into the mesh. Upon entering the space, the viewer-participant activated the piece, became "meshed" into it when a camera picked up his or her image. This image was digitally encoded, producing a grid effect, and was then displayed on the first of four monitors. Each person who entered the space generated a new image, which, when displayed on monitor one, cycled the previous image to monitor two, and so on.]

I didn't use discrete multiple channels in that piece—or *Primarily Speaking* and even *Glass Onion.* It's all dynamically controlled and interrelated, so that you're taking information and moving it in space, which is really interesting. I want to take this idea a lot further.

LF: You mean a kind of layering? I'm remembering *Soundings* [1979], where you put sand on an audio speaker, and it vibrates as the sound comes through. Then you go through variations—water, burning the speaker.

GH: I meant taking one or more images from cameras or tape and directing them out into different spaces, different monitors. Moving images in space. The work came about because I'd used a lot of mesh in my sculpture, and was interested in overlapping things to make a third element or pattern. Literally, the title refers not only to the material—the mesh—but compressing sound and image together. What was different about both *Mesh* and *Ring Modulation* was not only this preoccupation with physicality, but that an underlying concept was becoming increasingly more important. In the earlier works, there was much more of a visual orientation.

LF: Was *Mesh* your first video installation?

GH: Actually, the first was *Hole in the Wall,* done in 1974 at the Woodstock Art Association. Unfortunately, the only remaining element of the piece—a tape—was destroyed by accident. You have to see it in light of the political-social context of the Woodstock Art Association, where there's an old guard, and there are always new people around who want to get in. When I was involved with it, it was always a hotbed of controversy.

I set up a camera and zoomed in on a wall, framing an area approximately actual size when displayed on a 23-inch monitor. On the video screen, you saw a hand with a ruler drawing a frame on the edge of the screen. A matte knife entered the frame, cut the muslin surface on the wall, and then various tools were used to cut through a number of layers—plasterboard, fiberglass, etc.—to the wall outside. At one point, we reached structural beams. The camera zoomed in and framed a smaller frame. Then that was cut through to the outside. At the opening, a monitor was fitted into the hole, and played back the tape performing the action. When the camera zoomed in, I took the big monitor out, put a smaller one in, and then at the end of the tape, when you see outdoors, I took the monitor away.

Besides the fighting between the older, established artists and the younger ones trying to break into the scene, the Woodstock Art Association didn't consider video an art form. It wasn't until the mid-1970s that they accepted photography! So the political implications are obvious, and formally the piece contained reverberations of drawing, painting, sculpture, video, and conceptual art. What made it even more interesting at the time was that an art critic, Irwin Touster, mentioned the piece in the local paper, *The Woodstock Times,* with a statement like "Hill's *Hole* is a monumental act of hostility in the guise of art." I sent a letter to the editor which simply read: "Re: Irwin Touster's review . . .

a rebuttal," with a large photograph, taken in the gallery, of my ass sticking through the hole.

So that was my first installation.

LF: Getting back to how your work changed, *Around & About* seems like a big leap.

GH: It was. I was talking in the first person directly to the viewer. When I was making *Windows,* for example, I never dreamed—it was the farthest thing from my mind—that I would use language. Now language seems like it will never go away. It's like a monkey on my back.

In the summer in 1979, I just started writing. I wrote the texts that ended up in *Equal Time* [the tape was done in 1979; an installation of the same title was shown at the Long Beach Museum of Art in March 1982], *Picture Story,* and a few of the *Videograms* texts. In the first month of 1980, I made *Processual Video, Black/White/Text,* and then, shortly after, I made *Around & About.* That was a very prolific time for me.

LF: Someone told me *Around & About* came from your frustration with your class at the State University of New York at Buffalo—that you couldn't communicate with the students.

GH: That's not true. I had to move suddenly, and I was also going through some heavy changes in a relationship. I had to move all my things, my studio, into my office at SUNY. Those two things coinciding put me on the edge. I had a lot of anxiety, and was paralyzed in terms of what to do. I sat down and wrote the text very quickly, as if I were talking out loud. I think the idea of editing the images to the syllables of my speech came out of this frustrating situation. It was almost as if I wanted to abuse the images, push them around, manipulate them with words. Maybe I was trying to expand this tiny little space, persuade the woman I lived with of the art-life paradox in plain English. On both accounts, I failed. I did the whole thing in my office, and each shot was set up and edited as I went along.

LF: So you wrote the text, laid it down as an audio track, and then plugged in images as you were shooting?

GH: Right. Even the concrete wall—where there's one layer of wall over another? I had two cameras. I would set up the matte, then zoom in the camera, then set it up again for each edit. And I edited it by hand. I didn't use a controller.

LF: That's amazing, because it looks like you used sophisticated equipment.

GH: People ask me if I used a Quantel. It's great to tell people how it actually was made—especially students—because then they don't feel intimidated about equipment.

The thing about *Around & About* is that I was able to use the image and the text as a single unit. Suddenly I began to think about how far the images could get from what I was saying and still have the tape work. The images could be whatever I had at hand. Of course, the tape was also determined by the frustration of being in the closed space—stuff was everywhere. I couldn't have done anything else anyway.

LF: There seem to be two different strains in your most recent tapes. While they all are made from texts with nonsynchronous video, some—like *Around & About* and *Primarily Speaking* [1981–83]—make use of direct address. You establish an I/you relationship, and it's very confrontational. On the other hand, *Videograms* and *Processual Video* [1980] are much slower, descriptive, and you use the third person.

GH: There's an urgency in *Around & About* and *Primarily Speaking,* whereas the others are much more timeless, almost about beauty. *Videograms* and *Processual Video* are much more object-oriented—"Here, look at this." There's a relationship between these words and this image.

LF: When you make the *Videograms,* do you write the text first, and then sit down and figure out images? [In *Videograms,* abstract black-and-white images undergo subtle transformations as Hill recites short passages whose simplicity and compression resemble haiku poetry. Because the passages are variously concrete and abstract, descriptive and metaphoric, the images alternately become illustrations and counterpoints.]

GH: So far, the texts have been written beforehand. However, when I actually combine them with the video, a phrase or a word or the ordering might change here or there. Little details might change, but in essence, the text is written beforehand.

LF: What do you use to produce the abstract images in *Videograms?*

GH: A Rutt/Etra scan processor. [The Rutt/Etra, invented by Steve Rutt and Bill Etra in the early 1970s, allows one to manipulate the video image or raster. According to "The Electronic Image," an unpublished paper by the Experimental Television Center, Owego, N.Y., the raster can be described as the visible rectangle of light emanating from a cathode ray tube, and is normally constructed by a beam of electrons focused to a fine point. This point is moved around in an orderly and continuous manner—horizontally from left to right and vertically from top to bottom—so that the raster, or image, is described. The rate at which the raster is drawn is determined by a timing pulse called sync. The Rutt/Etra allows one to manipulate sync signals, providing an enormous amount of flexibility in altering a video input, or in generating new images by using other inputs, such as waveforms. The images produced are always black and white, and cannot be recorded directly; they must be recorded by pointing a camera at the display monitor.] The Rutt/Etra is interesting. Conceptually a lot more is possible on it than with commercial digital effects. It's a powerful machine, and relatively unexplored. It probably never will be because it's hard to find access to them, and people tend to bypass black and white like it's—well, you know, black and white is black and white, man, it's not color. And you have to rescan it. And that's primitive. It's not state-of-the-art.

LF: What's nice about the *Videograms* is that they're so spare.

GH: Some of the *Videograms* are more successful than others. Some are too literal, others I'll probably redo because the image isn't quite right. I'm working on a new work, *Happenstance,* which has similarities to *Videograms,* but it's not a series. It's continuous, and it uses sound and character-generated text in addition to the voice-over. The images are more developed, also.

LF: Something more like *Processual Video?* [In *Processual Video,* a single white line revolves clockwise in the center of the monitor. Its movement is synchronized to a text read by Hill, so that the mental images conjured up by the text are often reinforced by the location of the line. For instance, when a line is in a horizontal or vertical position, there are references to surfing and skiing, the ocean and mountains. Into these visually suggestive sentences, Hill interweaves seemingly random, but highly self-conscious musings, about the text and the line.]

GH: Actually, I did a performance out of *Processual Video* for the "Video Viewpoints" series at the Museum of Modern Art. In fact, the piece was written as my lecture for the series.

LF: How did it work?

GH: There was a large monitor facing the audience, and the text was scored on paper. I watched a small monitor so I knew approximately where the bar was in relation to what I was reading. In different readings, there would be slight variations, but it all remained pretty close to the score. In that tape, there are references to me, references to the audience sitting in chairs, but it's more allegorical than *Around & About* and *Primarily Speaking*. In those tapes, the address is acutely direct. *Primarily Speaking* is probably the most complex work I've done. It still isn't finished. Its complexity gets subverted by the use of idiomatic expressions. I still haven't unwound it because it exists on so many different levels.

LF: In *Primarily Speaking,* why did you use color bars as a background for the two boxes? Was it a reference to broadcast television? [In the single-channel piece, the screen is divided into two boxes which are framed top and bottom by vertical bars of color—a standard test pattern for adjusting the color video signal. Inside the boxes, two sets of images are rapidly edited—like *Around & About*—to the syllables of the text, which is constructed entirely from idiomatic expressions.]

GH: It's a general reference, an idiom of television. To me, it becomes a kind of social frame. The tape has a very superficial layer to it, which I love, in that the whole thing is constructed from idioms. It's curious, when someone says something using an idiomatic expression, it's taken with a grain of salt (*laughs*). And yet, idioms are the heart of the matter, expressions that originally put a thought or feeling in a nutshell (*laughs*). I really constructed the text. It wasn't like writing. When I was doing the text, I thought of Matisse's cutouts, these reenergized primal shapes. Idioms seem like language cutouts. Once you get inside of idioms, they're incredibly rich. Television is the most advanced communication system and yet it's one big idiom. Everything that's spewed out is an idiom—the corporate world takes on how life should be.

LF: Did you divide the screen into two boxes to designate one box as the speaker and the other as the viewer?

GH: Not specifically, but to set up the idea of oscillating relationships.

LF: You establish some very literal connections between the images and what your voice is saying in the tape. For example, when you say, "So," an image of a pig flashes by; when you say, "Listen," there's a conch shell. But the tape doesn't operate just on that level. Most of the word-image connections are impossible to pin down, and I found myself reading into the tape, trying to figure out what the nonliteral connections meant. At one point, I was convinced that the tape was a comment on industrial pollution, because there were all these images of pipes and industrial waste, and you say, "They've done it again." At another point, I thought you were talking about the inability of two people to communicate. Finally, I felt that that was what the tape was designed to do—bring me to this process of making associations. But I also felt that it didn't matter if the associations I was making were the "right" ones, because there really could be no "correct" interpretation. On the one hand, the tape seemed extremely tight and structured, and on the other, the relationships were completely ambiguous.

GH: All those things are there, they exist, a lot are intentional. But then again, all those things—the images, the puns—are to me distractions from the heart of the work, which is the text. Consequently, *Primarily Speaking.* It's like a spear, and everything else is outside that. At the same time, it's an internal dialogue and a monologue addressing someone: Who is talking to whom? There's a section where the images are just black-and-white rectangles—I thought of this process as standing in front of a mirror for a long time, of the way you can separate the reflection from yourself and kind of have a conversation.

When you're trying to focus an idea, you're always in the context of everything else. All the external distractions are still going to exist, and they're going to affect that honed-in moment you're having. But the text is the heart of it. Language can be this incredibly forceful material—there's something about it where if you can strip away its history, get to the materiality of it, it can rip into you like claws, whereas images sometimes just slide off the edge of your mind, as if you were looking out a car window.

LF: Well, one always has an ongoing mental dialogue. One thing you seem to be doing to make that apparent is editing the video to the pace of the audio. The video becomes subservient. The images pass by faster than you can assimilate them.

GH: That gives a contradictory feeling. It makes the text-image construct, the syntax, the way it's coming at you, seem very purposeful. They're one unit, yet so much of the time they're disparate; they're pulled apart. The video is forcing associations—you could easily wander off—but the text continues straight ahead, getting larger than life, almost. At certain times, I try to second guess the viewers, fill in their minds with their own thoughts.

LF: Are the images completely arbitrary then?

GH: Yes and no. If I went out and did that tape right now, I could take the text, erase all the images, and put in a whole new set. The work would be archetypically the same; it would be a variation on a theme.

LF: In *Primarily Speaking,* the rapidly edited images in the boxes are interrupted a number of times by short breaks or interludes in which your voice says or sings a puzzling rhyme. One of them is "Time on our hands is blood on our hands." Your voice sounds like it's been processed—it has a very eerie tone, especially in the break where you have two dangling telephones.

GH: It's vocoded speech [a Vocoder breaks down an audio input into sixteen different frequency bands, then imposes those frequencies onto another carrier frequency]. I was trying to come up with almost idiomatic, harmonic sounds analogous to what's being said. The telephone is a rather pessimistic reference to communication. I remember that when I shot it I wanted the dangling phone to turn around so that the ITT on it could be read. The receiver hanging there conjures up, to me, images of something that happened to someone while they were on the telephone, or they simply left, or the telephone's dead.

LF: What about the rhyme that goes with it?

GH: In that section, I say: "Blue, green, red, cyan, magenta, yellow, food, feed, fed, I have the time of dayglow." It's a way of saying that television feeds us constantly. It even gives us the time of day. In the section, "Time on our hands is blood on our hands," when the two GASLAND signs appear, that's probably the most synchronous segment in the tape. First of all, you have the rhyme, the political implications of blood and gas. Then you have the actual sign being in language—words—on a sign that's designed to look like a television set, which coincides with the frame of the monitor television.

LF: I don't know that I would have made those connections, but I read them as general references to communication. You also made an installation from *Primarily Speaking,* and there the interludes work very differently. [In the installation, two walls of four monitors face one another, forming a corridor about the width of outstretched arms. The images which appear inside the two boxes in the single-channel tape are two separate tapes in the installation: one rectangle fills up the entire screen. On one end of each side of the corridor, the two videotapes are played on monitors facing each other. On the other three monitors are solid fields of color: one set of monitors displays red, green, blue; the other set displays cyan, magenta, yellow. Each wall of monitors alternately functions as a "speaking" wall, in that the text emanates from the speakers on that side only. As in the tape, the video is edited to each syllable, as if Hill's voice were activating the movement of the images. The other wall functions as a "listening" wall, in that no sound emanates from its audio speakers while the other wall is "speaking." The video on the "listening" wall is also activated by the audio, but rather than being edited to the beat of every syllable, the image actually rotates from one monitor to the next at a pace slower than the rapid video edits of the "speaking" wall. During the breaks, the images on all the monitors are rapidly sequenced, so that they ripple up and down the bank of monitors in a fixed relationship to one another.]

How do you think the tape differs from the installation in terms of how each is experienced?

GH: The tape in very linear. You sit in front of it; it locks you in—your eyes fix on two squares that are almost like horse blinders, spatially. The installation expands the idea of the images being an element that distracts from the text. In the tape, you're on the outside—watching. In the installation, you're inside. It's as if the two walls are speaking to each other; there's much more of a sense not only of talking back and forth, but on the images relating back and forth. You're constantly looking over your shoulder, walking up and down in a thoroughfare of images. The movement constantly distracts. The solid fields of color soften this, wash the space in a kind of sensuality, another distraction.

LF: Do you have a preference for installations over tapes?

GH: Installations. I like the complexity of working spatially, combining materials and media in different ways. I generally have ambiguous feelings about the experience of watching tapes on television.

LF: You mean sitting in a gallery and watching tapes?

GH: Yes, even more so with seeing video work on television. But it's more that the tape, the images, don't have a surface. They're encased behind glass. Yet at the same time, I really like the quality of emitted light.

LF: In the pieces that exist as both tapes and installations, you always change them in the process of going from one to the other, don't you?

GH: Definitely. A lot of times, in the middle of making a tape, I'll be thinking of an installation. It's not an afterthought. Some people think that one compromises the other, but for me, it's all raw material, even the texts. It's not pristine—this text belongs to this tape, and anything that's done outside its original context compromises it.

LF: It really depends on how it's realized as an installation or as a tape. Some people show tapes from installations as unaltered tapes, and it often doesn't translate.

GH: Yeah. For instance, there isn't a *Mesh* tape, and there's not a *War Zone* [a 1980 installation at Media Study, Buffalo, N.Y.] tape, although I do have a tape documenting it. But I don't show it as a "tape."

LF: You've called *War Zone* a metaphor for the empty mind thinking to itself. That seems very similar to the "internal dialogue" in *Primarily Speaking*.

GH: There's a similarity in dealing with image and language, but *War Zone* deals with it more directly. The scenario was image and language being at war. It also refers to the left and right sides of the brain, the perceptual and conceptual faculties battling for control. It's definitely a battle within myself, but the experience of the two pieces is very different.

The original idea for *War Zone* was to have many speakers in a room whispering single words, so that the experience would be walking through a room of white noise. As you walked around, individual words naming the objects would become audible. In the end, this became the basic texture of the piece. The large sound-space [at Media Study] determined certain details. It's insulated for sound recording, and feels quite raw, with exposed fiberglass on all the walls and ceiling. The pink of the fiberglass and the deadness of the sound changed my thinking about it, and I constructed the piece much more literally, picturing the space as "inside the mind."

LF: In using the metaphor of fighting, the camera represents a machine gun, the audio speakers function as mines in a mine field, the panning lights become surveillance lights. How did you choose the objects you used?

GH: A lot was determined by what I found around Media Study. Once I got a few things, it gave me the idea of using objects that would become analogous to thought processes, psychologically symbolic. For instance, a ladder represented a kind of hierarchy of thought; the dolly represented a stable thought, moving horizontally in any direction, but never shaken; a mirror represented reflection; and various things, such as a rope hanging from the ceiling, represented escape. There were sixteen objects identified with speakers. These references were not intended to be perceived exactly the way I described them, but rather as a kind of map or diagram for constructing the piece.

LF: What about the white rabbit?

GH: That rabbit was the only live element; it represented illusion. When I think of the way rabbits dart around, it represents to me the creative aspects of the mind. Among the identified objects in the space, it served as the unidentified, nonverbal, unconscious element.

LF: Your other installations, *Glass Onion* [1981] and *Equal Time* [1982], also seem to set up physical spaces in which language and image play off one another. In *Glass Onion,* you used a rectangle constructed from video feedback as the only image. What was the thinking behind that? [*Glass Onion* consists of four concentric rectangles. In the outermost layer are four monitors; in each of the next two layers are four audio speakers; in the center is a single monitor displaying a tape of an image of a black-and-white rectangle which was constructed from video feedback. The central monitor and the speakers all lie on the floor facing up. Pointing down from the ceiling is a camera with an automated zoom lens: when zoomed all the way in, it frames the single monitor; when zoomed all the way out, it frames the outermost rectangle of monitors. This undulating image is displayed on the outer monitors. It is also altered whenever a person enters the space, because his or her image is picked up by the camera. The rate at which the rectangle shrinks and expands—or the rate at which the lens zooms in and out—is determined by the sound track, which is measured by the enunciation of these three syllables: *rec·tan·gle.* Based on the rhythm of these syllables, a mathematical structure of enunciation is set up for the entire text: one phrase overlaps another at a certain rate, mimicking and thereby describing the process of video feedback.]

GH: I did *Glass Onion* right after *Black/White/Text* [1980, the single-channel work that *Processual Video* is based on]. They're similar in that both take a very basic image and try to question image versus language—what happens when you use a very simple image with a text that gets very complex. *Glass Onion* is much more anchored to the original tape than my other installations. It uses a known image and process as a foundation.

The curious thing about feedback is that it's about delay—that's what makes the squares within the squares—but you see it all at once. You don't experience the time until you know what it is, and then you can conceptualize the delay. The problem with any feedback is that it just keeps feeding on itself, and you're pulled into it without any kind of external check. It's like two people who begin by having a conversation and get into an argument. If you listen to it later, it oscillates into oblivion. That's what I think of when I watch video feedback—it's meaningless after a while.

The text provides a check, a kind of third party. It isolates segments of time, so that you don't fall into the feedback. The experience of text is perceived as time passing; the image, the parts, are not separated. There is no isolation of the individual loops or segments of time that construct the image.

LF: In other words, the video feedback flows continuously, whereas the text is composed of discrete syllables and words that provide an overall structure?

GH: It's more specific than that. It's the way the description is structured. The idea was to try to isolate the individual rings in the feedback, and to have an analog in language, something that would be comparable to video feedback, but without actually using audio feedback. The text literally describes feedback, and is structured as a process of feedback. It is read backward so that the phrases pile up on one another until they invert and you actually hear it from beginning to end. The end of the sentence is said first, and then each phrase is repeated, overlaps with the phrase before it, until the whole paragraph is constructed. Each phrase is twice as long as the one before it, and so there's a mathematical relationship almost like a pyramid. The installation itself is laid out like a pyramid, topographically.

LF: So you layered the phrases in order to create an experience similar to looking at video feedback?

GH: Yes, you don't follow the words linearly; it's a kind of linguistic maze that one gets lost in and every once in while, when the individual phrases double up on each other, "objects of meaning" appear.

LF: What do you mean by "objects of meaning"?

GH: That term is a little obtuse, isn't it? The text literally defines the outer parameter of the space as a character-generated image that crawls along the bottom of each monitor. This outlining is again reinforced by the quadrature movement of the sound (speech) between each set of four speakers, which mark the corners of concentric rectangles. The character-generated text consists of the individual phrases or units that make up the text you're hearing, but in linear order. The first barrier is the "reading" of the text. This describes what you're entering. With each successive barrier or rectangle, the "description" gets more complex—that is to say, it's no longer a word-for-word interpretation. Experientially, something else is taking place. The sound of the text feeding back on itself is becoming that object of meaning, which finally leads us to go to the central monitor, the image "tomb," and there it is, in living black and white—this graphic image of where you're standing. One tends to retrace one's steps, to feed back on one's own movement, and construct this "object of meaning."

LF: How does this installation compare to *Equal Time?*

GH: *Glass Onion* is autonomous in the sense that the installation defines its own space. In fact, the height of the overhead camera and the focal length of the lens are the determining factors. When the camera is zoomed out to the widest view, that becomes the outer rectangle. *Equal Time* was set up in a given, almost symmetrical space, with all the components set up as oscillating pairs, everything in a kind of reciprocal relationship, all trying to cancel each other out. This cancelling relationship is prevented by the viewer's own participation, because of the nature of perception when seeing and/or hearing two or more things simultaneously. This idea was the structuring principle of the work.

In the original tape, there are two texts. Each is a long paragraph. One describes the opening of a fictional art show. It's kind of a joke: one gallery wall is painted white, but it's still wet. That's the exhibit. People are at the opening, drinking and talking, and at the end, they notice that they have paint all over them. The other text is a description of a private performance, very solitary. Both texts are very image-oriented and descriptive—except one's public and one's private. Both texts are the same length, and the last part of each is the same: "I left the room, exiting to a hallway. It was long enough to form extreme perspective looking in either direction with doors to other rooms on both sides. I crossed the hall and entered the room opposite me."

This is another instance where the text could be replaced with other texts, and the piece would still be the "same." The content would be different, but *Equal Time* isn't about *the* content. It's about how content is experienced when structured in this field of simultaneity. I considered having other pairs of texts, which would change every other time I crossed the hall and entered the room opposite me. I felt this would have made it unnecessarily complicated, giving the impression of rooms with many scenes. The repetition of just the two texts reinforces the static quality of being inside an object and figuring out how it's constructed.

In the installation, there are two adjacent rooms connected by a narrow passage. In the center of each room there are monitors facing the passageway, and each other. The monitors display separate tapes which consist of the same images, images which refer to the text. The only difference is that on one monitor the images corresponding to, say, text A are prioritized, or keyed over, the images of text B. The opposite exists on the other monitor.

LF: So while you can always hear both texts, one text always dominates, depending on where you are. And in the room where one text dominates, its accompanying video also dominates?

GH: Right. At the end of both tapes, one hears the same last sentence, and then the two audio tracks are reversed, along with the images, and repeated in opposite rooms. Inside the passageway there are two more monitors, also facing each other, displaying another videotape. In that tape, there's an abstract image of two shiny, grid-like panels that slowly move until they overlap each other. They overlap at the point where the two texts overlap, creating a moiré pattern; and then, when the texts start up again, the panels start to move again.

LF: What was the reasoning behind using the abstract imagery in the small space?

GH: The abstract imagery was the original tape for *Equal Time*. It functions similarly to *Black/White/Text*, somewhat diagrammatically, mirroring the movement of the sound/text. There are also a lot of textural, abstract references to the text. Because the location of those inner monitors becomes so narrow, you almost have to turn sideways to get through. It became a kind of synaptical point, where all four monitors pointed toward each other. It was the "hot spot," especially when there were several people in the space. It was the ambiguous zone, where one asked where one space met another.

LF: Given that you're literally saying in *Equal Time* that people in the art world are all wet—covered with paint—I'm interested in what you think about video being plugged into that world.

GH: I think that essentially it's not.

LF: No?

GH: Peripherally, but not really, basically because it's not marketable.

LF: They said that about photography, too.

GH: It may be in the future, but right now it's not. Video as an art form proving itself . . . for me the whole idea of the singularity of an art form is backward, dead, reactionary. So much is manipulated and defined by the market.

LF: Don't you think that there's an imperative to intellectualize, institutionalize, and legitimize video?

GH: Sure. The Paik show [*Nam June Paik,* a retrospective originating at the Whitney Museum of American Art, April 30–June 27, 1982]. It was still a great show though. I don't know. I could see some point—not necessarily far away—where I wouldn't be doing video, but something else. I don't see myself as a video artist. Any time I feel like I'm falling into "this is what I do," I don't like it, and I want to push it away. I worked in sculpture longer than video. I could see working with just about anything, working with nothing, not doing anything for two years. Just thinking.

Stephen Sarrazin

A Discussion with Gary Hill

The following interview with Gary Hill took place in Paris, in February 1992. It is essentially divided into several parts: a discussion of the evolution of his work within the context of the histories of video; the evolution of contemporary art and the possible affinities shared between Gary Hill's tapes and installations and the works of other artists; a retrospective discussion of his tape production and its relationship with language; a general discussion of his installations. It is important to understand that Gary Hill did not experience a formal university training; nor did he go through the process of having access to art history through academia. His experience of electronics developed as his tapes became more ambitious, while his encounters with language came out, for the most part, of chance meetings (individuals, books, etc.). It was clearly a didactic method, which removes him, in spite of the intensely cerebral nature of his work, from a generation of artists trained in art as well as in the business of art through the structure of a curriculum. The naturally accidental encounters with the art market, via his installations, demonstrate how art which is made with video is still very much perceived as a risk; few galleries are willing to take this kind of gamble, although the number is rising. But recognition is now undeniably happening at a more balanced pace; Nam June Paik was well into his 50s when he finally experienced the kind of financial independence artists of his generation had appreciated decades before. Nowadays, artists like Gary Hill, Bill Viola, Klaus vom Bruch, Tony Oursler, and a few others, artists in their late 30s to early 40s, are showing pieces in galleries, museums, major contemporary art exhibits.

Originally published as a *Chimera* monograph (Montebeliard: Centre International de Creation Video Montebeliard, Belfort, 1992).

Nevertheless, the economy of this recognition radically differs from the one which surrounds painters, or other media artists. The case of Gary Hill is also of interest as it retraces the move from alternative exhibit spaces to larger venues, and how video participated in the latters' respective relationships with media-based arts and new technologies. This artist is now working with sophisticated tools, such as a computer matrix for his installations. But prior to this, there is more than twenty years of creative output, ranging from sculpture to sound experiments and music, to performance and video. This discussion takes into account the social-political context during which Gary Hill began working with video, and the various crossings of histories are retraced through the artist's recollections of them. All remarks in brackets are mine.

Stephen Sarrazin: How did you first get involved in art? Were you still in your teens when you began making sculpture?

Gary Hill: I was 15 years old and I was doing a lot of drawing as well. I covered the walls of my entire room with intricate psychedelic drawings. My best friend, who turned me on to LSD—one always remembers who turned them on to acid—had a brother, Tony Parks, who made metal sculptures. This was like 1966–67 and there was a nice mix of music, drugs, and surfing at least for a short time. I was really fascinated by this welding he was doing and eventually I got my own tanks and learned to weld. I pretty much took up his style and he was probably influenced by Giacometti, even though his work had this California psychedelic attitude to it. I don't think he was involved at all in mainstream contemporary art.

SS: He wasn't aware of contemporary American sculpture? Smith, Di Suvero, Chamberlain . . .

GH: I don't know but it wasn't apparent. I certainly wasn't; I had no idea about Pop Art or Minimalism until a few years later when I moved to the East Coast and then very quickly the world of art appeared, so to speak.

SS: When you moved east, did you set out with idea that you would become a sculptor, that this would be the definite art form you would work in?

GH: Well, I knew I was going to make art and at least for the time being that was going to be welded metal sculpture, but I also went you might say with an open mind. I mean I was 18 and incredibly optimistic and hungry for whatever.

SS: So once you got there you began to spend more time looking at sculpture, instead of just wanting to make things?

GH: Going to the East Coast was at first tied to this expectation that one goes to college after high school but I wasn't really sure about this. On the other hand I was 1A and ripe for the draft, in fact eventually I was number 35 on the lottery so it was a sure bet that I would be called up. I had seen something on the Arts Students League in Woodstock, New York, and I received a little scholarship to go there. Bruce Dorfman was my instructor and later he set up a small workshop for a handful of people. He was really instrumental in my decision to stay on the East Coast. I also worked for him for a while in his studio. His neighbor happened to be Bob Dylan and I did some odd jobs for him: gardening, painting, mowing the lawn—and we're talking about a pretty big lawn (*laughs*). At one point Bruce took me to an exhibition at the Metropolitan in New York, called *New York Painting and Sculpture, 1940–1970*. This was the first time I saw any of these artists. It simply blew me away completely.

SS: Once you encountered these works, did you begin to lean toward any one of the sculptors mentioned previously?

GH: No. My first enthusiastic reactions were for the paintings of Frank Stella and Morris Louis, whom I don't like as much anymore. As far as sculpture goes, Giacometti, for me, was and is a much more interesting artist than the celebrated David Smith. . . . The one sculptor I was looking at at the time was Robert Morris. Later on Robert Smithson was important to me.

SS: What did this discovery do to your work?

GH: I went very quickly from figurative work into abstraction. I started using solid forms with paint, then I would layer these forms. That was the Stella influence. So the kind of abstract work I was doing had more to do with formalism that with representation. I was also quite attached to this material I was working with, copper-coated steel rods, which I stayed with for some time [it's there as well in *Full Circle*]. So that became my material, and it was raw, but I wasn't working from a Minimalist perspective, the way Carl Andre and Richard Serra did. It was still very compositional and then I got into wire mesh. This freed me up a bit, getting more and more construction-oriented.

SS: Were you aware of how sculpture had evolved, from the chisel, or the molding of clay, to the use of steel, the Constructivists, Picasso, the American artists . . . ?

GH: No, not really. But I was in awe of Picasso for a while.

SS: Did you ever want to go and live in New York City itself?

GH: No, but I would go there regularly. Overall I stayed in that general area (Woodstock, Barrytown) for about fourteen years.

SS: Was there a lot of experimenting with drugs by artists who were there with you?

GH: By that time it wasn't so much about experimentation. It had really become part of the fabric of everyday life.

SS: And do you think that played a significant role in your work?

GH: Most definitely. I would say that taking acid is one of the most important things I've ever done, in the sense that it changed my life. This went on for a few years until the time when we weren't sure what we were getting anymore.

SS: Were you aware of a history of literature in which writers had experimented with drugs, from Baudelaire to Cocteau, or Michaux, Burroughs . . . ? Was this at all a possible model or reference?

GH: No. I wasn't aware of those people at the time. For me it really started as a generational kind of thing a couple of years before moving east. You have to remember that I was only 15 when I turned on and it happened to be a good dose. Wham! Life will not be seen the same way again. I mean everybody wanted to turn everybody on. I wanted to turn my mother on. Instead of drinking and throwing up we were taking acid and smoking pot and going to human be-ins, surfing in the middle of the night and going to see the Doors, Jefferson Airplane, and the Grateful Dead. It was a special time. In the middle of all that I started making art and I'm sure it was all very influential on my work. Jumping back and forth and trying to see how it all fits is difficult. But without a doubt LSD precedes deconstruction in the most profound sense.

SS: You know that Timothy Leary is now a spokesperson for virtual reality systems.

GH: Yes, I know. He's very sharp.

SS: How influenced were you by music and television, growing up on the West Coast on one hand, and on the other being part of that first generation of artists working the tools of television and music?

GH: Music was very important. It was social too, I watched television, but I never bothered to think about it one way or another, including when I began to work with video. My tapes weren't about a position on television, locating myself for or against the language of television. Coming back to music, I remember walking in a record store and hearing something by Terry Riley! Then I got very interested in La Monte Young, Alvin Lucier . . . Other ideas of structuring sounds.

SS: As you were discovering contemporary art, were you also becoming aware of filmmakers like Warhol, Michael Snow, or Godard? Other ideas of structuring images . . .

GH: No, not at that time. I wasn't thinking about images in that sense, and I didn't know people making films or who were film buffs in a big way.

SS: If you weren't interested in television or in film, how did you connect with video? Had you heard of Nam June Paik, Vito Acconci, or of Bruce Nauman's early tapes?

GH: I don't think so. Perhaps some of Nauman's pieces but I wasn't aware of video as an art form. There are two reasons why I started do-

ing video: (1) I had started doing some sound work with a little synthesizer and processing sounds made from my sculptures.

SS: Derrida called them the singing sculptures.

GH: Yes, in the *Passages de l'Image* catalogue. I liked the instantaneous
results, the transformation of my relationship with time; welding could
be a very long process. (2) Then Woodstock Community Video, which
used to be the People's Video Theater from NYC, moved up to Woodstock. They were going to do community access television. They had
their own local station. So I went to see them to find out if I could just
make something with them, like a movie . . . This was in 1973, I was 22.
What hit me immediately about video was that in looking at things
with a video camera everything had a very intense presence. The image
on the monitor has something to do with hyperreality, and with phenomenology, as Woody Vasulka explained. The other significant step
for me—and there was nobody there to tell me to try this—was when I
first recorded myself with a portapac, I asked if I could borrow another
one in order to record myself in front of the monitor which was already
playing back the previous image of me. This had nothing to do with
the moving image, it had to do with the process and feedback. So naturally at that time I was not thinking about framing, or shot composition, or about film and television languages. I was in this mode of self-
consciousness. I first did a couple of tapes in which there was no
editing, no effects. Then I did sort of a performance piece with a
friend: we painted color rectangles all around the city at night. After
three or four nights, there were a lot of them, but we got caught and
were arrested. Then I did a documentary about it, asking people about
what they thought of the rectangles: should we put more, should we
take them off . . .

SS: But what seems significant here is reproducing one shape in a space,
the way you eventually structured various numbers of pixels within the
geography of the screen, like in *Bathing* or *Electronic Linguistics.*

GH: Perhaps in retrospect but I don't really connect the two. I was just
trying a lot of different things. Later on I tried a little narrative. It was
a short piece called *Feathers* in which a friend and I improvised a story.
It was very European, with Erik Satie music in the background and

playing off some of Duchamp's ideas. But this was a coincidence because I had never seen René Clair's *L'Entr'acte*. I suppose I was just discovering a number of genres without really knowing what was going on
historically.

SS: Did you keep on doing those sound sculptures?

GH: Yes, I did both video and sculpture, for about three years, before
dropping the welding completely. I didn't want to give up the sculpture because I was so attached to this material. I began texturing the copper into moiré patterns [there's a reference to this in *Videograms*], and besides, the copper rods were able to produce such incredible harmonics.

SS: You had no formal training in recording and electronics?

GH: No, it was pretty much trial and error. It came to a point where I
would have hundreds of tape loops on the floor, trying different combinations, wiring the tape recorder differently, this kind of thing. At
the time though, I didn't know a capacitor from a resistor.

SS: But I've seen you time and time again taking monitors apart.

GH: That's now. But I don't really know circuitry. And I'm not a computer programmer. A circuit board is no longer an alien thing to me,
but if your television set was broken I'm not sure I could fix it. However, 50 percent of the time I could guess what's wrong with it. I was
discovering technology as I went along.

SS: Did you ever sell some of your sculptures?

GH: Yes, in fact some of the very early ones, when I was still in California, to a gallery in Los Angeles. But not a lot.

SS: What about the California art scene? Had you picked up on Ed
Ruscha?

GH: Not at all. Although I like Ruscha very much now, and obviously
I'm interested in how he uses idioms. But keep in mind that at the time
I wasn't making contemporary art as we know it. I was welding pat-

terns and pictures together, coming from what I knew: the drug culture and the music, skateboarding and surfing . . .

SS: Keeping with the times, was your decision not to serve in the Army politically motivated?

GH: No, it wasn't. The only form of protest I did against the war was my own act of deciding not to go. In fact I wasn't that aware of all the political movements going on. The People's Video Theater were politically active, and I did encounter people from those various video collectives who were socially engaged in the early 1970s. But I was focusing on my art.

SS: In what type of context did you become a video coordinator for that TV Lab in upstate New York?

GH: In the early 1970s, funding became available for media projects and collectives started to get money. Groups like Raindance and TVTV. Then the Arts Council got mandated to have more projects dealing with art and I happened to be there, the sole artist working with video in Woodstock. So I became a coordinator for the television lab, and that plugged me into government and grants which allowed Woodstock Community Video and myself to survive.

SS: The earliest tapes that I've seen are *Bathing* and *Windows;* did these get made while you were in Woodstock or did you do them much later?

GH: Some time later. I had invited Dave Jones to come live in Barrytown, build me some electronic tools and some collaborations. He created tools which made it possible to mix digital and analog images together. I learned a lot from him. When you look at *Windows* now, it seems so primitive but at the time nobody, not even the Vasulkas, had done a tape like that, except perhaps the big corporate electronic laboratories. The Vasulkas didn't have a frame buffer yet, and the one that Jones had was primitive: 64 × 64 pixels. So I was examining what was going on behind the image, as in *Bathing* when I tried to play around with the use of color through processing by welding and unwelding various circuits. I didn't become aware of video art per se until I started showing my work. I showed my very first tape as an artist at the Kitchen in 1973, and soon after at the Anthology of Film Archives.

SS: This was relatively exceptional for the Anthology to show tapes of a young new artist, at the same period as the work is being produced. So right from the beginning your work in video enjoyed some recognition.

GH: I suppose so. It was pretty informal. The atmosphere was one of sharing tapes and experiments.

SS: Did you meet the Vasulkas, who you say had a considerably significant influence on you, as far as thinking about video is concerned, at the Kitchen?

GH: No, but they were aware of my work. Later on we ended up teaching at the same place in Buffalo in 1979–80. This was where I did *Around & About* and *Commentary, Processual Video,* all in a matter of months. At that point I was really trying to break out of that image-processing thing.

SS: So what's the transitional tape? In which tape did you find your subject?

GH: Well, in the tape which is now called *Full Circle.* You begin to perceive how the sound and the voice are having an influence on the image itself. It also involved the idea of collapse and paradox, which has carried over in later works.

SS: A lot of people would have thought it was *Electronic Linguistics.*

GH: I never developed the notion of what that could be. It became the signifier of that possibility which materializes to some extent in a tape like *Happenstance.* Whereas in a tape like *Around & About,* the process was much more naïve in that I was wondering what it would be like to match an image to a syllable as opposed to the linguistic connections of speech, sound, electronics . . .

SS: It's once you begin seriously to write the texts which constitute the sound tracks to your tapes that the deconstruction process begins, the reversal of the image dominating the sound.

GH: Yes, although there have been occasions on which other things were involved. In *Around & About,* for instance, that was written very quickly and it was meant for one particular person.

SS: Had you been writing prior to the tapes?

GH: At one point when I was 18 I'd decided I was going to write a book, and I remember it was going to be about everydayness. I did about two pages, on which I worked for a very long time, very hard, which is still how I write now. It's completely constructed a phrase at a time and has nothing to do with stream of consciousness writing. The first things I really did write ended up in *Videograms* and *Equal Time.* By that time I had met George Quasha, a poet and writer, who did sound poetry performances, and was a publisher [Station Hill Press, which published two important anthologies of experimental American poetry]. We became very close friends and this put me in touch with writers like Jackson MacLow, Franz Kamin, Charles Stein. I'm sure this had something to do with me beginning to write. Writing was a release from image processing and pure image exploration, which was really getting boring. Speaking and talking became necessities. Finding a syntaxical weave between speech and image signaled itself as a direction for me. Suddenly I had the feeling that I was doing something that nobody else was doing, in video anyway.

SS: Were you looking at other forms of language art, conceptual art (Kosuth, Barry, Weiner . . .)?

GH: By that time, certainly. I remember being impressed by a Sol Lewitt show at Castelli which included drawings on the walls with all the descriptions of the drawings; the artwork including in itself a commentary on the process. And I liked Acconci and Smithson, who was not per se a conceptual artist . . .

SS: But the ephemeral nature of much of this art is linked to the immaterial dimension of video. Did you ever do performances like Acconci, or other video artists who combined performance with video?

GH: I did, but not a lot. George Quasha had opened this place called the "Arnolfini Art Center," which was a multimedia space and I did a few there.

I didn't really follow what was going on in performance art. I would see a few at the Kitchen and those which came upstate. The ones I was really interested in were the ones in which the artists were alone and self-sufficient.

SS: Like those performance videos in which Acconci, Jonas, Hoover, Wegman . . . were doing everything [performer, camera operator, editor . . . which meant turning the camera on and off].

GH: Exactly. There's such an obvious difference between people who came out of art and started doing video, and those who had a film background.

SS: This is something very difficult for film students to imagine or understand: that people working in video were not immediately concerned with mise-en-scène.

GH: Which is something I only began exploring in 1984, more than ten years after my first tapes, when I started working on *Why Do Things Get in a Muddle;* that was made in between two stays in Japan, the year I'd gotten a grant to go and work there. It was a very self-conscious work. The tape begins with two people reading books, as if they were reading their lines. So on one hand it looked very self-conscious, and on the other hand I didn't know how to direct these two persons. I'd never worked with actors. And I only had two lights and I didn't know anything about lighting; I had no assistants so I would run to the upstairs of the house to start the sound recording, then run back downstairs and pick up the camera. It was absurd. I was doing it like a one-person video. It could have been a better looking tape if I'd had a crew, but it would have had nothing to do with the essence of what it was about: the breakdown of meaning, reversibility, entropy, and chaos. It was Paul Ryan who introduced me to the work of Gregory Bateson.

SS: Let's go back to *Full Circle.*

GH: Which was called *Ring Modulation* originally. But I changed it because it sounded too much like electronics. This was in 1978, about two years after I'd met G. Quasha.

SS: What's the first tape in which you talked? *Full Circle* is about sounds.

GH: So you mean with words which are recognizable? I suppose it's *Elements,* in which you hear portions of the words which make up the four elements: fire water . . .

SS: We've talked about this before: at the time artists like Acconci, Wegman, or Baldessari were doing video, there was an explicit concern with real time. Their tapes would last as long as the event which was being represented, as in Baldessari's *Trying to tune two glasses of water for four minutes,* in which we see these glasses next to an alarm clock, and the tape is a 4-minute shot. The event was in the image. In your tapes, language becomes the event and the image is there as long as there is language; it completely challenges the nature of editing.

GH: That's right, language allowed the image to exist. The image is more like a compass or a graph of the language. It's a measure which helps to center you within the space of language.

SS: At what point does this become strategy for you?

GH: I would say I felt I was on to something when I did *Processual Video* and *Black/White/Text* which has a very precise structure derived from a text that is a literal description of negative video feedback (the Sol Lewitt lesson). The text grows mathematically, based on the exact number of syllables in each additive phrase. In a sense it accumulates phrases backward; it backs up into time. The image is simply expanding and contracting video feedback that tracts the text. It's pretty static looking really. In the case of *Around & About* or *Primarily Speaking,* the strategy changes significantly. The image's existence is directly tied to the speech; unless I speak the image does not change or does not move. This really puts one inside the time of speaking since every syllable produced an image change; suddenly words seem quite spatial and one is conscious of a single word's time.

SS: So these also function as representations of syntax through the editing process. Were you reading philosophers of language, linguistics?

GH: No. This wasn't based on linguistics. I don't think of myself as a language artist, or as a writer. My work doesn't come out of the practice of reading and writing. It's more about the web of rereading and rewriting in the electronic domain. At some point the image is touched by language and this produces something physical. It's very much of an internal process where the structure of the work might be representing what's going on in my head, and this is why in some pieces you not only hear my voice but you see me appearing in the tape, like in *Commentary*. In fact, in that tape my relationship to the things around me is similar to the one in *CRUX*. But if you take a work like *Incidence of Catastrophe*, it's another thing. The choice for me to be in it had more to do with my own experience of reading *Thomas the Obscure*. I didn't want to verbalize it; I wanted to "be" this. I wanted to put myself against this text.

SS: I think that besides language, your work deals with themes of solitude and isolation. On one hand there's the solitary voice and the absence of what is termed figurative content, as in the processed image tapes. Or there are those tapes in which we find the closed-in spaces, as in *Around & About, Primarily Speaking*. And when characters begin to appear, we have this breakdown in communication, or at least this difficulty in reaching meaning, as it's represented by such figures as the muddle, the palindrome, the catastrophe . . . I'm thinking here also of Bruce Nauman's work which can also be discussed in terms of violence, of a very dark humor (Beckett, Borges).

GH: Yes. Well this difficulty of communication you've mentioned is not to be restricted to an exchange between people, but should also include one communicating with himself. Obviously in *Muddle*, it becomes a trick question: the text is not by me and it's more about not being able to reach a resolution in a narrative. Existence without resolution is also an existence of possibilities, as well as risks and uncertainty. In that tape there is an incredible display of the struggle to speak and to mean something. In *Muddle*, you have two characters who are able to agree on something, then go off in different directions. *Primarily Speaking* anticipated this idea of a connection between sound and image which breaks off then connects again.

SS: The idea of order within disorder. *Primarily Speaking* anticipates much more than *Muddle:* there's *CRUX, Site Recite* . . . And there is also the construction of possible narratives through the use of such charged images of yourself in a fetal position, or the wine spilling on a table, etc.

GH: Actually, I was trying to "recharge" such images. It also had to do with the sheer number of images which were necessary for the two-channel exchange. You might think there is an infinite number of images, but at one point you ask: What can I do now? It becomes a collecting process. Like for the idioms: I just went through the dictionaries and phrase books and listed all the ones which were acceptable to me. I eliminated those which were too figurative, like "you can't lead a horse to water," and focused on those like "point of fact." Glue phrases. Once I started putting them together, they would flow so easily. It was like putting a puzzle together.

SS: Were you still working alone by that time?

GH: Yes, the camera, the editing. Friends would come in, hold something up, etc. But that was all. There was no time code editing. *Around & About* was hand-edited by manually punching the record button.

SS: What about now? Do you still shoot yourself or do you use a camera operator?

GH: Generally I prefer recording myself, but sometimes that just isn't possible. When I first used someone else, Rex Barker in *Incidence of Catastrophe* (he was used to films, commercials), I had to fight with him: "just leave the camera on and get away from it." It came out of the need to have someone "with" the camera while I was working on the Thomas character in front of the camera. Now he's more familiar with what I do, but I still prefer to do it myself. For instance, it would have been a lot easier to do *Inasmuch As It Is Always Already Taking Place* with someone else, but it's such a private space. I don't want to talk while I'm doing it, so I prefer running back and forth and pushing a button. In *Muddle* I did everything, placed cue cards, set up props, did sound and camera . . . But that was also a matter of budget, and anyway I didn't know of a better way. That tape was done with no funding at all. I rented a camera with a credit card. Kathy, Chuck Stein, and I were extremely committed to doing this. You're right, no one asked me about mise-en-scène, but what I was doing there certainly addressed issues of film language, even if I wasn't reproducing or articulating that language. *Muddle* was shot from the end to the beginning in order to keep continuity. The script was basically the text and some scribbled pictures. And then we had backward phonetically written cue cards everywhere. This being the case, the sound of speech gets "worse" as one watches the tape, since the learning curve has been reversed. People don't pick up on the incredible amount of visual references to *Alice Through the Looking-Glass.* There's a lot going on. It ended up being shown on Channel 4 in England, and on Channel 13 in New York.

SS: Did several of your tapes get shown on PBS?

GH: Not really. In fact Channel 13 didn't want to show *Muddle* because it would not have been a "première" thing.

SS: Channel 4 produced *Incidence of Catastrophe.*

GH: Right, but they did not show it. There was a change of structure and management; I guess they didn't care for the tape . . . I've never really done a big-budget production as far as tapes go.

SS: Was there a point when you felt people started recognizing you as an artist working with video, rather than as a video artist? Were you getting grants regularly?

GH: Well it really took about eight years before I got my first video grant . . . Then six weeks later I got another one, and yet another one from PBS, from Channel 13. So three grants in a row, for a total of $10,000. With PBS I could have gone to their television lab, but I chose to use the money. I made *Soundings* with it. But they never showed it. They thought it was too rough. All of this was still going within the context of video art.

SS: What was your first installation?

GH: It was something I made at the Woodstock Artists' Association, which really only supported painting and very traditional sculpture, but I managed to sneak in a proposal . . . I brought in a camera and zoomed into an outside wall, and started cutting into the wall, and into that image of the cutting, until I hit the beams and couldn't go any farther; it was like a Gordon Matta-Clark piece. It was called *Hole in the Wall.* Then I did performances which included multimonitor setups. But the next installations happened years later, *Mesh* in 1979 and *Glass*

Onion in 1980–81. The later ones, like *In Situ, CRUX, Media rite* were happening almost simultaneously.

SS: What has been the evolution process, from *DISTURBANCE (among the jars)* to *I Believe It Is an Image?* Are installations no longer possible sites for narratives?

GH: After making *DISTURBANCE* I was asked to do an exhibition at the Galerie des Archives in Paris, which is a very small space. I saw it as a limitation/opportunity that might derail me from my current thinking into something else. Although *And Sat Down Beside Her* uses the stripped tube element like in *DISTURBANCE,* a strategy I first used in *In Situ* [1986], the object and narrative are much more embedded in one another. The pieces really function more as object narratives in a sense, whereas the narrative of *DISTURBANCE* is linked up with the "editing." I think that the metaphorical aspects of the object developed in *And Sat Down Beside Her* were carried over to *BEACON* too. And then recently with *Suspension of Disbelief,* which is silent, I can already see extended possibilities of woven narratives taking place over the whole line of displays which in certain ways returns to *DISTUR-BANCE* but meanwhile has picked up the "electronic linguistic" of computer-controlled switching begun in *Between Cinema and a Hard Place.* So it's apparent that there's no linear development going on here, that narrative by no means is an exhausted idea for me, and that my works tend to feed off one another.

SS: How significant is Derrida's influence on your work and how explicit is your relationship to philosophy (and to Heidegger)?

GH: Contrary to what many people might think, Derrida has had little influence on my work in any kind of "direct" way. First of all I am simply not up on his writings in that way. I've read a few books and parts of several more but I'm not a big reader and so I can't possibly follow all the references. Nevertheless I can easily hold inspirational thoughts derived from certain passages and there's no question that I play off some of these ideas, even single words that he lights up in certain ways. But it's not a case of truly studying deconstruction, working out a parallel equivalent, and doing it. I would say that Heidegger and even more so Blanchot have struck deeper chords within me and have certainly influenced my work explicitly. In general I would say that my work is closer to philosophy and epistemology than art and politics. So in that sense there is a circle of interrelated influences that is in constant flux.

SS: Are you familiar with Heidegger's writings on technology, and his criticisms of modern art, in which he anticipates the issue of reproduction, crucial to video? What do you think of this question of reproduction in video; is making installations a way in which to define a position?

GH: I'm somewhat familiar with his discussion of technology in *The Nature of Language,* which I used passages from in *Between Cinema and a Hard Place.* I try to explicate through the syntax of video certain things Heidegger talks about when he differentiates the neighborhood that thought and poetry share from parametric notions of time and space. I am using a particular technology that in ways contradicts but at the same time suggests a different kind of poetics, a kind of electronic linguistics, that plays directly into the reproduction question. Time is divided up so more images can exist—however, not at the same time. As far as positions go I just don't think of it that way. The issue for me is not literal in the sense that a videotape or a video image can be reproduced. The important thing is the fractal nature of the medium—its ability to disseminate an image as something that is not so much an object but rather something that permeates space . . . and then how does one delimit this illumination.

SS: Could you comment, again, on the absent body in *CRUX* in light of a fragmented work like *Inasmuch?*

GH: It's interesting to compare the different ways the images were obtained in the two works. In *CRUX* a camera without subjective control, that is, an image that is essentially an extension of my struggle, nails my extremities to a cross. Whereas in *Inasmuch* a rather fixed gaze cycles through what is much more a collection of images that are sort of holding on for fear of disembodiment. In ways the pieces are almost inversions of one another. *Inasmuch* seems apocalyptically pessimistic and *CRUX,* I think, in an active way, gives the final testimony back to the viewer.

SS: You've been working with concepts of scale in recent works, from small pieces like the *CORE SERIES* to miniature works like *And Sat Down.* What's your idea of video's relationship to space?

GH: Again I don't have a global notion or position regarding video's relationship to such things as space. It would appear that video can't have a relationship with space because it is already everywhere—the image is everywhere; space is now image. If I have a position, it's to question the privileged place that image, and for that matter sight, hold in our consciousness.

SS: Will you keep on exploring computer sequencing in your work?

GH: Well, *Suspension of Disbelief* [1992] uses the same technology in such a way that the image never stabilizes. This is also true of the *CORE SERIES* but it's not perceived in the same way since there are only two monitors. They flicker continuously but they still define where they are. In *Suspension of Disbelief,* the image is much more of an ongoing trace that never remains long enough to constitute itself. I'm working on a new piece that will project images in rapid succession all over the space. As in the Documenta piece, *Tall Ships,* there won't be any video frame borders so that the images will be object-like and won't last but a few frames, leaving afterimages to pile up in dark space.

SS: We'll end with this question: What role has the body played in the installations?

GH: The body for me is a kind of built-in referent. It's important to realize that most of the time I work with my own body. It is close at hand, intimate, and at different times annoyingly and pleasurably real. When you turn the camera and the ideas back on yourself it's a way of not working with the subjective visuals of images because although you see your own body displayed you feel it being seen. It is always mediated by the skin that separates you from Image.

Regina Cornwell

Gary Hill:

An Interview

You walk into a long, corridor-like space. It is completely dark and totally silent. You hesitate, adjusting to the conditions, wondering if anyone else is there. Time is skewed by the absence of light and sound. You happen to be alone in the space. You walk along the wall and a figure appears from a distance as though coming forward to greet you, then it hesitates, turns, and walks away. You continue walking and another figure approaches you. In all there are sixteen figures whose images are projected against the walls of a 90-foot-long space, one at the end, the others along the sides. Only the figures are illumined. There is no framing to give borders of light. You may be alone or with others in *Tall Ships*. Walking through the space, each viewer triggers electronic switches which, in turn, activate the projections, one at a time. Depending upon the number of visitors, any or all of the sixteen figures may be activated, each totally independent of the others, moving forward, hesitating, or returning into the distance.

Regina Cornwell: Tell me about *Tall Ships,* about the title itself and the experience you wanted to create through this installation.

Gary Hill: The title comes from seeing an old photograph taken in Seattle around 1930. The last tall ship is being moved out of Lake Union before the final section of the Aurora Bridge is put into place. The bridge is actually quite high but still would have clipped the ship's masts. I saw this photograph right around the time of recording the people for the piece. I imagined a sailing ship on the high seas—that

Originally published in *Art Monthly* (October 1993).

frontal view of extreme verticality coming toward you. It has a kind of
majestic buoyancy of something very sure of itself—something that will
come forth with a kind of terrifying grace no matter what. It's dark, it's
very dark, but you can see clearly this beautiful thing cutting through
the night—a night that isn't referenced by day. To think of a person
like this—the human approaching—the notion of "ships passing in the
night" took a certain poetic space that felt very open. I don't think I
was really clear about the piece until I had this title.

RC: What were your production methods? How did you direct the participants and then transcribe the results for the kind of extreme space
of a corridor?

GH: I wanted the whole situation to be as unassuming as possible. All
the people in *Tall Ships* are family or friends or friends of friends. My
daughter, brother, mother, and stepfather are all in the piece. From the
time of conceiving of it to actual production, I simplified the movement of the people involved so that they only came forward and then
returned to a particular place and position of either standing or sitting.
There are a few interruptions to that, for instance, after coming forward they would pause and go back or they would come back a second
time after starting to return. It was shot in a long, dark room—it was a
50-foot walk toward me and the camera. As each came forward, together we would be almost holding an imaginary ball between us.
Some would get more and more uncomfortable, others would pass
through this threshold of "how long have I been out there?" In other
words, what all the viewers do, I went through with each filmed person. Originally, the figures were to speak to the visitors, but even after
I decided to delete the speaking, I considered the sounds important: I
imagined filling the space with silence.

I didn't want any theater or aesthetic. In terms of the piece as a
whole, I wanted to avoid it being an experience to do with technology
or anything to do with a multicultural agenda. It's simply the idea of a
person coming up to you and asking, "Who are you?" by kind of mirroring you and at the same time illuminating a space of possibility for
that very question to arise. Basically, I wanted to create an open experience that was deliberate and at the same time would disarm whatever
particular constructs one might arrive with, especially in a museum.

I would like to do more work, as I have in *Tall Ships,* that involves stripping down, breaking down to something very close to absence. It was very easy to make; I only shot for two days, then there was a few days' editing. That easiness somehow reassured me about the work. Rather than thinking "this is so easy, there must be something wrong," this easiness seemed to come out of the work and it became a case of accepting it, going through with it, and not saying "I must do something else."

RC: Would you say a few words about the child at the end of the corridor? She is the only child among the participants and assumes the central position.

GH: Originally I hadn't intended to have someone there but as we were installing it seeing that blank void suggested too much a sense of the infinite. Without any figure there the others would seem to go on forever like a hall of mirrors. I wanted the space to retain a sense of place somehow. I decided on having the child there which would produce a certain amount of closure but at the same time suggest an openness, a future, the possible.

RC: You mentioned that producing *Tall Ships* was quite easy. Would you say something about the installation's technology?

GH: All the images are on one laserdisc, and there are twelve to sixteen copies, depending on the number of projections, all of which are linked to one computer. There are things called "switch runners" under the carpet which trigger the images, and there's a 5-foot section for each projection. I've used 4-inch black-and-white monitors with lenses placed on top of them. And the reason that they're angled so much—it becomes somewhat of a compromise, but I really don't mind that—was that if you do it that way the viewer can get really close to the wall and not interrupt the projection. In other words, they're projected from about 9 feet up, directly down on the wall. To do that extreme angle the whole recording was digitally keystoned to cancel out the distortion. So if you look at the images on a regular monitor the figures are distorted with large heads and small feet.

RC: At *documenta IX* I had a sense of anxiety in the space. I couldn't see, it was really dark, but at the same time it was an extraordinary experience . . .

GH: I think this anxiety is very much a part of the ingress. Once you are in and over your initial trepidation then perhaps some questions arise, "What kind of a space am I in?" "How long is it?" "Who are these figures?" "How long will they look at me?" "Am I making them move?" "Can I talk?" These questions are not so much answered as slowly illuminated both figuratively and literally. As the figures come forth they provide the light in the space. Silhouettes of other viewers begin to appear. In a sense, the "ships passing in the night" become not only the figures and you, but you and other viewers. You begin to see the shapes and shadows and light cast by the figures onto people's faces. It's very subtle, but the viewers begin to mix with the projections.

RC: Is this a radical departure from other installations?

GH: Well, yes and no. There are technical aspects and to some extent the "content" is very close to *BEACON (Two Versions of the Imaginary)*. There are two projections of two different images out through the ends of a tube. The tube rotates very slowly in an equally darkened space and the images continually expand and contract around the room. Technically, the projections of both works were obtained the same way, so the visual quality of the images is very similar. The same kind of "assemblage" projections are used—very primitive, black and white, with the same monitors and surplus projection lenses. As in *Tall Ships* there are a number of full-figured images along with portrait-like shots. All were recorded with a rotating camera that moved counter to the projections in the installation. This in effect canceled out the movement so that it looks like a spotlight (or beacon) passing across the people, illuminating them in the space which also happens to the viewers in the space.

RC: How is this related to *Tall Ships*?

GH: I used a similar approach in recording the people. With the exception of the two readers in *BEACON,* whom much of the time you see reciting the text, the remaining people are seen looking or watching. So in both works the viewers and viewed are intertwined in a number of ways. I hadn't thought of it before but it's interesting to think about the relationship of the metaphors at play in the two pieces—beacons and tall ships.

RC: Given the complexities of the textual layering in most of your work, does the absence of sound in *Tall Ships* point in a new direction?

GH: *Suspension of Disbelief* is silent too, but I think that the silence in *Tall Ships* is more active—it feels present and brings the impending contact with the figures really out in the open. It's as if you are out on "mind island" with this or that person and you feel there must be something to say. I think this kind of radically stripped-down space is also very uncomfortable for some people. Instantly they want to fill it with talking.

The possibility of working with interactive systems has always been in the back of my mind, or a thorn in my side depending on the context I'm thinking in. I wanted the interactivity to be virtually transparent to the point that some people would not even figure it out. I didn't want somebody going in there and, in a sense, playing. I mean "play" like cause and effect—I'm pushing this and this is happening. I think this is the major problem with interactive work in general. You have to find a way around the mind being told where and when it may make a choice. It has to "dawn" on the mind.

RC: You have been quoted as saying "If I have a position it is to question the privileged place that image or, for that matter, sight holds in our consciousness." Would you comment on this?

GH: About the image being privileged, even in the most obvious sense, when we say "seeing is believing" or "I have to see it," so much of our culture tends to rely on the image. Images are so all-pervasive; in a sense we walk around with our eyes—the given gaze; it's a passive process in a way. Because the image's existence in *Tall Ships* is directly related to the viewer's activity and is always blurring the distinction between lightness and darkness, it resists passivity; the light directly involves the viewer in the space. It becomes something shared by the viewer and the image as an active relationship.

RC: In the light of your strong concern with language, especially in your single-channel tapes, would you comment on this quote: "Language can be this incredibly forceful material: there's something about it where if you can strip away its history, get to the materiality of it, it can rip into you like claws, whereas images sometimes just slide off the edge of your mind as if you were looking out of a car window."

GH: Quotes, like anything, have their context. I'm really looking for another way outside the theoretical dualism concerning language and image. I am still very interested in the image being experienced self-consciously rather than merely being a given. I think this comes through particularly in my installation work—the way that one has to complete the image or at least negotiate with it in space. At times it's an image on the edge of visibility as in *Tall Ships* and *BEACON* or one that exists for a very brief moment that only becomes "seen" as part of a "swarm" of other brief moments making a kind of trace as in *Suspension of Disbelief* and *Between 1 & 0.* But text and all that that implies has also become suspect to me. I'm really interested in the newer possibilities of intermedia, particularly the electronic forms with their inherent feedback attributes. This is why I've continued to work with video and electronic media for so long.

RC: Do you see *Tall Ships* and other recent works as phenomenological, insofar as you are interested in language and thinking about the problem of the mind/body, subject/object split?

GH: When I work, I don't work theoretically. I am not a Heideggerian; I am not a Derridean. I'm not any of these things, although people may assume that I am. I'm more physical; I'm posthistorical in the sense that I don't really work much with history. I'm very interested in the way that my body rubs up against the world, the sound of my speech, how we see. I might begin a work on a pinpoint of an idea; but I don't *know* what will happen. I'm committed to the idea that the event takes place within a process and one has to be open to that event, able to kind of wander in it, see it through until some kind of release feels inevitable.

RC: Are you still making single-channel tapes?

GH: The last tape I made was literally on December 23, 1990, commissioned by LA SEPT, for a series called *Live,* in which the artist had to produce a work in real time (no editing) that would be an hour long. This proved to be extremely difficult. Although it's not successful in a number of ways, it renewed my interest in real time.

I'm also interested in making film. It's a different scale. With video, it's so cheap you can shoot as much as you want. In film, real time is replaced by "you've got to get this, this is the one time." It's that sort of intensity.

Tape is so far from being something that's about something visual; it's very much a conceptual medium. If you put a camera, a person, and a monitor together you have that totality of the loop: a seer being seen and then something that's showing both what is being produced at the same time. That is embedded in the medium, whether you use it literally or not. I'm really talking about feedback, of things folding back on other things, affecting them. Then there's response and interaction which folds back again in a sort of ongoing process of seeing oneself being seen.

RC: Today, while there is more installation work involving media such as video or new technologies, the interest in it is still slight. In terms of a response from the art press, why do you think that it is so minimal and why, when it is there, is it so critically and theoretically underdeveloped?

GH: The object has been revered for so long and is so much a part of the economic base of art that people really have to have an experience that turns their minds and breaks the habit of wanting *things.* Even conceptual art was assimilated more easily into art culture because, in the end, there was still some sort of static object.

Once you ask the viewers to enter time, or tell them that in fact you want their time, there's another kind of expectation. Performance and media art, in their own ways, reside somewhere between theater and cinema, respectively, and the plastic arts. I think this is what lends them a certain flux—their "cultures" have more inputs and outputs—by nature they are more interactive and driven by intermedia tendencies.

Most of the time this kind of work falls between the cracks. Either you have theoreticians applying the theories of the likes of Baudrillard and/or stealing from McLuhan—but nevertheless completely missing simply because they are not attending to the work itself—or you have the art critic who comes from an historical base of objects and images but doesn't have a clue about technological systems and can't begin to consider epistemological or ontological questions pertaining to art.

RC: For a time you were better known in Europe than in the States. Why do think this was so?

GH: I suppose as far as the art world is concerned that was true. But I really matured as an artist through the media/video community in the

States, most notably New York. Maybe in time the art world will see the significance of many things that were done which weren't looked at because video simply wasn't a commodity. Toward the beginning it really functioned as an alternative supported by grants; media arts survived independently of the art world.

My reception in Europe, which really gained momentum in France, was perhaps first due to my concerns with language, in particular the writings of Maurice Blanchot. But I think, too, it had a lot to do with timing. I had been exhibiting a great deal more in Europe at the time and European spaces, whether it was museums, galleries, or other spaces, had been quicker to show video installations. Even though I've shown quite a bit in the States—I think I've been in every Whitney Biennial since 1981—so much of the time the context is compromised. It's still a situation of video being ghettoized, although this seems to be changing in both Europe and the States. Last year at *documenta* there were a number of media works, and you could hear curators, critics, museum directors, etc., saying something to the effect of "video has finally come of age." You just felt like saying, "No, video has not finally come of age, *you* have finally come of age."

Louis-Jose Lestocart

Surfing the Medium

Louis-Jose Lestocart: I believe you were influenced by the music of La Monte Young and Cage. Could Cage's idea of prepared piano be applied to your work?

Gary Hill: Young was more of an influence than Cage. Two things he wrote have stayed with me. One of them is the idea of being inside a sound. I think this comes across in my relation to physicality. For instance in the switch pieces like *Between 1 & 0* (1993) and *Circular Breathing* one has the sense of being in the space with the images. In *BEACON (Two Versions of the Imaginary)* (1990) and *Tall Ships* (1992) the viewer is in relationship to the projections. The other idea that rings in my ears is that "tuning is a function of time." That also resonates with Heidegger's notion of living in time or being face to face.

As for "prepared video," that has more to do with Nam June Paik. In relation to Cage's silence work (4:33) there's La Monte Young's piece where he released a butterfly into the performance space. It's cinematic in a way, you have the image of sound through the flapping wings— something like a flicker film.

LJL: You have done a lot of work on the physicality of language since *Elements* (1978), *Around & About* (1980), and *Primarily Speaking* (1981–83). But silence is increasingly prominent in your recent works. What is the meaning of this fading of the voice?

GH: Certainly in these earlier works the connection between image and speech is particularly physical. The speaking—the output of voice—is

Originally published in *Art Press* 210 (February 1996).

in some sense generating the images. But I don't think it's a matter of the voice disappearing. It has more to do with extending intertextuality, with treating images as a kind of language using markings and erasure or the generating of sentences. In *Suspension of Disbelief* (1991–92) the presence of the bodies has an urgency, a continuity not unlike the process of writing. I have an ambiguous relationship to language.

Obviously I'm in the thick of it but I can't quite give myself to it the way a writer would. The key word here being "it." In that sense I share the event of "it" with the writer and anyone else who looks for the cracks between words, images, and meanings—that is, the fallibility of "techknowledgy." I suppose *Remarks on Color* (1994) has something of this attitude with the child reading, or phonetically negotiating a philosophical text. The relationship of language to visible color phenomena is questioned with the kind of wonderment one associates with a child. One begins to empathize with the child reader while the misreading of a word here and there spins the meanings off in other directions. In a way there is a similar identification with the performers in *Why Do Things Get in a Muddle?* (1984).

By the Thread of Reading

LJL: Talking of cracks in meaning, how did Blanchot influence *Incidence of Catastrophe* (1987–88)?

GH: In fact, *Incidence* came after an installation called *In Situ,* where there are scenes inspired by Blanchot's *Thomas the Obscure.* In particular there's one where I am sitting alone at a dinner table, reading, and you see me falling backward, pulling the tablecloth and all the food and plates along with me. Anyway, while reading this book I had the rather strange experience of the book reading me—we were reading each other somehow. And the experience was quite physical. It reminds me of a scene in *Incidence:* at first you see two totem-like forms outlined by light. Suddenly they move and you realize it's a person from the back leaning over a book supporting their head with their forearms. It's like being outside yourself seeing yourself read and the narrator is in the same room. Originally I considered this as the opening shot of the piece.

In Situ (1986) was the first work in which I pulled the television tube from its enclosure. The frame, as it were, was still there, so it gave an impression of the tube being an eye shrinking from its skull. This relationship was mirrored in an easy chair facing the set; its seat cushion was about two-thirds normal size. So these elements of catastrophe and entropy have been ongoing, as in *Muddle* and *CRUX* (1983–87).

LJL: *Inasmuch* (1990) seems to reflect Blanchot's ideas about the suffering or despair created by writing as a process occurring in the present.

GH: Well, I have to say that I'm beginning to suffer more as time goes on with making images (*laughs*). I don't know if that reflects. *Inasmuch* was sort of an explosion or magnification of the last scene of *Incidence.* I also recently "discovered" that the text from one of the *Videograms* (1980–81) is very close to a literal description of this same scene. In all these works language, meaning, and in a sense the vessel from which these flow—the body—are going through an entropic process toward either some prelinguistic state or a process of death—it's rather ambiguous.

LJL: What about the idea of still life and *vanitas* painting in this work—Zurbaran, say, or Cotan?

GH: Certainly there is a play off that. Imagistically I was thinking more along the lines of catacombs—you have to hunch over a bit and lean into the work to get at its "liveness." But when I make a piece I'm not thinking about *vanitas* or deconstruction, or the fragmented body. References and relationships come in retrospectively, but the actual making occurs in a cybernetic or feedback environment with cameras, monitors, and signal flow; it's me and this media. *Inasmuch* came from the idea of putting parts of the body into different sized spaces or video tubes that would display them actual size, giving them a kind of autonomy. The other essential element was the processual event of each image. They are circuitous loops about 5 to 40 seconds long repeating from frame A to frame B, which are identical. I did this by monitoring my body and mixing it with the superimposition of a freeze-frame: the moment the freeze-frame is activated my body would leave that image and then I took as long as was necessary to return to the frozen image, making a loop. It was interesting finding the body in space—there are infinite positions possible. I could sense the texture of my skin, the marks and hairs.

LJL: What is the significance of the sound of murmuring or rustling pages in your work?

GH: I wanted to give a physicality to the text-as-body and body-as-text idea. I mean, the horizontal inset the piece lies in could be used for books. Maybe the figure could be a sort of bookkeeper like in Greenaway's *The Cook, The Thief, His Wife, Her Lover.* The sound of paper and breathing, of skin on skin and the little noises the mouth makes between and among its utterances all seemed connected—I wanted their intertextuality to be felt.

CRUX has a similar relation to physicality, although more centered on the image and body. The idea was to attach view to the body and not the eye. The body parts are always seen pinned to the frame. The cameras become nails in a crucifixion and the cameraman and his image are one and the same. One is in a real-time physical process and the environmental space is completely fragmented.

LJL: Your movements often seem to take place in the same kind of environment, a forest with branches, and then you come to the sea. Is this a representation of your own inner space?

GH: I've certainly used numerous images of the forest and the sea literally and metaphorically. I have lived in or near these two environments for most of my life, it affects how I see and think about things in very particular ways. Maybe this is why I got so much from Bateson's *Steps to an Ecology of Mind,* his ideas about the mind or at least thoughts as being an ecosystem like a forest, where some trees or thoughts live and some die. The formation and breaking of waves are rich metaphors for media, but then, as Bateson said, "What are Metaphors" anyway?

The Topology of Mind

LJL: Would you agree that *Happenstance* (1982–83) offers the best approach to your work, in that it both initiates and sums up?

GH: Considering the subtitle—"part one of many parts"—I'm not surprised you ask. In terms of its intertextual nature and the way it reflects a kind of working methodology, of interacting with the event as it arises . . . yes, *Happenstance* has provided many seeds. The relationships among sound, image, speaking, and writing are perhaps the most complex in all my work. There is a kind of topological enfolding of thinking made visible—its physicality, that in different ways has continued in other pieces.

LJL: In *Site Recite* (1989) the out-of-focus and in-focus views of the objects on the table can be compared to the focused and unfocused bit at the beginning of *Why Do Things Get In a Muddle?* Was the idea of *Site Recite* contained in this beginning of *Muddle?* Also, could you tell us how in *Site Recite* you made a complex montage look like one long, continuous shot?

GH: The table in *Muddle* was built to fit a hexagonal space in the Stained Glass Studio, which belongs to George Quasha. It's true, there is something of a play on focus with the objects. It's not as specified as in *Site Recite*. It's a kind of cosmology of things that are referred to during the muddle that takes place after. In *Site Recite,* a large round tableau with found objects consisting mostly of what I like to call a cosmology of death was surrounded with a dolly track. Thirteen circular tracking recordings were made, each with a different fixed focus length. Additionally, focus pulls in and out across the table were made at 64 points on the circle. These overlapping circles and intersections created 832 matched frames. The original idea was to do an interactive work in which, through some kind of interface, one could travel through these objects in real time while at the same time generating a spoken text. The text would continuously unfold in a reflexive manner and also maintain syntactical sense so that one would have the experience of meaning being generated physically in real time. I wanted to avoid the collage aspect of so many interactive works that ultimately just point out the quantity of possibilities. In the end I just made a single travel with a linear text, representing one possible way. But this piece is really what led to *Withershins* (1995), where the interaction is not image-based but sound-based, the same text being spoken by a man and a woman depending on which side you entered. Two people can be tracked—can trigger the speech—and any number of people can be in the maze. The text deals with left- and right-handedness and plays off Matthew's words from the Bible—"And if the right hand did not know what the left hand is doing." Not only is the text continuous no matter where you go, the content reflects the architectural topology of your movement. In certain places the text is six layers deep so even if you go back and forth along a path the text will continue to unfold new passages. There is one area of the maze that is symmetrical and the text is only one or two layers deep but is structured in such a way that alternating phrases kind of mirror one another.

The Role of the Mirror

LJL: What about the role of mirrors in your work? The idea of two opposing paradigms—say nonsense or sense, or order and entropy—seems to be a recurring theme. In *Muddle,* voices or actions and meanings change or turn around, as if we were on the other side of the mirror. The same kind of process occurs in *URA ARU (the backside exists)* (1985–86), where the other side is shown by the Noh actor.

GH: I work the in-between of these opposing elements. The dominance of one or the other is always deflected in some way. I think the question of symmetry is fundamental in my work. *URA ARU* has remained problematic for me. I went to Japan and just kind of groped for six months. When I came back to the States I made *Muddle* and during the production a number of acoustic palindromes cropped up, one being "flesh-shelf." When I returned to Japan I began to think of this in terms of Japanese, because the phonetic sounds of Japanese are easier to reverse and are oftentimes symmetrical; there are no diphthongs like in English. But I don't speak Japanese, so I had to take dictionaries and look up the meanings of words, finding sounds that could be reversed by trial and error and making a lexicon. As it turned out, many of these words were archaic but still used in Noh. I was very interested in Noh and its multiple concepts of time—"split time," "reverse time," "simultaneous time"—all of which had implications for electronic media. The first version of the tape, the Japanese version, does not have the English text encrusted in the image, it's just sound. Somehow I was really estranged from this work and I had to "remake" it with my own language as a kind of response. The problem though is that this eliminates the phenomenological aspect of the experience of the sound itself. Only a Japanese person, or someone who speaks Japanese really well, can experience the physicality of the reversal and that it means something—a sort of origami-like unfolding of language. But then there's a kind of paradox, which is that the Japanese do not relate to language phonetically in that way: Japanese is image-based. So the work exists in a strange space. It's interesting to think that the place where the Noh actor prepares himself is called "the mirror room," and to ask: what would the video room be, as a metaphor for the difference between them? How would the idea of video play out in some virtual idea of Noh? In a mirror you don't see yourself as someone else sees you, the image is reversed, whereas in video you do. What would happen if a Noh drama took place after being in the video room?

LJL: Why did you choose gnostic texts for *DISTURBANCE (among the jars)* (1988), and those specific poets, and Derrida, to read them?

GH: George Quasha suggested I look at these texts and subsequently became involved in the work. George and I both selected the parts of the text and then gave them to specific people who would do what they wanted with it. It was all very spontaneous. In the case of Derrida it was something of a long shot but with a little persuasion he went for it. We also tried Blanchot and the phone call was quite interesting. A woman answered the phone and said, "It would be better if you wrote a letter." Unfortunately we didn't have time to do that, but in terms of Blanchot's relation to writing the reply made perfect sense. Seconds after putting down the phone we looked up at each other with the same expression on our faces and George says, "Maybe that was Blanchot" . . . speaking through the other. I remember asking Derrida if he thought there was some connection between *Thomas the Obscure* and the Gospel according to Thomas and he just said, "It's possible."

The way that work came about was highly interactive and collaborative, at least during the initial production stage. There was no scenario. In the end, I had this material of highly performative works from which I constructed the piece. It's strange because the work looks highly scripted. This was a commissioned work done at the Pompidou and the studio there had trouble dealing with the improvisational impulse we brought into their space. Without a script I was not a professional! By summer's end this produced a kind of good and bad energy that played into the whole gnostic idea. The gnostic texts had a similar kind of effect on me as reading Blanchot's writing, in that they seemed very present, very alive. They seem to open up as you read them. Their meaning seems to only hold if kept from freezing up. By their nature these texts were open to new readings and voices.

LJL: How does the installation of *DISTURBANCE,* with the platform and people seated around it like in a school, relate to the desk and the video image of a wave in *Learning Curve* (1993)?

GH: There's something to do with distancing that relates the two works and I suppose the notion of something forming or unfolding before you is similar. The use of the wave as a metaphor for a state of perpetual becoming in *Learning Curve* no doubt has a connection to my experience as a surfer. The goal of surfing is to get inside the space of the wave—what surfers call "the green room." Another theme is the difference of the learned position and experiential position. Formally, there's the visual relation between the curve of the table around your body and the curve of the wave. I wanted the site, including the seated viewer, to be an experience of this perpetual becoming. Heidegger comes to mind here. Thierry de Duve pointed out to me a passage McLuhan wrote about Descartes riding the mechanical wave and Heidegger riding the electronic wave. I wrote a little text called *Surfing the Medium* which asks what would have happened if, rather than coming out of the landlocked forest, where his etymological play has its metaphor in roots, he had lived by the sea working from an amphibious point of view? I was also thinking about John C. Lilly's work with dolphins and isolation tanks. The difference is worth pondering. That was when I saw a piece by a Spanish artist in the form of a street sign, or maybe a station sign, which said, "Heidegger sur mer." Interesting.

LJL: What are your current projects?

GH: I've just finished editing a piece for the Lyon Biennale, *Placing Sense ↔ Sens Placé*. It consists of four 32-inch color monitors positioned on low dollies. Each are attached to cables 75 feet long and can be moved by the viewer with the instruction that all four image displays can be at least partially seen from one fixed vantage point. All the images are shot in the house. I'm not looking through the camera but carrying the "object of seeing" with me, and putting it down here and there. And this happens at exactly the same time on all four monitors: suddenly there are four places, images, objects, sites, and then they're ripped from view. You hear the sound, you can feel the physical placement of the camera object. There's a return to the physicality of the thing. By moving the image/objects—the monitors —the viewer extends the process from the house to the space housing the work. In the context of the Biennale this "interactive" aspect could be construed as a little tongue-in-cheek. The interaction is merely physical, not electronic or virtual.

Christine van Assche

Six Questions to Gary Hill

Christine van Assche: Would you create work without the use of machines?

Gary Hill: Who knows and why not? On the other hand I've been using machines in my work for a long time. Perhaps the decision to not use a machine would only arise as a self-conscious gesture. I always work with the kept catastrophic threat to pull the plug—to pull the rug out from under the system. Part of it comes down to one's definition of machines in the larger lexicon of technology and I am presuming we are speaking about "thinking" machines, that is, the cybernetic kind. Machines breed a systems approach and much of the time I'm looking elsewhere. Machines don't really think, they only humor you to think that they think. Machines pretend to think. Contrary to AI pundits I won't consider it a milestone when IBM's Big Blue beats all humans at chess. That all has to do with calculation and speed, albeit tremendous quantities of both, but when the mind is called into thinking, something else altogether is taking place.

CVA: Is there an internal necessity to the use of machinery or is it just a sign of the times?

GH: Machines are not only a sign of the times but they affect our relation to time directly. Speed has infiltrated everything. One's sense of place, physicality, the body, communication, economy, and media are all changing at exponentially faster rates. And yet this speed/time

Originally published in *Parachute* 84 (October, November, December 1996), pp. 42–45.

doesn't have much to do with being(s) in relation to the ontological questions of time. Nevertheless, we are face to face with technology because we are technological. It's not something you choose to partake in or not; the question of necessity is moot. Even a painter's relation to paint has been dramatically affected by the invention of acrylics. Not only are color and viscosity different but even the painter's relation to (drying) time has substantially changed.

CVA: Which comes first, the machinery or the idea?

GH: It all depends. Ideas come from many different and, for the most part, serendipitous occasions. I could be driving in a car and see something when I'm thinking about something completely different, and the images and thoughts collide and trigger something. Ideas are not units of thought isolatable from other ideas/thoughts. On a map the actual birth of an idea would be like going back into a forest where you think you saw a specific plant and finding it. Working with electronic media becomes second nature like anything else. It's integrated into the tools at hand.

CVA: What do you think of the new technologies—the internet, hypermedia, virtual reality, artificial intelligence?

GH: In a sense I've already been using computers, hypermedia, virtual reality, and artificial intelligence for a long time—just not in the way that it's packaged now. Wordplay is hypermedia, isn't it? As Gregory Bateson asks, "What are Meta fors anyway?"

CVA: With whom do you feel closest in the art world?

GH: I don't know. I suppose the closest person that's dead center in the art world I continue to look at is Bruce Nauman. His use of language has a particular attraction for me. Cindy Sherman, too. I've always been interested in the idiomatic use of images and she continues to make brilliant pictures. I will still go and see Robert Ashley, Laurie Anderson, and La Monte Young when I can and hopefully I'll get a chance to see Steelarc again. Most recently I've seen interesting performances by the choreographer Meg Stuart of Damaged Goods and the sound poet Chris Mann from Australia. So I guess one could say that I am most near to "time-based art."

CVA: If you lived in the nineteenth century, what kind of artwork would you have produced?

GH: Perhaps something that would reflect the conjoining of Eadweard Muybridge and Lewis Carroll—a kind of hybrid of thinking with machines with a helix of logic and nonsense usurping the system.

George Quasha and Charles Stein

Liminal Performance:

Gary Hill in Dialogue

George Quasha: Your identity as artist seems complex virtually from the beginning: sculptor, sound artist (also sculptural), video artist, creator of installations involving electronics (especially video), language art ("video poetics," as we have called it), and performance art. The latter is perhaps the least well defined and therefore the most interesting ground to break in the present context. But you started out as a sculptor, working with metal. Let's begin by tracing why you turned to video.

Gary Hill: There were a number of overlapping events that took place from 1969 to 1973 when I was living in Woodstock, New York. I did a lot of sound work with my sculpture—sounds generated by the metal constructions themselves. Then I began using tape recorders working with tape loops, feedback, and other electronic sound. I had a little EMS synthesizer in a briefcase. At around the same time, and for the most part by chance, I did some recording with a portapak that I borrowed from Woodstock Community Video. The fluidity of taping and viewing in real time freed up my thinking in a very radical way. Suddenly the sculpture I had been doing for several years seemed overwhelmingly tedious and distant from this present-tense process. Video allowed the possibility to "think out loud" as if with some "other" self. It was a continuously self-renewing situation—like "reality," yet the monitoring gave it a sense of hyperreality. Here was an immediately accessible process that was a seemingly much closer parallel to thinking than basic sculpture.

The very first thing I did was to record myself as I watched myself on a monitor. Then I played *that* back on the monitor and recorded my-

Originally published in *PAJ* 58 (1998).

self interacting with this prerecorded image of myself on the same monitor to combine the recorded and the "live." This really had nothing to do with making images but was rather a kind of externalized thinking pertaining to coherences between mind and body. After this initial discovery I first made a couple of tapes in which there was no editing, no effects. Then I did sort of a performance piece with a friend: we painted colored rectangles all around the town at night. After three or four nights, there were a lot of them, and we got caught and were arrested. I made a documentary about it that included individual responses and suggestions to questions as to whether we should put up more, remove them, etc. It was interesting how the responses correlated with property ownership and private/public space. "Decorating" the war memorial in the center of town was a lot more taboo than we had imagined.

GQ: Sculpture, sound, performance, street performance—this sequence touches a lot of bases that reappear in your work. Perhaps video, given its history of increasing portability, "takes to the streets" even more easily than theater and performance art. Perhaps video is intrinsically performance art, particularly with the advent of the portapak, which if I'm not mistaken also marks the beginning of self-conscious "video art."

GH: Often, especially during those early days, I would indeed "take to the streets"—just to see what I could see, so to speak. And, as you say, inevitably there was a certain self-consciousness. There was something about the extension of one's nervous system through the camera that made for the possibility of connecting to the environment in a very new way. But even when I worked with a conscious idea, with a conceptual parameter, there was always a lot left up to the "medium" and to the event itself. This usually involved feedback loops of some sort— some way of looking at oneself looking and/or performing some kind of activity. Many of my early single-channel video pieces were in a sense "system-performances" that generated their *own* time in relation to *real* time. There are really so many folds in time involving media, feedback, delay, writing, speaking, and the body. Time becomes more like a Möbius band or Klein bottle without an absolutely "real" side.

Charles Stein: So even though there is a real-time element—going into the street and recording what you see—this gets played off in relation to another sense of time that emerges in the specific piece.

GQ: Both senses of time involve "performance": street performance and in a sense studio performance. We'll be looking at the question of studio performance as we go along here, but for the moment I'm wondering about how the notion of performance functions in relation to installation. In both tape and installation work you create structures in which certain kinds of performance are released into action. The difference is that in installation work, which will perhaps be more like theater, the structure and its resulting performances are happening in a physical space rather than on tape. Some of your installations are, from very early on, in some sense performance pieces, most obviously *War Zone* (1980), an early "interactive" piece in which the viewer/visitor in a sense "performs" the work in a way that is specific to each viewer and each viewing. That piece, with its objects whispering their own names through tiny exposed speakers that viewers had to approach, made me think of an experimental/interactive theater set.

GH: Except for the obvious fact of a charged activated space, I'm not sure about the installation/theater connection, at least as a generalization. There have certainly been self-conscious approaches to bridging these forms—Robert Wilson comes to mind, but in his work, however architectural its origins, there is always that "theatrical" tinge. From the other side, where the theatricality is really at a minimum, it's interesting to look at something like Vito Acconci's *Seed Bed.* The differences certainly have to do with scale and perhaps intended audience. I myself, even though at times I come dangerously close to theatricality, try not to let the work cross the line. Rather, there is always a sense of opaqueness in the way that the work is *not* calling out for an audience, or for that matter, not calling outside itself at all. Perhaps this is left over from my sculpture days, but the autonomy of the work itself is still something that I'm very aware of, at least in terms of keeping theatricality at bay.

At this point perhaps it's worth mentioning my first video installation, *Hole in the Wall* (1974), as a kind of bridge from sculpture to video that was a conceptual formal piece installed at the time in somewhat of a political context. The work took place at the Woodstock Artists' Association, which like many other places at the time didn't accept video as an art form. It consisted of setting up a camera in front of a wall and "framing" a section of the wall through the viewfinder that is equal in size and shape to the 20-inch black-and-white monitor, which would later be inserted there. Then, using this fixed camera, I recorded a real-time process of cutting through all the layers of the wall—muslin, wood, aluminum paper, and fiberglass—until finally the last boards were penetrated and the outside world appeared. The tape of the entire process was then repeatedly played back on the monitor, now fitted to the hole in the wall. The image on the monitor was of course on exactly the same scale as its content. Here then is a work in which the performance itself is seen as a video memory, shown at the site where "it" happened; and yet the object/sculpture aspect of the work modulates the performance time by its stasis, its physical presence. Is it still performing? It was certainly a political act in the art world of Woodstock.

CS: You were in fact "installing" video itself into the space of visual art! It's as if you abandon one familiar territory without crossing entirely over to another, but remain in a liminal space between.

GQ: The notion of "liminality," which I have found useful in poetic practice and in defining a "metapoetics" (circa 1969: the inquiry into the principles of open possibility in language), struck us as a necessary notion in discussing your work when we were working on HAND HEARD/*liminal objects* (1995–96), and even before that in my 1988 piece ("Disturbing Unnarrative of the Perplexed Parapraxis: A Twin Text for *DISTURBANCE*"). Indeed your attraction to the notion is expressed in your acceptance of the phrase *liminal objects* for those strange computer-generated object-entities—folded hands whose fingers pass through each other, a wheel that rolls through the pudding-like substance of a bed, etc. They are objects on the threshold of being something other than objects, "animated" in a sense deeper and stranger than the technical. And beyond this we quickly saw that much of your work occurs in a space that is "liminal" to one or several categories of art/thought/behavior; for instance, your work often straddles a productively unsettled space or "threshold" (Latin: *limen*) between mediums.

GH: I suppose that in thinking about my own work I use the more vernacular idea of things that exist "between." "Liminal" had a particular resonance with the computer works you mentioned, suggesting in fact many kinds of liminality and opening onto important philosophical issues. I think my involvement with this kind of issue began early on with thinking about the difference between videotape and installation works—for example, *Around & About* (1980), first a videotape, then an installation, in which a spoken monologue manipulates images, each syllable connecting to a new image. It not only speaks directly to the viewers to the point of seeming to "second guess" their responses, but also, through this image/voice linkage, draws attention to the space *outside* the monitor. One sees images "spoken" on and off the screen; the viewer's position becomes more and more complex in terms of architectural and linguistic space.

CS: So the piece is liminal not only between video and installation but between image and language as well. Both these liminal spaces seem to be developed again and again in your work. It's true for the piece that George mentioned, *War Zone.* Relations among all three elements—video, installation, and languages—proliferate in a context in which each viewer is a performer. In a sense, there is no way that the piece can be taken in as a whole; rather the viewer devises his or her own itinerary through it: what you hear depends upon how you approach the various "talking" objects. What you see depends on how you choose to operate the optical equipment, such as the odd binocular machine with one eye seeing into the room and the other eye viewing animated versions of the objects in the room as seen from the rabbit's point of view. These would switch left/right and even sometimes become a stereoscopic image of one or the other. Here the liminality is in the shifts between objects as animated or real, between objects and brain/eye reception, and between all of this and cognition. Even what you think is happening depends directly on your own acts of attention.

GH: It's a kind of activated field and a field at play. Objects *announce* themselves, and a living rabbit scampers through the space already littered with both visual and auditory representations, interrupting the intellect with pure, immediate intuition. The thing about *War Zone* is that even though there are infinite paths and "takes," I do see it as decodable as a whole to a large degree; but the sense of the piece comes with knowledge slowly discovered as one participates in it, so that the work can contribute to one's questions both about it and about the world at large. To a lesser degree the installation *Primarily Speaking* (1981–83) functions along similar lines. Here you have two facing rows of monitors with images flashing between them, accompanied by a text composed of ready-made phrases that are read out loud on a tape broadcast into the space. The phrases go in and out of connectivity to the images. As different viewers walk along the corridor between the monitors, they identify with the text variously regarding its relationship to the images on the monitors and to their own body. Perhaps one could say that this was a "performance for two walls"! I once received a request for a copy of the text from a man who wanted to give it to his girlfriend—it said "exactly" what he wanted to say to her. Rather strange, but it gave me confidence that I was successful in recharging idiomatic expression.

CS: Again, there is no sense in which the presentation of the material of the piece is "theatrical": whatever content an individual experiences there is not something that is being expressed in a simple fashion by "Gary Hill," either as the creator of the piece or the speaker of the verbal aspect of it. It is rather a spontaneous response of the individual who picks up on a specific set of possible combinations of image, speech, and rhythm at the moment.

GQ: And the sense of the whole of the piece, as with *War Zone,* is something that one discovers slowly as one gains in experience with it.

GH: Maybe in performance in its most theatrical sense you have to get the story *across,* even if this amounts to nothing more than expressing the character of a person. That obviously is not the case with *Primarily Speaking* or *War Zone,* but in a piece like the videotape *Why Do Things Get in a Muddle? (Come on Petunia)* (1984), which does seem to tell a story and to express the personalities of the "characters," there's a quite different raison d'être. The whole matter of character and plot just sort of implodes. The viewer isn't concerned about either character or plot, but rather ends up plumb in the middle of a process wherein the texture of involvement itself is the content/information of the work. The viewer becomes part of the work's unfolding. I can even imagine an audience identifying as a whole and going through something rather strange. In any case there is no theatrical projection from the "performers" out to an intended audience.

GQ: Let me recall the "embedded story" of *Why Do Things Get in a Muddle?* This involved the merging of aspects of two unrelated pieces of writing. One was a "metalogue" from the anthropologist Gregory Bateson's *Steps to an Ecology of Mind.* "Metalogues" for Bateson are conversations where the structure of what happens between the inter-locutors repeats the content of the conversation—an instance of life imitating art at the formal level.

CS: This kind of thing happens in conversation more often than we think. For instance, perhaps this "liminal performance" is itself a metalogue.

GH: Liminally speaking, maybe.

GQ: (*laughs*) What's striking is how *dramatic* the dialogue is in and of itself. That particular metalogue is a conversation between Bateson and his daughter. The other text was *Alice in Wonderland.* Bateson's metalogue becomes the "Alice" dialogue. At the beginning of the piece, Chuck [Charles Stein, who "performed" in it during its creation in Barrytown, N.Y.] simply read the part of Bateson while holding the book on camera, and Kathy [Bourbonais] read the part of his daughter. But after a few minutes, things develop strangely where Kathy turns into "Alice," and the language itself undergoes a bizarre transformation. What is actually happening is that the characters are speaking their lines and performing their actions backward, but the tape re-reversed the speech and movement so that everything seems to be happening in the right direction, only crazily distorted.

GH: The performers in fact are completely concentrated on the job at hand with all they can muster. The engagement with these tasks generates all kinds of emotive content that has nothing to do with skill in acting, and which for the most part is unknown to the actors or even actually felt by them. The viewer identifies with them as people who are going through some kind of strange trip—"through the looking glass," as it were.

CS: Certain weird emphases occur in both speech and gesture that were not even "unconscious" in the actual "take." Neither Kathy's long, sultry gazes nor the frenzied quality of my impatience with her were actually present in the energy of the shooting situation. They seem very expressive, but expressions of what exactly? It is quite peculiar, really. I remember how while working on *Why Do Things Get in a Muddle?* we were constantly talking about the different possibilities of meaning that what we were doing supported. We had the Gregory Bateson text, *Alice in Wonderland,* the commitment to work with talking backward, and just about everything else was a matter of continuous discovery along the way. We had an intuition that reversing language, perhaps in its violence and even perversity, would be a fruitful field for exploration. But it was as if the richness of the intellectual content that I believe the piece ends up having, was itself something that emerged "in process," and not at all something that *guided* the piece as its intention from without.

GH: *Why Do Things Get in a Muddle?* is a good example of how a lot of ideas begin for me as questions that arise from possibilities close at hand, like one's own body or speech or the way a system is patched together. I had begun to think about the piece after experimenting with talking backward using a reversible tape recorder. That seemed possible, but I had nowhere to go with it. In fact, at first it was talking backward itself, without re-reversing the output, that seemed interesting. The ploy of performing the double reversal only came to mind after reading the "Metalogues" in the Bateson book and deciding to use one of them as a text. And then it turned out that Bateson mentions *Alice in Wonderland* so many times that what was in fact an encrustation—turning the character in the "metalogue," who actually is Bateson's daughter, into Alice—became natural. Of course the "Alice" books are filled with reversals, so there was an enormously rich area for the play of analogies and concepts, and for working with images whose import lay not in their character as images but in their logical or pseudo-logical implications. And once those ideas were in place, the work began, in the Red Hook Diner, actually.

You remember how every morning we'd go to breakfast and play this game where one of us would say a word backward and the other one would have to figure out what it was. We were in fact studying what was really involved in talking backward, which, as should be obvious, is quite different from just spelling words backward. While we practiced in this way, I was transcribing the Bateson text into a kind of phonological score—writing it out so that we would have a way to work on talking backward. As a matter of fact, this is the only piece of mine that I can think of offhand that, ironically, had to be completely scripted out; the reversed language/sound had to be worked out phonetically in detail and then scored for the rise and fall of pitches. But, even so, there were always unexpected happenings. And, as you say, there was a continuous discussion of the possibilities of meaning regarding what we were doing. Basically moving and speaking backward is something like swimming upstream.

GQ: In terms of viewer/audience, I would think the projective installation *Remarks on Color* (1994) would have had a similar relationship to performance in the sense that, here again, the qualities the audience perceives in "the character" performing in the piece are in no way things that the young girl is trying to get across.

GH: Absolutely. You see an 8-year-old child reading Wittgenstein's book of that title, struggling with pronouncing the words of a text she can't possibly understand. The piece "frames" her 45-minute action (facing us as a video projection on a wall) as if she's on stage, but she never looks up; she's objectified as "the reader." The whole performance has a "random" character in that it's impossible to know what she will come up with, and for her it's just a difficult and strange thing to be doing in front of a camera. It's a completely unprecedented and unrepeatable performance of the text, analogous in a way to bringing an unsuspecting person on stage in a theater event, so that the outcome is just an actual extension of who she or he is in that context.

GQ: In this way it's also related to such pieces as *DISTURBANCE (among the jars)* (1988) and *Tall Ships* (1992), which bring "real people" (nonactors/performers) into highly structured contexts, asking them to do something that is not a matter of their expertise or previously focused abilities—to perform the unknown, so that they reveal something unique to their presence there. In *Tall Ships* there are "ordinary people" who seem to walk up to you in the dark and just stand and stare—the effect of which is to make the viewer, paradoxically, feel somewhat "onstage." In *DISTURBANCE* very sophisticated people, such as Jacques Derrida, have to read unfamiliar texts from the gnostic gospels (the Nag Hammadi library)—a sort of adult version of the child reading Wittgenstein; a public meditation with an unexampled sense of wonder. Indeed, the particular sense of liminal performance here consists in the apparent fact that Derrida felt free in the context of a "performance piece" to manifest himself in an unpremeditated way. He didn't have to "perform" at all; yet he was at once in an exciting way both at hazard in, and protected by, the performance context.

GH: I think that this is pretty much the space that I often attempt to work in. Many of the single-channel works were structured in such a way as to allow that unpremeditated activity on my part in producing them. I'm thinking in particular of works where I myself appear on camera. I'm not really performing as an actor performs, but rather taking part in an open system that I myself have devised. Again, in many instances they are similar to the performances in *Why Do Things Get in a Muddle?* and *Remarks on Color* and several other installations as well. For example, in the installation *CRUX* (1983–87) you see five monitors mounted on a wall suggesting the form of a crucifix. On the screens are tapes of myself: at the top, my head; horizontally to the left and right, my hands; at the bottom close together, my feet. The tapes show me moving strangely through the difficult terrain of a ruined castle on an island in the Hudson River, and, of course, there is the symbolic suggestion of the crucified body, a kind of "Stations of the Cross" and Crucifixion all in one. But the visceral nature of my activity—walking with cameras attached to my body along with the weight of the recorders—breaks through these representations very quickly. My movement is at best awkward, and there is a distinct sense of separation from the environment around me. I'm "nailed," as it were, to a continuously changing ground and sky by the cameras, which have fixed frames focused on my extremities. What is actually happening is that I'm just trying to make it from point A to point B [on an island in the Hudson River a few miles south of the Beacon-Newburgh Bridge, in and around the ruins of an abandoned turn-of-the-century armory called Bannerman's Castle] without falling down, and all the nuances, facial contortions, and distortions of scale between the body and the environment simply occur given the "happenstance" of the paths I take.

The relationship to performance, at least in the way we are speaking about it now, shifts in an interesting way with a work like *In Situ* (1986). Rather than setting up a frame/context in which I or someone else goes through a process, each viewer walks into a system performance: a single monitor turns on and off, revealing the collapse of the raster; electric fans in all four corners of the room also go on and off, stirring up the air, into which printed copies of images from the screen are ejected down from the ceiling on and around a chair. This chair obviously occupies *the* viewing position. It has a shrunken cushion doubling the "shrunken" cathode ray tube that looks to be falling from its larger frame. The work physically presents ruptures between public media and private space—my first encounter with Blanchot's *Thomas the Obscure*. This was the precursor to *Incidence of Catastrophe* (1987–88).

CS: Most recently, in *Viewer* (1996), performance in a sense faces itself: the day-workers perform their own being by just standing in front of the camera, standing, that is, projected, on the gallery wall. Performance is reduced to the raw element of bare human presence on the part of the "performers" and bare presence of attention on the part of ourselves as "viewers." The viewers *perform* the act of viewing. The performers just stand and *view*.

GQ: How is this raw sense of viewing informative of "video," which is, after all, Latin for "I see"?

GH: Well, I've always downplayed the etymological root of the word *video* and its direct connection literally with seeing, because of the emphasis on image. I've even gone so far as to attack "video" as ultimately the wrong word for what I, at any rate, think I'm involved with. For me, this would hold true for the meaning of the title of *Viewer* too, even though of course it does draw upon the site of seeing. It all depends on how much "I see" can be extended ontologically.

GQ: Often "to see" does have a broad ontological extension. We say "I see" to mean the mind's recognition, and of course the root of the Latin word itself is related to "wisdom," "wit," and "vision" in all its senses. There is also the connection with the Greek root of "idea" (*idein*) and the close connection between seeing and thinking in Greek thought. Visual sensation, visualization, thinking as envisioning, and insight, both psychological and spiritual, are potentially alive in the root sense of "video," so perhaps we can say that "video art"—particularly a video art that does not focus primarily on asserting images—restores the root meaning to the word. "Video art" as opposed to video as television, say, protects and recovers possibility. Certainly our choice of "Viewer" for your piece and for our book (*Viewer: Gary Hill's Projective Installations—Number 3*) was meant to do just that, by making the title "performative" of the reflexivity in the viewing situation and the liminal state of any image/object so consciously engaged.

GH: Yes, and getting further into the roots through titling the work *Site Recite* (1989) I discovered an interesting etymological twist where "cite" in its relationship to "read aloud" and to "instigate" (e.g., "incite") goes back to something like to "make move" and eventually connects to the Greek (*kinesis*) which generates "cinematograph." In other words, speaking is directly connected to moving images. This is only a syllable within what turns out to be a very complex title, and titles that come the closest to distilling works into words have always been important to me, as you are well aware, having collaborated on several of mine—for instance, *Tale Enclosure,* HAND HEARD/*liminal objects, Viewer, Standing Apart/Facing Faces,* and indirectly (the parenthetical part of) *Learning Curve (still point).*

GQ: Over the years, however, we *have* noticed a certain impatience on your part as regards the distinction "video artist," which still tends to follow your name. Certainly there was a tactical advantage to using that term in the late 1970s and early 1980s when we were applying for grants at Open Studio in Rhinebeck and Barrytown—video was young and exciting and very fundable. But you came from sculpture, were attracted to sound, and very soon to language as medium, no doubt furthered by your interaction with poets, and then moved toward performance. Certainly, it was true of the early experiments with video synthesis in Woodstock, where you were collaborating with Walter Wright and were doing mixed-media performances under the name Synergism, and later working with the electronic designer David Jones in Barrytown. All of this was inherently performative and quickly led into our actual intermedia performances at the Arnolfini Arts Center in Rhinebeck.

GH: I'm definitely not comfortable with the tag of "video artist." Once again, it foregrounds a passive sense of *image.* Virtually all my work in one way or another has something to do with putting into question the hierarchical position of the image. For me, working in video involves a *thinking space* that is part of the milieu of working with electronic media. It includes feedback processes, cybernetics, and various I/Os from and to the world, all on an equal footing with the aspect of the work that has to do with recording and processing visual images. So the term *video art,* even for my work that is technically single-channel video, can be very misleading. Also, keep in mind that the art world didn't so to speak discover video art until *documenta IX* (1992). I think a lot of this comes out of habit and laziness but above all economics.

GQ: Okay. Let's return for a minute to an installation piece that goes far beyond the category "video" and into root issues of language, which to extend the active ground of the creative function of language I might call *metapoetic,* namely, *DISTURBANCE.* The poets—like Bernard Heidseick, performance art master (*poésie sonore*)—for obvious reasons readily accepted our invitation to read gnostic gospels in front of the camera. It's interesting to speculate about why Derrida—a philosopher with no apparent connection to ancient heretical religious texts—would be willing to participate, to perform (does he "act"?). We mentioned the self-protectiveness of the art context, even when it is revealing in an uncomfortable or inconvenient way. Your sense of performance as sculpturally autonomous and not addressed to an audience is, I think, connected to issues that Derrida deals with in the process of his writing and that make it rather exciting even when one doesn't particularly "agree" with him—writing *as* performance. I've had the fantasy that he saw the connection between this opportunity to perform and his mode of "writing/thinking"—a stage on which he could be "meditatively heretical" even to himself.

There are several fairly recent texts of Derrida that are actually lectures—I'm thinking of *Of Spirit: Heidegger and the Question* (1987), for instance, which interestingly dates it around the time of *DISTURBANCE.* That is, the lectures/texts are writing-performances, addressed to a certain audience at a certain time on a certain issue with a certain background, yet they are driven by an internal textual dynamic. A book publishing such language-events is very much like an installation. Perhaps this liminal performance/installation quality is present in the thinkers that you are attracted to—Blanchot even more than Derrida—who seem to work in a way somehow related to how you are working. How do you see this connection between performance and writing?

GH: One might think that performance, even within the context of various self-conscious delimitations, would be closer to Derrida's ideas on grammatology, whereas editing, working with "post-performance" recorded material, might be closer to the space of writing which, by its nature, gives distance and mediation. In one sense the making of *DISTURBANCE* was a two-part ordeal: the performance events and the editing/writing events. And the complexity of the relationship between these two stages of composition could be thought about in terms of the complexity of the relationship in Derrida's thought between speaking and writing. (Derrida thinks that speaking-performing is *already* a kind of writing.) Or perhaps, if we open up performance as we've been speaking about it, by structuring it through other media, other questions such as "What is performance time?" come into play, as well as all the ontological issues that swirl around the very questions we are asking—*then* we might begin to see performance within the domain of writing.

As you know, George, since you were there as collaborator, the production time of *DISTURBANCE* was short indeed—about two weeks. And although we worked hard on the textual base, we didn't produce a script. I had some drawings and structural notes for the initial piece I had planned (called *Vanishing Points*) which at least gave an inkling of the images moving through a sequence of monitors. This was not much to go on, given the level of poets and performers arriving at our doorstep in a steady stream. So various on-the-spot decisions by us and the performers alike became very important, since in retrospect the collected recorded "events" would in some sense become almost "found objects," perhaps something like the Nag Hammadi manuscripts themselves (which were found preserved in ancient *jars*). I suppose a completely different final text could be made from the same raw material.

Long before this, I had similar notions about *Primarily Speaking*—that a completely different set of images could be plugged into the text, although not just *any* images. So our on-the-spot decisions became very important—decisions about the framing and the movement of the performers became deciding factors in structuring the work. Basically I had to work with what I had after everything had been recorded. During the taping, we tried to capture something from each individual performance without thinking about how everything would be woven together in the end. So the improvisational energy along with the inspiration that those heretical texts seemed to engender in the writers produced very powerful results. Given that we rarely did more than a single take, it was remarkable.

More than with the other performing writers, the pressure was on when Derrida came. It was an on-the-spot decision to have him walk back and forth full-bodied all the way through the frame each time. The fact that this made it possible, later in editing, to have him continue through the space of multiple monitors determined a major thread of the piece. (The illusion of his walking continuously from screen to screen across several monitors in a row involved reversing the image each time.) On a subtler level, since he held the text in one hand, every time he walked through and appeared on another monitor, the text would otherwise have changed hands due to the image's having become reversed. This played right into the issues of left and right that appear throughout the work and became one of the major factors in building the fundamental structure of the piece. In the end, the monitors became a fragmented sentence that he was weaving through. But it also made sense in terms of the simple act of walking, thinking, and pacing. There's an interesting connection, which I believe you expressed at the time, to Heidegger's *Conversation on a Country Path,* at least as image.

. . . . .

CS: This sense of language as a kind of walking—the sense that the body activates language—becomes literally the case in *Withershins* (1995), where the participant wanders through a labyrinth laid out on the ground of the installation and each step activates a phrase that is broadcast through the space of the work, so that a text is generated by the act of walking. The labyrinth becomes a kind of brain, and one becomes, as it were, one's own homunculus, walking inside the folds and passageways of one's own cranium. Or again, language itself becomes a brain.

. . . . .

CS: We have been talking about performance in a number of different senses, and perhaps this is the moment to call attention to a meaning of the word *performative* that we have used in discussing your work elsewhere. We borrow the philosopher J. L. Austin's use of this term for utterances that literally *perform the action* of which they speak: I promise, I wish, I accuse, I name, etc.—actions accomplished in their very saying. Such verbal actions close the gap between word and meaning, but can only do their work within the specific contexts that call them forth. . . .

GQ: Performative language is always site-/occasion-specific—it happens here and now.

CS: In some sense, each artistic gesture, each decision or choice, is a performative act, calling into being, or allowing to emerge into being, the particular artistic value with which it is concerned.

GH: Ultimately every word and every moment in a tape (or life for that matter) could be performative almost in and of itself in that sense. I think of La Monte Young's saying, "tuning is a function of time." Each event enters into an evolving relationship with the developing piece, spiraling around and folding in so that at any moment you might "begin" again from a different place. I mean even repeating an image or a sequence can be part of a continuous event; in working on a piece, relistening to a sequence folds a past event back into the present. One just has to be patient, believing something will emerge. But what is it that is the source of this emergence when it does happen? It happens in "the present" but the present has now gained a complexity that quite literally includes the replayed past. This really complicates the question of "real time."

GQ: Everything emerges in the present, but the present is the occasion of a "performance" that includes the replay of real-time taped sequences captured in the past.

Your "every word is performative" expresses the condition of poetry —each word accomplishes its meaning immediately and concretely. In this sense poetry is not the special case of language but the emergence—the eruption—of its deepest nature. We watched your already active awareness of language possibilities grow through your relations to poets in the late 1970s. Your tape *Happenstance* (1982–83), with its literal "spiraling around and folding in" of language, as you say, is as fresh today as the first day I saw it, *as* it was being made, in Barrytown. For me it belonged to the history of what I had already long been calling—thinking of Blake's nonlyric works—"poetic torsion." And frankly *Happenstance* was like a read-out of a part of my own brain, because it proved something I fantasized was true, that in the deepest sense a poem is an animate force that is active in all of the mind's projections, visual/aural/tactile. Blake invented a high-tension open interaction of text and image that rendered both "mind-degradable." *Happenstance* carries that process into territory Blake would have loved. Your sense of textuality sets the viewer-reader *inside* the experience of reading, recognizing that alert acts of reading are actually performative: the world or content of the text is performed on the mind of the reader, or *by* the mind of the reader, as reading takes place. But reading is also a bodily act and a bodily performance, and a book is also a physical occasion, and its physical properties can become part of the reading performance itself. I think this is very much the sense of things that you evoke in *Incidence of Catastrophe* (1987–88), which "takes place" inside the act of reading a text by Maurice Blanchot, *Thomas the Obscure.*

GH: When I read that work, it was as if the edges of the book ceased to exist or that the book took on enormous proportions.

CS: As of course it does for you at the end of your tape.

GH: In *Thomas* the differentiation of the space of the book from that of the author and of the reader collapses, and this creates a state of incredible vertigo; your position is constantly being challenged in terms of where you fit into the narrative as a reader. All you can do is *hold* the book, *feel* the pages, *see* the words as pure things being there, generating a cocoon around you. That experience of reading itself belongs to the main character in the book, but it also is forced upon you as you read it. It's one of the most hallucinatory books I've ever read, not just in the images it creates but in the play of that space. That aspect of the book really rattles me, actually.

GQ: There's a sense that every time one comes to it, it's like a new text—you forget what you've read. Blanchot is the most continuously forgettable unforgettable writer I know! (Except maybe Blake!)

CS: I remember rereading *Thomas the Obscure* a few years after experiencing it the first time. I returned to the text with very sharp memories of certain scenes and certain passages; but when I had read it through, those scenes had completely vanished—they just weren't there. There was, this time, a completely different distribution of images and events —it was quite startling.

GH: The last time I read the book—quite recently, actually—I had a similar experience—even after my close and intense use of it in *Incidence of Catastrophe.*

GQ: What you capture in that work by emphasizing the physicality of the book—the textures of its pages, the sounds of turning them, the resonance between those sounds and the sounds of the surf—is not just an imaginative extrapolation from the subject matter of the book, but a direct portrayal or projection of the book itself—of that aspect of it that is always right in your face, that means to grab hold of you and demonstrate something of the terror and mystery of the ontology of reading. *Incidence of Catastrophe* is as much an intensive commentary on *Thomas the Obscure* as it is a work of art informed by it—a work of art that *performs* the act of reading another.

GH: The impulse to put myself in the place of the protagonist was to make that happen—because otherwise I would have just been outside, trying to *tell* you what reading that book was like. But like I say, that book really rattled me, and the whole point of *Catastrophe* was to deal with that experience.

CS: Yet, once again, that tape was not put together by following a theatrical scenario.

GH: Certainly not. I never really acted in it, per se, as I mentioned before. Most of the scenes were tableau-like. We would set them up and just *perform.* Many times we just left the camera on, recording well past the time limit we had initially decided upon. Generally speaking, that was when interesting things would start to happen. I think that extending the recording time turned out to be key to actually projecting the experience of reading,—the connection between real time and reading time. There are portions of *Catastrophe* where the scenes are purposefully *elongated.* Pages of the book are seen for extended periods of time, considerably longer than mere spectator time. Yet these sequences need to be there to submerge the viewer into the *time of reading*—an actual reading time that's parenthesized in the work—there had to be some actual event of reading: time spent sitting with the book, being with the book.

GQ: There's real time, performance time, and *reading* time—

GH: It's interesting to think in this respect about Noh drama: how in the theory of Noh there are different kinds of times: split time, reverse time, and others. I think there are four or five differentiated concepts of time.

GQ: Perhaps there is something that we could call "deep time" that runs underneath them all and makes them possible—a time that's always there and that you know you can count on, it doesn't have any structure in itself, but it allows whatever time structure is necessary to become available.

GH: It's zero time—as something like the *still point.* In surfing (I just had to get this in) this could be described as the moment in which the surfer finds a position in the "green room" (inside the curl of the wave). And that curving/breaking line is so steadily evolving that it appears to be still. Consequently, the surfer is in the perfect position "infinitely." I think when one is in the creative act, the desire is to find and stay with this kind of still point as long as possible. But it is the unavoidable breaks from it that allow the still point to reveal itself *outside* itself. Paradoxically it needs disturbance of some kind to exist so as to be what it is: the consummate tuning fork.

GQ: "At the still point of the turning world. Neither flesh nor fleshless; / Neither from nor towards, at the still point, there the dance is, / But neither arrest nor movement . . ." (T. S. Eliot, *The Four Quartets: Burnt Norton,* Part II).

So direct experience of the still point—whether in an activity like surfing, or in a "nonaction" activity like tai chi chuan or certain types of bodywork (in the osteopathic offshoot, craniosacral therapy, "still point" is a technical term for deep and transformative suspension of rhythmicity), or in the process of working in a specific artistic medium or between mediums, or in the actual ongoing activity of transforming the material with which one is working—the still point would be that poise of mind and hand, mind and body, where awareness and activity click in and the work is really under way. And this *still-point* experience is simultaneously the access to *deep time*—to the very time that engulfs and surrounds and underplays and nourishes and *is* the very heart of the process and the activity itself.

CS: The deep issue behind process, then, behind the creative potentialities of real time, as well as behind the complex folding of time upon itself, behind the self-referential aspects of the "performative"—is *this deep time* as the strange source or wellspring of what is truly creative in the work. This reminds me of that incredible image of the mask rising abruptly to the surface of the water in *URA ARU* (1985–86)—as if there were a certain trust expressed in this moment, that the image, in this case the mask, has been trusted to arise, to return from the depths—that you don't always have to plan out beforehand the effects you are after, but that there is a fundamental trust in this deep time itself that you have to acknowledge, and in acknowledging, in a certain sense prepare for—but that all the planning, the contriving, the structuring is only to create occasions where a certain emergence can be allowed to happen; that given the right kind of permission, or solicited in the right manner, deep time will deliver what is needed; and I think that this is true in a great variety of ways in your work. I would say that it is what is most profound even where the issue seems to involve the relationship between language and image, and precisely where the ordinary understanding of those relationships is most challenged; that these are occasions strategically contrived so that new species of events of meaning might emerge from deep time—the time in which the work is being generated but also the time in which the work is being *viewed.* For since the image/event itself is not contrived but solicited, the moment of creation and the moment of viewing are the same.

GH: In terms of the mask I hope you are speaking figuratively because the reality of the situation was thus: throwing the mask in a small pond, hoping that it would "arrange" itself just so, and at that moment, using the end of an old broomstick to push the mask down through the water until it was all but invisible; then recording it as it surfaced in hope that it did it in "just the right way." If not, do it again . . . and again. Certainly I couldn't plan how the mask would arise in terms of all the nuances nor could I hang out by the local swimming hole waiting for an *otafuku* Japanese mask to suddenly come from the deeps! So in this sense the actual event that I wanted was thought out, knowing full well that not everything could be controlled (by a long shot). Also, if one were to imagine a Japanese person watching this activity, it would practically be a form of sacrilege!

GQ: "A line will take us hours maybe; / Yet if it does not seem a moment's thought, / Our stitching and unstitching has been naught" (W. B. Yeats, "Adam's Curse").

CS: Indeed. My point was just that the meaning of the image's arising, in the context of our discussion, seems capable of such a *reading.* . . .

In the 1970s, there was a lot of talk among poets—and I mean the poets in our scene—George, myself, Robert Kelly, and a few others—to valorize the "processual" over the "procedural" in work—and what we meant was that the life of the work came from the actual doing of it—that you felt your way along toward the emerging poem; you didn't think it up beforehand and work out a procedure that would guarantee the value of the work no matter what it turned out to be. Even "process" wasn't valued as a concept, as if anything at all could be justified because it illustrated "process" as such. But everything important came in the application of actual attention—it required a continuous alertness to the emerging possibilities with a view to realizing them, working them out, finding out what they would yield; and that this happened in the actual process of working. The work was not an *example* of its concept, but something that issued, that was projected, in the process of doing it. In that way, every poem was an improvisation, a performance—not because it was impromptu or even because it happened "live," but because the life of the activity of producing it was what made possible whatever vital qualities the work itself might show.

GQ: Perhaps we could create a useful distinction between "real time" and "actual time." Real time, following computer science, is "the time in which a physical process under computer study or control occurs"; so in video one does something like suppose a "camera time" that operates within literal clock time. Actual time, on the other hand, may or may not follow literal clock time—because it's interruptible without loss of deeply linked intensities. Here the issue is *present time* in the sense of *being present in time*—what happens with the special intensity of the emergent and creatively unfolding *composition process itself*. It stands in relation to the temporal/auditory as *concreteness* and *particularity* do in relation to the spatial/visual. This actual-time distinction—or, paradoxically, *concrete time*—may draw out what was of interest to you in the "processual" and why you chose to apply it to video—for example, *Processual Video* (1980)—much in the sense we had been using it for in poetics in the 1970s.

GH: Whatever language I used in the early 1970s—and I'm sure "process" was clearly central to it—I think it was very much along the lines of your description of the processual. There is a certain difference, though, between the processual in writing and the way I was taking it in video. Except for hard core conceptual art and perhaps what became known as "process art," which as you say was about procedure, all the work I've done, with a few exceptions, from sculpture to sound and video, emerged *in* time much in the way you speak about it. Once I became aware of your scene and aware also of the term *processual* as you were using it, I took it as a way to delineate a working space/time to yield something between an emphasis on process and on concept. Yet

I'm wondering if what I hear as a certain modulated difference has to do with how the various mediums—writing and video, say—are differently informed by the same principle of emergence.

I think Heidegger's notion of *techne* is important here as suggesting that any specific technology can be transformed in its own specific way by its use in artistic work. There is a *techne* of harnessing electronic media, and in particular the complexities of multiple overlapping systems and feedback situations, that is quite distinct and offers, at times, specific opportunities for dealing with the issues and ideologies surrounding technology as such. And these issues however much they are constantly fluctuating for me, may at times enter the fold of a work. That said, the crucial point is how to remain *in* time in relation to the *techne*—the transformation of the medium and the working through of its work-specific implications. There are types of feedback that are experienced in electronic media that don't come up in writing. Certainly the differences between writing on a computer, on a typewriter, or by hand enter into the discussion, but I think what we are searching for here is something that occurs on a deeper level.

CS: So for you the crucial issue is the possibilities of feedback that electronic media offer.

GH: I think so. And how they differ, not only from writing, but other feedback situations. I feel that feedback phenomena really dominate the whole issue of video. Actually, this seems more important than, say, the fact that a tape is made in "real time" as such, even though, of course, feedback occurs through real-time process. So the deep time/actual time distinction from "real time" is interesting. But the important *result* is the feedback; feedback is what gives you something different from the more ordinary ways of working with a medium. The feedback situation that arises when you are working with videotape can involve a certain cognitive element—an implication of abstract thinking that has nothing to do with, say, the way your hands work some material, that is, the ordinary sense of feedback that has to do with craft. If you focus a video camera on yourself—there you are, outside yourself.

GQ: As in *Standing Apart/Facing Faces* (1996).

GH: Right. But it is even more than that. I was thinking about this while driving today. A car is always used as a good example of cybernetic feedback—the most prosaic notion of it. You're driving a car. Your eyes see the road. You turn the wheel. The car turns. Now the *road* appears to turn because *you* have turned. There's a continuous loop. Feedback. But in the kind of space that arises in the video situation, you find yourself forced into an involvement with more abstract ideas that arise quite naturally in relation to the simple facts—ideas about identity, the nature of inner and outer, the relation between image and actuality, the meaning of presence, the role of information or real time, and so forth. And these ideas are part of your immediate, ongoing negotiation with what is actually happening, not at all at an academic or "philosophical" level, but part of the difficulty of simply existing in the situation that you have conjured up through electronic media. And once you find yourself involved in this, very unusual spaces open—spaces that can seem to hold the promise of real insight into these very difficult issues.

CS: Of course if you claim that this is happening, it all becomes quite questionable—people can say that referring to those issues is a kind of pretension, particularly if they don't enter into that kind of experience.

GH: Exactly. And at this point it really becomes a matter of belief or faith. There's nothing that's going to *prove* that you are on any said "level." You do know, say, that you're in a feedback process—there's a camera on you; there's a monitor in front of you and you're looking at it. But once you enter into what we could call "meta feedback," the space that opens up when you are simultaneously in your own body looking out and out there on a monitor or projected onto a wall being looked at—you have to make a deal—you have to commit yourself to the connection, to the fact that you believe that there's a kind of feedback that comes from this total situation that is beyond the mechanical, first-order feedback of the camera and the monitor. I think that the interest in this marks a difference between my work and that of a lot of other artists who use video feedback in one way or another.

CS: This shows up, I would say very powerfully in works like *Tall Ships* or *Viewer,* or HAND HEARD—George and I have dealt with this question extensively in our series of books about those works. The experience of *Tall Ships,* say, has the possibility of initiating a state where something like the "common mind" of the piece manifests—where the participant enters into what you are calling the meta feedback space of a collective participation in an inquiry.

GQ: Aren't we also dealing here with something very close to biofeedback and psychofeedback? Biofeedback in some respects is the best model for discussing a whole range of processes human beings are involved with—even the crude instance of biofeedback where you put an electrode on your head and watch a gauge that tells you when you're agitated. The feedback situation allows you to reflect upon your own productive energy—what you are producing in the way of energy waves, mind waves, which exist along some kind of a spectrum of electronic impulses. One of the things that has always been attractive about video feedback is the strange way that video seems to engage the mind's sense of itself as if there were a resonance between the bioelectricity of the nervous system and the emission of electrons by the cathode ray tube—a sense, obviously, that film doesn't excite. I don't know that I have any satisfactory notion of what it means, but it does seem to relate to the biofeedback that occurs in doing hands-on bodywork, for instance, or touch-oriented movement like Contact Improvisation or tai-chi push-hands. Perhaps we need a notion like "biointerfeed" to suggest that the feedback—the engaged "listening/signaling"—is going both ways, as it obviously is in many performance situations where the performer is modulating behavior according to audience response.

GH: I think the real difference between the kind of feedback that occurs in video and bodywork or biofeedback, on the one hand, and film, on the other, is that neither biofeedback nor video is essentially *pictorial.* The end result is not an image, even if it involves images, in a sense, along the way. One is not engaged in setting up a scenario to represent something through an image. The outcome, the output, is more a blueprint *after the fact* of what occurred in the feedback situation. That's not true of all my work, but take pieces like *Dervish* (1993–95) or *Between 1 & 0* (1993) or anything where the image is really *agitated*—the whole thing has to do with keeping you in an agitated state, to force you to remain or become aware of the process of seeing and looking and being in a certain place and becoming engaged in what it means.

GQ: An excited feedback situation.

GH: An excited feedback situation.

GQ: It moves somewhat close to a "flicker" effect at certain times. It engages you at a neurological level. Certainly you get that in *Dervish:* a strange, neurological, even *trippy* quality.

GH: *Circular Breathing* (1994), too—a continuous pulsation at the same rate. And what's interesting—and this is something I want to pursue more—is, like you say, this kind of *trippy neurological* thing which is embedded with some notion of narrative or of there being something *underneath.* In other words, it's not solely a mechanical or biochemical effect, but an opening up of another view on what a story is, what a narrative is, what images are, and what do images mean when they are next to each other flickering at such and such a rate.

GQ: The great forbidden subject—how this all works in with actual transformation, actual states of mind, the work as initiation into our "further nature," to use Charles Olson's projective term. But here we are on the threshold of another dialogue, one that leads us into the *further life* of all our genuine work.

"I'm so foolish," Olson also wrote, "a song is heat!"

Selected Bibliography of Texts Related to the Dialogue

Note: Texts are listed chronologically.

Cybernetics of the Sacred, by Paul Ryan (Garden City, N.Y.: Anchor/ Doubleday, 1974).

Glass Onion: Notes on the Feedback Horizon, text by George Quasha (Barrytown, N.Y.: Station Hill Press, 1980).

Gary Hill: DISTURBANCE (among the jars), texts by George Quasha ("Disturbing Unnarrative of the Perplexed Parapraxis [A Twin Text for DISTURBANCE]"), French and English, and Jean-Paul Fargier ("Magie Blanche"), French only, exhibition catalogue for the Musée d'Art Moderne, Villeneuve d'Aseq, 1988.

Passages de l'Image, including a text on Gary Hill by Jacques Derrida ("Videor") in a group show catalogue for the Musée National d'Art Moderne, Centre Georges Pompidou, Paris, 1990. Also available in English in the exhibition catalogue of the same name for the Centre Cultural de la Fundacio Caiza de Pensions, Barcelona, 1991.

Gary Hill, joint catalogue for solo exhibitions at Stedelijk Museum, Amsterdam, August 28–October 10, 1993, and Kunsthalle Wien, November 17, 1993–January 9, 1994.

Gary Hill: Sites Recited, 60-minute videotape, directed and edited for the

Long Beach Museum of Art by Carole Ann Klonarides, media arts curator, in collaboration with Gary Hill, George Quasha, and Charles Stein (in performance and on-site dialogue), as catalogue for the exhibition *Gary Hill: Sites Recited* at the Long Beach Museum of Art, December 3, 1993–February 20, 1994. Includes printed catalogue with texts by Carole Ann Klonarides, Steven Kolpan, George Quasha, and Raymond Bellour.

Gary Hill: Spinning the Spur of the Moment, a retrospective collection of single-channel videotapes in three laserdisc volumes, including texts by Michael Nash, George Quasha (with Charles Stein), Lynne Cooke, and Bruce Ferguson (Irvington: The Voyager Company [a joint venture of Janus Films and Voyager Press], 1994).

Gary Hill, catalogue for solo exhibition at the Henry Art Gallery, Seattle, 1994.

Cut to the Radical of Orientation: Twin Notes on Being in Touch in Gary Hill's (Videosomatic) Installation Cut Pipe, by George Quasha and Charles Stein, in *Public 13,* "Touch in Contemporary Art" (Toronto: Public Access, 1996).

HanD HeaRD/*liminal objects, Gary Hill's Projective Installations—Number 1,* by George Quasha and Charles Stein (Paris: Galerie des Archives; Barrytown, N.Y.: Station Hill Arts/Barrytown, Ltd., 1996).

Tall Ships: Gary Hill's Projective Installations—Number 2, by George Quasha and Charles Stein (Barrytown, N.Y.: Station Hill Arts/Barrytown, Ltd., 1997).

Viewer: Gary Hill's Projective Installations—Number 3, by George Quasha and Charles Stein (Barrytown, N.Y.: Station Hill Arts/Barrytown, Ltd., 1997).

Gary Hill: Midnight Crossing, exhibition catalogue for Westfälischer Kunstverein Münster, 1997. Includes Heinz Liesbrock, "Loss Illuminates," and Robert Mittenthal, "Presubjective Agency: Outside Identity."

III Gary Hill's Writings

Primarily Speaking

well
you know what they say
we've all heard it before
it never ceases to amaze me
this time
it's more than just a change in the weather
they've really outdone themselves
how they ever got it past us I don't know
in many circles it's considered the unspeakable
these types of goings-on surface every so often
statistically
one of us is probably involved
there's always someone willing to run the risk
at this point though
there are no tell tale signs to speak of
I wonder if the better thing to do is refrain from speculation
hang in there but hold back
not get caught up in the missing link syndrome
of course there's an ulterior motive
when is there ever not
that it's been dropped in our laps I'm sure is no accident
we can't just stand around though
where to go from here is the question
do you have any ideas
one thing's for certain

Transcription of spoken text in the work *Primarily Speaking*, © 1981 by Gary Hill. First published in *Video Communications*, no. 48 (Paris, 1988).

they don't know we'll go to any length to do what has to be done
for the time being
if we can hold our own
we're bound to come across something in that near future

Blue Green Red Cyan Magenta Yellow
Food Feed Fed I have the time of Day-glo

there's no way in the world I'm going to get framed this time around
chances are you're thinking along similar lines
stick close to me and remember
I'll be calling the shots from now on
if at any time l drop back
you pick up where l left off
if we find ourselves losing touch here's a little piece of advice
there can never be an eye for an eye
there will always be a middle man
who will whisper in your ear at every turn
something to the effect of
"we can go by the book or you can eat my words"
no reason to go to such extremes
think little or nothing of it
then again
just to be on the safe side
better file it away for future reference
so
let's get on with the business at hand
we can cover a lot of ground in the time we've allotted ourselves
we have our choice
living in suspended animation
or under the auspices of supply and demand

when you buy and we sell we both trade

I've swallowed a good many hook line and sinker
in light of the fact
I've been a fish out of water for a long time
it's pretty safe to assume you're in the same position
sure
I know that you know that I know that you know
so on and so forth
you've got it all staked out

I know you were playing for keeps from the beginning
why do I sense a note of skepticism
listen
we can part company anytime
in case you've forgotten
this is all at your convenience
still
it's necessary if not by design that we cross paths in some way shape
or form

Blue Green Red Cyan Magenta Yellow
Food Feed Fed I have the time of Day-glo

off the record
this is somewhat out of character for me as I imagine being closed
mouth is for you
if it all seems a bit too high and dry
take comfort in the fact
that coming up face to face would eliminate our time for reflection
look
on the surface
what do we have to lose
aesthetic persuasion
leisure time
what is it
why has it come to this
I've never turned on you before
or vice versa
have our shortcomings finally met
one of us must accept the other
if not the two of us accept each other
the remaining possibility is out of the question

objects in the mirror are closer than they appear

in light of the situation maybe it's wrong to carry on like this
we've been on delicate ground before
should one of us back off
wait
let's try to be objective
there's no sense in running ourselves into a ditch
in the midst of it all

let's try to be objective for a moment
point blank
who are you
I mean it
just this one time
we don't have to split hairs or anything
within reason
who
are
you
come on
shift gears for a minute
take a deep breath
you know the ropes
you're one of those in their right mind
take a deep breath and face the music
start now and work backwards
start in the middle and dream
think it over
rattle off a list if that's all that's left
never mind the images
they always return
if not new ones will replace the old ones
it's their destiny
even those permanently lodged
sooner or later lose their grasp
it's the nature of the beast

Blue Green Red Cyan Magenta Yellow
Food Feed Fed I have the time of Day-glo

where did you leave off
did you take the plunge
what was the cut off point
maybe you need more lead time
there's a long way to go before hitting rock bottom
come on
put your best foot forward
move on it
cover some ground
get the feel of it

re-enter
you're not a backseat driver are you
I know what you're thinking
it's not in the scheme of things that you take me for a ride
afterall
I'm your monkey business
I can never really touch you
I can only leave word
still
there's not much separating us
we're like minded
I ask the same questions
you give the same answers
you can't teach an old dog new tricks
or can you
I don't know
you tell me
what's what
maybe you prefer sight seeing and i'm better off leaving well enough
alone

time on our hands is blood on our hands

I think we're off the track
I know we're off the track
I never for one moment thought I could railroad this through
I knew it was coming
this is the diminishing return I failed to negotiate
sad but true
less is more
more or less
more and more of the time
oh well
such as it is

Blue Green Red Cyan Magenta Yellow
Food Feed Fed I have the time of Day-glo

in the meantime
let's not lose sight of the facts
they do not need reiterating
there's a time and place for everything

I hope we haven't come here under false pretenses
there are things that should be said and things that should be done
you've been around
and I've been around
double talking will get us nowhere and second guessing is a lost art
quite simply
we are an act of faith
there's no reason we can't walk out of this together
face facts
the controlling factors of our little mise en scène are untouchable
take my word for it
put me above suspicion for a moment
accept it
you are on the receiving end
the distances we imagine are next to close by
at arms length
easily penetrable
we are at each other's disposal
we can concentrate on our discrepancies or we can split the difference
that which takes the edge off
in any event
it is on our consciences

don't don't block block the the box box
a a void void grid grid lock lock

the fixation moves from left to right
as time goes on it becomes clockwork
you will have your way and i will make do
in the end we can double back or play the field
I don't want to deny you your own flesh and blood
who am i but a figure of speech
free standing
in advance of a broken arm
these things can happen when one gets ahead of themselves
I'm just going to sit tight
take refuge in the picturesque
things travel fast by word of mouth
I can be long-winded at times as well as drag my feet
the logical conclusion
I'm always putting my foot in my mouth

of course you understand
this is all in a manner of speaking
I don't want to underscore my place here that would be misleading
afterall
it's not an open door policy
by the same token
it's very touch and go here
anything can happen at anytime and no one's privy to that bit of
information
I don't want to make a production out of it though
all I want is to walk through it with you
we don't have to go to the four corners of the earth to discover we
speak the same language
savvy
the place is here
the time is now
zero hour
and so on

Blue Green Red Cyan Magenta Yellow
Food Feed Fed I have the time of Day-glo

I want to come to terms with where we began and let the rest fall into
place
granted
there are many simultaneities
that goes without saying
but for practical purposes
we should respect our limits
so
take a good long hard look at yourself
never mind me
i'll just go in one ear and out the other
complications can arise in the simplest of forms
and should be played out
watch it
perhaps the most we can do is try and remain true to form
however short-lived these moments may be we can never return to the
killer instinct
listen
the floor has been mine now for longer than i care to remember

do you want to talk
do you want to talk it over
do you want to talk about it
feed it intravenously
and have it be over with as soon as possible
I know the position you're in
if you can pull it off
more power to you
it's never clear cut and you'd be wasting your time with the clean
break idea
i'll bend over backwards to meet you halfway
in view of where you stand where does that put me
where does that leave us
in the mercenary position
perpendicular
but right side up
no
we can't go by rote memory
there's nothing tying you down and there's nothing letting you go
make up your mind
get a grip on things
your modus operandi
square off and break ground

put your head on the table tangent to your ear
talk to yourself and smile know that you are still here

on the level
perhaps I'm not coming across
I know it's difficult in these close quarters
I've tried to make it as easy as possible
I assure you
one can adapt to this neck of the woods
I'm not out of bounds
you know it and i know it
i'm not going to walk off with it
and you're not going to let it get away
when I'm through
you are going to know what I am talking about
word for word
let's face it

we are too few and far between to let generalities get the best of us
up to this point
when all is said and done
so far so good
when it gets down to the wire perhaps it will be a different story
again
let's not get ahead of ourselves
we're bound to end up in the red that way
you might think the grass is greener on the other side
but it's once in a blue moon a situation the likes of this can occur
in all seriousness
you're dead center in the sightlines of a tour de force
etcetera
etcetera
etcetera

Primarily Speaking

The title *Primarily Speaking* should pretty much be taken at face value. This is to say that prying into things merely for orientation should be avoided at all costs. Nobody wants to be riding a bicycle, especially at top speed, only to discover that the wheels are spokeless and wonder how they got as far as they did in the first place. The work, consisting of eleven parts segmented by anthemic songs, is founded in a monologue construed from idiomatic phrase units—language at large residing in the public domain. The voice ping-pongs up and down a corridor stacking the idioms, placing linguistic objects in their appropriate places, sometimes answering and sometimes questioning. The given is always reciprocated. An image of a seesaw comes to mind. (I remember playing seesaw and in my neighborhood the object of the game was to leave your partner high and dry by jumping off at the instant your end touched ground, leaving said partner to come crashing down with his or her own weight—in effect sawing off the seeing.)

The text provides the attention span offered as a crossing. Images are signposts syllabicated by the tongue, pushed out and left by the wayside—discards, there is always room for more. The snake sheds its skin. This isn't something new, nor is it a recapitulation, it's a different take on talking pictures—talking pictures breaking the story. (Words and images move together like old roads and their placements sometimes do, and every once in a while they share a stretch of time where the scenario doesn't permit the necessary excavations.)

Really, it all boils down to this: I walked in on a tell a vision set and all the dialogue was provided and there were countless props, props

Originally published in *Primarily Speaking, 1981–83* (New York: Whitney Museum of American Art, 1983).

upon props, more than I could ever use in a lifetime and it was all in living color colors colored—everything just as you or I might expect. Eye level and surprised, I found myself staring at arm's length cross-eyed into the palm of a hand. It was a glimpse of actual size which bespeaks my preoccupation with the notion of face value.

URA-ARU:

The Acoustic Palindrome

The distinctive nature of *URA-ARU* lies in its use of the Japanese language in a unique way. The spoken text of the work is entirely made up "acoustic palindromes." Palindromes are written words or phrases which, when reversed, spell another word or phrase. It follows that acoustic versions are spoken words which, when reversed, become another word. For example, if one speaks into a microphone the word "amai" (sweet) and records it on tape, then plays the tape backward, one will hear "yama" (mountain). As the tape is played back and forth one hears "amai-yama" or sweet mountain. Another example is the title itself, *URA-ARU*: "ura" (the back or reverse side) and "aru" (there is), or there is a back/reverse side. "Ura" can also mean a hidden meaning. To eliminate confusion, written palindromes, or *kaibun,* and acoustic palindromes are different and are not interchangeable. Although the same word might function as both types of palindrome, its reversal will be different in each case. For instance, "ima" (now, or living room) as an acoustic palindrome becomes "ami" (net) and as a written palindrome becomes "mai" (dance).

Currently I have a growing list of seventy-five acoustic palindromes. Since there are hundreds of possibilities, a selection process becomes necessary. I chose the following albeit somewhat subjective criteria: Can the forward/backward words combine in what seems to be a natural way, and, more important, can the acoustic palindrome be coupled to an image in a similarly unforced and meaningful way—a way which is perhaps deeply suggestive, subtle, even profound? Or, appro-

Originally published in *Video Guide,* vol. 7, issue 34, no. 4 (Vancouver, B.C., 1985).

priating a Japanese concept, can each realization in some way embody *yugen?*

The acoustic palindrome can only exist as a form of media, where the processes of recording and playback are inherent. In fact, it really only becomes operational as a cybernetic process, and only in this way can its specific qualities be fully appreciated. A description of the process is as follows: a single word and image, called the "source," is recorded onto videotape. When two or more words are heard in any given sequence of the completed videotape, they are recognized, via the bidirectional playback (or "rocking") of the videotaped sound and image, as being derived from one initial source—one spoken word and one real-time image.

Stressing the importance of the sense of physicality that the acoustic palindrome conveys, we might compare the experience to viewing sculpture "in the round." The first word is heard (first view); the tape reverses and the first word is heard backward making the second word (second view); the tape continues on past the starting point revealing a third word which, when coupled with the second word, becomes a phrase (third view); the tape reverses again, reversing the third word and transforming it into the fourth word (fourth view).

The majority of these words are chanted by an offscreen chorus, to obtain a resonant texture of sound that envelopes the videospace which might otherwise be dominated by the image symbology. The "big" sound further emphasizes the physical nature of the process so far discussed. When the recording of a larger sound is reversed, the moment of directional change is magnified almost as if there were weight to the sound; somewhat like shifting gears of a large vehicle compared to a small one. On a subtler note is the change in awareness of reverberation. Even the lowest levels become noticeable when recorded on tape and reversed, since the reverberation is heard first, without interference from the fundamental sound which then immediately follows. This aspect of the sound is somewhat controllable and, if effectively used, can be hauntingly beautiful.

Each acoustic palindrome, which may be a single word caused by symmetrical phonetics, or two words, or in some instances a short phrase, combined with an image forms a sound/image construct or "scene"—not to be confused with the "shot by shot" continuity that can only move toward establishing, developing, and concluding. These are processes of make believe. In *URA-ARU* any sense of "story" (line) is only the by-product of a kind of accumulation process which plays with our perceptions of time. On a more radical and fundamental level, within each scene, time is continually being contradicted.

The viewing experience greatly simplified might be described like this: a word is heard in context with an image on the screen, the tape reverses and the viewer is caught expecting nonsense and instead receives another word which works together with the initial word and "changes" the perception of the image. (See attached detailed treatments.) There is no attempt through some sort of trickery or special effects to make the viewer think that everything is forward, which would of course negate the process and the tension of the work. This very tension together with the notion of *yugen* is in fact the central theme of the work.

And if not the concept of continuity, then what? The "scene" as view (the veranda of extremes—entertainment and contemplation)? And if not that, then perhaps, with no sense of finality, traces—brief moments of inscription, of time upon time—a series of "strokes" that are really but one where the brush tip never leaves the surface. *URA-ARU,* then, is a collection of media etchings, an array of suspended meanings—dare I say it—haiku, or "uki-ah" . . . word for word, "a float, ah!" A play on words, a play on time; the acoustic palindrome thus creates a kind of nodal tension between the two, seen not so much as a manipulation of time (applied more appropriately to the brute force edit) but a folding of time—origami time—where a single piece of paper (time/space segment of videotape) enfolds upon itself. A mirror relationship occurs wherein the soul of the language is not lost to the process of feedback transpiring to infinity, rather, it embraces its reflection and steps through the looking glass. Here is where the very nature of the word, quite literally its branches, twigs, leaves, and embedded stones, overgrows the notion that a word is worth .001 pictures

Details of Three Sound/Image Constructs

AME
Source word: ame
ame–ema
Length: 15 seconds

Here I will describe two possible takes of the same scene, each with a slightly different connotation. In fact, the emotional impact resulting from different interpretive visualizations may well be an integral part of the project, especially in terms of the videodisc. In the first version, the scene is shot in late afternoon during a pouring rain. An ema (votive picture tablet) is lying on the ground, perhaps along a muddy dirt path. The shot is a medium close-up, using a tripod to provide an image which is rock steady except for the falling rain hitting the wooden tablet. After 3 to 5 seconds of just the sound of the rain, the chant "ame" (rain) is heard, lasting 3 to 5 seconds, followed again by silence except for the sound of the rain. The tape reverses, causing the rain to "fall" back up into the clouds. Then the chant "ema" is heard, followed again by only the rain.

The second version is shot at night when there is also a pouring rain. Artificial light is used to highlight the rain. Instead of one ema being the central image, a typical shrine picture votive offering pavilion is used as the location, and the camera frames all of the ema into a grid pattern. As in version one, a tripod is used to provide a steady image except for the rain. The scene will then be realized in the same way as in version one. In comparison, version one might be experienced in a more personal light, suggestive of one's own fate, whereas version two, presenting a formal image, creates a more meditative spiritual feeling.

OTAFUKU
Source word: otafuku
ato–otafuku–uku–f
Length: 20–30 seconds

A white painted otafuku is seen floating near the surface of a pond. It is a nighttime scene and the otafuku is artificially lit, suggestive of moonlight. The camera pans across the water revealing the otafuku (moon-faced woman). The movement is quick enough to cause a smear or delay of the image due to videolag. The word "otafuku" is chanted and dubbed onto the tape with the recorded image. Considering this as the source material, the image seen starts as a still of water. The tape then plays backward; the otafuku comes into view screen left and smears across the screen; at the same time "ato" (trace, trail) is heard. (The taped segment begins playback in the middle of the word "otafuku.") The otafuku disappears screen right and the tape continues for a few seconds during which only water is seen. The tape reverses, backtracking over what has already been seen: the otafuku comes back into view from screen right, passes across the screen, absorbing the smear—unsmearing—and "otafuku" is heard. Since the tape playback began in the middle of the word "otafuku," the image that accompanies the sound "-fuku" is new material. The camera is seen to catch up with the otafuku image and sees it sink a little below the surface. The tape reverses one more time and the otafuku rises to the surface; simultaneously is heard "uku" (to float, to rise to the surface), after which the tape pauses. Another possibility at this point is that after "uku" is heard the tape goes into extreme slow motion and the sound of the "f"—drawn out and with a much lower pitch—becomes white noise suggestive of the sound of water. The tape then pauses (still shot) after the "f" sound, and is back again at the starting point of the segment. This construct might be viewed as an omen of the woman's suicide.

IKIMONO
Source word: ikimono
ikimono—on—omiki
Length: 20–30 seconds

A priest and a man are seated at a low table. The man has come to the priest for help in dealing with his inner turmoil. The scene is framed by a camera that points directly down from the ceiling. All that is seen is the topology of the table and the two men's hands on it. Also on the table are a sake bottle and cups, an uchinarashi (bowl-shaped bell) and mallet, and a small, live snake. The image appears as a kind of still life with a snake winding through it. The priest's hands are moving in an almost choreographed way—the hands are "living creatures." He picks up the mallet and strikes the uchinarashi, then pours the sacred sake. The action lasts as long as the word "ikimono" (living creature) is chanted. The uchinarashi is struck exactly as the "n" sound of ikimono is heard. The sound of the bell is allowed to die out and the tape reverses. One hears this sound now get increasingly louder as the priest appears to pick up the mallet and (un) ring the bell, while the chanted word "on" (sound) is heard. The tape pauses the moment after the bell sound abruptly ends. A moment later the tape continues in reverse and one hears "omiki" (sacred sake) as the priest (un) pours the sake.

BEACON (Two Versions of the Imaginary)

Always I become snared in this text of a work. Is it a forward or an after(word)? Is there anything to be gained by description—a walk through with words? Is it to remind the viewers who have already seen the work of what they saw? But wouldn't this be a trampling of their memory, a false recollection, a mere outline of their fascination, a coarse approximation as to the nature of their adjustment to the light (or was it the darkness)? And what about the viewers-to-be, can they be forewarned, foretold (their witness shadowed by original intent)? These uneasy viewerships passing through the text, one coming the other going, might just as well be the two versions of the imaginary.

No—let us imagine that *nothing* is imagined . . . that *BEACON* is suspended off center in a darkened room. It is a motorized object: an aluminum tube, 54 inches long with a 6-inch diameter, capped with lenses at either end, the innards consisting of two 4-inch television monitors facing out in opposite directions, their screens magnified through the glass. What is it? A device, a machine, a technological apparatus that quickly recedes to its function. It is a projection instrument that turns and returns one cycle per 6 minutes. (Why is it that the moment we become precise in description the mind withdraws to double check its memory of time and distance only to come back and find them renewed?) And this object with its emission of light wavers between what might be a searchlight sweeping empty dark nights and a form of organized light of an image: a standing figure that seems to float. We wonder (for the sake of imagination): Are they images?—these projections that inch across the walls, the light of which grows

Originally published in the exhibition catalogue *ENERGIEEN* (Amsterdam: Stedelijk Museum, 1990).

287

trapezoidal as they blur (or resolve), leaving a kind of apparition of images behind.

One sweep catches a child's face and transports it as if it were in a carriage of light. The viewer is caught up in the fascination of her gaze and follows it across the room, where it meets the gaze of a woman (mother?) projected from the opposite end of the beacon. Perhaps one forms the Other's projection across time:

mother when child—child when mother

The duplicity of the source, an object, whose beam reveals and inevitably confronts us, suddenly becomes aggressive—a telescope with its terrifying optics of harsh mirrors and polished cut glass—eclipses the viewer, penetrates the eyes, interrupting the passive gaze. An 'arc' occurs between the nodes of origin and destination, between light and image, awakening the mind's eye from its stupor, our melancholy for image. The pupils contract from the directed beam of light that only moments before was seen passively from within the peripheral scape, as that which clothed darkness nd held fast our fascination of image (with the image of fascination) suspending our thought.

> After the object comes the image, 'after' means that first the thing must move away in order to allow itself to be grasped again. But that distancing is not the simple change of place of a moving object, which nevertheless remains the same. Here the distancing is at the heart of the thing. The thing was there, we grasped it in living motion of a comprehensive action—and once it has become an image it instantly becomes ungraspable, noncontemporary, impassive, not the same thing distanced, but that thing as distancing, the present thing in its absence, the thing graspable because ungraspable, appearing as something that has disappeared, the return of what does not come back, the strange heart of the distance as the life and unique heart of the thing.[1]

Someone asks, "Why Blanchot?"[2]
Blanchot asks, "Why fascination?"
One might ask Blanchot, "Why text?"

It is perhaps not only the song of the sirens but ironically the enchanting light of the beacon that seduces and leads to a shipwreck of consciousness.

What will you do when you are in the light?

Notes

1. Maurice Blanchot, *The Gaze of Orpheus* (Barrytown, N.Y.: Station Hill Press, 1981), pp. 80–81. (One of several excerpts used in *BEACON [Two Versions of the Imaginary]*).

2. Raymond Bellour, *The Last Man on the Cross,* from the catalogue *OTHERWORDSANDIMAGES: Video by Gary Hill* (Copenhagen: Video Gallerie/Ny Carlsberg Glyptotek, 1990), pp. 20–26. Translated by Alison Rowe.

Inter-View

You started as a sculptor working with steel. What brought you to video?

I first used video in 1973. At the time I was doing a lot of sound work with sculpture. I worked almost exclusively with steel welding rods which by chance had rich sonic possibilities. This got me into tape recorders and tape loops, feedback, and ultimately electronically generated sound. I did some recording with a portapak and the fluidity of videotape freed up my thinking in a very radical way. Suddenly, the sculpture I had been doing for several years seemed overwhelmingly tedious and distant from this present-tense process. Video allowed a kind of real-time play, the possibility to "think out loud." Here was a process immediately accessible and seemingly a much closer parallel to thinking.

Within contemporary art what would you say is the primary difference between video and other mediums, particularly in the context of conceptual art and related practices?

Time, this is what is central to video, it is not seeing as its etymological roots imply. Video's intrinsic principle is feedback. So it's not linear time but a movement that is bound up in thinking—a topology of time that is accessible. This experience of time exists within specific electronic parameters that, to the eye, is a rectangular screen but which is very distant from a cybernetic process that includes oneself. I think this paradox of being intimate with time and estranged from it is what brought me to speech and specifically speech rather than some form of

Excerpts of interviews with the Centre Georges Pompidou, Paris, 1992. Rewritten by Gary Hill.

written text on the screen. Vocalization was a way to physically mark the time with the body through utterance—the speaking voice acting as a kind of motor generating images. This really puts one inside the time of speaking. Every syllable is tied to an image; suddenly words seemed quite spatial and the viewer becomes conscious of a single word's time.

The most extensive illustration of these image/word constructs is perhaps *Primarily Speaking*. This seems to be a pivotal work that also anticipated much later ideas, for example, order within disorder as seen in *Why Do Things Get in a Muddle?*, *CRUX*, and *Site Recite (a prologue)*, among others. There is also the possible construction of multiple narratives from a single set of images. There are a number of charged images such as yourself in a fetal position, or the wine spilling on a table, etc.

Primarily Speaking also had to do with the sheer number of images which were necessary for the two-channel exchange, given the image-to-syllable ratio I wanted to maintain. You might think there are an infinite number of images, but at one point you ask: What can I capture, frame, record, (have) now? It becomes a collecting process. Have you ever noticed the relationship between possession and seeing—you see it and you gotta have it? Anyway the idioms were easy, they had already been gathered in dictionaries and phrase books. I simply selected some and eliminated others. Once I started putting them together, they just sort of fell into place.

Your art has moved from sound into language, and incorporated a number of literary texts. There doesn't seem to have been a singular approach to these investigations. Comparably speaking, your work, at least from the outside, changes fairly dramatically over short periods of time. Is there an identifiable thread here?

I would say that the commonality is linked to getting at the physicality of language and in breaking those categories down. I suppose I share some concerns with the language poets, but on the other hand I generally start a little closer to the norms of "meaning" and proceed to look for the cracks. I want to suspend the either/or relation of sense and nonsense; see what happens inside the experience of language, as meaning is taking root or being uprooted, as the case may be. My questioning lies more in what the nature of language is as it moves among sound, linguistics, and literature. The composer La Monte Young speaks of getting inside the sound; that tuning is ultimately a function of time (very long times). He seems to be saying that music/sound is not a dead object in the air but rather vibrations moving through the air and that one must continually listen and tune. It's interesting to think about an analogous relationship with language; as a processual continuum that "tunes" the world.

Most of your work deals with the interrelationship of words and images—confrontations between them. Would you say this is more of a European concern than an American one, let's say, in the tradition of semiology?

Certainly with a number of my works from the early 1980s, *Primarily Speaking, Around & About, War Zone,* it would be hard to deny the relationship to semiology, but this was never a focal point. The works are not grounded in theory in that way; I'm rather distrustful of polemics and prone to look for inconsistencies—breakdowns. My ideas seem to shift, turn, invert, contradict, rather than develop, refine, and serialize. Of course, working in this manner I come face to face with particular writers, or artists that are identified with certain theories. The significant difference is that my preoccupation with language began with very sculptural notions coming out of sound, the body, utterance, and speaking. Furthermore, this took place within the discourse of electronic media: when you work in real time the mediation of signs is very different than in a reading/writing context. If one is going to talk about my work in a deconstruction context, I think it's worth keeping in mind that Derrida, whom the origin of this notion comes from, is said to be primarily a reader. I am primarily an image maker. Video embodies a reflexive space of difference through the simultaneous production of presence and distance. I think it has a visceral reality more encompassing than writing and still allows for mediation without falling prey to the image. And yet, although my art is based on images, I am very much involved in the undermining of those images through language.

It's once you begin seriously to write the texts which constitute the sound tracks to your tapes that the deconstruction process begins, the reversal of the image dominating the sound.

Writing was a release from an intense period of focusing on the possibilities of the electronic image and its transformation. I went as far as I could go and just wanted to make some noise, I felt very disconnected. Speaking and talking were a kind of reentry. Finding a syntaxical dependency between speech and image signaled itself as a direction for me.

What is the first tape in which you spoke?

In *Elements,* you hear portions of the words which make up the four elements—fire, water, air, earth—which were electronically intercut together. Occasionally there is a recognizable word. But it wasn't until I started writing my own texts that I began to see that there was a connection to be made between electronic systems and linguistics. This is when I made *Picture Story, Processual Video,* and *Black/White/Text.* This latter work is precisely structured around a text that is a literal description of negative video feedback. The text grows mathematically based on the exact number of syllables in each additive phrase. Starting from the end, "rectangle," "within a rectangle," "The frame of reference within a rectangle," and so on, each successive phrase has twice the number of syllables. In a sense it accumulates phrases and spoken voices backward until the entire paragraph is heard forward; it backs up into time. The image barely changes. Slowly expanding and contracting video feedback tracks the layers of the text. In these tapes, the image becomes more like a compass or a graph of language. The image centers you within the space of language.

In terms of language being the impetus for "moving the image," how does this relate to the notion of narrative within your work?

Except for perhaps *Incidence of Catastrophe,* where even the flirtation with traditional narrative is highly self-conscious, I am working within a different domain of narrative having more to do with a kind of meta narrative; the works evolve from a self-reflexive practice that includes me as author/performer in the mise-en-scène. Rather than characters and locations, whether or not they exist literally, my subjects are more akin to entropy, memory, consciousness, and death. This other narrative brings about a web of interrelated questions which again I feel are strongly embedded in time. Once a word is spoken or a word is read (or an image is "read") time becomes an element in which the viewer "narrates" experience. Even cognition becomes part of the narrative scheme.

In Site Recite, we see bones, leaves, shells, texts from a very mechanical point of view—the movement is labyrinthine and machine-like. Similar to some of your earlier work, the connection between speech and the movement of the images is practically seamless. You've said that this piece was a precursor to an interactive videodisc. Was this a way to expound upon this "other narrative" you speak of?

The images of *Site Recite* were meant to be viewed as a sort of cosmology of death. I used objects that were particularly associated with the decay of seeing. And yes, they were shot for an interactive videodisc and that's partially why it's called "a prologue." Because of the nature of the disc project the segments of images had to be completely planned out ahead of time so that later they could all be interconnected together by identical frames. The fact is, that although it appears as a continuous camera take, every change—left, right, in, or out—is an edit point. In a sense *Site Recite* could be seen as a recording of one reader/writer/viewer's sitting with the disc. So this labyrinthine movement that you mentioned is partially a technical solution that will make it possible for someone to wander through the site without montage or flagging that would inform the participant to interact—to make a choice. The intent of the disc, through a kind of phenomenological insistence, will be to make the participants hyperaware of their own mediation process as they uncover a text while wandering through a kind of still life.

You mentioned reader, writer, viewer as one. Did this perhaps come out of the making of *Incidence of Catastrophe* and its relationship to *Thomas the Obscure* by Maurice Blanchot? Can you talk about the connection between the video and the book?

I've used Blanchot texts or have been directly inspired by them a number of times for both tapes and installations. *Incidence of Catastrophe* came about from having a unique and powerful experience while reading that particular book. As you read this book, it reads you. It personifies that kind of enfolding of physicality back onto consciousness that is so indigenous to video—there would have been no way *not* to have done something with it. Being the protagonist was not a choice. I wasn't about to verbalize my experience of this book to a third person; I wanted to "be" this; I wanted to confront this text and its body (the book), as another real body (myself).

I'm interested in pursuing this question about narrative which perhaps I use in a similar way that you refer to time. What about installations, both *DISTURBANCE* and *Between Cinema* seem intrinsically narrative. . . .

Obviously these works are very much embedded in narrative space but it is always in relationship to a specific self-referential structure. Once again time and metaphorical spaces for texts to unfold are the parameters I begin with. In *DISTURBANCE* people are moving through a kind of broken sentence seen as seven monitors as they recite fragments of texts. There's a continuous weave and unraveling of different languages, people, questions, and inquiry; it is layered almost like a stratum; the point of view is constantly shifting. *Between Cinema and a Hard Place* plays with the construct of frames as it relates to photography and cinema. Images from single sources are distributed by computer-controlled electronic switching to several monitors. There are certain sections where scenes divide into two scenes, three scenes, and so on. With each division all the scenes slow down—half speed, third speed, quarter speed, etc. It is a kind telescopic time that makes the viewer aware of the process of seeing—of beholding the world through sight that exists in the folds of time. Images of the landscape and domesticity are precisely structured spatially and temporally juxtaposing with Heidegger's text, which speaks about a neighboring nearness between thought and poetry and differentiates this from parametric notions of time and space, using nature as a metaphorical referent for the place of thought.

You've worked with both single-channel tapes and installations for quite some time. Conceptually, what do you see as the difference in terms of time, the use of scale and methodology?

Making tape, and likewise viewing tape, has similarities to reading and writing. Videotape lives in linear time; it's always an assemblage—one image/sound after another (one single pixel after another)—it writes left to right. Although the nonlinear nature of memory can be played with extensively through editing, a single-channel work is not *in the world* the way installation and sculpture are. The moving image in a box cannot have the same physical relationship with the viewer. There's a definite trade-off. With installation there's an inevitable theatricality which I try to minimize. I want the viewers incorporated into the work; to be self-conscious about their sense of place within the conceptual strategy of the specific piece. The experience of time is displaced by the physical experience to a much greater degree. Hopefully, the viewer is viscerally confronted with things, images, and ideas.

   I think the most difficult aspect of using video in an installation is decentralizing the focus on the television object itself and its never-ending image. How does one get away from that everyday seduction of the continuous flow of images couched as information? I tried to do this in different ways. For instance, in *BEACON* the television object disappears completely and is seen as the dual beacon of a lighthouse. Light as source and image as source become interchangeable. Not only has the television been physically removed from its frame of reference, but the object producing the image is a metaphor turned on itself conversing with its own image. In *And Sat Down Beside Her,* the television is seen as a spider and in *I Believe It Is an Image in Light of the Other* the display has been incorporated into a canister—something like an oxygen bottle perhaps. We only see projected images in which the borders are defined by open books.

And Sat Down Beside Her is more object-oriented than any other of the recent past. How did this piece come about? . . . What was the inspiration to combine video, text, and spiders, for instance?

I was working with these miniature dissected monitors that were hanging from bundles of black wire and trying to figure out how to get at the image without losing the object. I collected all kinds of secondhand lenses (perhaps like idioms) to experiment with a kind of projection, of diffusing images through the object. Probably through the association of these dangling monitors I came up with the title and then as I began researching spiders, things started falling into place. The floor piece with multiple lenses came from the fact that spiders have eight eyes. The glass tube piece started from a description of silk tubes, a certain kind of spider's web, and I had a piece of text I had written that mentioned arachnids and had to do with the process of writing. The table and chair piece was also a combination of solving the image/object problem and remembering a passage from *Thomas the Obscure* (Blanchot again) having to do with the image of a female spider. Maybe working with those lenses so intensely is what led to the idea of constructing the table and chair to look like they were seen through a wide-angle lens. It's really hard to know how ideas occur.

Your recent installations differ radically in their outward appearance and yet one is aware of a conceptual thread, or at least an interconnectedness of divergent ideas and, cautiously I might add, systems that embody your thinking.

For the most part my recent work has developed around two strategies. *And Sat Down Beside Her, BEACON, I Believe,* and most recently, *Tall*

Ships came about in varying ways from the notion of this diffused image I spoke of earlier. It has to do with making something that is already immaterial lose its identity even further; watch it sprawl over things and dissipate into the space. In *Tall Ships* this is brought to the extreme where, in a darkened 90-foot corridor the only things seen are "projected" figures that at once are images of reality (people) and the only source of illumination for the passer-by. Light, image, and representation become a singular ontological presence that confronts the viewer. This is all the more amplified since the figures' movements are interactive with the presence or absence of viewers.

The "switch pieces" originated with *Between Cinema and a Hard Place,* which was followed by the *CORE SERIES.* After the complexity of *Cinema,* I wanted to reduce the possibilities down to the essential element of the switch—on/off, either/or, etc. I wanted to deal with the image as something written in time without the extraneous issue of rhythm or compositional schemes. I positioned two monitors like an open book and worked with the image as a double—as two co-dependent upon one another; an image that only exists as "down time" of another and vice versa. At no time is there symmetry or not symmetry in a sense. It had more to do with the notions of an image dividing and multiplying like a cell. These pieces were very problematic for me, which is why I think they brought me back to generating texts. I tried to deal with them by writing them out; something having to do with a construct of time/image/text. The two texts are widely different but at the same time deal with elements of counting and the asymmetry of right and left. Even though the pieces did not resolve as I would have liked, I still find myself wondering about them and unwilling to let go of the idea.

What about *Tall Ships?* The relationship to the viewer seems like a new direction. Can you say something in general about your intentions with this work, perhaps beginning with the title?

The title comes from seeing an old photograph taken in Seattle around 1930. The last tall ship is being moved out of Lake Union before the final section of the Aurora Bridge is put into place. I imagined a sailing ship on the high seas—that frontal view of extreme verticality coming toward you. It has a kind of majestic buoyancy of something very sure of itself—something that will come forth with a kind of terrifying grace no matter what. It's dark, it's very dark but you can see clearly this beautiful thing cutting through the night—a night that isn't referenced by day. To think of a person like this—the human approaching—the notion of ships passing in the night took on a certain poetic space that felt very open. I don't think I was really clear about the piece until I had this title. I wanted the whole situation to be as unassuming as possible. All the people are family or friends or family and friends of friends. From the time of conceiving the piece to actual production, I simplified the movement of the people to only coming forward and then returning to a particular place and position of either standing or sitting. There are a few interruptions to that, for instance, after coming half way forward they would pause and go back or they would come back a second time after beginning to return. I gave very little instruction during the recordings. I only wanted there time up front but I wanted the time spent there to really open up. I left them kind of hanging there considerably longer than I told them it might be. I didn't want any theater or aesthetic. And in terms of the piece as a whole I wanted to avoid it being an experience with technology or anything having to do with a multicultural agenda. It's simply the idea of a person coming up to you and asking, "Who are you?" by kind of mirroring you and at the same time illuminating a space of possibility for that very question to arise. Basically, I wanted to create an open experience that was deliberate and at the same time would disarm whatever particular constructs one might arrive with, especially in a museum.

Site Recite (a prologue)

Nothing seems to have ever been moved. There is something of every description which can only be a trap. Maybe it all moves proportionately, canceling out change and the estrangement of judgment. No, an other order pervades. It's happening all at once. I'm just a disturbance wrapped up in myself, a kind of ghost vampirically passing through the forest passing through the trees.

The sun will rise and I won't know what to do with it. Its beak will torture me as will its slow movement, the movement it invented that I can only reiterate. Too much time goes by to take it by surprise. Bodily sustenance is no longer an excuse. The quieter and stiller I become, the livelier everything else seems to get. The longer I wait, the more the little deaths pile up.

A vague language drapes everything but the walls—what walls? The very walls that never vary—my enclosure, so glorious from a distance, stands on the brink of nothing like a four-legged table. What is it? An island with a never ending approach? A stopgap from when to where? Something to huddle over with my elbows like trestles without tracks, the bases of which are scattered with evidence of unsolved crimes? The overallness of it all soaks through, runs through the holes in my hands and continues to run amok, overturning rocks that should not be overturned, breaking bread that should not be broken.

So much remains. No doubt it can all be counted. Starting with any one, continuing on with any other one until all is accounted for, a con-

Transcript of the text in the work *Site Recite (a prologue)*, 1989. First published in "Unspeakable Images," *Camera Obscura*, no. 24 (San Francisco, 1991).

sensus is reached. That it can all be shelved in all its quantized splendor, this then is the turf.

These sightings. This scene before me made up of just so many *just* views (nature's constituency) sits with indifference to the centripetal vanishing point that mentality posits so falsely. Brain, minding business, incessantly constructs an infinite series of makeshifts designed to perpetuate the picture—the one like all others that holds its breath for a thousand words, conversely exhales point zero zero one pictures. This insidious wraparound, tied to the notion "I have eyes in the back of my head," binds me to my double, implodes my being to a mere word as it winds the world around my mouth. A seamless scroll weaves my view back into place—back to back with itself—the boomerang effect, decapitates any and all hallucinations leaving (lo and behold) the naked eye, stalking each and every utterance that breaks and enters the dormitories of perception.

I must become a warrior of self-consciousness and move my body to move my mind to move the words to move my mouth to spin the spur of the moment.

Imagining the brain closer than the eyes.

Site Re:cite

Site, The place where something was, is or is to be located. *Recite,* from Latin *recitare,* to read out, cite again; *re-,* back, again + *citare,* to set in motion, summon. From the Indo-European root, kei; Suffixed form, *ki-neu*—in Greek, *kinein,* to move; (-KINESIS), . . . , CINEMATOGRAPH, . . . TELEKINESIS [*kei-*: from *Pokorny's Indogermanisches Etymologisches Wörterbuch,* 538]

Herein: bracketed off, framed, safe from incision, a verified moment akin to a photograph, however cropped, of the life (and "little deaths") of a text—a transcription from a videotape entitled *Site Recite (a prologue).*[1] Why not the epilogue to *Incidence of Catastrophe?*[2] What might it be a prologue to? Is this writing a prologue to it? What am I prolonging? Am I logging on to the text?

The image folded in the double bind of frame and context. Permanence of the act was marginal with a perforated edge of light heartedness. The hand reciprocated with one swift movement. Damage was negligible to the remaining back to back facades.[3]

The transcription (a text in question) is but a fragment among fragments from a larger textual weave. Perhaps it could be said that it is holographic—any "fragment" contains the whole (the same but not identical).

Moving back words to the text (in) question, *Site Recite* has been seen, heard, recorded, erased, coded, transcribed, and published. These "versions" will have existed for reasons other than varied dissemination.

Originally published in "Unspeakable Images," *Camera Obscura,* no. 24 (San Francisco, 1991).

They are in fact uneasy outside the hybrid media spaces from which they arose. (Surely there are others in hiding.) The question here becomes how to mark the differences, if there are any, between writing and what I have come to refer to as an *electronic linguistic*.[4]

Notwithstanding the play of the seen/unseen, the traces and (re)re-markings of beginnings and ends, and other intertextual modalities, the scoring here will be along the *trans*textual—how the text is intimately entwined in a process of overwriting itself as it passes between media. Rather than being a referential body for mapping out the evolutionary progression of a "script"—notations of amendments, insertions, deletions, or simply bedded down for a closed reading—the transcription is a momentary flashing, or perhaps, an epistle from a text (in question). One more of however many more re-presentations surfacing in the wake of video. What follows then is a tale of the text, the threads of which are entangled in a briar patch of picture, *The Evil Demon of Images* (Baudrillard). It shall be a reconnaissance to situate the debris, the textual shrapnel in the aftermath of brisance within the garden of inscription. Here then will be a writing work of excavation; pourings at an archeological site later to be overturned. What kind of cracks and fissures will appear as text and cast separate?

The outline separating the mouth and the words was prerecorded.[5]

I could say that the progenitor, the mythic seeding of *Site Recite* took place in the midst of writing *Primarily Speaking*[6] . . . sometime in 1981 or was it 1980? Could there have been a specific day, an exact time, a moment, a pause between the sewing of idioms, a burr in the twine . . .

think it over   rattle off a list if that's all that's left
never mind the images   they always return   if not
new ones will replace the old ones   it's their destiny
even those permanently lodged   sooner or later
lose their grasp   it's the nature of the beast

. . . a phrase set aside, a single word that resonated in the margins—a verbal cocoon, a pinpoint (no-body, not even I heard the needle drop)?

The mind can't help but mince and suddenly you're beside yourself entertaining a party of two only to fall back a few steps, a few words gone by, a few instructions on how to get from point A to point B [points known only by the needle that records everything].[7]

From a catalogue statement excerpted from what was then the (text in) question. A marginal thought for the screening of *Why Do Things Get in a Muddle? (Come on Petunia),* wherein an exception to a slippery entropic dialogue comes to mind. After having heard her father explain by enumerated examples why things tend toward chaos rather than toward tidiness, the daughter cites the examples in the exact reverse order from the way she had heard them during the course of the dialogue: "Then Daddy, are you saying the same thing about pennies, and about Come on Petunia, and about sugar and sand, and about my paint box?"[8]

What happens with these recitations, historicities, circuitous extra-texts that (dis)figure the (con)text? There is a kind of pileup; an exquisite corpse leading a procession of dancing, flip-flopping parentheses (Greek: "a putting in beside"). They begin to take on something other than abstract grammatical marks—pliers with unseen handles wiring the syntax with shifting -vexes and -caves tripping the gait of the eye; amassing pairs of upright bows diking the script. Brute metaphors somehow won't do. The heap of language still seeps. The parenthetical is but a meandering line that whispers what one hears, which side is (a)side and which is (be)side?

It's Time to Turn the Record Over was the title of a proposed work,[9] a five-channel/screen video installation that would display synchronous recordings of my feet and hands, made by attaching four cameras to my limbs, and my head, recorded with a fifth camera attached to my trunk and positioned out in front of my body looking back at my head. The screens were to be configured as a cross.

> In effect, [my] body films its own absence, metaphorically pinning or nailing its extremities to the cross with the camera's "objective" view, (dis)embod[ying] the "video." . . . Only the extremities of the body are seen, a body crucified and impassioned by the cameras that have entered it.[10]

These parts, versions, shards, titles, de-scriptions, sutures, occlusions, excerptual reverberances, quotations, and all the other generic simulacra of text cited above, bled into *CRUX.*[11] During that time, the text developed metaphorically *with* the location and process of making the work: the topology of the site, a river island laden with castle ruins; labyrinthine paths, stairways, and rooms through which the body might gain passage; perceptual discovery; moments of abandonment and physical pain were all to bear upon "scripting" the walk. Even the anecdotal seemed to ripple the text:

It was nearing dusk. Having completed the last walk, we were preparing to leave the island when a late fall storm came in from nowhere. We were left with an either/or decision: to leave at that moment in hopes of reaching the mainland before the storm worsened, or wait it out, hedging it would only be a squall. We took our chances with movement and packed the canoe with our gear and all the tape we had recorded. By the time we entered the water, the wind had worked up a menacing brew of cross-currents and choppy water. Taking the drift into account, we headed for the single lacuna in the moat surrounding the island. If we missed it (which felt like a given), there was the risk of shipwreck—the hull would be torn open by the dead heads hidden by the tide. Needless to say, we made it; bodies, equipment, tape, sediment intact.

CRUX was premiered at the Museum of Contemporary Art in Los Angeles with what was at that point the most fabricated version of the (text in) question. It was foregrounded in the work as a spoken monologue. In describing *CRUX,* Raymond Bellour wrote, "The text that accompanies the gait of this disconnected body is itself a 'blank' text . . . it is a text of desperation and of wandering, close to some of the writings of the nouveau roman, and in particular to those of Blanchot, whose dislocating and decentering force is [witnessed]. . . . From this solitary destiny, that in fact isn't destiny at all because it has neither beginning nor end, the hero bears the cross, alone."[12] It is not only the *neither beginning nor end* that rears here, but in a strangely prescient way, the "blank" text. Bellour wrote this not knowing that the text (in) question had been re-moved from the work prior to his writing. Had he known, how would Bellour have treated this erasure? Or, as it seems, hadn't he divulged the site? Was the text a temporary tool, a scriber, used to dislodge the image (of flesh); to excavate the site (of absence); to break the spine of the book? Is the absent body the word/image crux? Is it Freud's mystic writing pad, everyone's desire, every one's death, zEros' wait state?[13]

The crux of the matter . . . A talismanic depression left over from *Primarily Speaking*? (My mouth couldn't quite fit around the words?)

So far, the traces of historicity have only referred to the public domain of the text (in question). What of that which has been left behind; the sediment that accumulates in folds, files, discs, and onion skin? In the margins of one such scrap, I had counted syllables from selected parts. Each part had the same number of syllables. What was this numerological encrypting about?

Decoding my own code, the idea was a kind of möbius interlocutor of speech and writing for videotape. A similar notion was applied, though sparingly, in *Happenstance (part one of many parts)*.[14] The text is folded on itself (textual rorschach); one part is spoken, the utterance of which dictates the other part on the screen, syllabically corresponding one to one. Each part minding the other—logosfrog and leapscript fraying the play of meaning.

And then there's the forthcoming, where the (text in question), entitled "And If the Right Hand Did Not Know What the Left Hand Is Doing," is the left side of a double-sided text and the column between is a meandering crack.[15] Left with these unrelenting beginnings and ends—the unravelings of disembodied text(s)—its "prologue," *Site Re-cite* paronomastically disturbed, there is little recourse but to enter the current work. *Site Recite* (the videotape) can be seen as a single reading/writing from an "interactive" videodisc entitled *Which Tree*.[16] I mark this word interactive with its tendency to attract an optimism of infinite possibilities, contrary to the fact that it is not only delimited by if/then scenarios, but thoroughly collapses when the viewer finds his or her self forced to make decisions inscribed by "multiple choice."

To subvert this technocratic illusion prescribed by interactive media, *Which Tree* is an attempt to create a field of play wherein the modus operandi is one of wandering, where one makes way through a metaphorical wood entangled in a web of reflexivity. Description: a single line scribbled on a page makes points of intersection where the line overlaps itself. These labyrinthine intersections (points of "interactivity") the viewer wanders "through" are embedded in the "paths" rather than announced by signposts. Neither image nor text (the scribbled line) breaks up into multiple plots, stories, or non-sequiturs (collage, montage, juxtapositions, cut-ups, etc.). Rather, by continuous passage through said intersections, the viewer/*writer* unfolds a scenario in real time. No matter which way one turns (wanders), the camera obscura and (spoken) text continue seamlessly, uninterrupted by edits or syntactical quirks.

The viewer/*reader's* primary impetus to engage the work is atypically other than seeing. She or he conjoins with a voice[17] to (dis)cover "their" text (tracks) within a self-reflexive mental terrain of (th)ree-(de)construction. Is a phenomenological experience of thinking possible? Traversing the fold between consciousness and self-consciousness, the viewer reads as he or she writes in the shadows of presence. Here, the linear (author)ity of text, meaning, origin, and sight begins to implode. The *viewer/reader/writer* is continually thrown back (to) incite the text.

Notes

1. *Site Recite (a prologue),* color videotape, stereo, 1989 (4 minutes).

2. *Incidence of Catastrophe,* color videotape, stereo, 1987–88 (43:51 minutes).

3. *Videograms,* excerpts from *Videogram 2,* b/w videotape, 1980–81 (13:27 minutes).

4. Gary Hill, "Processual Video," program notes, *Video Viewpoints,* Museum of Modern Art, 26 February 1980.

5. Excerpt from *Processual Video,* b/w videotape, 1980 (11:13 minutes).

6. *Primarily Speaking* exists as both a single-channel videotape and eight-channel video installation. The text was closer to being "constructed" than "written." I literally surrounded myself with the cinerama-like scroll of hundreds of idiomatic expressions and "watched" them fall together, 1981–83.

7. Gary Hill, *Focus,* Scan Program notes, Video Gallery Scan (Tokyo), April–May 1985.

8. *Why Do Things Get in a Muddle? (Come on Petunia),* color videotape, 1984 (33:09 minutes). This work was based on the metalogue by Gregory Bateson published in *Steps to an Ecology of Mind: Essays in Anthropology, Psychiatry, Evolution and Epistemology* (New York: Ballantine Books, 1972), 3–8. Curiously, now, in comparing my script notes with the original text, it was I who had performed this mirroring of the text. The original has an additional "pennies" at the end. (Also, *Come on Petunia* replaced Donald in the original text. The daughter used anagrams, Once Upon a Time and Old Dan, respectively, to mix up the father's logic.)

9. "Video Installations 1983," *Afterimage* 11.8 (December 1983). Also, the "same" work for a time had the working title, "The Writing's on the Wall and I Can't Stop Reading It."

10. Robert Mittenthal, "Video's Event: Gary Hill's Catastrophe," *Reflex* 3.6 (1989).

11. *CRUX,* five-channel video installation, collection of the artist, 1983–87.

12. Raymond Bellour, "Video Writing," trans. Alison Rowe. Included in *Illuminating Video* (New York: Aperture Press, 1990) and originally in a separate article, "Le dernier homme en croix," *Cinq pièces avec vue,* exhibition catalogue (Geneva: Centre Genevois de Gravure Contemporaine, 1987).

13. The wait state of a computer works in conjunction with its speed (in megahertz). The lower the number the faster the CPU computes. A zero wait state suggest the hypothetical ideal of no waiting.

14. *Happenstance (part one of many parts),* b/w videotape, stereo sound, 1982–83 (6:47 minutes).

15. One of a collection of essays in *Illuminating Video.*

16. Although the images appear continuous (real time), all directional

changes—left and right movements, "in" and "out" focusing—are edit points that join separately recorded images. All the segments were recorded for an interactive videodisc project, *Which Tree* (1986–).

17. The spoken text of *Which Tree* is an electronic combine of a male and female voice. Unlike a sample mix (chorus) of the two, the sound is a harmonic weave of the two sources that can be dynamically weighted one way or the other at different points in the labyrinthine text.

Biography

Born: 1951, Santa Monica, Calif.
Resides: Seattle, Wash.

1998   John D. and Catherine T. MacArthur Foundation Grant

1998   Artist-in-residence, Capp Street Project, San Francisco, Calif.

1996–98 Performed and collaborated with Meg Stuart and the dance company Damaged Goods in *Splayed Mind Out,* a multimedia performance that was rehearsed in Brussels, Belgium, and traveled in Europe and South America

1995   Leone d'Oro, Prize for Sculpture, Venice Biennale, Venice, Italy

1991   Artist-in-residence, Hôpital Éphémère, Paris

1985–92 Art faculty, Cornish College of the Arts, Seattle, Wash.

1988   National Endowment for the Arts, France/United States exchange fellow

        Commissioned by the Musée National d'Art Moderne, Centre Georges Pompidou, Paris, France (to produce a new video installation)

1987   Artist-in-residence, California Institute for the Arts, Valencia, Calif.

1986   Artist-in-residence, Chicago Art Institute, Chicago, Ill.

1985   Artist-in-residence, Sony Corporation, Hon Atsugi, Japan

        Established video program, Cornish College of the Arts, Seattle, Wash.

1984–85 Lived in Japan under a Japan/United States exchange fellowship

1983   Visiting professor of art, Bard College, Annandale-on-Hudson, N.Y.

        Participant, *Intersection of the Word and Image,* Women's Interart Center, New York

1982   Media panelist, New York State Council on the Arts, Ithaca Video Festival, Ithaca, N.Y.

            Visiting artist, American Center, Paris, France

1981–82   Member, board of directors, Media Alliance, New York

1981   Video panelist, Creative Artist Public Service Program, New York

1979–80   Visiting associate professor, Center for Media, State University of New York (SUNY), Buffalo, N.Y.

1978   Artist-in-residence, Portable Channel, Rochester, N.Y.

1977–79   Founder and director, Open Studio Video Project, Barrytown, N.Y.

1975–77   Artist-in-residence, Experimental Television Center, Binghamton, N.Y.

1975–76   Conceived and directed *Synergism,* a series of intermedia performances for dance, music, and video, Woodstock, N.Y.

1974–76   Artist-in-residence and artists' television lab coordinator, Woodstock Community Video, Woodstock and Rhinebeck, N.Y.

Grants and Fellowships

1998   John D. and Catherine T. MacArthur Foundation Grant

1990   Guggenheim Fellowship

            Rockefeller Intercultural Media Arts Fellowship (stage two)

1989   Rockefeller Intercultural Media Arts Fellowship

1988   *Seattle Artists 1988* (selected for the City Light portable works collection), Seattle, Wash.

1987   National Endowment for the Arts Fellowship

            Artist Trust Fellowship

1986   American Film Institute Fellowship

            Guggenheim Fellowship

            National Endowment for the Arts Production Grant

1985–86   New York State Council on the Arts Production Grant

            New York State Foundation on the Arts Fellowship

1985   National Endowment for the Arts Fellowship

1984   New Works Grant, Massachusetts Council on the Arts

1983–84   New York State Council on the Arts Production Grant

1982   Channel Thirteen/WNET Artist-in-Residence Production Grant

            Japan/United States Exchange Fellowship sponsored by the National Endowment for the Arts and the Japan/United States Friendship Commission

| 1981–82 | Rockefeller Video Artist Fellowship
National Endowment for the Arts Media Production Grant
New York State Council on the Arts Production Grant |

1980–81   New York State Council on the Arts Production Grant

1979   Channel Thirteen/WNET Artist-in-Residence Production Grant
National Endowment for the Arts Fellowship

1978–79   Creative Artist Public Service Fellowship
New York State Council on the Arts Production Grant

Awards

1996   CAA Artist Award for Distinguished Body of Work, College Art Association, New York

Second Prize, 1996 United States Chapter of the International Association of Art Critics Awards, Best Video or Installation, *Gary Hill: Withershins,* at the Institute of Contemporary Art, Philadelphia, Pa.

1995   Leone d'Oro, Prize for Sculpture, Venice Biennale, Venice, Italy

First Prize, 1994–95 AICA (International Association of Art Critics) Best Show Awards, Best Video Show or Installation, *Gary Hill,* at the Guggenheim SoHo, New York, organized by the Henry Art Gallery, University of Washington, Seattle, Wash.

1991   Prize Winner, "ARTEC 91" International Biennale, Nagoya, Japan

1989   Prize Winner (Performance Video), 13th Atlanta Film/Video Festival, Atlanta, Ga.

1988   Grand Prix, World Wide Video Festival, The Hague, The Netherlands

Honorable Mention, 3rd Bonn Video Art Festival, Bonn, Germany

Prix Alcan (video), 18th Annual Montreal Film and Video Festival, Montreal, Quebec, Canada

1987   1st Prize, Structuralist Video, Athens International Video Festival, Athens, Ohio

Grand Prize, 6th Annual Daniel Wadsworth Video Festival, Real Art Ways, Hartford, Conn.

1986   1st Prize (shared), Narrative Video, Athens International Video Festival, Athens, Ohio

James D. Phelan Art Award, San Francisco Foundation, San Francisco, Calif.

Honorable Mention (Non-Narrative Video), Video Culture International, Toronto, Ontario, Canada

1985   Grand Prix (shared), 1st Tokyo International Video Biennale, Tokyo, Japan

Sony Grand Prize, 3/4 Inch Video/New Media, Video Culture International, Montreal, Quebec, Canada

1st Prize, Art Video/New Media, Video Culture International, Montreal, Quebec, Canada

1st Prize, 3/4 Inch Non-Narrative Art Video/New Media, Video Culture International, Montreal, Quebec, Canada

1983   1st Prize (shared), San Sebastian International Video Festival, San Sebastian, Spain

Merit Award, Chicago International Film/Video Festival, Chicago, Ill.

1982   2nd Prize, Video Art, United States Film/Video Festival, Salt Lake City, Utah

1981   The Video Art Award, 3rd Annual Daniel Wadsworth Memorial Video Festival, Hartford, Conn.

1978   Merit Award, Experimental Video, Athens International Video Festival, Athens, Ohio

1976   Merit Award, Experimental Video, Athens International Video Festival, Athens, Ohio

Solo Exhibitions

1999   Aarhus Kunstmuseum, Aarhus, Denmark

School of the Museum of Fine Arts, Boston, Mass.

Gary Hill: Video Works, NTT InterCommunication Center (ICC), Tokyo, Japan

Barbara Gladstone Gallery, New York

Galleria Lia Rumma, Milan, Italy

1998–99 Whitney Museum of American Art, New York

Barbara Gladstone Gallery, New York

1998   Musée d'Art Contemporain de Montréal, Montreal, Quebec, Canada

Gary Hill: Reflex Chamber, Rice University Art Gallery, Houston, Tex.

Fundação de Serralves, Porto, Portugal

Donald Young Gallery, Seattle, Wash.

Capp Street Project, San Francisco, Calif.

St. Norbert Arts and Cultural Center, Manitoba, Canada

Museu d'Art Contemporani, Barcelona, Spain

Saint-Gervais, Genève, Switzerland

The Kitchen, New York

1997 Westfälischer Kunstverein, Münster, Germany

o lugar do outro/where the other takes place, Centro Cultural Banco do Brasil, Rio de Janeiro, Brazil, and Museu de Arte Moderna de São Paulo, Brazil

Tall Ships: Gary Hill, Museum of Art, University of California, San Diego, Calif.

Midnight Crossing and *Remarks on Color,* Ujazdowski Castle, Centre for Contemporary Art, Warsaw, Poland

1996 *Gary Hill: Withershins,* Institute of Contemporary Art, Philadelphia, Pa.

Galerie des Archives, Paris, France

Kunst und Ausstellungshalle der Bundesrepublik Deutschland (Forum), Bonn, Germany

Galleria Lia Rumma, Naples, Italy

Donald Young Gallery, Seattle, Wash.

Barbara Gladstone Gallery, New York

White Cube, London, England

1995 *Gary Hill,* Moderna Museet, Stockholm, Sweden (Scandinavian traveling exhibition organized in collaboration with Riksutställningar, Stockholm, Sweden). Museet for Samtidskunst, Oslo, Norway; Kunstforeningen, Copenhagen, Denmark; Helsingfors Konsthall, Helsinki, Finland; Bildmuseet, Urneå, Sweden; Jönköpings Läns Museum, Jönköping, Sweden; Göteborgs Konstmuseum, Göteborg, Sweden

Busch-Reisinger Museum, Harvard University Art Museums, Cambridge, Mass.

Gary Hill: Remarks on Color, Fundació "la Caixa," Barcelona, Spain

1994–95 Gary Hill (traveling exhibition organized by the Henry Art Gallery, Seattle, Wash.), Hirshhorn Museum and Sculpture Garden, Washington D.C.; Henry Art Gallery; Museum of Contemporary Art, Chicago; Museum of Contemporary Art, Los Angeles; Guggenheim Museum SoHo, New York; Kemper Museum of Contemporary Art and Design, Kansas City, Mo.

1994 Gary Hill, Musée d'Art Contemporain, Lyon, France

Imagining the Brain Closer than the Eyes, Museum für Gegenwartskunst, Öffentliche Kunstsammlung, Basel, Switzerland

1993–94   *Gary Hill: In Light of the Other,* Tate Gallery Liverpool, Liverpool, England; Museum of Modern Art, Oxford, England

1993   *Gary Hill: Sites Recited,* Long Beach Museum of Art, Long Beach, Calif.

     Gary Hill, Donald Young Gallery, Seattle, Wash.

1992–93   *Gary Hill* (traveling exhibition organized by the Centre Georges Pompidou, Paris, France), Musée National d'Art Moderne, Centre Georges Pompidou; IVAM Centre Julio Gonzalez, Valencia, Spain; Stedelijk Museum, Amsterdam, The Netherlands; Künsthalle, Vienna, Austria

1992   Stedelijk Van Abbemuseum, Eindhoven, The Netherlands

     Gary Hill, Le Creux de L'Enfer, Centre d'Art Contemporain, Thiers, France

     I Believe It Is an Image, Watari Museum of Contemporary Art, Tokyo, Japan

1991   Galerie des Archives, Paris, France

     OCO Espace d'Art Contemporain, Paris, France

     Nykytaiteen Museo: The Museum of Contemporary Art, Helsinki, Finland (retrospective of videotapes)

1990   Galerie des Archives, Paris, France (installation)

     Galerie Huset/Ny Carlsberg Glyptotek Museum, Copenhagen, Denmark (installation)

     YYZ Artist's Outlet, Toronto, Ontario, Canada (screening, installation)

     Museum of Modern Art, New York (installation)

1989   Beursschouwburg, Brussels, Belgium (screening)

     Kijkuis, The Hague, The Netherlands (installation)

     Musée d'Art Moderne, Villeneuve d'Ascq, France (installation, screening)

     Pacific Film Archives, San Francisco, Calif. (screening)

1988   Western Front, Vancouver, B.C., Canada (screening)

     Video Wochen, Basel, Switzerland (performance, screening)

     Espace lyonnais d'art contemporain (ELAC), Lyon, France (retrospective of videotapes)

1987   Museum of Contemporary Art, Los Angeles, Calif. (installation)

     Los Angeles Contemporary Exhibitions (LACE), Los Angeles, Calif. (screening)

     Cornish College of the Arts, Seattle, Wash. (installation)

2nd Seminar on International Video, St. Gervais-Genève, Geneva, Switzerland (retrospective of videotapes)

1986   Whitney Museum of American Art, New York (retrospective of videotapes)

Nexus Gallery, Philadelphia, Pa. (screening)

1985   Scan Gallery, Tokyo, Japan (videotapes)

1983   International Cultural Center, Antwerp, Belgium (screening)

The American Center, Paris, France (retrospective of videotapes)

Whitney Museum of American Art, New York (installation)

MonteVideo, Amsterdam, The Netherlands (screening)

1982   Galerie H at ORF, Steirischer Herbst, Graz, Austria (installation)

Long Beach Museum of Art, Long Beach, Calif. (installation)

1981   The Kitchen Center for Music, Video and Dance, New York (installation)

And/Or Gallery, Seattle, Wash. (installation)

Anthology Film Archives, New York (screening)

1980   Media Study, Buffalo, N.Y. (installation)

Video Viewpoints, Museum of Modern Art, New York (screening)

Image Dissector Screening Series, University of California at Los Angeles, Los Angeles, Calif. (screening)

1979   The Kitchen Center for Music, Video and Dance, New York (installation)

Everson Museum, Syracuse, N.Y. (installation)

Meet the Makers: Gary Hill, Donnell Library, New York (screening)

1978   Rochester Memorial Art Gallery, Rochester, N.Y. (screening)

1976   Anthology Film Archives, New York (screening)

1974   South Houston Gallery, New York

1973   Woodstock Artists' Association, Woodstock, N.Y.

1971   Polaris Gallery, Woodstock, N.Y.

Selected Group Exhibitions

1999–2000 *The American Century: Art & Culture, Part II 1950–2000,* The Whitney Museum of American Art, New York

Seeing Time: Selections from the Pamela and Richard Kramlich Collection of Media Art, San Francisco Museum of Art, San Francisco, Calif.

1999   *Somewhere Near Vada,* Project Arts Centre, Dublin, Ireland

TV Gallery, Moscow, Russia

Passage a l'art: des lieux et des choses, Forum Culturel du Blanc-Mesnil, Le Blanc-Mesnil, France

Umedalen Skulptur 99, organized by Galleri Stefan Andersson, Umeå, Sweden

The Hand, The Power Plant Contemporary Art Gallery, Toronto, Ontario, Canada

Transmute, Museum of Contemporary Art, Chicago, Ill.

Romancing the Brain, Pittsburgh Center for the Arts, Pittsburgh, Pa.

Re-Structure, Grinnell College Art Gallery, Grinnell, Iowa

Searchlight: Consciousness at the Millennium, CCAC (California College of Arts and Crafts) Institute, Oakland/San Francisco, Calif.

1998–99   *Silent Treatment,* Aspen Art Museum, Aspen, Colo.

Surrogate: The Figure in Contemporary Sculpture and Photography, Henry Art Gallery, Seattle, Wash.

Voices, Witte de With, Rotterdam, The Netherlands; Fundació Joan Miró, Barcelona, Spain; and Le Fresnoy, Studio national des arts contemporains, Tourcoing, France

Crossings, Kunsthalle Wien, Vienna, Austria; Rudolfinum, Prague, Czech Republic

1998   *Anos 80,* Culturgest—Gestão de Espaços Culturais, Lisbon, Portugal

Tuning up #5, Kunstmuseum Wolfsburg, Wolfsburg, Germany

Made in Corpus, Odyssud, Blagnac, France

Personal Effects: The Collective Unconscious, Museum of Contemporary Art, Sydney, Australia

3rd Werkleitz Biennial, Werkleitz, Germany

1997   *Angel, Angel,* Kunsthalle Wien, Vienna, Austria

Citta' Natura, Palazzo delle Esposizioni, Rome, Italy

The Twentieth Century: The Age of Modern Art, Martin Gropius Bau, Berlin, Germany; traveled to: Royal Academy of Arts, London, England

Biennale d'Art Contemporain, Lyon, France

Unimplosive Art, Milan, Italy

Water: The Renewable Metaphor, University of Oregon Museum of Art, Eugene, Oreg.

Kwangju Biennale, Kwangju, Korea

World Wide Video Festival, Amsterdam, The Netherlands

The Objects in Hangar 2, Seattle Arts Commission, Sand Point Naval Base, Seattle, Wash.

Human References: Marks of the Artist: A Ten Year Retrospective Exhibition of the Seattle Artists' Program Collection, The Seattle Center Pavilion, Seattle, Wash.

Grand Opening, Montevideo/TBA, Amsterdam, The Netherlands

Surveying the First Decade: Video Art and Alternative Media in the United States, San Francisco Museum of Modern Art, San Francisco, Calif.

Amours, Fondation Cartier pour l'art contemporain, Paris, France

1996–97 *Being and Time: The Emergence of Video Projection* (traveling exhibition organized by the Albright-Knox Art Gallery, Buffalo, N.Y.; Albright-Knox Art Gallery; Cranbrook Art Museum, Bloomfield Hills, Mich.; Portland Art Museum, Portland, Oreg.; Contemporary Arts Museum, Houston, Tex.; Site Santa Fe, Santa Fe, N.M.)

1996 *One and Others: Photography and Video by Juan Downey, Angela Grauerholz, Gary Hill, Alfredo Jaar, Annette Messager,* Galerie Lelong, New York

NowHere, Louisiana Museum of Modern Art, Humlebaek, Denmark

Worldwide Video Festival, Den Haag, The Netherlands

Kunstmuseum Wolfsburg, Wolfsburg, Germany

fremdKörper—corps étranger—Foreign Body, Museum für Gegenwartskunst, Basel, Switzerland

Ex-Libris/home page, Paço das Artes, São Paolo, Brazil

Sonambiente, Akademie der Kunste, Berlin, Germany

Le Printemps de Cahors Photographie & Arts Visuels, Fondation Cartier pour l'art contemporain, Paris, France; Portalen Koge Bugt Kulturhus, Greve, Denmark

The Last Supper, Donald Young Gallery, Seattle, Wash.

Hamburger Bahnhof—Museum für Gegenwart, Berlin, Germany

The Red Gate, Museum Van Hedendaagse Kunst Gent, Belgium

Moderna Museet Stockholm, Kunst- und Ausstellungshalle der Bundesrepublik Deutschland, Bonn, Germany (video program)

1995 *ARS '95 Helsinki,* The Finnish National Gallery, Helsinki, Finland

Pour un couteau, Le Creux de l'Enfer, Le Centre d'Art Contemporain, Thiers, France

Altered States: American Art in the 90's, Forum for Contemporary Art, St. Louis, Mo.

Immagini in Prospettive, Cinema "Verdi," Serre de Rapolano, Italy

Multimediale 4, ZKM, Karlsruhe, Germany

Sculptures Sonores: Une Certaine Perspective Communique, Ludwig Museum im Deutschherrenhaus, Koblenz, Germany

Identità e Alterità, Venice Biennale, Venice, Italy

Video Spaces: Eight Installations, Museum of Modern Art, New York

Longing and Belonging: From the Faraway Nearby, Site Santa Fe, Santa Fe, N.M.

Carnegie International, Carnegie Museum of Art, Pittsburgh, Pa.

Biennale d'Art Contemporain, Lyon, France

1994   *Beeld,* Museum van Hedendaagse Kunst, Ghent, Belgium

Múltiplas Dimensões, Centro Cultural de Belém, Lisbon, Portugal

São Paulo Bienal, São Paulo, Brazil

Facts and Figures, Lannan Foundation, Los Angeles, Calif.

Light into Art: From Video to Virtual Reality, Contemporary Arts Center, Cincinnati, Ohio

Cocido y Crudo, Centro de Arte Reina Sofia, Madrid, Spain

Intelligent Ambience and Frozen Images, Long Beach Museum of Art, Long Beach, Calif.

1993   Forumbhzvideo, Festival Internacional de Video, Belo Horizonte, Minas Gerais, Brazil

London Film Festival, London, England

Gary Hill, Between Cinema and a Hard Place, and recent works by Lewis Baltz, Jac Leirner, and Glenn Ligon, The Bohen Foundation, New York

"Strange" HOTEL, Aarhus Kuntsmuseum, Aarhus, Denmark

Anonymity and Identity, Anderson Gallery, Virginia Commonwealth University, Richmond, Va.; and The Art Gallery, University of Maryland, College Park, Md.

American Art in the 20th Century, Painting and Sculpture 1913–1993, Royal Academy, London, England

Centro Cultural Arte Contemporaneo, Mexico City, Mexico

1993 Whitney Biennial in Seoul, National Museum of Contemporary Art, Seoul, Korea

Fifth Fukui International Video Biennal, Fukui, Japan

American Art in the 20th Century, Painting and Sculpture 1913–1993, Martin-Gropius-Bau, Berlin, Germany

Eadweard Muybridge, Bill Viola, Giulio Paolini, Gary Hill, James Coleman, Ydessa Hendeles Art Foundation, Toronto, Ontario, Canada

Passageworks, Rooseum, Malmö, Sweden

The 21st Century, Künsthalle Basel, Basel, Switzerland

The Binary Era: New Interactions, Künsthalle, Vienna, Austria

Biennial Exhibition, Whitney Museum of American Art, New York

Doubletake: Collective Memory and Current Art, Künsthalle, Vienna, Austria

1992   *Performing Objects,* Institute of Contemporary Art, Boston, Mass.

Metamorphose, St. Gervais-Genève, Geneva, Switzerland

Manifest, Musée national d'art moderne, Centre Georges Pompidou, Paris, France

Art at the Armory: Occupied Territory, Museum of Contemporary Art, Chicago, Ill.

The Binary Era: New Interactions, Musée d'Ixelles, Brussels, Belgium

Filmladen Festival, Kassel, Germany (also Botschaft Festival, Berlin, Germany, and Hinterhaus, Wiesbaden, Germany)

Dance, California Museum of Photography, Riverside, Calif.

documenta IX, Museum Fridericianum, Kassel, Germany

Passages de l'image, San Francisco Museum of Modern Art, San Francisco, Calif.

Japan 92 Video and Television Festival, Tokyo, Japan

Doubletake: Collective Memory & Current Art, Hayward Gallery, London, England

Japan: Outside/Inside/Inbetween, Artists Space, New York

Donald Young Gallery, Seattle, Wash.

1991   *Biennial Exhibition,* Whitney Museum of American Art, New York

Currents, Institute of Contemporary Art, Boston, Mass.

The Body (2), The Renaissance Society at the University of Chicago, Chicago, Ill.

In Public: Seattle, 1991, Security Pacific Gallery, Seattle, Wash.

Metropolis, Martin-Gropius-Bau, Berlin, Germany

Topographie 2: Untergrund, Wiener Festwochen, Vienna, Austria

Artec '91, International Biennale, Nagoya, Japan

Glass: Material in the Service of Meaning, Tacoma Art Museum, Tacoma, Wash.

Passages de l'image, Fundacio "la Caixa," Barcelona, Spain, and Wexner Art Center, Columbus, Ohio

1990   *Tendances multiples (Videos des Annees 80),* Musée national d'art moderne, Centre Georges Pompidou, Paris, France

Energieen, Stedelijk Museum, Amsterdam, The Netherlands

Video Poetics, Long Beach Museum of Art, Long Beach, Calif.

Passages de l'image, Musée national d'art moderne, Centre Georges Pompidou, Paris, France (traveling exhibition)

L'Amour de Berlin: Installation Video, Centre Culturel, Cavaillon, France

A Force of Repetition, New Jersey State Museum, Newark, N.J.

Bienal de la Imagen en Movimiento '90, Centro de Arte Reina Sofia, Madrid, Spain

God & Country, Greg Kucera Gallery, Seattle, Wash.

1989   *Video-Skulptur Retrospektiv und Aktuell 1963–1989,* Kolnischer Künstverein, Cologne, Germany (traveled to Berlin and Zürich)

Electronic Landscapes, National Gallery of Canada, Ottawa, Ontario, Canada

Video and Language, Museum of Modern Art, New York

Delicate Technology, 2nd Japan Video Television Festival, Spiral Hall, Tokyo, Japan

Les Cent Jours d'Art Contemporain, Centre International d'Art Contemporain de Montreal, Montreal, Quebec, Canada

Selections from the Permanent Collection: Recent Acquisitions—Video, San Francisco Museum of Modern Art, San Francisco, Calif.

Filmer à tout prix, no. 4, Brussels, Belgium (festival selection)

Eye for I: Video Self-Portraits, Whitney Museum of American Art, New York

3rd Seminar on International Video, St. Gervais-Genève, Geneva, Switzerland (festival selection)

Japan 89 Video Television Festival, Tokyo, Japan

1988   *Infermental VII,* Buffalo, N.Y.

Degrees of Reality, Long Beach Museum of Art, Long Beach, Calif.

Art Video American, CREDAC, Paris, France

As Told To: Structures for Conversation, Walter Philips Gallery, Banff, Alberta, Canada

4th International Manifestation of Video and TV, Montbéliard, France (festival selection)

London Film Festival, London, England (festival selection)

The World Wide Video Festival, Kijkhuis, The Hague, The Netherlands (festival selection)

3. Videonald, Bonn, Germany (festival selection)

1987   *documenta VIII,* Museum Fridericianum, Kassel, Germany

Video Discourse: Mediated Narratives, Institute of Contemporary Art, Boston, Mass.

Video Discourse: Mediated Narratives, La Jolla Museum of Contemporary Art, San Diego, Calif.

Infermental VI, Western Front, Vancouver, British Columbia, Canada

Contemporary Diptychs: Divided Visions, Whitney Museum of American Art, New York

Avenues of Thought: Cultural and Spiritual Abstractions in Video, Rutgers University, Newark, N.J.

The Situated Image, Mandeville Gallery, University of California at San Diego (UCSD), La Jolla, Calif.

15th Avenue Studio #2: The Mechanics of Contemplation, Henry Art Gallery, University of Washington, Seattle, Wash.

The Arts for Television, international traveling exhibition organized by the Museum of Contemporary Art, Los Angeles, Calif., and the Stedelijk Museum, Amsterdam, The Netherlands

Cinq Pièces Avec Vue, Centre Génevois de Gravure Contemporaine, Geneva, Switzerland

Japan 87 Video Television Festival, Tokyo, Japan

Video Transformations, organized by Independent Curators Incorporated (ICI), New York (traveled to: Goldie Paley Gallery, Moore College of Art, Philadelphia, Pa.; Modlin Fine Arts Center, Richmond, Va.; Oklahoma Art Center, Oklahoma City, Okla.; Bass Museum of Art, Miami Beach, Fla.; Museum of Art, University Park, Pa.)

Computers and Art, Everson Museum of Art, Syracuse, N.Y.

1986   *Video: Recent Acquisitions,* Museum of Modern Art, New York

Video and Language/Video as Language, Los Angeles Contemporary Exhibitions (LACE), Los Angeles, Calif.

National Video Festival, American Film Institute (AFI), Los Angeles, Calif.

Cryptic Languages, Washington Project for the Arts, Washington, D.C.

Resolution: A Critique of Video Art, Los Angeles Contemporary Exhibitions (LACE), Los Angeles, Calif.

The Image of Fiction: International Videoart, Infermental 5, Con Rumore, Rotterdam

Collections Videos—Acquisitions Depuis 1977, Musée National d'art Moderne, Centre Georges Pompidou, Paris, France

The World Wide Video Festival, Kijkhuis, The Hague, The Netherlands

San Francisco Video Festival, San Francisco, Calif.

II National Video Festival of Madrid, Circulo de Bellas Artes, Madrid, Spain

Poetic License, Long Beach Museum of Art, Long Beach, Calif.

International Festival of Video Art, Saw Gallery, Ottawa, Ontario, Canada (traveled to: Centre for Art Tapes, Halifax, England; Forest City Gallery, London, England; EM Media, Calgary, Alberta, Canada; A Space, Toronto, Ontario, Canada; Video Pool, Winnipeg, Manitoba, Canada; Monitor North, Thunder Bay, Ontario, Canada; PRIM Video, Montreal, Quebec, Canada)

Video Transformations, organized by Independent Curators Incorporated (ICA), New York (traveled to: University of Arizona Museum of Art, Tucson, Ariz.; Ball State University Gallery, Muncie, Ind.; Grand Rapids Art Museum, Grand Rapids, Mich.; de Saisset Museum, Santa Clara, Calif.; Hillwood Art Gallery, Greenvale, N.Y.; Stevenson Union Gallery, Ashland, Oreg.; Closely Watched Films, Doylestown, Pa.; Video Free America, San Francisco, Calif.; Weatherspoon Art Gallery, Greensboro, N.C.; Visual Studies Workshop, Rochester, N.Y.; Tyler Art Gallery, Oswego, N.Y.; Ohio State University Gallery of Fine Art, Columbus, Ohio; Alberta College of Art Gallery, Calgary, Alberta, Canada)

1985   *Biennial Exhibition,* Whitney Museum of American Art, New York

Image/Word: The Art of Reading, New Langton Arts, San Francisco, Calif.

San Francisco Video Festival, San Francisco, Calif.

National Video Festival, American Film Institute (AFI), Los Angeles, Calif.

The World Wide Video Festival, Kijkhuis, The Hague, The Netherlands

Video Art: Stockholm International Festival '85, Kulturhuset, Stockholm, Sweden

A Video Sampler, American Museum of the Moving Image, Astoria, N.Y.

1984   *Biennale di Venezia,* Venice, Italy

So There, Orwell 1984, The Louisiana World Exhibition, New Orleans, La.

Video: A Retrospective, Long Beach Museum of Art, Long Beach, Calif.

Videographia, Escoia I Centre d'Activtats Video, Barcelona, Spain

National Video Festival, American Film Institute (AFI), Los Angeles, Calif.

1983   *Art Video Retrospectives et Perspectives,* Palais des Beaux-Arts, Brussels, Belgium

Video as Attitude, University Art Museum, University of New Mexico, Albuquerque, N.M.

Electronic Visions, Hudson River Museum, Yonkers, N.Y.

The Second Link: Viewpoints on Video in the Eighties, Walter Philips Gallery, Banff, Alberta, Canada

XXXI Festival Internacional de Cine de San Sebastian, San Sebastian, Spain

1983 Biennial Exhibition, Whitney Museum of American Art, New York

San Francisco Video Festival, San Francisco, Calif.

1982   *The Sydney Biennale,* Sydney, Australia

Gary Hill: Equal Time, Long Beach Museum of Art, Long Beach, Calif.

1981   *Projects Video XXXV,* Museum of Modern Art, New York

National Video Festival, John F. Kennedy Center for the Performing Arts, Washington, D.C.

New York Video, Stadtische Galerie im Lenbachhaus, Munich, Germany

7th Annual Ithaca Video Festival, Ithaca, N.Y.

1980   *San Francisco Video Festival,* San Francisco, Calif.

1979   *Projects Video XXVII,* Museum of Modern Art, New York

Video Revue, Everson Museum of Art, Syracuse, N.Y.

Beau Fleuve, Media Study, Buffalo, N.Y. (traveled to: The Center for Media Art, American Center in Paris, France; L'espace lyonnais d'action culturelle, Lyon, France; Musée Cantini, Marseille, France)

Political Comment in Contemporary Art, Brainerd Art Gallery, Potsdam, N.Y.

1978   *4th Annual Ithaca Video Festival,* Ithaca, N.Y.

Sums & Differences (performance), Arnolfini Arts Center, Rhinebeck, N.Y.

1977   *New Work in Abstract Video Imagery,* Everson Museum of Art, Syracuse, N.Y.

1976   *Video Expovision '76,* Woodstock Community Video, Woodstock, N.Y.

Athens International Film Festival, Athens, Ohio

Synergism, performance with Walter Wright and Sara Cook, Woodstock Artists' Association, Woodstock, N.Y.

1975   *Projects Video VI,* Museum of Modern Art, New York

An Evening of Video, Walnut Street Theatre, Philadelphia, Pa.

Woodstock Video Exposition, Woodstock, N.Y.

Annual Avant-Garde Festival of New York, New York

1974   *Artists from Upstate New York,* 55 Mercer Gallery, New York

1972   *Electronic Music: Improvisations* (performance with Jean-Yves Labat), Woodstock Artists' Association, Woodstock, N.Y.

Performances

1998   Performance by Gary Hill, George Quasha, and Charles Stein at the Musée d'art contemporain de Montreal, January 30, 1998.

1996–98 *Splayed Mind Out,* Collaboration with Meg Stuart and the dance company Damaged Goods. Performed in Europe, South America, and the United States.

1996   *Touching,* and other works, at the Speakeasy Cafe, Seattle, Wash., on September 19, 1996.

1993   *Performance by Gary Hill,* George Quasha, and Charles Stein for Gary Hill: Day Seminar, on November 7, 1993, at the University of Oxford in Oxford, England, in conjunction with the exhibition entitled *Gary Hill: In Light of the Other.*

Selected Video Works, 1973–1992

Videotapes*

The Fall, 1973. Black and white; 11:00

Air Raid, 1974. Black and white; 6:00

Rock City Road, 1974–75. Color, silent; 12:00

Earth Pulse, 1975. Color; 6:00

Improvisations with Bluestone, 1976. Color; 6:00

Mirror Road, 1976. Color, silent; 6:00

Bits, 1977. Color; 2:59

Bathing, 1977. Color, silent; 4:25

Windows, 1978. Color, silent; 8:00

Electronic Linguistics, 1978. Black and white; 3:45

Sums & Differences, 1978. Black and white; 8:00

Mouth Piece, 1978. Color; 1:00

Full Circle, 1978. Color; 3:25

Primary, 1978. Color; 1:40

Elements, 1978. Black and white; 2:00

Objects with Destinations, 1979. Color, silent; 3:40

Equal Time, 1979. Color, stereo sound; 4:00

Picture Story, 1979. Color; 7:00

Soundings, 1979. Color; 17:00

Processual Video, 1980. Black and white; 11:30

Black/White/Text, 1980. Black and white, stereo sound; 7:00

Commentary, 1980. Color; 0:40

*Videotapes are listed chronologically.

325

Around & About, 1980. Color; 4:45

Videograms, 1980–81. Black and white; 13:25

Primarily Speaking, 1981–83. Color, stereo sound; 18:40

Happenstance (part one of many parts), 1982–83. Black and white, stereo sound; 6:30

Why Do Things Get in a Muddle? (Come on Petunia), 1984. Color; 32:00

Tale Enclosure, 1985. Color, stereo sound; 5:30

URA ARU (the backside exists), 1985–86. Color; 28:00

Mediations (towards a remake of Soundings), 1979–86. Color, stereo sound; 4:45

Incidence of Catastrophe, 1987–88. Color, stereo sound; 43:51

Site Recite (a prologue), 1989. Color, stereo sound; 4:00

Solstice d'Hiver, 1990. Color, sound; 60:00

Installations*

Hole in the Wall, 1974
Site-specific, single-channel video/sound installation
Two monitors

Mesh, 1979
Mixed-media installation
Three live cameras, four black-and-white monitors, wire mesh, electronics, and speakers

War Zone, 1980
Mixed-media installation
Live stereo camera/viewfinder, two videotapes, sixteen loudspeakers, objects, motor-controlled lights, and live rabbit

Around & About, 1980 (destroyed)
Video/sound installation
Two versions:
1. Two monitors (black-and-white and color) and videotape
2. Eight monitors (four black-and-white and four color), videotape, and controlling electronics

Glass Onion, 1981
Two-channel video/sound installation
Live camera with remote-controlled zoom lens, two videotapes, five monitors, eight speakers, and controlling electronics

Primarily Speaking, 1981–83
Two-channel video/sound installation
Two versions:

*Installations are listed chronologically.

1. Eight monitors, four speakers, and controlling electronics
2. Two monitors, chairs, and mirrors

Equal Time, 1982
Three-channel video/sound installation
Four monitors and two speakers

CRUX, 1983–87
Five-channel video/sound installation
Five color monitors, five speakers, five laserdisc players, and synchronizer

In Situ, 1986
Mixed-media installation
Modified easy chair, modified monitor, six electric fans, sculptural elements, motorized paper feeder, controlling electronics, and speakers

Mediarite, 1987
Site-specific mixed-media installation
Three videotapes/VTRs, six monitors, four electric motors, lenses, mineral oil, sculptural elements, controlling electronics, and speakers

DIG, 1987–92
(based on *Mediarite*)
Mixed-media installation
Three-channel video, six monitors, four electric motors, lenses, mineral oil, sculptural elements, computer-controlled electronics, and speakers

DISTURBANCE (among the jars), 1988
Seven-channel video/sound installation

And Sat Down Beside Her, 1990
Mixed-media installation consisting of three works:
1. Single-channel video and hanging television tube with table, chair, lens, book, and speaker
2. Single-channel video and glass tube enclosing 1-inch television tube, text applied on floor and speaker
3. Two-channel video and two 1-inch television tubes with four lenses

BEACON (Two Versions of the Imaginary), 1990
Two-channel video/sound installation
Two television tubes mounted in aluminum cylinder, projection lenses, motor, and controlling electronics

Inasmuch As It Is Always Already Taking Place, 1990
Sixteen-channel video/sound installation
Sixteen 0.5-inch to 21-inch black-and-white television tubes positioned in horizontal inset in wall

Between Cinema and a Hard Place, 1991
Three-channel video/sound installation
Twenty-three modified monitors and computer-controlled switching matrix

CORE SERIES (two works: *Glasses* and *Leaves*), 1991
Single-channel video/sound installations
Each work: two modified monitors and electronic switch with tone decoder

Split Time Mystery, 1991
Site-specific temporary installation produced for the Vienna subway system as part of the exhibition *Topographie II: Untergrund*

I Believe It Is an Image in Light of the Other, 1991–92
Mixed-media installation
Seven-channel video, modified television tubes for projection, books, and speaker

Suspension of Disbelief (for Marine), 1992
Four-channel video installation
Thirty 12-inch television tubes mounted on aluminum beam, four channels of video, four laserdisc players, and computer-controlled switching matrix

CORE SERIES (*No Evil*), 1992
Single-channel video/sound installation
Three modified monitors and electronic switch with tone decoder

Tall Ships, 1992
Sixteen-channel video installation
Sixteen black-and-white monitors, sixteen projection units, sixteen laserdisc players, and computer-controlled interactive system

Cut Pipe, 1992
Single-channel video/sound installation
Black-and-white video monitor, projection lens, two aluminum cylinders, and three loudspeakers

Some Times Things, 1992
Nine-channel video/sound installation
Nine modified monitors, nine projection lenses, nine loudspeakers, and nine aluminum tubes

If Two People, 1993 (destroyed)
Two-channel video/sound installation
Ten black-and-white monitors mounted on two aluminum ladders, two speakers, and spoken text

Between 1 & 0, 1993
Two-channel video/sound installation
Thirteen black-and-white monitors mounted on aluminum cross, computer-controlled video switcher, and audio

House of Cards, 1993
Seven-channel video/sound installation
Five black-and-white monitors mounted on an aluminum ladder, two color monitors

Learning Curve, 1993
Single-channel video installation
Video projector, custom-made screen, and plywood chair/table construction

Learning Curve (still point), 1993
Single-channel video installation
One 5-inch color monitor, plywood chair/table construction

Searchlight, 1986–94
Single-channel video/sound installation
Aluminum tube, black-and-white video monitor, motor, two laserdisc players, and controlling electronics

Circular Breathing, 1994
Single-channel video/sound installation
Five color video projectors, laserdisc player, computer-controlled video switcher, amplifier, and two loudspeakers

Clover, 1994
Four-channel video/sound installation
Four modified black-and-white 20-inch monitors, four laserdisc players, steel platform, synchronizer, loudspeaker, and stereo amplifier

Remarks on Color, 1994
Single-channel video installation with color video projection

Red Technology, 1994
Single-channel video/sound installation with two projectors

Bind, 1995
Single-channel video/sound installation
Combination video monitor/video cassette recorder with attached book

Dervish, 1993–95
Video/sound installation
Aluminum and wood structure, mirrors, strobe light, two video projectors, motor, speakers, computer, and controlling electronics

Withershins, 1995
Interactive sound installation with video projections
25 × 35 feet floor maze constructed from 2 × 4 inch aluminum rectangular tubing, electronic switch mats, two video projectors, two laserdisc players and synchronizer, two computers with sound cards, computer-controlled location of sound on four loudspeakers, and lights

Placing Sense↔Sens Placé, 1995
Video/sound installation
Four color monitors, four metal dollies, four laserdisc players, amplifiers, and synchronizer

HaND HeaRD, 1995–96
Five-channel video installation with five color projections

Five projectors, five laserdisc players, and synchronizer

Viewer, 1996
Five-channel video installation
Five laserdisc players, five projectors, one five-channel synchronizer

Standing Apart, 1996
Two-channel video installation
Two laserdisc players, two projectors, one two-channel synchronizer

Facing Faces, 1996
Two-channel video installation
Two laserdisc players, two monitors, two monitor shelves, one two-channel synchronizer

Reflex Chamber, 1996
Single-channel video/sound installation
Video projector, mirror, strobe light, loudspeakers, computer, and 60 × 60 × 34 inch square table

Midnight Crossing, 1997
Single-channel video/sound installation
Custom-made 12 h. × 14 w. × 8 d. foot aluminum screen, projector, laserdisc player, six strobe lights, speakers, amplifier, and computer

Conundrum, 1995–98
Single-channel video installation
Laserdisc player, six video monitors, switcher, and steel armature
10.5 h. × 13 d. × 71 l. inches

Liminal Objects #1–#8, 1995–98
Single-channel video installations
Each installation: one 14-inch monitor, one laserdisc player, custom-made metal stand

23:59:59:29 The Storyteller's Room, 1998
Twelve-channel video/sound installation
Twelve laserdisc players, twelve-channel synchronizer, twelve 4-inch black-and-white monitors with projection lenses and mounts, audio amplifier with multiple loudspeakers, ten strobe lights, strobe controller, computer, foam, rope, and miscellaneous cabling
Dimensions variable

Switchblade, 1998–99
Single-channel video/sound installation
Projector, monitor, laserdisc player, one laserdisc, switcher, and stereo system

Crossbow, 1999
Three-channel video/sound installation
Three 13-inch LCD video displays with speakers, three DVD players, three DVD discs, and synchronizer

Bibliography

Writings by the Artist*

"Processual Video." *Video Viewpoints* (New York: Museum of Modern Art, February 1980).

"War Zone." *Media Study/Buffalo* (January–May 1980).

"Videograms." *Themes in Electronic Image Processing* (New York: The Kitchen Center for Music, Video and Dance, December 1981).

Primarily Speaking, 1981–83 (New York: Whitney Museum of American Art, 1983).

"URA ARU: The Acoustic Palindrome." *Video Guide,* vol. 7, issue 34, no. 4 (Vancouver, B.C., 1985), pp. 10–11.

"Happenstance (explaining it to death)." *Video d'Artistes* (Geneva: Bel Vedere, 1986).

"Processual Video" (videotape transcription). *2nd International Week of Video* (Geneva: St. Gervais, 1987).

"Primarily Speaking." *Video Communications,* no. 48 (Paris, 1988).

Paragraph and photograph in "Reordering the Hierarchy," by Willard Wood, *Reflex* (May–June 1988).

"And if the Right Hand Did not Know What the Left Hand is Doing." *Illuminating Video,* ed. Doug Hall and Sally Jo Fifer (New York: Aperture Press in association with the Bay Area Video Coalition, 1990), pp. 91–99. German translation reprinted in *Noëma Art Journal* 49 (October–November 1998), pp. 83–89.

"*BEACON* (Two Versions of the Imaginary)," essay from the exhibition catalogue, *ENERGIEEN* (Amsterdam: Stedelijk Museum, 1990). Reprinted in the catalogue, *Bienal de la Imagen en Movimiento '90* (Madrid: Museo Nacional Centro de Arte Reina Sofia, 1990).

"Inasmuch As It Is Always Already Taking Place." *OTHERWORDSAND-*

---

*Writings are listed chronologically.

IMAGES: Video by Gary Hill (Danish and English) (Copenhagen: Video
Gallerie/Ny Carlsberg Glyptotek, 1990), p. 27.

"Site Recite" from "Unspeakable Images." *Camera Obscura*, no. 24 (San
Francisco, 1991).

"Split Time Mystery." *Topographie II: Untergrund, Videoinstallations in the
Vienna Subway System* (Vienna: Wiener Festwochen, 1991).

"Leaves." *Gary Hill—I Believe It Is an Image* (Tokyo: Watari Museum of
Contemporary Art, 1992).

"Entre-vue." *Gary Hill* (Paris: Centre Georges Pompidou, 1992), pp. 8–13.
Also available in Spanish with an English translation as "Entre-vista" in
the exhibition catalogue of the same name (Valencia: IVAM, 1993), pp.
12–17; and in English with Dutch and German translations, as "Interview" in the exhibition catalogue of the same name (Amsterdam: Stedelijk
Museum; Vienna: Kunsthalle, Wien, 1993), pp. 13–17.

"Entre 1 & 0." *Gary Hill* (Paris: Centre Georges Pompidou, 1992), pp. 74–76.
Also available in Spanish with an English translation as "Entre 1 & 0" in
the exhibition catalogue of the same name (Valencia: IVAM, 1993), pp.
78–80; and in English with Dutch and German translations, as "Between 1
& 0" in the exhibition catalogue of the same name (Amsterdam: Stedelijk
Museum; Vienna: Kunsthalle, Wien, 1993), pp. 37–39.

"The Electronic Gallery." *The New York Times Magazine* (Special Technology Issue), September 28, 1997, sec. 6, p. 93.

"Liminal Performance: Gary Hill in Conversation with George Quasha and
Charles Stein." *Performing Arts Journal (PAJ)*, no. 58, vol. 20 (January
1998), pp. 1–25.

Lectures*

Princeton University School of Architecture, Princeton, N.J., March 27, 1995.
Henry Art Gallery, University of Washington, Seattle, Wash., May 14, 1997.
University of Hawaii at Manoa, February 19, 1997.
Centre for Contemporary Art, Ujazdowski Castle, Warsaw, Poland, Decem-
ber 2, 1997.
Musée d'Art Contemporain de Montreal, Quebec, Canada, January 30, 1998.
San Francisco Art Institute, San Francisco, Calif., March 18, 1998.
Rice University Art Gallery, Houston, Tex., March 28, 1998.
Williams College Museum of Art, Williamstown, Mass., September 17, 1998.
TV Dinner No. 2, Conversation with Meg Stuart, The Kitchen, New York,
December 4 (moderated by Anney Bonney, The Kitchen) and 5 (moder-
ated by Chrissie Iles, Whitney Museum of American Art), 1998.
MacArthur Foundation Grant Recipient Panel Discussion, Henry Art
Gallery, Seattle, Wash., March 2, 1999.
Bard College, Annandale-on-Hudson, N.Y., March 24, 1999.

*Lectures are listed chronologically.

Other Projects*

Mac Low, Jackson. *Asymmetries 1–260* (Printed Editions, 1980). (book cover)
Davis, Christine, ed. *Public 7 (Sacred Technologies)* (Toronto: Public Access
Press, 1993). (project for journal; drawings by Anastasia Hill)

Exhibition Catalogues and Brochures*

Jenkins, Bruce, and John Minkowsky. "Gary Hill." *Beau Fleuve* (Buffalo:
Media Study, 1979).
Quasha, George. "Notes on the Feedback Horizon." *Glass Onion* (Barrytown,
N.Y.: Station Hill Press, 1980).
Hanhardt, John G. "Gary Hill." *The New American Filmmakers Series 12*
(New York: Whitney Museum of American Art, 1983).
Hanhardt, John G. "Commentary . . ." in *The 3rd Fukui International Video
Biennale* (Fukui, Japan, 1985).
Hanhardt, John G. "Gary Hill." *The New American Filmmakers Series 30*
(New York: Whitney Museum of American Art, 1986).
The Image of Fiction: International Videoart Infermental 5 (Rotterdam, The
Netherlands: Con Rumore, 1986), p. 41.
Kolpan, Steven. "Bateson: Through the Looking Glass." *1986 Saw Gallery
International Festival of Video Art* (Ottawa, Ontario: Saw Gallery, 1986).
Rankin, Scott. *Video and Language/Video as Language* (Los Angeles: Los
Angeles Contemporary Exhibitions, 1986).
Video by Artists 2 (Toronto: Art Metropole, 1986).
Video Transformations (New York: Independent Curators Incorporated, 1986).
Bellour, Raymond. "Le dernier homme en croix." *2nd Semaine International
de Video* (Geneva: Bel Veder, Centre Génevois de Gravure Contempo-
raine, 1987). Also published in *Illuminating Video,* ed. Doug Hall and Sally
Jo Fifer (New York: Aperture Press in association with the Bay Area Video
Coalition, 1990), pp. 425–26, and in *OTHERWORDSANDIMAGES:
Video by Gary Hill* (Danish and English) (Copenhagen: Video Gallerie/Ny
Carlsberg Glyptotek, 1990), pp. 20–26.
1987 Biennial Exhibition (New York: Whitney Museum of American Art,
1987), pp. 150, 168, 201–2, 211.
Goodman, Cynthia. *Digital Visions: Computers and Art* (New York: Harry N.
Abrams, 1987). Published in conjunction with the exhibition *Computers
and Art* organized by the Everson Museum of Art, Syracuse, N.Y., 1987.
Kain, Jackie. "L'intime du mot: l'oeuvre video de Gary Hill." *2nd Semaine
Internationale de Video* (Geneva: Bel Veder, Centre Génevois de Gravure
Contemporaine, 1987).

*Projects are listed chronologically.
*Catalogues and brochures are listed chronologically.

Riley, Bob. *Video Currents—Mediated Narratives* (Boston: Institute of Contemporary Art, 1987).

Artists 1/2 Inch Videotape Series 1988 (Toronto: Art Metropole, 1988).

Augaitis, Daina. "As Told To: Structures for Conversation," program essay for exhibition of same title at Walter Philips Gallery, Banff, Alberta, Canada, 1988 (Banff: Walter Philips Gallery, 1990). Also published in the book *Sound by Artists* (Toronto: Art Metropole, 1990).

Fargier, Jean-Paul. "Magie Blanche." *Gary Hill: DISTURBANCE (among the jars)* (French and English) (Villeneuve d'Ascq: Musée d'Art Moderne, 1988), unpaginated.

Quasha, George. "Disturbing Unnarrative of the Perplexed Parapraxis (A Twin for DISTURBANCE)." *Gary Hill: DISTURBANCE (among the jars)* (French and English) (Villeneuve d'Ascq: Musée d'Art Moderne, 1988), unpaginated.

3. VIDEONALE IN BONN (Bonn: Videonale, 1988).

Bellour, Raymond. Trans. Lynne Kirby. "Eye for I: Video Self-Portraits." *New American Film and Video Series* 48 (New York: Whitney Museum of American Art, 1989).

1989 Biennial Exhibition (New York: Whitney Museum of American Art, 1989), pp. 210–11, 252.

Biggs, Simon. "The Author and the Machine (The Electronic Artist in Relation to Evolving Conditions of Production and Consumption)." *Machinations Festival* (Geneva: St. Gervais MJC, 1989).

Selections from the Permanent Collection: Recent Acquisitions—Video (San Francisco: San Francisco Museum of Modern Art, 1989).

Video formes '89 (Clermont-Ferrand: Festival de la Création Vidéo, 1989).

L'Amour de Berlin (Cavallion: Centre Culturel de Cavallion, 1990).

Bellour, Raymond. "La Double Helice." *Passages de l'Image* (French) (Paris: Musée National d'Art Moderne, Centre Georges Pompidou, 1990), pp. 51–55. Also available in English in the exhibition catalogue of the same name (Barcelona: Centre Cultural de la Fundacio Caixa de Pensions, 1991), pp. 68–73.

Christoffersen, Agnete Dorph, Raymond Bellour, and Gary Hill. *OTHERWORDSANDIMAGES: Video by Gary Hill* (Danish and English) (Copenhagen: Video Gallerie/Ny Carlsberg Glyptotek, 1990).

Derrida, Jacques. "Videor." *Passages de l'Image* (French) (Paris: Musée National d'Art Moderne, Centre Georges Pompidou, 1990), pp. 158–61. Also available in English in the exhibition catalogue of the same name (Barcelona: Centre Cultural de la Fundacio Caixa de Pensions, 1991), pp. 174–79.

Huici, Fernando. "Gary Hill: *BEACON*." *Bienal de la Imagen en Movimiento '90* (Madrid: Museo Nacional Centro de Arte Reina Sofia, 1990).

Mittenthal, Robert. "Reading the Unknown: Reaching Gary Hill's *And Sat Down Beside Her*." *Gary Hill* (Paris: Galerie des Archives, 1990).

Parent, Sylvie. *Cent Jours D'Art Contemporain à Montreal* (Montreal: Centre International D'Art Contemporain de Montreal, 1990), pp. 9–11.

Van Assche, Christine. "Video Story." *Le Temps des Machines* (Valence: CRAC, 1990). Also reprinted in *Galeries Magazine,* no. 38 (August–September 1990), pp. 10–11.

1991 Biennial Exhibition (New York: Whitney Museum of American Art, 1991), pp. 102–5, 378.

The Body (2) (Chicago: The Renaissance Society at the University of Chicago, 1991).

Glowen, Ron, and Kim Levin. *Glass: Material in the Service of Meaning* (Tacoma, Wash.: Tacoma Art Museum, 1991).

Joachimides, Christos M., and Norman Rosenthal, eds. *METROPOLIS* (Berlin: Martin Gropius Bau, 1991), pp. 154–55, 290.

Lageira, Jacinto. "Sprachen Video." *Between Cinema and a Hard Place* (French) (Paris: OCO Espace d'Art Contemporain, 1991).

Sarrazin, Stephen. "Berlin, Metropolis, La Création, Le Désarroi." *Chimera* Monograph no. 3 (Montbéliard: Edition du Centre International de Creation Video Montbéliard, Belfort, 1991), pp. 56–61.

The 2nd International Biennale in Nagoya ARTEC '91 (Nagoya, Japan: Nagoya City Art Museum, 1991), pp. 30–31.

Videocroniques (Marseille: IMEREC, Vielle Charité, 1991).

Zippay, Lori. "Gary Hill." *Video* (New York: Electronic Arts Intermix, 1991).

Art at the Armory: Occupied Territory (Chicago: Museum of Contemporary Art, 1992), pp. 88–91.

Cooke, Lynne, Bice Curiger, and Greg Hilty. *DOUBLETAKE: Collective Memory and Current Art* (London: Hayward Gallery, 1992), pp. 31, 156–59, 225–26, and addendum.

documenta IX (Stuttgart: Edition Cantz, 1992), vol. 1, p. 157; vol. 2, pp. 222–25, 308. English-language edition published in association with Harry N. Abrams, New York, 1992.

L'Ere Binaire: Nouvelles Interactions (Brussels: Musée Communal d'Ixelles, 1992), unpaginated.

Gary Hill, Video Installations (Eindhoven: Stedelijk Van Abbemuseum, 1992).

Massardier, Hippolyte. "Gary Hill." *Video et Après* (Paris: Musée National d'Art Moderne, Centre Georges Pompidou, 1992).

Sarrazin, Stephen. "Channeled Silence (Quiet, Something 'is' Thinking)." *Gary Hill—I Believe It Is an Image* (Tokyo: Watari Museum of Contemporary Art, 1992).

Watari, Shizuko, and Gary Hill. Interview with Gary Hill, in *Gary Hill— I Believe It Is an Image* (Tokyo: Watari Museum of Contemporary Art, 1992).

Sarrazin, Stephen. "In a Crowded House." *Passageworks* (Malmö: Rooseum— Center for Contemporary Art, 1993), pp. 58–69.

Van Assche, Christine. "Introduction." *Gary Hill* (Paris: Centre Georges Pompidou, 1992), pp. 4–7. Also available in Spanish with an English translation in the exhibition catalogue of the same name (Valencia: IVAM, 1993), pp. 8–11.

Mignot, Dorine. "Introduction." *Gary Hill,* in English with Dutch and German translations (Amsterdam: Stedelijk Museum; Vienna: Kunsthalle, Wien, 1993), pp. 8–9.

Cooke, Lynne. "Gary Hill: au-dela de Babel." *Gary Hill* (Paris: Centre Georges Pompidou, 1992), pp. 78–115. Also available in Spanish with an English translation as "Gary Hill: mas alla de Babel" in the exhibition catalogue of the same name (Valencia: IVAM, 1993), pp. 82–119; and in English with Dutch and German translations as "Gary Hill: Beyond Babel" in the exhibition catalogue of the same name (Amsterdam: Stedelijk Museum; Vienna: Kunsthalle, Wien), pp. 40–99.

Lageira, Jacinto. "L'image du monde dans le corps du texte." *Gary Hill* (Paris: Centre Georges Pompidou, 1992), pp. 34–71. Also available in Spanish with an English translation as "La imagen del mundo en el cuerpo del texto" in the exhibition catalogue of the same name (Valencia: IVAM, 1993), pp. 38–75.

Massardier, Hippolyte. "Du bec et des ongles." *Gary Hill* (Paris: Centre Georges Pompidou, 1992), pp. 118–29. Also available in Spanish with an English translation as "Con unas y dientes" in the exhibition catalogue of the same name (Valencia: IVAM, 1993), pp. 120–33.

1993 Biennial Exhibition (New York: Whitney Museum of American Art, 1993), pp. 13, 168–69.

Kellein, Thomas. "Interview with Gary Hill," and Gary Hill, "Transcription of spoken text for *If Two People.*" *The 21st Century* (Basel: Kunsthalle Basel, 1993), pp. 81–88.

Joachimides, Christos M., and Norman Rosenthal, eds. *Amerikanische Kunst im 20. Jahrhundert—Malerei und Plastik 1913–1993* (Munich: Prestel-Verlag, 1993), pp. 160, 161, 480, 481, Kat. 247.

Van Weelden, Willem. "Primarily Spoken." *Gary Hill,* in English with Dutch and German translations (Amsterdam: Stedelijk Museum; Vienna: Kunsthalle, Wien, 1993), pp. 21–35.

Quasha, George. "Tall Acts of Seeing." *Gary Hill,* in English with Dutch and German translations (Amsterdam: Stedelijk Museum; Vienna: Kunsthalle, Wien, 1993), pp. 99–109.

Brothers, Leslie A., Dorit Cypis, and Steven S. High. *Anonymity & Identity* (Richmond: Virginia Commonwealth University, 1993), pp. 9, 32, 33.

Sorensen, Jens Erik, ed. *Strange Hotel International Art* (Aarhus: Aarhus Kunstmuseum, 1993), pp. 82, 83, 121, 122.

Diserens, Corinne. "Inasmuch As It Is Always Already Taking Place." *Gary*

Hill: In Light of the Other (Oxford: The Museum of Modern Art Oxford; Liverpool: Tate Gallery Liverpool, 1993).

Ferguson, Bruce. "I Believe (That) It Is an Image (in Light) of the Other." *Gary Hill: In Light of the Other* (Oxford: The Museum of Modern Art Oxford; Liverpool: Tate Gallery Liverpool, 1993).

Morgan, Stuart. "Tall Ships." *Gary Hill: In Light of the Other* (Oxford: The Museum of Modern Art Oxford; Liverpool: Tate Gallery Liverpool, 1993).

Nittve, Lars. "Between 1 & 0." *Gary Hill: In Light of the Other* (Oxford: The Museum of Modern Art Oxford; Liverpool: Tate Gallery Liverpool, 1993).

Mittenthal, Robert. "Standing Still On the Lip of Being: Gary Hill's 'Learning Curve.'" *Gary Hill: In Light of the Other* (Oxford: The Museum of Modern Art Oxford; Liverpool: Tate Gallery Liverpool, 1993).

Bruce, Chris, Lynne Cooke, Bruce W. Ferguson, John G. Hanhardt, and Robert Mittenthal. *Gary Hill* (Seattle: Henry Art Gallery, 1994).

Gary Hill: Tall Ships, Clover (Stockholm: Riksutställningar, 1995). Texts by Tom Sandqvist, George Quasha, and Måns Och Pål Wrange.

cocido y crudo (Madrid: Museo Nacional Centro de Arte Reina Sofia, 1995), pp. 106–7. Foreword by Carmen Alborch and José Guirao. Texts by Dan Cameron, Jean Fisher, Gerardo Mosquera, Jerry Saltz, and Mar Villaespesa.

Private/Public ARS '95 Helsinki (Helsinki: Museum of Contemporary Art, 1995), pp. 70–71. Texts by Yonah Foncé-Zimmerman, Jonathan Friedman, Michael Glasmeier, Maaretta Jaukkuri, and Asko Mäkelä.

Altered States: American Art in the 90's (St. Louis: Forum for Contemporary Art, 1995), p. 14. Organized by Jeanne Greenberg and Robert Nickas.

London, Barbara. *Video Spaces: Eight Installations* (New York: The Museum of Modern Art, 1995), pp. 22–23, 48–53.

Identity and Alterity: Figures of the Body 1895/1995: La Biennale di Venezia, 46. esposizione internazionale d'arte (Venice: Marsilio, 1995), pp. 455, 565.

David, Catherine, and Corinne Diserens. *Immagini in Prospettive* (Siena: Comune di Rapolano Terme, 1995).

Vischer, Theodora, ed. *Gary Hill: Imagining the Brain Closer than the Eyes* (Basel: Museum für Gegenwartskunst, 1995). Published in English and in German.

Mayer, Marc. *Being and Time: The Emergence of Video Projection* (Buffalo: Albright-Knox Art Gallery, 1996).

Klangkunst—Sonambiente festival für hören und sehen (Berlin: Akademie der Kunste, 1996).

Quasha, George, and Charles Stein. *Gary Hill: Hand Heard—Liminal Objects* (Paris: Galerie des Archives, 1996).

Diserens, Corinne, and Francis Gomila. *Colisiones* (San Sebastián: Arteleku, 1996).

de Rode Poort (Gent: Museum Van Hedendaagse Kunst, 1996), pp. 78–79.

Hamburger Bahnhof / Museum für Gegenwart—Berlin (München: Prestel-Museumfuhrer, 1996), p. 110.

4e biennale d'art contemporain de lyon: l'autre (Lyon: Réunion des Musées Nationaux, 1997), pp. 114–15.

Pichler, Catherin, ed. *Engel, Engel* (Vienna: Kunsthalle, Wien, 1997).

Città Natura: mostra internazionale di art contemporanea (Roma: Fratelli Palombi Editori, 1997).

97 Kwangju Biennale: Unmapping the Earth (Kwangju, Korea: Kwangju Biennale Press, 1997), p. 90.

o lugar do outro/where the other takes place (Rio de Janeiro: Centro Cultural Banco do Brasil, 1997). Essays by Marcello Dantas, Arlinado Machado, and George Quasha.

Midnight Crossing (Münster: Westfälischer Kunstverein, 1997). Essays by Heinz Liesbrock and Robert Mittenthal.

Quasha, George, and Charles Stein. *Tall Ships: Gary Hill's Projective Installations—Number 2* (Barrytown, N.Y.: Station Hill Arts, 1997).

Quasha, George, and Charles Stein. *Viewer: Gary Hill's Projective Installations—Number 3* (Barrytown, N.Y.: Station Hill Arts, 1997).

Water: The Renewable Metaphor. Essay by Blake Stimson (Eugene: University of Oregon Museum of Art, 1997).

Bélisle, Josée. *Gary Hill* (Montreal: Musée d'art contemporain de Montréal, 1998). Essay by George Quasha and Charles Stein.

Tuning up #5 (Wolfsburg: Kunstmuseum Wolfsburg, 1998).

Phillips, Christopher. *Voices* (Rotterdam: Center for Contemporary Art; Barcelona: Fundació Joan Miró; and Tourcoing: Le Fresnoy, Studio national des arts contemporain, 1998).

Crossings: Kunst zum Hören und Sehen (Vienna: Kunsthalle Wien, 1998), pp. 166–67.

Gary Hill: HanD HearD—Withershins—Midnight Crossing (Barcelona: Museu d'Art Contemporani de Barcelona, 1998). Essays by Heinz Liesbrock, George Quasha and Charles Stein, and José Lebrero Stals.

Memory/Book: Personal Effects/The Collective Unconscious (Sydney: Museum of Contemporary Art, 1998).

Anos 80/The Eighties (Lisbon: Culturgest, 1998).

Kold, Anders, ed. *Gary Hill* (Aarhus: Aarhus Kunstmuseum, 1999). Essays by Julie Harboe, Anders Kold, Gitte Ørskou Madsen, and George Quasha and Charles Stein, and interview by Jérôme Sans.

Gary Hill: Video Works (Tokyo: NTT InterCommunication Center, 1999).

Amalfitano, Lelia. *Gary Hill: Placing Sense↔Sens Placé* (Boston: School of the Museum of Fine Arts, 1999).

Umedalen Skulptur 99 (Umeå: Galleri Stefan Andersson, 1999). Essay by Jan-Erik Lundström.

Monographs*

Devriendt, Christine. *L'Oeuvre Video de Gary Hill* (French and English). (Rennes: Université de Rennes-II, 1990–91).

Gilbert, Christophe. *Maurice Blanchot/Gary Hill: d'une Ecriture l'Autre (et Son Double)* (Paris: DEA Université Paris-III, 1992).

Sarrazin, Stephen. *Chimaera Monographe No. 10 (Gary Hill).* (Montbéliard: Centre International de Création Vidéo Montbéliard, Belfort, 1992).

Selected Articles and Reviews*

Ament, Deloris Tarzan. "Artist Uses Videos to Tease Viewers." *Seattle Times* (February 22, 1993).

Anello, Laura. "Una rassegna sul rapporto fra spazio urbano e ambiente." *Stampa/Qui Roma* (April 21, 1997).

Aquin, Stephanie. "Gary Hill—Vague de fond." *Voir,* Montreal (February 12, 1998), p. 25.

Artner, Alan G. "Veni, Vidi, Video." *Chicago Tribune* (October 9, 1994).

Azzi, Francesca. "Poeta das novas mídias faz individual." *O Tempo,* Brazil (July 2, 1997).

Bækgaard, Bjarne. "Livsnær kunst." *Stift* (January 17, 1999).

Baker, Kenneth. "Capp Street Opens Doors of Perception." *San Francisco Chronicle* (May 27, 1998).

Barcott, Bruce. "Gary Hill." *New Art Examiner* (May 1993), p. 51.

Barrett, David. "Gary Hill" (White Cube exhibition review). *Art Monthly,* no. 203 (February 1997), p. 22.

Barter, Ruth. "DOUBLETAKE." *Art Monthly* (April 1992).

Bassan, Raphael. "Murs d'Images pour un Art Mur." *Liberation,* Paris (July 31, 1990).

Beckmann, Angelika. "Gary Hill." *European Photography*, no. 58, vol. 16, issue 2 (Fall 1995), p. 60.

Bellemare-Brière, Véronique. "La vidéo s'éclate." *Esse,* Montreal, no. 4 (1998), pp. 2–5.

Bellemare-Brière, Véronique. "Gary Hill—La vidéo reine au MAC." *Séquences,* Montreal, no. 196 (May–June 1998), p. 55.

Benichou, Anne. "From Exhibition to Event." *Espace Magazine* 6, no. 2 (Winter 1990).

Berland, Jody. "International Video/Images in Translation." *Vanguard* (April–May 1987), pp. 26–27.

Bonde, Lisbeth. "Renæssancemaleriet ført op til vort århundrede." *Informationer,* Aarhus (January 19, 1999).

Borum, Poul. "Fravaerets Film." *Tusinoe Ojne,* no. 116 (July 1989).

*Monographs are listed alphabetically (by author).
*Articles and Reviews are listed alphabetically (by author).

Bosco, Roberta. "Gary Hill, en el Macba: En busca de un nuevo lenguaje." *El Periodico del Arte* 14 (August–September 1998).

Bourriard, Nicolas. "Vagabondages européens." *Globe,* no. 47 (May 1990), p. 130.

Brown, Richard L. "God and Country." *Tacoma News Tribune* (October 12, 1990).

Bufill, Juan. "El laberinto parlante de Gary Hill: El Macba muestra tres instalaciones audiovisuales del artista." *La Vanguardia,* Barcelona (July 15, 1998).

Burnham, Scott. "Currents Review at ICA." *Boston University Daily Free Press* (January 1991).

Campeau, Sylvain. "Epistémologie de la réalité visuelle." *Vie des Arts,* Montreal, no. 170 (1998), pp. 81–82.

Casabella, Carla. "Sala de estar: Im-presentable." *ABC,* Barcelona (October 7, 1998).

Chaimovich, Felipe. "Tecnologia Bem-Aproveitada." *Jornal da Tarde,* Brazil (November 1, 1997).

Chion, Michel. "La bouche et la video." *L'Image Video,* no. 3 (April–May 1990), pp. 20–22.

Coen, Esther. "Artisti tra eccessi ed equivoci." *La Repubblica,* Rome (March 10, 1997).

Conomos, John. "Verbal executions on Gary Hill's videography." *Photofile* 35 (1992), pp. 35–38.

Cooke, Lynne. "Gary Hill: 'Who am I but a figure of speech?'" *Parkett,* no. 34 (1992), pp. 16–27.

Cornwell, Regina. "Gary Hill—Museum of Modern Art, New York." *Sculpture* (May–June 1991), p. 69.

Couvreur, Bram. "Video en de kunst van de verbeelding." *Uit In Amsterdam* (January 7, 1998).

Croft, Williams Janis. "Caps Video: Wegman, Hill, Koplan, Lucier." *Afterimage* 7 (November 1979).

Darke, Chris. "Gary Hill: Museum of Modern Art, Oxford." *Frieze* 14 (January–February 1994), pp. 54–55.

De Barros, Paul. "Video Artists Reveal One-of-a-Kind Image." *Seattle Times* (May 10, 1990).

Decter, Joshua. "Gary Hill: Galerie des Archives." *ArtForum,* vol. 35, no. 3 (November 1996), p. 108.

Degener, Patricia. "A Too-Brief Chance to See Video Pieces at Their Best." *St. Louis Post-Dispatch* (November 12, 1985).

"Del paraíso de Delvaux a las instalaciones de Gary Hill y Baldessari." *El Punto de las Artes,* Barcelona (July 17–31, 1998), p. 11.

Devriendt, Christine, and Paul-Emmanuel Odin. "L'image comme une aiguille qui ecrit au bout des mots *Site Recite (a prologue)* une video de Gary Hill." *Kanal,* no. 6 (May 1990), pp. 54–56.

Dithmer, Monna. "Mester i videosurfing." *Politiken,* Aarhus (January 18, 1999).

Dollar, Steve. "Image Festival Explores New Frontiers." *Atlanta Journal and Constitution* (May 7, 1989).

Doran, Anne. "Seeing is Believing." *Time Out,* issue 173 (January 14–21, 1999), p. 49.

Duncan, Michael. "In Plato's Electronic Cave." *Art in America,* vol. 83, no. 6 (June 1995), pp. 68–73.

Durland, Steven. "CRUX." *High Performance,* no. 37 (1987), pp. 97–98.

Estado, Agência. "São Paulo tem mostra de arte multimediática." *O Tempo,* Brazil (October 2, 1997).

Fargier, Jean-Paul. "Z. Rybczinski et G. Hill: La Ligne, Le Point, Le Pli." *Cahiers du Cinema,* no. 415 (January 1989), pp. 60–63.

Fargier, Jean-Paul. "Defense de Doubler." *Art Press,* no. 147 (May 1990).

Fioravante, Celso. "Imagem de vídeo ganha nova dimesão com Gary Hill." *Folha de São Paulo* (October 2, 1997).

Fitzsousa, Michael. "Focus of Videos is People." *Waterbury Republican* (April 23, 1987).

Folha, Agência. "Hill colta ao país para festival de dança em BH." *Folha de São Paulo* (October 27, 1997).

Fontaine, Mario. "Pour les amateurs d'insolite." *La Presse,* Montreal (February 8, 1998), p. B5.

Fox, Catherine. "Video Poet Sees Things in a Muddle." *Atlanta Journal and Constitution* (March 20, 1987).

Freudenheim, Susan. "Video Art Show a Mixed Bag." *San Diego Tribune* (June 3, 1987).

Frohne, Ursula. "Warheit des Scheins: Gary Hill: Suspension of Disbelief." *Mediagramm,* Museum für Gegenwartskunst 11 (April 1996).

Furlong, Lucinda. "A Manner of Speaking: An Interview with Gary Hill." *Afterimage* 10 (March 1983), pp. 9–16.

Galloway, David. "Cologne Exhibit is Milestone for Video Sculpture." *International Herald Tribune* (April 2, 1989).

Gattinara, Federico Castelli. "Gli artisti d'oggi? Figli naturali delle metropoli." *Il Giornale Dell'Arte,* Italy (April 1997), p. 22.

Gauville, Hervé. "Gary Hill, le maître du temps." *Liberation* 31, Montreal (February 14–15, 1998), p. 31.

Gay, Jean-Jacques. "Deux temps trois mouvements." *Genlock,* no. 15 (December 1989).

Gay, Jean-Jacques. "Surf, drogue et video." *Museart,* no. 26 (December–January 1992–93), pp. 122–24.

di Genova, Arianna. "Giardino di Cemento." *Il Manifesto,* Italy (April 23, 1997).

Glowen, Ron. "Camera of the Mind." *Artweek* (February 22, 1990).

Goggin, Kathleen. "Review of the *Gary Hill* exhibition catalogue published by the Editions du Centre Georges Pompidou." *Parachute,* no. 70 (April–June 1993), p. 49.

Goodman, Jonathan. "Gary Hill." *Contemporary Visual Arts,* issue 22 (1999).

Gragg, Randy. "The Waning of Modernism." *Seattle Weekly* (November 21, 1990).

Grey, Meg. "Res Ten." *RES,* vol. 2, no. 2 (1999), pp. 20–28.

Grillo, Cristina. "Gary Hill procura una criança brazileira." *Folha de São Paulo,* Brazil (July 1, 1997).

Grout, Catherine. "Gary Hill—La condition humaine de la pensee." *Arte Factum,* no. 48 (June–August 1993), pp. 8–12.

Grundberg, Andy. "Gary Hill at the Museum of Modern Art." *New York Times* (December 21, 1990).

Gudis, Catherine. "Interview with Gary Hill at MOCA." *The Contemporary 4,* no. 1 (Winter 1987).

Hackett, Regina. "Gary Hill and Gary Reel at And/Or Art Center." *Seattle Post-Intelligencer* (January 21, 1981).

Hackett, Regina. "Gary Hill's Stark Videos Lack Charm but Pack Power." *Seattle Post-Intelligencer* (November 14, 1985).

Hackett, Regina. "Gary Hill's 'Tall Ships' a Hit at the Henry." *Seattle Post-Intelligencer* (1997).

Hackett, Regina. "Seattle Video Artist Wins Prestigious Prize." *Seattle Post-Intelligencer* (June 14, 1995), p. C3.

Hackett, Regina. "Thought Becomes Physical in Hill's Video." Seattle Post-Intelligencer (June 2, 1998), pp. D1, D2.

Hackett, Regina. "20th-Century Art Takes a New Turn at Donald Young." *Seattle Post-Intelligencer* (January 24, 1992).

Hackett, Regina. "Video Sculpture Compels Viewer to Stay Tuned." *Seattle Post-Intelligencer* (February 19, 1993).

Hagan, Charles. "Gary Hill, 'Primarily Speaking' at the Whitney Museum of American Art." *Artforum* (February 1984).

Hagen, Charles. "Tube Art (Take Out)." *The Village Voice* (May 14, 1985).

Hall, Charles. "DOUBLETAKE." *Arts Review* (April 1992).

Hankwitz, Molly. "Gary Hill: 23:59:59:29—The Storyteller's Room." *RES* (Summer 1998), p. 8.

Hara, Hélio. "A arte dependente do olhar do outro." *O Globo,* Brazil (July 1, 1997).

Hara, Hélio. "As imagens reencantadas: Gary Hill diz que percepção basta entender sua mostra no CCBB." *O Globo,* Brazil (June 12, 1997).

Hara, Hélio. "Luz e percepção." *O Globo,* Brazil (March 14, 1997).

Hara, Hélio. "O lugar do outro: Trocas de emoção e sensaçöes num acúmulo de idéias." *O Globo,* Brazil (July 3, 1997).

Hara, Hélio. "O outro à mostra segundo Gary Hill." *O Globo,* Brazil (July 3, 1997).

Helfand, Glen. "Lost in Space: Gary Hill's Illuminations Lodge in the Memory." *San Francisco Bay Guardian* (May 27, 1998).

Hirszman, Maria. "Hill brinca com tempo e espaço." *Jornal da Tarde,* Brazil (October 4, 1997).

Horn, Lawrence. "On Video and Its Viewer." *Millennium Film Journal,* nos. 14/15 (Fall–Winter 1984–85).

Hulser, Kathleen. "National Video Award Festival." *The Villager* (October 1982).

Huntington, Richard. "'Zone' Animates Common Objects." *Buffalo Courier-Express* (May 15, 1980).

Hürzeler, Catherine. "Kann man auf abstrakte Weise surfen? Ein Gespräch mit dem Videokünstler Gary Hill." *Das Kunst-Bulletin* 9 (September 1997), pp. 12–19.

Jarque, Fietta. "La Ier Bienal de la Imagen en Moveimiento ofrecera video y cine interdisciplinar." *El País,* Madrid (December 8, 1990).

Jørgensen, Dorthe Rugaard. "Virtuos videokunst." *Kunstavisen* (February–March 1999).

Jørgensen, Ulla Angkjær. "Vedkommende videokunst." *Stift* (January 17, 1999).

Jowitt, Deborah. "Taking It Apart: Radical Expats Drop by New York." *The Village Voice,* vol. 43, no. 51 (December 22, 1998), p. 145.

Juncosa, Enrique. "Gary Hill, Poeta de la Oscuridad." *El País,* Barcelona (September 12, 1998).

Kandel, Susan. "Gary Hill, Museum of Contemporary Art." *ArtForum,* vol. 33, no. 8 (April 1995), pp. 86–87.

Katz, Helena. "Gary Hill usa tecnologia para desvendar o corpo." *O Estado de São Paulo,* Brazil (July 5, 1997).

Kolpan, Steven. "Bateson Through the Looking Glass." *Video and the Arts* (Winter 1986), pp. 20, 22, 35, 56.

Kozinska, Dorota. "Brave New Space: The Art of Gary Hill." *The Montreal Gazette* (February 7, 1998), p. K5.

Kremer, Mark. "Geef me een licham met vleugels van papier." *Metropolis M,* no. 6 (December 1997–January 1998), pp. 22–35.

La Chance, Michaël. "Vidéognose." *Spirale,* Montreal (May–June 1998), pp. 12–14.

Lageira, Jacinto. "Gary Hill: The Imager of Disaster." *Galeries Magazine* (December 1990–January 1991), pp. 74–77, 140, 141.

Lageira, Jacinto. "Une Verbalisation du Regard." *Parachute,* no. 62 (April–June 1991), pp. 4–11.

Lajer-Burcharth, Ewa. "Real bodies: Video in the 1990's." *Art History,* vol. 20, no. 2 (June 1997), pp. 185–213. (Polish translation also published in *Magazyn Sztuki,* no. 15 [March–April 1997], pp. 287–317.)

Lamarche, Bernard. "L'art de la syncope." *Le Devoir,* Montreal (February 2, 1998), p. D8.

Lapointe, Josée. "Angoisses sur grand écran." *Le Soleil,* Quebec (March 7, 1998), p. D12.

Larson, Kay. "Art Through a Screen Dimly." *New York* (September 12, 1983), pp. 86–87.

Leão, Tom. "A revanche carioca do camaleão do pop." *O Globo,* Brazil (November 4, 1997).

Leduc, Louise. "Le vidéaste Gary Hill au MAC." *Le Devoir,* Montreal (January 30, 1998), p. B10.

Lee, Thomas. "March Screening Series at BF/VF." *Visions Magazine* (March 1983).

Lestocart, Louis-Jose. "Gary Hill: Surfer sur le medium / Surfing the Medium." *artpress* (February 1996), pp. 20–27.

Libbenga, Jan. "Videokunst Verlengt Het Bewustzijn." *NRC, Donderdug* (September 15, 1988).

Lopez, Nayse. "A videoarte de Gary Hill." *Jornal do Brasil* (July 3, 1997).

Lord, Catherine. "It's the Thought That Counts." *Afterimage* (October 1983), pp. 9–11.

"Los museos catalanes hacen su agosto: menú de exposiciones a la carta." *ABC Cataluña,* Barcelona (August 8, 1998).

Marshall, John. "Three Local Artists Win 'Genius Grants': MacArthur Awards Honor Creativity." *Seattle Post-Intelligencer* (June 2, 1998), pp. A1, A7.

Marziani, Gianluca. "Città Natura." *L'opinione,* Rome (March 7, 1997).

Mays, John Bentley. "Five Fingers on the Pulse of Video Art." *Globe and Mail,* Montreal (March 7, 1998), p. C4.

McManus, Michael. "Video and the Literary Imagination." *Artweek* (March 1987).

Meuris, Jacques. "Art et science ou science et art?" *Art et Culture,* Brussels (September 1992).

Millner, Sherry, and Ernest Larsen. "The Problems of Pluralism: AFI Video Festival." *The Independent* (January–February 1985).

Mittenthal, Robert. "Overpowering Ideas." *Reflex* (March–April 1992).

de Moraes, Angélica. "Gary Hill mostra sua arte eletrônica em SP." *O Estado de São Paulo,* Brazil (September 2, 1997).

de Moraes, Angélica. "Gary Hill no CCBB: Instalação do artista pode ser vista até 15 de setembro." *Jornal do Commercio,* Brazil (July 13–14, 1997).

de Moraes, Angélica. "MAM abre hoje mostra individual de Gary Hill." *O Imparcial,* Brazil (September 2, 1997).

de Moraes, Angélica. "Rio vai ter individual de Gary Hill em junho." *O Estado de São Paulo,* Brazil (October 2, 1997).

345 Bibliography

Moreau, Yvan. "Montreal—Là et nulle part." *ETC Montreal,* no. 43 (1998), pp. 53–54.

Morgan, Robert C. "Gary Hill / Barbara Gladstone Gallery." *Review,* vol. 2, no. 7 (December 15, 1996), pp. 29–30.

Morgan, Stuart. "Thanks for the Memories." *Frieze* (April–May 1992).

Morrison, Wolf. "Wizard in Videoland." *The Daily Yomiuri,* Tokyo (April 8, 1985).

Movin, Lars. "Video er Skrift." *Information Onsdag,* Copenhagen (April 18, 1990).

Movin, Lars. "Kroppen som impuls i det elektroniske kredsløb." *KUNSTmagasinet 1%,* no. 5 (1999), pp. 42–45.

Nash, Michael. "Video Poetics: A Context for Content." *High Performance,* no. 37 (1987), pp. 67, 70.

Nash, Michael. "Poetic Oversights and Critical Misgivings." *High Performance,* no. 39 (1987).

Nash, Michael. "AFI Video Festival." *Artscribe International* (Summer 1989).

Nash, Michael. "What Time is Television? or The Importance of Being Boring." *Art Issues,* no. 16 (February–March 1991).

Neimann, Susanne, and Agnete Dorph Christoffersen. "Blinde i Billedstormn." *Information Onsdag,* Copenhagen (September 27, 1989).

Parent, Sylvie. "L'entrevue—entrevue avec Gary Hill." *Le Magazine électronique du CIAC,* Montreal, no. 4 (February 1998), pp. 1–6.

Pavlova, Adriana. "Festival Internacional de Dança leva canguarda do movimento belga a MG: Coreógrafa Meg Stuart mostra hoje à noite parceria com o videoartista Gary Hill." *O Globo,* Brazil (November 21, 1997).

Pencenat, Corinne. "L'Experience Limite de Gary Hill." *Beaux Arts* (October 1991), p. 113.

Perron, Joel. "Video Show Reflects on Technology's Role." *Japan Times,* Tokyo (March 18, 1990).

Phillips, Christopher. "Between Pictures." *Art in America* (November 1991), pp. 104–14, 173.

Pieroni, Augusto. "La natura della città." *Liberazione,* Rome (April 26, 1997).

Pincus, Robert L. "Watching Machines Ignore Us." *San Diego Union* (May 28, 1987).

Preisner, Brenda. "Sound, Images Conflict in Video 'War Zone.'" *Buffalo Evening News* (May 15, 1980).

"Primera Bienal De La Imagen En Movimiento." *RTV Magazine di los Mercados Audiovisuales,* no. 20 (January 1991).

Provencher, Louise. "Catastrophe(s) en ou le bégaiement du temps." *Espace 44,* Montreal (1998), p. 26.

Quasha, George, and Charles Stein. "Touch in Contemporary Art." *Public 13* (Toronto: Public Access, 1996), pp. 65–83.

Renouf, Renee. "Video." *Artweek* (July 3, 1982).

Rocha, Daniela. "Gary Hill torna humana a tecnologia." *Folha de São Paulo,* Brazil (October 3, 1997).

Rocha, Daniela. "Furto muda rumos da exposição de Hill." *Folha de São Paulo,* Brazil (September 19, 1997).

Ross, Trine. "Mod beskueren som høje skibe." *Politiken,* Aarhus (January 19, 1999).

Sá, Fátima. "A busca pelo lugar do outro: Videoinstalaçøes de Gary Hill interagem com o espectador que se aproxima." *Jornal do Brasil* (July 4, 1997).

Sandbye, Mette. "Se og bliv set." *Avisen,* Aarhus (Weekend: January 22–28, 1999).

Sarrazin, Stephen. "Gary Hill at Galerie des Archives." *Art Press,* no. 147 (May 1990).

Sarrazin, Stephen. "La parole aux objets." *Art Press,* no. 165 (January 1992).

Sarrazin, Stephen. "Things Fall Apart: Gary Hill & Meg Stuart (with Damaged Goods) 'Splayed Mind Out'/Gary Hill: Installations and Videotapes." *Intercommunication* 25 (Summer 1998), pp. 82–83.

Schneider, Irmela. "Wörter sehen und Bilder lesen. Einige Betrachtungen zur Veränderung von Grundlagen innerhalb der Medienästhetik." Soziale Wirklichkeit, Jena, Germany (Winter 1997), pp. 299–315.

Simøes, Alessandra. "As esculturas falantes de Gary Hill." *Gazeta Mercantil,* Brazil (October 10–12, 1997).

Slemmons, Rod. "Gary Hill—Under New Skins." *Reflex* (May–June 1993), p. 13.

Smallenberg, Sandra. "Een seconde per gefilmde geweldsexplosie." *Nrc Handelsblad,* Amsterdam (January 3, 1998).

Smallenberg, Sandra. "Mediakunst weg can 'in crowd.'" *Nrc Handelsblad,* Amsterdam (December 11, 1997).

Smallwood, Lyn. "The World as They Know It." *Seattle Weekly* (March 18, 1992).

Stadler, Matthew. "A Theater of Perception: Picture This." *The Stranger,* Seattle (June 18–24, 1998), p. 27.

Sterritt, David. "Multichannel Show (*Primarily Speaking*)." *The Christian Science Monitor* (December 8, 1983).

Stiftel, Ralf. "Unter die Netzhaut: Gary Hill's Midnight Crossing im Westfälischen Kunstverein." *Westfälischer Anzeiger* (September 7, 1997).

Sturken, Marita. "Electronic Visions." *Afterimage* (November 1983).

Tablyn, Christine. "Video Art: An Historical Survey." *High Performance,* no. 37 (1987), pp. 35, 36.

Taubin, Amy. "The Whitney Biennial: Video." *Millennium Film Journal,* no. 13 (Fall–Winter 1983–84).

Tietenberg, Annette. "Die Augen, sie sind blödsinning und beinahe blind: Bilder, die entstehen und vergehen: Gary Hill's *Midnight Crossing* im Westfälischer Kunstverein Münster." *Seite* 34 (August 30, 1997).

Tougas, Colette. "Gary Hill." *Parachute* 90 (April–June 1998), pp. 43–44.

Uberquoi, Marie-Claire. "Dos manipuladores de la imagen, John Baldessari y Gary Hill, exponen en BCN." *El Mundo* (July 15, 1998).

Updike, Robin, et al. "3 Local Residents Named 'Geniuses': Prestigious MacArthur Grants Go to Writer, Poet, Video Artist." *Seattle Times* (June 2, 1998), pp. A1, A11.

Van Assche, Christine. "Tendances Multiples." *Tendances Multiples, Videos des Années 80, Petit Journal,* no. 22 (March–May 1990).

Van Assche, Christine. "Restless Images." *Galeries Magazine* (April–May 1990).

Van Assche, Christine. "Interview with Gary Hill." *Galeries Magazine* (December 1990–January 1991), pp. 77, 140–41.

Van Assche, Christine. "Six Questions to Gary Hill." *Parachute 84* (October–December 1996), pp. 42–45.

Vernay, Marie-Christine. "Tactique Plastique." *Liberation* (February 14–15, 1998), p. 30.

Vidal, Jaume. "Gary Hill, pionero de la videocreación, muestra en el Macba su obra junto a la de Shamberg y Baldessari." *El País* (July 15, 1998).

Von Graevenitz, Antje. "Living Funeral Art—Video Installations by Bill Viola and Gary Hill." *Archis* 7 (1993), pp. 45–53.

Wakefield, Neville. "Let's Go to the Videotape." *Art and Auction,* no. 21, vol. 4 (October 19–November 1, 1998), pp. 48–53.

Wißmann, Kathrin. "Der Moment vor der Ekstase: Katsushika Hokusai, Gustave Courbet, Gary Hill: Künstler, dem Geheimnis der Welle auf der Spur." *mare* 3 (August–September 1997), pp. 92–94.

Wivel, Henrik. "Sjaelfuldt." *Berlingske Tidende* (February 5, 1999).

Wooster, Ann-Sargent. "Manhattan Short Cuts." *Afterimage* (Summer 1985).

Wooster, Ann-Sargent. "The Heart of Darkness—Film and Video at the Whitney Biennial." *Arts Magazine* (October 1991), pp. 66–71.

Xexéo, Artur. "A estátua de Gandhi e a outra." *Journal do Brazil* (August 3, 1997).

Yamamori, Eiji. "Gary Hill." *Aera Magazine,* vol. 5, no. 27, Tokyo (July 1992), pp. 72–73.

Young, Lisa Jaye. "Electronic Verses: Reading the Body vs. Touching the Text." *Performing Arts Journal* 52, vol. 18, no. 1 (January 1996), pp. 36–43.

Electronic Publications

documenta I–IX: 1955–1992. Kassel: documenta Archiv, 1997. (CD-ROM)

3e biennale d'art contemporain de Lyon: cinéma, vidéo, informatique propos, et documents interactifs. Lyon: Réunion des Musées Nationaux, 1995.

Other Publications*

Brockhaus Enzyklopädie, Bd. 30 (Mannheim: Bibliographisches Institut and FA Brockhaus AG, 1996), p. 344.

Der elektronische Raum: 15 Positionen zur Medienkunst (Bonn: Kunst und Ausstellungshalle der Bundesrepublik Deuschland, 1998), pp. 146–59.

Marcoci, Roxana, Diana Murphy, and Eve Sinaiko, eds. *New Art* (New York: Harry N. Abrams, 1997), p. 65.

Petho, Bertalan. *post-postmodernism: The Nineties: Opinions and Philosophical Investigations Concerning Our Change of Era* (Budapest: Platon, 1997), pp. II. 97, 295, 315, 316, 318, 319, 320, 336, 342, M. vi, vii, xx.

The 20th Century Art Book (London: Phaidon Press, 1996), p. 202.

Walther, Ingo F., ed. *Art of the Twentieth Century: Painting, Sculpture, New Media, Photography*, vol. 2 (Cologne: Taschen, 1998), pp. 614, 615.

*Other publications are listed alphabetically.

Credits

Grateful acknowledgment is made for permission to reprint from the following writers and publishers: Barbara London: "Video Spaces: Gary Hill," *Video Spaces,* The Museum of Modern Art, New York, 1995; Jacques Derrida: "Videor," *Passages de l'Images* (Paris: Musée National d'Art Moderne, Centre Georges Pompidou, 1990); Jacinto Lageira: *The Image of the World in the Body of the Text,* show catalogue, Centre Georges Pompidou, Museum of Modern Art, 1992; Corinne Diserens: "Time in the Body," in *Gary Hill: In Light of the Other* (Oxford: The Museum of Modern Art; Liverpool: Tate Gallery, 1993); Stephen Sarrazin: "Surfing the Medium," *Gary Hill, Chimera* monograph, 1992; Raymond Bellour: "The Matrix," *Sites Recited,* catalogue, the Long Beach Museum of Art, 1994; Willem van Weelden: *Primarily Spoken,* exhibition catalogue from the Stedelijk Museum, Amsterdam, Kunsthalle, Wien, 1993–94; Robert Mittenthal: *Standing Still on the Lip of Being: Gary Hill's Learning Curve,* catalogue, Henry Art Gallery, University of Washington, Seattle, 1994; George Quasha: "Notes on the Feedback Horizon," in *Glass Onion* (Barrytown, N.Y.: Station Hill Press, 1980); John C. Hanhardt: *Between Language and the Moving Image: The Art of Gary Hill,* catalogue, Henry Art Gallery, University of Washington, Seattle, 1994; George Quasha and Charles Stein, *HAND HEARD/liminal objects* (Paris: Galerie des Archives; Barrytown, N.Y.: Station Hill Arts of Barrytown, Ltd., 1996); Lynne Cooke: "Postscript: Re-embodiments in Alter Space," *Parkett,* no. 34 (1992), Gary Hill, Henry Art Gallery, University of Washington, Seattle, 1994; George Quasha and Charles Stein: *projection: the space of great happening,* in Gary Hill, *O Lugar do Outro [Where the Other Takes Place]* (Centro Cultural Bauco do Brasil and Museu de Arte Moderna de São Paulo, Rio de Janeiro, 1997); Arlindo Machado: "Why Do Language and Meaning Get in a Muddle?" in Gary Hill, *O Lugar do Outro [Where the Other Takes Place]* (Centro Cultural Bauco do Brasil and Museu de Arte Moderna de São Paulo, Rio de Janeiro, 1997); Heinz Liesbrock: "Loss Illuminates," in *Gary Hill Midnight Crossing* (Münster: Westfälischer Kunstverein, 1997); Lucinda Furlong: "A Manner of Speaking—Interview with Gary Hill," *Afterimage,* March 1983; Stephen Sarrazin: *A Discussion with Gary Hill,* Chimera monograph, 1992 (Montbeliard: Centre International de Creation Video Montebeliard Belfort); Regina Cornwell: "Gary Hill: Interview," *Art Monthly,* October 1993; Louis-Jose Lestocart: "Surfing the Medium," *ArtPress,* issue no. 210 (1996); Christine Van Assche: "Six Questions to Gary Hill," *Parachute* 84 (October, November, December 1996); George Quasha and Charles Stein: "Liminal Performance," *PAJ* 58 (1997); Gary Hill: "Primarily Speaking," transcription of spoken text in the work *Primarily Speaking* © 1981 by Gary Hill; Gary Hill: *Primarily Speaking, 1981–83* (New York: Whitney Museum of Modern Art, 1983); "URA ARU (The Acoustic Palindrome)," *Video Guide 7* (no. 4, 1986); *BEACON (Two Versions of the Imaginary),* 1990, exhibition catalogue from the Stedelijk Museum, Amsterdam, 1990; *Inter-View,* Centre Georges Pompidou, Paris, 1992; *Site Recite,* 1994 from "Unspeakable Images," *Camera Obscura,* no. 24 (San Francisco, 1991). All photographs reprinted courtesy the Donald Young Gallery, Chicago, Illinois.

Library of Congress Cataloging-in-Publication Data

Gary Hill / edited by Robert C. Morgan.
      p.   cm. — (PAJ books. Art + performance)
   "A PAJ book."
   Includes writings by Gary Hill.
   Includes videography and bibliographical references.
   ISBN 0-8018-6401-1 (hc : alk. paper) — ISBN 0-8018-6402-X
(pbk. : alk. paper)
   1. Hill, Gary, 1951—Criticism and interpretation.   2. Video art—
United States.   I. Hill, Gary, 1951-   II. Morgan, Robert C.,
1943-   III. Series.

N6537.H533 G37 2000
709'.2—dc21   00-021626